Essentials of Mastering English

W
DE
G

Essentials of Mastering English

A Concise Grammar

by
Carl Bache

Mouton de Gruyter
Berlin · New York 2000

Mouton de Gruyter (formerly Mouton, The Hague)
is a Division of Walter de Gruyter GmbH & Co. KG, Berlin.

Library of Congress Cataloging-in-Publication Data

Bache, Carl, 1953–
   Essentials of mastering English : a concise grammar / by
Carl Bache.
        p.   cm.
Includes bibliographical references and index.
ISBN 3 11 016722 0 (pbk. : alk. paper)
   1. English language – Grammar. I. Title.
PE1106.B26 2000
428.2–dc21   99-057777

Die Deutsche Bibliothek – Cataloging-in-Publication Data

Bache, Carl:
Essentials of mastering English : a concise grammar / by Carl
   Bache. – Berlin ; New York : Mouton de Gruyter, 2000
   ISBN 3-11-016722-0

Printing and Binding: WB-Druck GmbH, Rieden am Forggensee.
Cover Design: Christopher Schneider, Berlin.
Printed in Germany.

Preface

This grammar covers much the same ground as its predecessor, *Mastering English: an Advanced Grammar for Non-native and Native Students* by Niels Davidsen-Nielsen and myself, but it is aimed specifically at undergraduate students of English (native and non-native) at universities, business schools and teachers' training colleges. It is correspondingly less detailed, and difficult topics have been made more easily accessible. Readers of *Essentials of Mastering English* who are interested in more detailed discussions and in references to the works on which they are based should consult *Mastering English*.

One of the many similarities between the two grammars is that the guiding principle is a rigorous form/function distinction at all levels of analysis. The basic sentence analysis system employed can be practised on the internet at the VISL-group's address: http://visl.hum.sdu.dk. This site contains a number of valuable linguistic tools and allows students to work with a wide range of languages. Exercises and analyses relating to *Essentials of Mastering English* will be made available at the site in the near future, as will updated and extended versions of the glossary at the end of the book.

I am extremely grateful to Niels Davidsen-Nielsen for trusting me to write this 'short' version of our joint efforts. Many parts of *Essentials of Mastering English* reflect his keen insights, elegant prose and illuminating examples. Needless to say, although Niels Davidsen-Nielsen has contributed substantially and significantly to the book, I alone am responsible for the final product.

I would like to thank Leo Hoye, Hans Jørgen Ladegaard, Fritz Larsen, Nina Nørgaard and Christian Heyde Petersen for reading the manuscript and giving me a great deal of valuable feedback. I am grateful also to Anders Hougaard for preparing the subject and word indexes.

When in doubt about the acceptability of examples I have conferred with native speakers of English, in particular John Dienhart, Leo Hoye, Sharon Millar and Tom Pettitt. My sincere thanks go to these colleagues for their invaluable assistance.

I am indebted also to Anke Beck, Chief Editor at Mouton de Gruyter, and her staff for constructive and friendly cooperation, and to the referees for their helpful comments on the manuscript.

Finally, I wish to thank SDU Odense University for generous support of the project.

Carl Bache
Odense, October 1999

Contents

Part I

PART I

The purpose of Part I is to introduce the reader to the basic grammatical terms and concepts necessary for the description of sentences in English. The account will thus form the basis for understanding English grammar and for using grammatical rules and explanations.

1. Grammatical description: getting started

1.1. Grammar: syntax, morphology and semantics

Consider first a few samples of English:

(1)   My sisters painted the old shed.
(2)   Was Andrew in London last week?
(3)   Give me a kiss!
(4)   What a jerk he is!

These examples are **sentences**. Provisionally we can define a sentence as a string of words expressing a statement (as in (1)), a question (as in (2)), a command (as in (3)), or an exclamation (as in (4)). One way to approach the description of sentences is to look at the individual **words** and see how they contribute to the meaning of the sentence as a whole. The sentence in (1) contains six words, but one immediately notes that some of these belong more closely together than others. Thus *My* and *sisters* are more closely related than e.g. *painted* and *the* or *My* and *old*. It appears that words often form larger units, which in turn form sentences. In example (1) there are three units, usually referred to as **constituents**: [My sisters], [painted] and [the old shed]. Two of these are **complex** in that they contain more words than one. The first constituent expresses who was engaged in painting the old shed; the second expresses what my sisters did to the shed; and the last expresses what my sisters painted. In the two complex constituents, the individual words are **constituents within constituents**. So instead of beginning one's analysis by saying that the sentence contains six words, it would be more appropriate to say that it contains three constituents. **Syntax** deals with the structure of sentences, i.e. the division of sentences into constituents and lower-level constituents down to word level, and with the relationship between these units.

It is quite possible to describe language below word level. For example, although *sisters* is simply a word, we can divide it into two smaller meaningful units and see how they contribute to the meaning of the word as a whole: [sister] and [s]. The first unit names a certain kind of person and the second adds plural meaning to the first. Similarly *painted* consists of [paint], which names a certain activity, and [ed], which adds the meaning of pastness to this activity. Other words, such as *My, the, old* and *shed*, cannot be divided into smaller meaningful units. The smallest meaningful units in language, whether individual words or parts of words, are called **morphemes**. The study of morphemes (and how they are combined to form words) is called **morphology**. The kind of morphology that deals with how words are inflected (e.g. to express plurality in *sisters* and pastness in *painted*) is called **inflectional morphology**.

In both syntax and morphology, **meaning** is of the utmost importance. We recognized e.g. *My* and *sisters* as belonging together (unlike *painted* and *the*) because together they expressed who was engaged in painting the shed. Without knowing the meaning of *My* and *sisters*, we would not recognize them as forming a constituent. In the case of *sisters*, we recognized [s] as an inflectional morpheme because it added plural meaning to [sister]. So we combine morphemes and we combine constituents in order to express meanings. The study of meaning in language is called **semantics**.

In **grammar**, all the three disciplines of syntax, morphology and semantics are relevant: grammar is concerned with the rules for combining morphemes, words and higher-level constituents in meaningful ways. Occasionally it will be relevant also to refer to other small units than the morpheme, namely **syllables** (i.e. clusters of vowels and consonants, e.g. *polite*: [po] + [lite]) and the individual sounds of language, the so-called **phonemes** (e.g. cat: /k/ + /æ/ + /t/).

1.2. The form and function distinction

To be able to read and use grammatical descriptions, e.g. for teaching purposes or for improving one's language proficiency, it is important to know the special terms used by grammarians for describing language. In this and the following sections, we shall examine some useful terminology.

To analyse sentences we must first of all distinguish between the **form** and the **function** of constituents. The terms 'form' and 'function' are here used in a somewhat technical sense: the form of a constituent corresponds to the make-up, or composition, of the constituent whereas the function corresponds to the way the constituent is used in relation to other constituents. This distinction is relevant not only in grammar but far more generally. Thus, there are two different but equally valid ways of describing, say, a pen. One would be to list its physical aspects (size, weight, shape, material, colour) – i.e. aspects of its 'form'. Another would be to specify what it is used for in relation to other things (typically writing) – i.e. its 'function'. To describe a pen exhaustively, it is necessary to include both kinds of description. Similarly, in language, constituents can and should be described in terms of both their form and their function. For example, in a sentence like:

(1)   Jack was kissing the beautiful girl.

each of the three constituents ([Jack], [was kissing] and [the beautiful girl] have both a form and a function. *Jack* is a 'noun' (form) serving as 'subject' (function); *was kissing* is a 'group of words' (form) serving as 'predicator' (function); and *the beautiful girl* is a 'group of words' (form) serving as 'object' (function). We shall look at the technical terms for different forms and functions in the following sections.

The important thing to remember about form and function is that most often there is **no one-to-one correspondence** between them: given the form, we normally cannot predict the function, and vice versa. Again this is true more generally: instead of using a pen for writing we may use a pencil, a piece of chalk, a typewriter, a word-processor, etc. These are all different 'forms' which may serve basically the same function, that of writing. Conversely, though a pen is normally used for writing it can easily be put to other uses: e.g. 'tapping impatiently on the desk to wake up students who have dozed off' or even 'throwing at somebody in anger'! In language it is the same. In example (1) the single word *Jack* is a subject and the group *the beautiful girl* is an object but, from a grammatical point of view, they might just as well change functions, as in:

(2)   The beautiful girl was kissing Jack.

Without looking at a constituent in the context of the sentence in which it occurs, we usually cannot establish its function.

1.3. Sentence functions introduced

We recognize five basic **sentence functions**, i.e. functions which may be used to form sentences:

subject	S
predicator	P
object	O
complement	C
adverbial	A

Here are some examples of these five basic sentence functions:

(1)   Sarah laughed.

   ^{S}[Sarah] ^{P}[laughed]

(2)   The old man wrote a long letter.

   ^{S}[The old man] ^{P}[wrote] ^{O}[a long letter]

(3)   He was writing very slowly.

   ^{S}[He] ^{P}[was writing] ^{A}[very slowly]

(4)   The letter was unbearably long.

   ^{S}[The letter] ^{P}[was] ^{C}[unbearably long]

In chapter 2 below, each of the five basic sentence functions will be examined in more detail.

1.4. Four form types

There are four different form types capable of assuming sentence functions:

single word	w
group of words	g
compound unit	cu
clause	cl

For example, in *Sarah laughed*, both the subject and the predicator are single words: ^{S}[Sarah] ^{P}[laughed]. In *The old man wrote a long letter*, the subject and the object are groups of words, the predicator a single word: ^{S}[The old man] ^{P}[wrote] ^{O}[a long letter]. All four types of form are present in an example like *That Helen left the party so early had bothered Jack and Jill immensely*: the subject [That Helen left the party so early] is a clause; the predicator [had bothered] is a group; the object [Jack and Jill] is a compound unit with two elements linked together, or coordinated; and, finally, the adverbial [immensely] is a single word.

Notice that we use lower-case letters for forms, capital letters being reserved for functions. Separating the two by a colon (:), we have a convenient way of describing both the function and the form of a constituent:

[That Helen left the party so early]	S:cl
[had bothered]	P:g
[Jack and Jill]	O:cu
[immensely]	A:w

Here are some more examples:

(1)   Richard was enjoying her company.

   $^{S:w}$[Richard] $^{P:g}$[was enjoying] $^{O:g}$[her company]

(2)   She had promised that they would come.

S:w[She] P:g[had promised] O:cl[that they would come]

(3)   The farmers laughed and danced until morning arrived.

S:g[The farmers] P:cu[laughed and danced] A:cl[until morning arrived]

Groups, compound units and clauses are **complex forms**, requiring analysis of their internal constituency, while individual words are **simple forms**.

1.5. Word classes

One of the forms introduced in section 1.4 will now be specified further: the individual word (w). Words are divided into eight main **word classes**:

nouns	=	n	(e.g. *car, letter, Jack, idea*)
verbs	=	v	(e.g. *write, be, receive, hear*)
adjectives	=	adj	(e.g. *long, old, afraid, big*)
adverbs	=	adv	(e.g. *slowly, gently, duly, very*)
pronouns	=	pro	(e.g. *he, she, who, any, this*)
prepositions	=	prep	(e.g. *by, at, to, from, in*)
conjunctions	=	conj	(e.g. *that, because, although*)
articles	=	art	(*the, a, an*)

In the brief description of these word classes below, use is made of quite a few technical grammatical terms (such as e.g. 'tense' and 'person'). The terms are simply illustrated at this point; definitions can be found in the glossary at the end of the book.

Nouns typically express things or persons. In doing so they are often combined with articles and inflected for the expression of 'number' (e.g. *the car* vs. *the cars*) and the 'genitive case' (e.g. *Jack* vs. *Jack's*).

Verbs typically express actions (terms of 'doing') or states (terms of 'being') and inflect for 'tense' and 'aspect' (e.g. *write* vs. *wrote*), 'person' and 'number' (e.g. *write* vs. *writes*).

Adjectives typically express qualities in relation to nouns and pronouns (e.g. *a long letter / Jack is old*) and often allow 'comparison' (e.g. *longer, longest / more afraid, most afraid*).

Adverbs typically express qualities in relation to verbs (e.g. *Jack moved slowly*), adjectives (e.g. *very big*), other adverbs (e.g. *so gently*), or the rest of the sentence (e.g. *Fortunately, everybody was saved*). Adverbs are often derived from adjectives by means of the ending *-ly* (a so-called 'suffix'): e.g. *slow → slowly, gentle → gently*. Like many adjectives, many adverbs allow 'comparison' (e.g. *more slowly, most slowly*).

Pronouns are a rather heterogeneous word class, comprising 'personal pronouns' (*I, me; you; he, him; she, her; it*, etc.), 'possessive pronouns' (*my, mine; your, yours*, etc.), 'reflexive pronouns' (*myself, yourself, herself*, etc.), 'demonstrative pronouns' (*that, those, this, these*), 'interrogative' and 'relative pronouns' (e.g. *who, which, what*), 'indefinite pronouns' (*some, something, any, anybody, no, nothing, every, everyone, all, (n)either, both*, etc.) and the grammatical prop words *it* and *there*.

Prepositions express relations (often spatial relations) between constituents. They typically do so by relating a noun or group (e.g. *the table*) to another noun or group (e.g. *the book*) as in *the book on the table*, or to some action or state (*The book was placed on the table / The book is on the table*).

Conjunctions also express relations between constituents. **Coordinating** conjunctions do so by combining constituents at the same level (e.g. *cars and books, clever but arrogant*). **Subordinating** conjunctions place one clause (e.g. *He didn't support her*) at a lower level in relation to another clause (e.g. *I said that he didn't support her*, where [he didn't support her] is at a lower level than [I said]).

Articles typically combine with nouns to express definiteness (e.g. *the car, the idea*) or indefiniteness (e.g. *a car, an idea*).

To the eight main word classes we may add **interjections** (intj) like *huh, ouch, well, oh, wow*, etc.), **numerals** (num) like *five, hundreds, 1993, tenth, twenty-first*, etc.), and the **infinitive marker** (infm) *to*, as in *To see her is to love her*.

The **classification of a word** is often difficult in isolation from its linguistic context. Many words are of course easily identifiable as members of one, and only one, word class: *policeman* is always a noun, *eliminate* is always a verb, *the* always an article, *always* always an adverb, etc. But there are also cases where we have to rely on the context to reveal the function of the word before we can classify it. Put differently, there are cases where word-class membership cannot be determined independently of function. For example, *blow* is a noun in *It was a hard blow to him*, but a verb in *The referee may blow his whistle any time now. Early* is an adjective in *He took an early train* but an adverb in *He left the party very early*.

To describe words precisely it is important to distinguish between words as **lexical items** and **words in use**. Consider the following examples:

(1)   We all *love* Sally.

(2)   Richard probably *loves* her more than the rest of us.

(3)   Even bad-tempered, old Graham *loved* her once.

(4)   As for myself, I cannot help *loving* her, too.

What we see here is **inflectional variation** of an item which does not result in a change of word class. Though distinct, *love*, *loves*, *loved* and *loving* 'belong' to the same word, or lexical item, the verb *love*. This means that we have to distinguish between a word in isolation – the **base form** as it appears in a dictionary – and its inflectional **manifestation form** in actual speech or writing. Henceforth capital letters are used to emphasize the status of a word as a base form, and italics are used to emphasize the status of a word as a manifestation form. Thus, for example, *love*, *loves*, *loved* and *loving* are manifestation forms of the base form LOVE.

Of the eight main word classes listed above, the first four (nouns, verbs, adjectives and adverbs) are **open classes** whereas the last four (pronouns, prepositions, conjunctions and articles) are **closed classes**. Open word classes have indefinitely many members and a fairly relaxed 'membership policy', admitting new members whenever there is a need for them. Closed word classes have relatively few members and rarely allow any change. Thus we often get new nouns (for example, as the result of new technology: LASER, VIDEO, SOFTWARE, etc.) but the classes of prepositions and articles stay the same for a very long period of time. Members of open word classes typically have one or more independently identifiable meanings. Thus, simply by looking at nouns like POLICEMAN and STORY we get a clear sense of their meaning. By contrast, members of closed word classes have little independent meaning. Instead they seem to get their meaning in relation to other words. For example, in isolation it makes little sense to discuss the meaning of, say, the definite article *the*, the conjunction *that*, the relative pronoun *which* and the preposition *at*. In appropriate linguistic contexts, however, these words assist open-class words in forming coherent sentences and utterances. The presence of e.g. the definite article in the context of a singular noun typically ensures that we interpret the noun as a word which refers to a specific, identifiable entity.

Having classified words into classes, we are now in a position to offer complete analyses of sentences consisting of one-word constituents:

(5)   John left her yesterday.

$S{:}n$[John] $P{:}v$[left] $O{:}pro$[her] $A{:}adv$[yesterday]

(6)   Predictably everybody liked chocolate.

$A{:}adv$[Predictably] $S{:}pro$[everybody] $P{:}v$[liked] $O{:}n$[chocolate]

1.6. Discontinuity

There is in language a tendency for things which belong together to be positioned together. Thus, in the examples we have looked at so far, all complex constituents (groups, compound units or clauses) have been **continuous** in the sense that all the elements making up the constituent appear in an uninterrupted string, one following the other. For instance, in:

(1)   Jack was kissing the beautiful girl

both the complex constituents, the P:g (*was + kissing*) and the O:g (*the + beautiful + girl*), are continuous: there are no intervening elements from other constituents in these strings. However sometimes the principle of continuity may be overridden by other considerations. One example of this is found in:

(2)   *Was* Jack *kissing* the beautiful girl?

Here *was* from the P:g in example (1) has been moved up in front of the subject noun *Jack*. The physical separation in example (2) of the two words *Was* and *kissing* does not in any way impair the sense that they belong together in a group, as a constituent. The fact that we have a 'broken relationship' seems closely related to the communicative difference between the two examples: the first sentence is a statement, the second is a question. In example (2), the predicator group is a **discontinuous** constituent: an element which does not belong to the P:g (namely the subject) intervenes between the two parts of the P:g.

In our analysis, discontinuity can be marked by hyphens as in:

(3)   Ildiko *did* not *send* the letter last night.
      S:n[Ildiko] P:g-[did] A:adv[not] -P:g[send] O:g[the letter] A:g[last night]

In this example, right-hyphenation in P:g- and left-hyphenation in -P:g indicate a discontinuous relationship between *did* and *send*. Together the two units make up the constituent P:g.

Here are some other examples of discontinuity:

(4)   *Where do* you *come from*? (A:g- P:g- S:pro -P:g -A:g)
(5)   I met *a girl* last night *who lives in Tasmania*. (S:pro P:v O:g- A:g -O:g)

1.7. Basic sentence structures

In English it is possible to define a number of **basic sentence structures**. These are the typical constellations of sentence functions in positive statements. The nature of the predicator is often decisive for the presence and absence of other functions and should therefore be further examined. There are three main kinds of predicator: **intransitive, transitive** and **copula**.

An **intransitive predicator** is a predicator which takes no object or complement. Some intransitive predicators take an **obligatory** adverbial (i.e.

an adverbial which must be present to make the sentence syntactically complete) and/or a number of **optional** adverbials (i.e. adverbials which are syntactically – though typically not semantically – redundant):

(1)   (Again) Richard *was sleeping* (heavily) (in my room).
       A:adv[Again] S:n[Richard] P:g[was sleeping] A:adv[heavily] A:g[in my room]

(2)   Jessica *was* in London.
       S:n[Jessica] P:v[was] A:g[in London]

In (1) the optional adverbials are in parentheses. In (2) the adverbial *in London* is obligatory. Disregarding the occurrence of optional adverbials, we can represent the possible basic sentence structures in statements with intransitive predicators in this way:

> S P
> S P A

A **transitive predicator** is a predicator which takes an object:

(3)   Richard *kissed* Jessica.
       S:n[Richard] P:v[kissed] O:n[Jessica]

(4)   The naughty boy *teased* his parents (at all times).
       S:g[The naughty boy] P:v[teased] O:g[his parents] A:g[at all times]

Transitive predicators are thus associated with the following basic structure (again we disregard optional adverbials):

> S P O

A **copula predicator** is a predicator which takes a complement:

(5)   Marion *is* such a nice person.
       S:n[Marion] P:v[is] C:g[such a nice person]

(6)   They *looked* so unhappy (when I met them in Paris).
       S:pro[They] P:v[looked] C:g[so unhappy] A:cl[when I met them in Paris]

The complement describes the subject and is therefore sometimes called 'subject complement'. Copula predicators are associated with the following basic structure:

> S P C

It is important to note that many verbs may serve in more than one of these basic types of predicator. Consider the following examples:

(7a)   James *smoked* an expensive cigar after dinner.

(7b)   Richard never *smoked*.

(8a)   Sally *was reading* the newspaper when I got back.

(8b)   Marion *was reading* while Tom did the dishes.

(9a)   She *got* pretty mad at me.

(9b)   I *got* little reward for my efforts.

In examples (7a) and (8a), *smoked* and *was reading* are transitive, taking an object (*an expensive cigar* and *the newspaper*, respectively). In the corresponding b-examples, these predicators are intransitive. In example (9a), *got* is a copula predicator followed by a complement (*pretty mad at me*). In (9b), *got* is a transitive predicator taking an object (*little reward*).

1.8. More sentence functions and structures

In addition to the basic sentence structures identified in section 1.7 above, there are a number of more complex structures which need to be introduced in this section. Consider, first of all, the following sentences, which contain two objects, a **direct object** (Od) and an **indirect object** (Oi):

(1)   John gave the little girl a new doll.

   $^{S:n}$[John] $^{P:v}$[gave] $^{Oi:g}$[the little girl] $^{Od:g}$[a new doll]

(2)   I bought my wife a new fur coat.

   $^{S:pro}$[I] $^{P:v}$[bought] $^{Oi:g}$[my wife] $^{Od:g}$[a new fur coat]

We use the abbreviation O if there is only one object present in a sentence, reserving Od and Oi for sentences with two objects. Predicators taking one object only are called **monotransitive**, those taking two objects are called **ditransitive**. In monotransitive constructions, the object is typically, though not inevitably, a direct rather than an indirect object. In ditransitive statements, the indirect object normally precedes the direct object:

   S P Oi Od

Sometimes we find combinations of an object and a complement, or an object and an obligatory adverbial, following the predicator. Predicators in such constructions are called **complex-transitive**. In complex-transitive constructions, a complement is called an **object complement** (Co), because it refers back to the object rather than to the subject:

(3)   We painted the wall yellow.

   $^{S:pro}$[We] $^{P:v}$[painted] $^{O:g}$[the wall] $^{Co:adj}$[yellow]

(4)   Actually, the staff elected Miss Johnson dean.

   $^{A:adv}$[Actually] $^{S:g}$[the staff] $^{P:v}$[elected] $^{O:g}$[Miss Johnson] $^{Co:n}$[dean]

Here are some examples of complex-transitive combinations of an object and an obligatory adverbial:

(5)   My father put the book on the shelf.
       S:g[My father] P:v[put] O:g[the book] A:g[on the shelf]
(6)   I slipped the key into the lock.
       S:pro[I] P:v[slipped] O:g[the key] A:g[into the lock]

Complex-transitive predicators thus yield two different types of structure:

> S P O Co
> S P O A

These sentence structures are obviously related to the copula S P C structure
and the intransitive S P A structure, respectively.

1.9. Summary of sentence functions and structures

We can now refine the list of sentence functions presented in section 1.3
above:

subject	S
predicator	P
direct object	Od
indirect object	Oi
subject complement	Cs
object complement	Co
adverbial	A

The typical sentence structures that these sentence functions form in
statements can be summarized thus:

S P	(intransitive predicator)
S P A	(intransitive predicator)
S P O	(monotransitive predicator)
S P Cs	(copula predicator)
S P Oi Od	(ditransitive predicator)
S P O Co	(complex-transitive predicator)
S P O A	(complex-transitive predicator)

2. Sentence functions

2.1. The predicator

The identification of subject, object, complement and adverbial often
depends on the prior identification of the predicator. Fortunately the form of
the sentence predicator is relatively stable and therefore fairly easy to
identify. It almost always consists of one or more verbs:

(1a)   Jack *treated* Sophia very badly.
(1b)   Jack *is treating* Sophia very badly.
(1c)   Jack *has been treating* Sophia very badly.
(1d)   Jack *may have been treating* Sophia very badly.

As we see in these examples, there are various ways of expressing a situation of 'Jack treating Sophia very badly': the key word is in each case TREAT. In fact, the italicized predicator in (1a) to (1d) can be regarded as different manifestation forms of the base form TREAT, involving one or more words. To describe the organization of the predicator, we distinguish between **full verbs** and **auxiliary verbs** (or simply 'auxiliaries'). A predicator may consist of just a full verb (as in example (1a)) or a full verb preceded by up to three auxiliary verbs (as in examples (1b) to (1d)).

The difference between a full verb and an auxiliary is normally one of semantic weight: full verbs have independently identifiable lexical meanings whereas auxiliaries are more like closed-class items (articles, prepositions, pronouns and conjunctions) in that they relate to other words. Formally, the two types of verb can be distinguished in terms of position: in predicators where both are present, the last verb is the full verb and the others are auxiliaries. If one wants to test whether a verb is a full verb or an auxiliary, one can convert a statement containing the verb into a **yes-no question** (i.e. a question of the type which tries to elicit either a *yes* or a *no* for an answer, e.g. *Do you like me?*). If the verb readily precedes the subject it is an auxiliary whereas if it cannot precede the subject it is a full verb (note that the symbol * is used in front of an unacceptable sentence, cf. (4b) and (5b)):

(2a)   Rob *was having* a nightmare.
(2b)   *Was* Rob *having* a nightmare?
(3a)   He *can run* a mile in six minutes.
(3b)   *Can* he *run* a mile in six minutes?
(4a)   Steven *finished* his cheeseburger.
(4b)   **Finished* Steven his cheeseburger?
(5a)   Cathy *kept* laughing.
(5b)   **Kept* Cathy laughing?

In examples (2) and (3) BE and CAN are shown to be auxiliaries. In (4) and (5) FINISH and KEEP are shown to be full verbs. To form a *yes-no* question from a statement containing a full verb only, **DO-support** must be used (see further below):

(4c)   *Did* Steven *finish* his cheeseburger?
(5c)   *Did* Cathy *keep* laughing?

In such cases DO is an auxiliary.

Note that three verbs, BE, HAVE and DO, are special in that they function sometimes as auxiliaries and sometimes as full verbs. In the latter case they may stand alone in the predicator:

(6a) Jack *is* now fully awake.

(7a) The old dancer *has* fond memories of Paris.

(8a) Her parents *did* nothing to change her mind.

The three verbs form a small closed class of so-called **primary verbs**. When functioning as a full verb, BE regularly precedes the subject in *yes-no* questions; HAVE occasionally allows this position in formal BrE; DO always takes DO-support:

(6b) *Is* Jack now fully awake?

(7b) *Has* the old dancer fond memories of Paris?

(7c) *Does* the old dancer *have* fond memories of Paris?

(8b) *Did* her parents *do* nothing to change her mind?

Auxiliaries other than the three primary verbs are called **modal verbs**. The central modal verbs are: *can, could, may, might, shall, should, will, would, must.* They have no base form, only a fixed present and past form. There can never be more than one central modal auxiliary in a predicator. In strings of auxiliaries, the others are typically forms of the primary verbs BE and HAVE.

A predicator is **finite** if it contains a finite verb. A predicator is **nonfinite** if all the verbs in it are nonfinite. A finite predicator may contain up to three nonfinite verbs in addition to the finite verb. The distinction between finite and nonfinite hinges on the presence or absence of present/past marking: a finite verb is either formally present (e.g. *(they) sing, (she) runs*) or formally past (e.g. *(they) sang, (she) ran*) whereas a nonfinite verb belongs to one of the following three form types:

(i) infinitives (with or without the infinitive marker): *(to) break, (to) think, (to) worry*, etc.;

(ii) present participles: *breaking, thinking, worrying*, etc.;

(iii) past participles: *broken, thought, worried*, etc.

In the following examples, all the predicators (marked in square brackets) are finite, containing a finite verb (in italics):

(9) Jack and Jill [*take*] a walk every morning.

(10) Jack [*takes*] things as they come.

(11) Jack and Jill [*have* taken] their stand on the issue.

(12) Both of them [*could* have been taking] the dog for a walk.

All the non-italicized verbs in these finite predicators (i.e. *taking, taken, have, been*) are nonfinite by themselves. The same is true of *take* when it is an infinitive, not a present form, as in the following examples:

(13)   To *take* a walk would be foolish.

In a string of verbs in a finite predicator, it is the first verb (the first auxiliary) which is finite. This verb is often referred to as the **operator**. Also the primary verbs BE and HAVE are usually operators even when they are alone in a predicator (cf. examples (6a-b) and (7a-b) above). The operator is called operator because it can do things which other verbs cannot. Thus, to form *yes-no* questions, the operator moves to a position in front of the subject. This is known as **subject-operator inversion**, sometimes referred to as 'partial inversion' because, typically, only a part of the predicator, the operator, is moved, cf. examples (2) and (3) above; for discussion see section 7.2.1 below. Another characteristic of the operator is that, unlike other verbs, it regularly precedes NOT in negative sentences:

(14)   I *could* not swim across.
(15)   She *may* not like us.

We can now explain the **two main uses of DO-support** in English: when there is no operator in a positive statement (e.g. *I swam across* and *She likes us*), DO is inserted as a 'dummy' operator to form a *yes-no* question (by moving in front of the subject) or a negative clause (by preceding NOT):

(16)   *Do* I swim across?
(17)   I *did* not swim across.
(18)   *Does* she like us?
(19)   She *did* not like us.

In addition to these two main uses, DO-support is also used to create emphasis. This is called **emphatic DO-support**:

(20)   I *did* swim across.
(21)   But she *does* like us.

In these examples DO – pronounced with nuclear stress – is used to emphasize the meaning of the whole sentence and can thus be used to express a contrast to the corresponding negative statement:

(22)   A: Why didn't you own up?
        B: I `did own up.

There can be **only one full verb in a predicator**. In examples like the following the second verb is thus by definition outside the sentence predicator:

(23)   My old friend [decided] *to leave* the party.

(24)   His girlfriend [stopped] *singing*.

In these examples, *to leave* and *singing* are part of, or fully constitute, the object rather than belong to the predicator (see further section 12.3).

Let us summarize the defining characteristics of the sentence predicator:

(i) A sentence predicator is always finite, containing a finite verb, showing formal present/past marking.

(ii) A predicator contains one, and only one, full verb.

(iii) Apart from the full verb, a predicator may contain up to three auxiliary verbs (a modal auxiliary and/or one or more forms of the primary verbs BE, HAVE and DO), the first of which is finite and called the operator.

2.2. The subject

Once the predicator of a sentence has been identified, it is usually quite simple to locate the subject. Typically, the subject expresses the person or thing which the predicator says, or predicates, something about. The subject is thus the **topic** of statements, whereas the predicator is part of what is being stated about the subject, the **comment** made about the subject. We can find the subject by asking 'Who or what' immediately followed by the predicator, i.e. 'Who or what + P?' The answer to that question is the subject. Consider:

(1)   The parish *vibrated* with gossip the next day.

(2)   Daphne *had enjoyed* the illicit character of our relationship.

(3)   It *was* a terrible shock to Mummy and Daddy.

To find the subject in (1) to (3) we simply ask the question 'Who or what P?':

(1')   Who or what *vibrated*?   *The parish* (did)

(2')   Who or what *had enjoyed*?   *Daphne* (had)

(3')   Who or what *was*?   *It* (was)

While this fairly simple test applies to the vast majority of sentences, there are instances where it does not really make sense to ask 'Who or what P?':

(4)   It *was raining* cats and dogs.

(4')   Who or what was raining?   **It*

More formally, the subject displays a number of defining characteristics:

(i) The subject typically precedes the predicator in simple statements (as we see in examples (1) to (4)).

(ii) The subject is always placed between the operator and the rest of the predicator in *yes-no* questions (if the predicator is the primary verb BE, it simply precedes the subject):

(1a)   *Did* the parish *vibrate* with gossip the next day?
(2a)   *Had* Daphne *enjoyed* the illicit character of our relationship?
(3a)   *Was* it a terrible shock to Mummy and Daddy?
(4a)   *Was* it *raining* cats and dogs?

(iii) Like the predicator, but unlike any other constituent, the subject is always obligatorily present in sentences expressing statements. This means that minimal sentences expressing statements consist of S and P:

(5)   John left.
(6)   The last glimmer of hope evaporated.

(iv) There is **concord** between subject and predicator, i.e. agreement between these constituents in terms of **number** (singular or plural) and **person** (first, second or third). With one exception (see below), subject-predicator concord is restricted to the present form of the finite verb: if the subject is in the singular third person (i.e. *he, she, it,* or anything potentially represented by these pronouns), the verb takes the suffix *-(e)s*, otherwise it appears in its base form:

(7a)   I *take* it easy.
(7b)   She *takes* it easy.
(8a)   The young woman *teaches* English grammar.
(8b)   The young women *teach* English grammar.

The verb BE is especially expressive with respect to concord, being the only verb showing concord in the past form and showing three person distinctions in the present form:

(9a)   I *am* better now than I *was*.
(9b)   You/We/They *are* better now than you/we/they *were*.
(9c)   He/She/It *is* better now than he/she/it *was*.
(10)   The book/books *was/were* far too expensive.

(v) With pronouns to which the distinction between the **subjective** and **objective case** applies (e.g. *I/me, he/him, she/her, we/us, they/them*), the subjective case is used when the pronoun functions as the subject of a finite predicator (see e.g. (7a-b) and (9a-c)).

(vi) Subjects, but not objects, complements or adverbials, can be represented by a pronoun in a so-called **tag question** (i.e. a question added to a sentence for emphasis) (curly brackets are here used to show the constituent referred back to):

(11)   {Bob} gave them extra work, didn't *he*?

(12)   {You and I} know better, don't *we*?

In some sentences there are *two* subjects, a **provisional subject** (Sp) and a **real subject** (Sr). Only *it* and *there* may function as provisional subject:

(13)   It was obvious that he disliked her.
        Sp:pro[It] P:v[was] C:adj[obvious] Sr:cl[that he disliked her]

(14)   There were five books on the table.
        Sp:pro[There] P:v[were] Sr:g[five books] A:g[on the table]

The provisional subject is semantically very light: it functions as a grammatical **dummy** (or prop) word in subject position, merely representing the real subject, which – for reasons to be discussed later – has been postponed. In the case of *it*, it is usually possible to move the real subject back to subject position, and in the case of *there* this is occasionally possible:

(15a)   It was obvious that he disliked her.

(15b)   That he disliked her was obvious.

(16a)   There were five books on the table.

(16b)   Five books were on the table.

Note that in sentences with *it* as the provisional subject, the real subject is said to be **extraposed**, i.e. it is placed at the end of the sentence, outside the actual sentence structure, and can sometimes be deleted without this affecting the grammaticality of the sentence (as in (15a): *It was obvious*). By contrast, the real subject in sentences with *there* as provisional subject is more closely integrated in the overall sentence structure: it is often followed by other constituents and it cannot be deleted without reducing the sentence to something that does not have sentence structure.

There is used as provisional subject in so-called **existential sentences**, i.e. sentences expressing the fact that something or someone exists somewhere. Existential sentences are always intransitive (i.e. 'object-less', cf. section 1.7 above). The real subject in such sentences is typically indefinite (e.g. *a book, books, some books, no book, something, somebody, nothing*) rather than definite (e.g. *the book, these books, John's books, that one, Bill, my parents,* etc.). The predicator is usually realized by a form of BE, by a modal verb + *be*, or by SEEM, APPEAR, HAPPEN or TEND followed by *to be*:

(17)   There *were* several students in the library.

(18)   There *could be* more than one kind of complexity.

(19)   There *seemed to be* no one left to talk to.

Other verbs are possible in existential sentences:

(20)   There *remained* a few unsolved problems.
(21)   There *emerged* in him a peculiar sense of affection for her.

Such constructions are fairly formal and the verbs are always semantically light, denoting either something stative (as in (20)) or the transition or arrival of something (as in (21)).

Occasionally the real subject of an existential sentence is realized by a definite construction to indicate that a known entity is an example or a possible solution to a problem, cf. the following data:

(22)   'Who could we ask?' 'Well, there's James, or Miranda, or Ann, or Sue, ...'
(23)   'Where can he sleep?' 'Well, there's always the attic.'

It and *there* as provisional subjects should be distinguished from *it* and *there* with **referential meaning**. *It* and *there* with referential meaning refer to, or represent, an entity (object, place, etc.) in the 'external world' or in the preceding text:

(24)   *It* came towards me with a fierce snarl.
        S:pro[It] P:v[came] A:g[towards me] A:g[with a fierce snarl]
(25)   *There* I finally found the letter.
        A:adv[There] S:pro[I] A:adv[finally] P:v[found] O:g[the letter]

In example (24), *It* obviously refers to something, e.g. an animal, in the (linguistic and/or extralinguistic) context. In (25), *There* refers to the place – contextually familiar to the speaker and hearer – where the letter was found (e.g. 'I opened the top drawer and *there* I finally found the letter').

Occasionally we find cases of *it* used as a non-referential grammatical prop word, i.e. with little or no meaning, as the only subject in a sentence (especially in expressions about **weather conditions**, **time** and **distance**):

(26)   *It* was raining again.
        S:pro[It] P:g[was raining] A:adv[again]

(27)   *It* was getting late.
        S:pro[It] P:g[was getting] C:adj[late]

(28)   *It* is a long way to Fitzroy Crossing.
        S:pro[It] P:v[is] C:g[a long way to Fitzroy Crossing]

2.3. The direct object

In section 2.2, we saw that the subject is commonly the topic of simple statements. To this **pragmatic** function (i.e. general communicative function) we can add one of a number of more specific semantic functions that constituents may have in relation to the action or situation expressed by the predicator. Often the subject has the role of **agent**, i.e. it is the participant performing the action expressed by the predicator. By contrast, the direct object (which like the predicator is considered to be part of the comment made about the subject) is typically the participant **affected** by the action expressed by the predicator, i.e. the thing or person towards which/whom the action is directed. We get a sense of these roles when we consider examples like the following:

(1)   Harris moved the bike.
        $S{:}n$[Harris] $P{:}v$[moved] $O{:}g$[the bike]
(2)   The little girl kissed the shaggy dog.
        $S{:}g$[The little girl] $P{:}v$[kissed] $O{:}g$[the shaggy dog]
(3)   They hit Sally on the head.
        $S{:}pro$[They] $P{:}v$[hit] $O{:}n$[Sally] $A{:}g$[on the head]

In these examples, the subjects are agents performing the actions of 'moving', 'kissing' and 'hitting', respectively. The objects are affected by these actions: the bike gets moved, the shaggy dog gets kissed and Sally gets hit. That both subjects and direct objects may express many other semantic functions is evident in examples like (4) to (6):

(4)   This bottle contains cold tea.
        $S{:}g$[This bottle] $P{:}v$[contains] $O{:}g$[cold tea]
(5)   I saw her very clearly.
        $S{:}pro$[I] $P{:}v$[saw] $O{:}pro$[her] $A{:}g$[very clearly]
(6)   Max has received detailed reports.
        $S{:}n$[Max] $P{:}g$[has received] $O{:}g$[detailed reports]

A more detailed description of the various meanings and roles attached to subjects and direct objects can be found in chapter 8.

Direct objects are identified by asking: 'Who(m) or what' followed by the relevant partially inverted S P construction. Applying this test to examples (1) to (6) above, we get the following appropriate answers:

(1')   Who(m) or what did Harris move?   *The bike*
(2')   Who(m) or what did the little girl kiss?   *The shaggy dog*
(3')   Who(m) or what did they hit?   *Sally*

(4')	Who(m) or what does this bottle contain?	*Cold tea*
(5')	Who(m) or what did I see?	*Her*
(6')	Who(m) or what has Max received?	*Detailed reports*

There are a number of formal characteristics of direct objects:

(i) The direct object usually follows immediately after the predicator in monotransitive statements, as in examples (1) to (6).

(ii) The direct object in a monotransitive **active** construction may often, though not always, serve as the subject in an intransitive **passive** construction. The active/passive distinction is a so-called **voice** distinction relating to **information structure** (i.e. the way information is presented) and the assignment of **focus** to constituents. Almost all the examples offered so far have been active. Passive counterparts to active sentences are formed by assigning subject function to the direct (sometimes indirect) object of the active sentence and by changing the active predicator into a passive one consisting of a form of BE followed by the past participle of the full verb of the active predicator. The original subject may be expressed by an adverbial *by*-group:

(7a)   Jack's secretary typed Bill's letters. (active)
   S:g[Jack's secretary] P:v[typed] O:g[Bill's letters]

(7b)   Bill's letters were typed by Jack's secretary. (passive)
   S:g[Bill's letters] P:g[were typed] A:g[by Jack's secretary]

(8a)   The terrorists blindfolded everybody. (active)

(8b)   Everybody was blindfolded (by the terrorists). (passive)

(iii) With pronouns to which the distinction between the subjective and objective case applies (e.g. *I/me, he/him, she/her, we/us, they/them*), the objective case is used when the pronoun functions as direct object:

(9)   She remembered *him* for his good manners.
   S:pro[she] P:v[remembered] O:pro[him] A:g[for his good manners]

(10)   They saw *us* from a mile off.

In some sentences there are **two** direct objects, a **provisional direct object** (Op) and an **extraposed real direct object** (Or). Only *it* may serve as provisional direct object:

(11)   They found *it* difficult *to work with him*.
   S:pro[They] P:v[found] Op:pro[it] Co:adj[difficult] Or:cl[to work with him]

(12)   I took *it* for granted *that they would leave early*.

The provisional direct object functions as a grammatical dummy or prop word in object position (immediately after the predicator), representing the extraposed real object. An extraposed real object is always a (finite or nonfinite) clause. It is not usually possible to move the extraposed object to normal object position:

(13a) I made *it* clear to her *that I accept no nonsense.*
(13b) *I made that I accept no nonsense clear to her.

It as a provisional direct object should be distinguished from *it* as a real direct object with referential meaning:

(14) They took it (= e.g. his loyalty) for granted.
      S:pro[They] P:v[took] O:pro[it] A:g[for granted]

In this example, *it* refers back to something mentioned in the previous discourse: *They never questioned his loyalty. I think they took it for granted.*

Occasionally, in more or less fixed expressions, we find *it* used as a non-referential grammatical prop word, i.e. with little or no meaning, as the only object in a sentence:

(15) They hit *it* off together.
      S:pro[They] P:v[hit] O:pro[it] A:adv[off] A:adv[together]
(16) I like *it* here.

2.4. The indirect object

An indirect object typically expresses the participant benefiting or suffering from the situation or action expressed by the combination of subject, predicator and direct object. The semantic function assigned to the indirect object is called **beneficiary**:

(1) Fred bought Sally a bunch of roses.
     S:n[Fred] P:v[bought] Oi:n[Sally] Od:g[a bunch of roses]
(2) Her little sister dealt Jack a severe blow.
     S:g[Her little sister] P:v[dealt] Oi:n[Jack] Od:g[a severe blow]

But sometimes the semantic function of indirect objects is less concrete:

(3) My wife gave going to France a good deal of thought.
     S:g[My wife] P:v[gave] Oi:cl[going to France] Od:g[a good deal of thought]

In addition to the semantic clue, there are a number of other characteristics of indirect objects which help us identify them:

(i) The indirect object usually appears immediately after the predicator and before the direct object, as in (1) to (3). There is, especially in BrE, an exception to this rule: when functioning as direct objects, *it* and *them* are sometimes seen to precede pronominal indirect objects:

(4)   I gave it him.

S:pro[I] P:v[gave] Od:pro[it] Oi:pro[him]

A third option is often chosen here to avoid ambiguity or confusion: an expression containing an adverbial *to*-phrase instead of an indirect object, as in *I gave it to him*.

(ii) Related to this last point is the general paraphrase relation between ditransitive constructions and monotransitive (or complex transitive) constructions containing an adverbial *to*- or *for*-phrase:

(5a)   They offered *the old man* a new job.

S:pro[They] P:v[offered] Oi:g[the old man] Od:g[a new job]

(5b)   They offered a new job *to the old man*.

S:pro[They] P:v[offered] Od:g[a new job] A:g[to the old man]

(6a)   My mother has baked *us* a chocolate cake.

(6b)   My mother has baked a chocolate cake *for us*.

(iii) Like the direct object, the indirect object may often serve as the subject in a corresponding passive construction. Thus, to a ditransitive construction, we often find two alternative corresponding passive constructions, one – much more common – with the active indirect object as the passive subject and one with the active direct object as the passive subject:

(7a)   Jack gave Sally a silver ring.

S:n[Jack] P:v[gave] Oi:n[Sally] Od:g[a silver ring]

(7b)   Sally was given a silver ring (by Jack).

S:n[Sally] P:g[was given] O:g[a silver ring] (A:g[by Jack])

(7c)   A silver ring was given Sally (by Jack).

S:g[A silver ring] P:g[was given] O:n[Sally] (A:g[by Jack])

When the active direct object becomes the passive subject, there is a preference for expressing the beneficiary in an adverbial *to*- or *for*-phrase:

(7d)   A silver ring was given *to Sally* (by Jack).

(iv) With pronouns to which the distinction between the subjective and objective case applies (e.g. *I/me, he/him, she/her, we/us, they/them*), the objective case is used when the pronoun functions as indirect object:

(8)   Granny was reading *them* a chapter.

(9)   Mr Smith ordered *me* a new radio.

From ditransitive constructions we can typically derive only monotransitive constructions with the direct object:

(10a)   Billy gave his brother a penknife.
(10b)   Billy gave a penknife.
(10c)   *Billy gave his brother.

With a few verbs, however, either the direct object or the indirect object in a transitive construction may function as the sole object in a monotransitive construction, cf. the following examples with TEACH:

(11a)   The young man taught us linguistics.
(11b)   The young man taught linguistics.
(11c)   The young man taught us.

Note that in clauses with TELL or TEACH, clausal direct objects require the presence of an indirect object:

(12a)   The young man taught us how to fix a lock.
(12b)   *The young man taught how to fix a lock.
(13a)   Jack told us that he missed his brother.
(13b)   *Jack told that he missed his brother.

2.5. The subject complement

A subject complement (for which we use the abbreviation 'Cs' or simply 'C') offers a **description** of the referent of the subject:

(1)   This is a misfortune.
         $^{S:pro}$[This] $^{P:v}$[is] $^{C:g}$[a misfortune]
(2)   Jack became my best friend.
         $^{S:n}$[Jack] $^{P:v}$[became] $^{C:g}$[my best friend]
(3)   My brother looks very intelligent.
         $^{S:g}$[My brother] $^{P:v}$[looks] $^{C:g}$[very intelligent]
(4)   My sister often gets more upset than Jack.
         $^{S:g}$[My sister] $^{A:adv}$[often] $^{P:v}$[gets] $^{C:g}$[more upset than Jack]

In examples (1) and (2), there is identity between the subject and the complement, the complement offering a (different) description of the thing or person referred to by the subject *This* or *Jack*, respectively. In examples (3) and (4), the complement simply assigns a quality to the subject, that of being 'very intelligent' and 'more upset than Jack', respectively.

   One diagnostic feature of the complement function is that – unlike subjects, objects and adverbials – it can almost always be realized by an adjective or adjectival construction (such as *very intelligent* and *more upset than Jack* in examples (3) and (4), respectively). Like subjects and objects, complements are however often realized by nominal constructions. But when a complement is realized in this way (as in examples (1) and (2)), one way of deciding that it is indeed a complement (rather than, say, an object) is to see if it can be replaced by an adjectival construction without this affecting the acceptability of the sentence:

(1')   This is *unfortunate*.
(2')   Jack became *very friendly*.

Exceptions to this diagnostic feature are rare:

(5a)   Sarah made (= became) a fine soldier.
(5b)   *Sarah made very brave.

The verbs serving as copula predicators fall into two groups: the **stative** 'BE' family and the **dynamic** 'BECOME' family. The members of the 'BE' family express 'identity' or '(possible) current possession of quality or characteristic feature' (e.g. BE, REMAIN, APPEAR, FEEL, LOOK, PROVE, SEEM, SOUND, STAY, TASTE). Examples:

(6)   She *remained* silent.
(7)   The decision *appeared* all wrong to me.
(8)   The directors simply *proved* far too inefficient.
(9)   That *sounds* good to me.
(10)   The cheese *tasted* sour.

The members of the 'BECOME' family express change and are resultative in meaning (e.g. BECOME, GET, FALL, TURN, GO, GROW, RUN and SPRING, particularly in set phrases). Examples:

(11)   Within a week my mother *fell* seriously ill.
(12)   Our teacher eventually *went* raving mad.
(13)   I *grew* quite fond of her despite our differences.
(14)   The river *was running* dry.
(15)   The lock *sprang* open.

The descriptive meaning associated with S P C constructions can sometimes also be expressed by intransitive constructions with adverbials; compare:

(16)   She was *happy*.
        S:pro[She] P:v[was] C:adj[happy]
(17)   She was *in high spirits*.
        S:pro[She] P:v[was] A:g[in high spirits]

The approach adopted in such cases is to distinguish between adverbial and complement on the basis of **form**: when the descriptive attribute is realized by a preposition group (like *in high spirits*), it is an adverbial; when it is realized by an adjective (like *happy*), it is a complement. This approach is consistent with the way we distinguish between adverbial and indirect object in sentences involving a beneficiary like *I gave the book to John* vs. *I gave John the book*: in the former example, the group *to John* is an adverbial, in the latter, the noun *John* is an indirect object.

Note finally that many verbs functioning as copula predicators may serve also as transitive and/or intransitive predicators:

(18)   He *proved* the point by singing the ballad himself.

(19)   My mother *fell* and hurt her knee badly.

(20)   We *grow* oranges in our garden.

2.6. The object complement

An object complement (Co) expresses further information about the referent of the object:

(1)   We painted the wall *white*.
      $S:pro$[We] $P:v$[painted] $O:g$[the wall] $Co:adj$[white]

(2)   They drove Stephen *mad*.

(3)   Jack considered Jane *his closest friend*.

In these examples there is a close relationship between the object and the object complement very similar to the one between subject and subject complement in S P C constructions: in (1) the wall becomes white; in (2) Stephen gets mad; and in (3) Jane is Jack's closest friend. In other words, there is in each case an implied S P Cs construction. Interestingly S P O Co constructions are actually turned into S P Cs constructions in the passive voice. Thus corresponding to (1) to (3) we get the following:

(1')   The wall was painted *white*.
      $S:g$[The wall] $P:g$[was painted] $C:adj$[white]

(2')   Stephen was driven *mad*.

(3')   Jane was considered *his closest friend*.

Object complements, like subject complements, are realized by nominal constructions or adjectival constructions. As with subject complements, the option of being realized by an adjectival construction is a fairly reliable diagnostic feature; but there are striking exceptions:

(4)   Her fellow students elected her *president* / **dutiful*.

(5)   The Vice-Chancellor appointed Penny *dean of the humanities* / **responsible*.

The kind of relation which exists between object and object complement may be expressed by other types of construction, notably S P O A constructions:

(6)   Many people regard *Jack as an eccentric.*

    S:g[Many people] P:v[regard] O:n[Jack] A:g[as an eccentric]

(7)   The professor took *her for a native speaker of English.*

2.7. Adverbials

Traditionally, the adverbial is regarded as the **default sentence function** in the sense that it characterizes any function at sentence level that is **not** a subject, predicator, object or complement. Here are some examples:

(1)   The Ford went *into the East Sector just after midnight.*

    S:g[The Ford] P:v[went] A:g[into the East Sector] A:g[just after midnight]

(2)   *Unfortunately*, his leg was broken *in three places.*

    A:adv[Unfortunately] S:g[his leg] P:g[was broken] A:g[in three places]

(3)   *As casually as she could*, she told me *about it.*

    A:g[As casually as she could] S:pro[she] P:v[told] O:pro[me] A:g[about it]

(4)   *Really*, he *never even* met this woman, *because he never got out of prison.*

    A:adv[Really] S:pro[he] A:adv[never] A:adv[even] P:v[met] O:g[this woman]
    A:cl[because he never got out of prison]

By looking at examples like these we get a sense of the price we pay for treating the adverbial as a default function: it is far more heterogeneous in its range of roles than the other sentence functions. It is in fact so heterogeneous that it is difficult, if not impossible, to define it positively with any degree of precision. There are, however, a number of noteworthy general features characterizing adverbials: optionality, mobility, multiplicity, functional and semantic diversity. The following is a brief comment on each of these features:

Optionality. Though adverbials participate as obligatory functions in the intransitive S P A structure type (e.g. *Jack was in London*) and the complex-transitive S P O A structure type (e.g. *Sally put the book on the table*), they are often far more peripheral to sentence structure than the other functions: they typically occur as syntactically optional constituents. Thus most of the adverbials in sentences (1) to (4) above could in fact be left out without this affecting either basic sentence structure or acceptability:

(1')   The Ford went into the East Sector.

(2')   His leg was broken.

(3')   She told me.

(4')   He met this woman.

Syntactic optionality should not be mistaken for semantic optionality: when we leave out syntactically optional adverbials, the meaning of the sentence is often radically changed. Thus in (4') the meaning of (4) is completely reversed. In the other examples, the adverbials offer additional information without which the sentences 'merely' lose specificity.

Mobility. That adverbials are often mobile (in the sense that they may freely appear in more than one position in a sentence) can be ascertained in an example like the following:

(5a)   *One night* the couple returned from a party in a happy mood.

(5b)   The couple *one night* returned from a party in a happy mood.

(5c)   The couple returned *one night* from a party in a happy mood.

(5d)   The couple returned from a party *one night* in a happy mood.

(5e)   The couple returned from a party in a happy mood *one night*.

Basically these variant sentences mean the same thing but differ slightly in terms of the speaker's presentation of the information. However, this is not to imply that anything goes with respect to the position of adverbials. There are restrictions:

(6a)   *With diligence* she has completed the play.

(6b)   *She *with diligence* has completed the play.

(6c)   (?)She has *with diligence* completed the play.

(6d)   ?She has completed *with diligence* the play.

(6e)   She has completed the play *with diligence*.

Sometimes the change of position has obvious semantic repercussions:

(7a)   *Clearly* Bill saw Jane.

(7b)   Bill saw Jane *clearly*.

(8a)   *Quite frankly*, Jack told me about all this.

(8b)   Jack told me about all this *quite frankly*.

In example (7a) what is clear is the fact that *Bill saw Jane* (i.e. it was clear to the speaker that Bill saw Jane), whereas in (7b) what is clear is Bill's visual experience of Jane. In (8a), *Quite frankly* is the speaker's comment on the rest of the sentence ('I am telling you this quite frankly'), whereas in (8b) this adverbial describes the manner in which *Jack told me about all this*. In other words, in the a-examples the adverbials are speaker-oriented and thus strictly outside the scope of the message conveyed, whereas in the b-examples they are fully integrated in the message, modifying the meaning of the predicator in terms of the manner in which the situation referred to is carried out.

Multiplicity. With optional adverbials (unlike other functions), we get an impressive multiplicity of occurrence within the sentence. Instead of simply saying:

(9a)   Jack left the room.

we might say:

(9b)   [1]*Well,* [2]*to tell the truth,* [3]*last Monday,* [4]*without really meaning any harm,* Jack [5]*curiously enough* [6]*once again* [7]*quietly* left the room [8]*for a few minutes,* [9]*without locking the door,* [10]*in order to catch a glimpse of her.*

Exactly how many optional adverbials we can get in a sentence seems more a question of stylistic consideration than of grammatical principle, but even in elegant speech or writing it is not unusual to have several.

This multiplicity of occurrence is clearly related to the functional and semantic diversity of adverbials. It is impossible to give a complete survey of the many uses and meanings of adverbials, but again there are certain noteworthy characteristics.

Functional and semantic diversity. Adverbials serve at least three main communicatively significant subfunctions, traditionally referred to as **adjunct, disjunct** and **conjunct**. An **adjunct** is fairly closely integrated in the sentence structure, typically relating closely to the predicator and somehow modifying or specifying its meaning. Adjuncts are commonly used to express 'negation', 'time', 'place' (including 'source' and 'direction'), 'manner', 'instrument', 'reason', 'purpose', 'condition', 'degree', etc., as in:

(10)   Owen did *not* believe in an afterlife.
(11)   I intend to leave for Rome *tomorrow*.
(12)   *In the distance* he heard the screeching tyres of a car.
(13)   Ursula chuckled *hoarsely* at her own choice of expletive.
(14)   He opened the lock *with a small pen-knife*.
(15)   Walter left the party *because he was angry with Enid*.
(16)   He rushed after her *to explain what had happened*.
(17)   I will do it *if you will*.
(18)   I *fully* agree that we ought to get rid of the vice dean.

As is evident in these examples, an adverbial serving as an adjunct is clearly a sentence function on a par with the subject, the predicator, the object etc., despite its frequent syntactic dispensability. By contrast, an adverbial serving as a **disjunct** takes on a broader scope in that it relates to the rest of the sentence and not just narrowly to the predicator. Disjuncts are commonly used to convey the speaker's or writer's comment on the information expressed by the rest of the sentence or on the style or form of the expression itself, as in the following examples:

(19)   James is *undoubtedly* a talented piano player.

(20)   *Fortunately*, Iris was not swept up in the Women's Liberation movement.

(21)   She *stupidly* tried to steer me off the subject of money.

(22)   Henry went to prison, *believe it or not*.

(23)   *Strictly speaking*, she should have reported the incident.

(24)   *Quite honestly*, I do not want you to leave Hawaii yet.

As can be seen, disjuncts concern the external relationship between the speaker or writer and the sentence and are thus more peripheral to sentence structure than adjuncts, which concern the internal relationship between sentence functions. **Conjuncts** are like disjuncts in being peripheral to sentence structure but differ from them in expressing a relationship between the sentence and its linguistic or non-linguistic context (thus often assuming a conjunction-like function). Typically, conjuncts serve to relate the sentence in which they occur to its linguistic context (often a previous sentence), and are thus important in the organization of texts, or they are used as discourse initiators:

(25)   He was beginning to feel better disposed towards Margaret. *All the same*, he would never allow John near her. (relation to linguistic context)

(26)   The rule seems to apply convincingly to all the Type A cases reviewed so far. *However*, there are important exceptions in the Type B material. (relation to linguistic context)

(27)   My wife is very busy this evening. *Nevertheless* she is likely to go to bed very early. (relation to linguistic context)

(28)   *In the first place*, I never wanted to get involved. *Secondly*, I do not like being bossed around. (relation to linguistic context)

(29)   *So* how are you these days, Sally? (discourse initiator)

(30)   *Well*, it feels good to be outside Makai Manor for a change. (discourse initiator)

Like the other sentence functions, adverbials will be dealt with more thoroughly at a later stage (see especially section 7.4).

2.8. Predicates and predications

In section 2.2, a distinction was drawn between the **topic** and the **comment** of the sentence. The topic is typically expressed by the subject, while the comment is typically expressed by all subsequent functions in the sentence:

	Topic	**Comment**
(1)	Harris	was fixing the bike
(2)	My parents	could have put the bottle in the bag
(3)	They	were in London
(4)	She	left
(5)	Barbara	seized a plate and gave it to Jack

The constituents expressing the comment belong more closely together than they do individually to the subject. In a sense, therefore, they form a higher-level constituent. This higher-level constituent is called the **predicate**. Many sentences can thus be said to consist of two parts: subject and predicate. The predicate is realized by combinations of sentence functions (e.g. P + O , P + O + A or P + A, as in (1), (2) and (3), respectively), or simply by P, as in (4). Sometimes, as in (5), the predicate is realized by a compound unit (cf. section 3.4 below), in which each coordinated element consists of a combination of sentence functions (*seized a plate* consists of P + O, and *gave it to Jack* consists of P + O + A) and could constitute a predicate of its own (as in e.g. *Barbara gave it to Jack*).

The predicate of a sentence is sometimes realized discontinuously:

(1')   *Was* Harris *fixing the bike?*
(2')   *Could* my parents *have put the bottle in the bag?*
(3')   *Were* they *in London?*
(4')   *Did* she *leave?*
(5')   *Did* Barbara *seize a plate and give it to Jack?*

In these examples, the operator has moved to a position before the subject, or, if there is no operator, DO has been inserted in that position, to form a *yes-no* question. It is often convenient to be able to refer to the two parts making up the predicate: the operator and the rest of the predicate. The term used to refer to the rest of the predicate is **predication**. In (1') to (5') the sequence of constituents is: operator + subject + predication. Note that in (3') the predication does not contain a verbal element because even as a full verb BE retains its status as an operator. In (5') the predication is realized by a compound unit in which each conjoint contains a number of clause functions.

3. Complex forms

3.1. Groups

It has already been noted that a sentence function may be realized by four different form types: a word, a group, a compound unit or a clause. Of these, only the word requires no further syntactic analysis. The other three forms are syntactically complex and must therefore be examined with respect to their internal structure.

A group always consists of a **head** (abbreviated as H) and one or more **dependents** (abbreviated as DEP):

(1)   may have been held
       DEP[may] DEP[have] DEP[been] H[held]

(2)   an extravagant party
       DEP[an] DEP[extravagant] H[party]

(3)   interestingly enough
       H[interestingly] DEP[enough]

(4)   in her honour
       H[in] DEP[her honour]

Groups are subclassified according to the form realizing the head. Here is a list of the most common kinds of group with a single word as head:

Verb groups have a verb as head:

(5)   might have been *dancing*
       DEP[might] DEP[have] DEP[been] H[dancing]

Noun groups have a noun as head:

(6)   the sad *result* of the affair
       DEP[the] DEP[sad] H[result] DEP[of the affair]

Pronoun groups have a pronoun as head:

(7)   *everyone* I know
       H[everyone] DEP[I know]

Adjective groups have an adjective as head:

(8)   extremely *miserable*
       DEP[extremely] H[miserable]

Adverb groups have an adverb as head:

(9)   very beautifully
       DEP[very] H[beautifully]

Preposition groups have a preposition as head:

(10)   *to* a small town
       H[to] DEP[a small town]

The head of a group is an **obligatory characterizing element** without which the group would have been some other kind of group, or simply ungrammatical. Dependents are obligatory or optional noncharacterizing elements. In principle, both heads and dependents may be realized by all four types of form (the word, the group, the compound unit, the clause), but there are many restrictions applying to the individual kinds of group.

It is necessary at this point to comment briefly on the distinction between groups and single words. With the exception of preposition groups, groups can be viewed as **expansions** of single words. For example, the noun group *the water* is an expansion of the single noun *water*, the adjective group *very honest* is an expansion of the single adjective *honest*, and so forth. Often single words and groups are used in the same way (e.g. with the same syntactic function, as in <u>She</u> was <u>honest</u> / <u>Her sister</u> was <u>very honest</u>) and display very similar grammatical features (e.g. *cars* and *the cars*, which are both plural expressions). Given this close relationship between single words and groups, it is often convenient to be able to refer to both form types with a single label. In traditional grammar there was a strong word-orientation: grammarians talked about e.g. **nouns**, often implying also noun groups. In modern linguistics, there is a tendency to focus more on the group level: grammarians now often talk about e.g. **noun groups** (or 'noun phrases', abbreviated 'NP'), implying also single nouns. In addition to these practices, which are difficult to avoid completely, the following explicit cover terms will be used:

verbal	=	verb group **or** single verb
nominal	=	noun group **or** single noun
pronominal	=	pronoun group **or** single pronoun
adjectival	=	adjective group **or** single adjective
adverbal	=	adverb group **or** single adverb

These cover terms are to be understood as **form** terms, not **function** terms.

3.2. Types of subordination in groups

There is no simple head-dependent relationship characterizing all the different groups that we have examined. By marking heads and dependents we simply indicate that there is **some** relationship rather than a particular kind of relationship. This relationship is one of **subordination**, the dependent being subordinate to the head, one way or the other.

There are in groups three main types of subordination, all of which can be illustrated by the following example:

(1)   By the time he left the Dean's room *the painful erosion of his self-respect was almost complete.* (S:g)

In *the painful erosion of his self-respect* – where the noun *erosion* functions as head – there are three dependents, realized by the article *the*, the adjective *painful* and the preposition group *of his self-respect*. The type of subordination realized by *the* is **determination**, that realized by *painful* is **modification**, and that realized by *of his self-respect* is **complementation**. In the example, *the* signals that the noun group has definite reference, *painful* attributes some quality to the meaning of the head noun, and the preposition group *of his self-respect* completes this meaning, i.e. the action specified by the deverbal noun *erosion* (derived from *erode*) is 'filled out' by this group. These three main types of subordination merit closer examination.

(i) Determination. Determination can be distinguished quite clearly from both complementation and modification. While a determiner always precedes the head of a group (typically a noun group), the unit realizing a complementation always follows it. The words which function as determiners are placed in the position before a premodifying adjective. They generally serve to signal what kind of reference a noun group has, for example definite as in *the girl* and indefinite as in *a girl*. The following forms are used as determiners (see section 13.3): articles (*the, a/an*), demonstrative pronouns (*this, that, these, those*), possessive pronouns (*my, your*, etc.), genitives (*Peter's, boys', the shrewd politician's*, etc.), the *wh*-pronouns *what, which, whose* (whether interrogative or relative) and a number of indefinite pronouns (*another, any, each, either, every, neither, no, some*). In the following sentence there are four instances of determination:

(2)   If *this* lamentable speech was anything to go by, *his* statements must have raised *some* hackles on *the* back benches.

(ii) Complementation. While determination applies mainly to noun groups, the type of subordination termed complementation is more generally applicable, not only to noun groups (e.g. *need for expansion*), but also to adjective groups (*immune to criticism*), preposition groups (*across the street*) and adverb groups (*fortunately for me*). Complements at group level often correspond to separate functions at sentence level, as is borne out by constructions like *We hesitate to accept your offer* (object at sentence level), *We are hesitant to accept your offer* (complementation in adjective group with *hesitant* as the head) and *He noted our hesitancy to accept your offer* (complementation in noun group with *hesitancy* as the head). Semantically, complementation contrasts with determination by **filling out** the meaning of the unit complemented. Thus *to accept your offer* fills out the meaning of *hesitant*. If we leave the complementation of a unit out, it can be assumed to be understood in the context, e.g. *We are hesitant* can only be used appropriately if it is clear from the context with respect to what we are hesitant.

(iii) Modification. The third main type of subordination is called modification. While a determiner typically serves to signal what kind of reference a noun group has and a complementation fills out the meaning specified by the word of which it is a dependent, broadly speaking a modifier **qualifies** the meaning of its head word, i.e. it attributes a property to the referent of this word. And unlike determination, which is restricted to the position before the head, and complementation, which is normally restricted to the position after the head, modification occurs both before and after the head. In groups like *depraved tastes, freely available* and *only rarely* there is **premodification** and in *a creature of habit, the woman I love* and *young enough* there is **postmodification**. Simultaneous pre- and postmodification is common as well and can be exemplified by a group like *the new house that they built last year*. Unlike missing complementation, missing modification is not implied. For example, by saying *the woman* instead of *the woman I love*, the speaker does not imply *I love* but simply assumes that he has offered enough information for the hearer to know whom he is talking about.

3.3. The preposition group

The preposition group is special in that it is not an expansion of a single word and the relationship between H and DEP is always one of complementation (note that DEP in a preposition group 'fills out' the meaning of the construction, compare *He helped an old lady across* and *He helped an old lady across the street*). The preposition group is always **binary**, i.e. it consists of two parts only, a head and one dependent. The dependent is traditionally referred to as the **prepositional complement**. The complement may be realized by a nominal, a pronominal, a compound unit, or a nonfinite *-ing* clause:

(1)   The clever girls objected *to the proposal*. (A:g)
       H:prep[to] DEP:g[the proposal]

(2)   No, I haven't heard *from her*. (A:g)
       H:prep[from] DEP:pro[her]

(3)   Richard flew *to Rome and Athens*. (A:g)
       H:prep[to] DEP:cu[Rome and Athens]

(4)   *By leaving so early* he offended my wife. (A:g)
       H:prep[By] DEP:cl[leaving so early]

The complement may also be realized by an **interrogative clause** (as in (5)) or by an **independent relative clause** (as in (6)), cf. sections 12.1-2:

(5)   I was wondering about *which doll to give her.*

(6)   You can give this book to *whoever wants to read it.*

Colloquially, finite clauses are used after *How about*:

(7)   How about *I take Jenny to her music lesson?*

Apart from examples like (5) to (7), finite clauses and nonfinite infinitive or past participle clauses cannot serve as prepositional complements. Thus, in examples like:

(8)   *Before he left*, he thanked me profusely.

(9)   *After she arrived*, everyone seemed far more relaxed.

Before and *After* are analysed as conjunctions (but in *Before dinner, he thanked me profusely* and *After her arrival, everyone seemed far more relaxed*, they are analysed as prepositions). And in examples like:

(10)   She told him nothing *except that Robert would soon join them.*

(11)   The case was very complicated *in that so many firms were involved.*

the sequences *except that* and *in that* are treated as complex conjunctions (like e.g. *as if, in case* and *in order to*).

Preposition groups typically have either adverbial function at clause level (as in example (12)) or dependent function in groups (as in example (13)):

(12)   *On Jack's advice* she will fly *to Rome.*

(13)   Someone *from our office* tapes the constant stream *of interviews she gives.*

The relationship between H and DEP in a preposition group is such that both constituents are in fact more independent than in other groups. Note in this connection the following points:

(i) The prepositional complement is often separated from the head preposition, thus realizing a discontinuous group; compare:

(14a)   You can draw water *from this well.*

(14b)   *This well* you can draw water *from.*

In such examples, the prepositional complement does not undergo a functional transformation but retains its dependent status.

(ii) The prepositional complement is occasionally capable of serving as the subject of a passive construction, leaving the prepositional head **stranded**:

(15a)   Someone has slept *in that bed.*

(15b)   *That bed* has been slept *in.*

(16a)   We must fight *for freedom.*

(16b)   *Freedom* must be fought *for.*

In the b-examples the prepositional complements of the a-examples have undergone a functional transformation and become syntactic subjects.

(iii) The prepositional head may grow more closely related to a preceding verb, forming a so-called 'prepositional verb' (cf. section 13.2.2):

(17)   Alfred's wife always *stood by* Jack.
         (i.e. 'Alfred's wife always supported Jack')

(18)   Miranda *waited on* the Wilson family.
         (i.e. 'Miranda served the Wilson family')

If the preposition is here analysed as part of the predicator, the 'prepositional complement' (*Jack* and *the Wilson family*) assumes direct object function.

3.4. The compound unit

Like groups, compound units may realize sentence functions:

(1)   *Rolf and Werner* were devious devils. (S:cu)

(2)   Bernard was *angry but calm.* (C:cu)

(3)   He gave *Tessa or Fiona guns and bullets in London and in Berlin.* (Oi:cu; Od:cu; A:cu)

A compound unit typically consists of two or more **conjoints** (abbreviated as CJT) bound together by a **coordinator** (abbreviated as CO). Thus the internal functional structure of the examples above looks like this:

(4) ^{CJT}[Rolf] ^{CO}[and] ^{CJT}[Werner]
         ^{CJT}[angry] ^{CO}[but] ^{CJT}[calm]
         etc.

Conjoints may be realized by any of the four types of form (word, group, compound unit, clause); coordinators are realized by conjunctions:

(5)   *Wendy and Kim* sat round the kitchen table.
         $^{S:cu}$[Wendy and Kim]
         $^{CJT:n}$[Wendy] $^{CO:conj}$[and] $^{CJT:n}$[Kim]

(6)   They saw *your daughter and my son* at the party.
         $^{O:cu}$[your daughter and my son]
         $^{CJT:g}$[your daughter] $^{CO:conj}$[and] $^{CJT:g}$[my son]

(7)   The two winning teams were *Walter and Sally and Peter and Helen.*
         $^{C:cu}$[Walter and Sally and Peter and Helen]
         $^{CJT:cu}$[Walter and Sally] $^{CO:conj}$[and] $^{CJT:cu}$[Peter and Helen]

(8)   I thought *that Jack had left and that Di would come to see me*.

O:cu[that Jack had left and that Die would come to see me]

CJT:cl[that Jack had left] CO:conj[and] CJT:cl[that Di would come to see me]

3.5. Types of coordination

There are several types of coordination:

(i) Linked versus unlinked coordination. The examples listed in the previous section are all examples of linked coordination, where the conjoints are explicitly connected by a coordinator. Sometimes we get unlinked coordination, where there is no overt coordinator (as in example (1a)), but where a coordinator could be inserted (as in example (1b)):

(1a)   Who blew *the landing party, the coordinates, the beach, the time?*
(1b)   Who blew *the landing party, the coordinates, the beach and the time?*

In linked coordination of more than two conjoints, usually only the last two conjoints are separated by a coordinator (as in example (1b)). However, all the conjoints may be separated, as in examples like the following where there is emphasis on each of the conjoints:

(2)   It was only too easy to mistake our tortuous structures of *codenames and symbols and cutouts* for life on the ground.

The missing coordinator in unlinked coordination is practically always *and* but we cannot rule out examples of open-ended questions with missing *or*:

(3)   Would you like beer, port, claret, Madeira ....?

(ii) Recursive versus non-recursive coordination. There is in principle no limit to the number of conjoints that may be joined together by *and* and *or*. Nothing in the structure of English prevents us from keeping adding conjoints as long as the explicit or implicit conjunction is *and* or *or*. Such coordination is called **recursive**. Coordination with *but* is non-recursive because here the number of conjoints is always restricted to two:

(4a)   I like claret but not port.
(4b)   *I like claret but not port but Madeira.

In examples like *It wasn't cheap, it wasn't easy, but it's the best solution*, the understood coordinator between the first two clauses is *and*, not *but*.

(iii) Reversible and irreversible coordination. In coordination the units joined together have the same syntactic status, and they can sometimes be interchanged with little or no difference of meaning:

(5a)   Jane and Albert arrived before noon.

(5b)   Albert and Jane arrived before noon.

(6a)   Henry is always friendly but James can be rather reserved.

(6b)   James can be rather reserved but Henry is always friendly.

Often, however, the order of the units joined together is fixed. In the first place, coordinated clauses cannot be interchanged if the second describes an event which is subsequent to or follows from that described by the first:

(7)   She slammed the door *and* Philip pulled out from the kerb. ('and then')

(8)   I have forgotten my keys *and* there is nothing I can do to help you. ('and therefore')

Nor is reversal of order possible if the second clause of a compound unit contains a pro-form that refers back to a word in the first clause, or if there is ellipsis in the second clause (cf. chapter 5):

(9)   The new constitution will enable Fujimori to stand for election in 1995, and *it* will give *him* the power to close congress again.

(10)   John likes apples and Bob cherries.

(iv) Simple versus complex coordination. Simple coordination involves functionally unitary constituents: by itself each conjoint would serve only one function outside the compound unit, and it is always realized by one of the established form types of the system (w, g, cu, cl). Thus, in e.g. *My neighbour and his daughter laughed*, each of the conjoints might serve as the subject realized by a group (*My neighbour* laughed and *His daughter* laughed). In cases of complex coordination, each conjoint contains a combination of separate functions:

(11)   He gave *Barbara a kiss* and *Ann some good advice.*

(12)   *She sold* and *I bought* the house.

The conjoints in these examples are combinations of functions which do not form groups, compound units or full clauses: indirect object + direct object in example (11) and subject + predicator in example (12). By definition, coordination of predicates (as in (13)) and of predications (as in (14)) is also complex coordination:

(13)   My sister *lives in Norwich and works for the council.*

(14)   He might *drop into a bar and down some liquor*.

Coordination of whole clauses (as in *Sally laughed and Jack got up*) is simple coordination because each conjoint forms a full clause.

(v) Appended coordination. Additional information is often added to a clause in the form of an appended construction consisting of a coordinator and a conjoint:

(15)   Barbara sings beautifully, *and Joan too.*

(16)   She is brilliant, *but not her husband.*

Such appended coordination typically involves elliptical clauses.

(vi) Pseudo-coordination. Sometimes we have coordination of completely identical constituents:

(17)   Jack became *more and more* upset.

(18)   They *talked and talked and talked.*

(19)   Well, you know, there are *teachers and teachers.*

This is called pseudo-coordination. In the first two examples the effect of pseudo-coordination is intensification. In (19) the expression implies that there are different kinds of teacher (e.g. good teachers and bad teachers).

3.6. Coordinating conjunctions

Coordinating conjunctions merit further attention. Semantically, **and** is inclusive and non-contrastive, **but** inclusive and contrastive and **or** exclusive, positing an alternative, as illustrated by respectively *clever and reasonable*, *clever but unreasonable* and *clever or stupid*. Besides having additive meaning, *and* sometimes appears to signify 'subsequent to' or 'following from', as in e.g. *He knocked three times and went in* and *She felt nervous and took a tranquillizer*. These meanings – which can be made explicit by inserting *then* or *therefore* after *and* – are not expressed by *and*, however, but are due to the conjoints, which describe temporally or causally related situations (and which are therefore irreversible). Similarly, *or* sometimes seems to signal a negative condition (*if not ... then*), as in *You must put on winter woollies or you'll catch a cold*. This meaning – which can be made explicit by inserting *else* after *or* – does not belong to *or* either, but is due to the conjoints, which describe conditionally related situations (and which are irreversible here as well). Occasionally, the coordinating conjunctions are used more loosely than in the examples above:

(1)   Could you try and find another?

(2)   I only drank two or three glasses of wine.

(3)   Speaker A: 'My daughter is getting married'
        Speaker B: 'But that's wonderful!'

In example (1), *and* is not used to coordinate two verbs but as an informal variant of the infinitive marker *to*. In example (2), *or* is used between two numbers to convey 'approximation' (i.e. roughly how many). And in example (3) *but* is used to signal sudden emotion rather than contrast.

There are three pairs of **correlative conjunctions**: *both ... and, either ... or* and *neither ... nor*:

(4)   He decided *both* to leave his wife *and* to sell his Porsche.

(5)   Baroness Thatcher is one of those politicians you *either* love *or* hate.

(6)   Women priests tend to be *neither* authoritarian *nor* submissive.

Both ... and and *either ... or* can be regarded as expansions of *and* and *or*, and like these they express inclusive and exclusive meaning, respectively. They differ semantically from *and* and *or*, however, in that they give extra prominence to the individual conjoints, i.e. *both* and *either* underscore the bipartite nature of the following unit. Distributionally, *both ... and* differs from *and* in being unable to link finite clauses. For example we cannot say **Both his hair was rumpled and he wore a raincoat over his pyjamas.* Otherwise there are no restrictions on the type of conjoints it can connect. *Neither ... nor* is the negative counterpart of *either ... or.*

3.7. Clauses

Functionally, many clauses differ from sentences in that they cannot occur on their own. But they are like sentences with respect to their internal structure. Clauses may contain all the functions identified at sentence level: subjects, predicators, objects, complements and adverbials. In addition, there is sometimes a formal marker of **subordination**, a subordinator (abbreviated as SUB) realized by a conjunction (conj), as in the following examples:

(1)   They figured *that Jack was a double agent.*
       $O{:}cl$[that Jack was a double agent]
       $SUB{:}conj$[that] $S{:}n$[Jack] $P{:}v$[was] $C{:}g$[a double agent]

(2)   *Whether he talked her into it* I simply do not know.
       $O{:}cl$[Whether he talked her into it]
       $SUB{:}conj$[Whether] $S{:}pro$[he] $P{:}v$[talked] $O{:}pro$[her] $A{:}g$[into it]

Like sentence functions, clause functions may be realized by single words, groups, compound units or clauses, as in:

(3)   Richard suspected *that Jack would tell Ursula and me if he got the chance.*

where the object clause consists of a SUB:conj (*that*), a S:n (*Jack*), a P:g (*would tell*) an O:cu (*Ursula and me*) and an A:cl (*if he got the chance*).

It is customary to distinguish between **main clauses** and **subordinate clauses** (henceforth referred to as **subclauses**). The main clause corresponds to the whole sentence, including subclauses. The terms sentence and main clause are therefore often used interchangeably. A subclause is a clause which functions within a main clause, either by realizing a clause function (such as the subject in *Being with you is far more important*) or by realizing some lower-level function (such as the DEP in *The house which my parents bought last year*). A further distinction which is sometimes useful is that between main clause and **matrix clause**. The term matrix clause is used about a superordinate clause minus its subclause (especially if the subclause functions as object or adverbial in the main clause). In the examples above, the matrix clauses are *They figured, I simply do not know* and *Richard suspected*, respectively.

An important difference between main clauses and subclauses is that while main clauses (and sentences) are finite, containing a finite predicator, sub-clauses are often nonfinite, containing an infinitive or participle as predicator (cf. section 12.1). Here are some examples of nonfinite subclauses:

(4)   *To see her* is *to love her.*

(5)   *Having finished my homework*, I went out.

A clause consists of at least two clause functions. As already noted, there is almost always a predicator in a clause. But the presence of a predicator is not actually criterial for the definition of clauses. Occasionally there are 'predicator-less' clauses, i.e. clauses where the predicator (and sometimes also other clause functions) is implied, and where the remaining constituents can only be analysed appropriately in terms of clause functions (cf. section 12.1):

(6)   I am sure he will help you, *if necessary.* (A:cl)
      SUB:conj[if] C:adj[necessary]

3.8. The functions of subclauses

Subclauses may assume one of the following functions:

(i) Obligatory sentence or clause function, as in examples (1) to (4) in the previous section, and the following:

(1)   The governments indicated *that they were looking for a new beginning.* (O)

(2)   His favourite pastime is *writing letters to his sister.* (C)

(3)   She gave *sacking him* some thought. (Oi)

(4)   You can put it *where you like.* (A)

The nature of the subordination is here typically **complementation** at clause level because the constituent realized by the subclause 'completes' the meaning of the basic sentence or clause (cf. section 3.2 on complementation at group level).

(ii) Optional adverbial function, as in examples (5) and (6 in the previous section), and the following:

(5)   He got depressed *after she left.*

(6)   I left my wife *because I realized I had made an awful mistake.*

(7)   I'll write it *if somebody wants it.*

(8)   The twins don't look alike, *which puzzles me.*

The nature of the subordination here is what may be termed **supplementation** because the subordinate clause provides further information in relation to the obligatory clause functions.

(iii) Dependent within group, as in:

(9)   He will be missed by all *who knew him.* (DEP in pronoun group)

(10)   Sarah dances more beautifully *than you can imagine.* (DEP in adverb group)

(11)   The assumption *that James took an earlier train* turned out to be correct. (DEP in noun group)

(12)   My wife is most anxious *that you would dine with us one evening.* (DEP in adjective group)

The nature of the subordination here is **modification** at group level in examples (9) and (10) and **complementation** at group level in examples (11) and (12) (cf. section 3.2).

(iv) Head of group, as in:

(13)   His *telling everybody about it* did make life easier for her.

(14)   There was to be no *fooling around with girls.*

In such examples the subclause is of course not subordinate but **super-ordinate** to the other constituent in the group (*His* and *no*, respectively).

3.9. Markers of clausal subordination

Clausal subordination is typically signalled in one of the following ways:

(i) by a subordinating conjunction:

(1)   *That* she should do a thing like that is unbelievable.

(2)   I wonder *if* he's got the qualifications for that job.

(ii) by a nonfinite verb form:

(3)   *Having finished* the book, he went to bed.

(4)   It is refreshing *to describe* a major Russian company that is successful.

(iii) by a relative pronoun:

(5)   Ian, *whom* I trusted with the money, has disappeared.

(6)   She talked to the students *whose* parents had complained.

For subordination signalled by constituent order, see sections 7.2.1 and 7.3.
 The commonest subordinating conjunction is *that*:

(7)   What is needed is *that* the two governments signal quite clearly *that* they are
        looking for a new beginning.

(8)   My wife is most anxious *that* you should dine with us one evening.

In *yes-no* interrogative clauses subordination is signalled by the conjunctions
if and *whether*:

(9)   I wonder *if* he's got the qualifications for that job.

(10)   I am uncertain *whether* we should go ahead as planned.

There is a fairly large class of conjunctions which are used to introduce
adverbial clauses:

(11)   I know that the world has always been and will always remain *as* it is.

(12)   I will write it *if* somebody wants it.

(13)   The 80-year-old woman was attacked on her doorstep *when* she answered a
        knock on her door.

(14)   He wants Anglo-Catholics to be able to join the Roman Catholic Church
        while retaining an Anglican liturgy and identity.

The class of subordinating conjunctions introducing adverbial clauses also
includes *after, before, because, once, since, (al)though, till, until, whenever,
where, whereas, whereupon* and *wherever*. In British English, furthermore,
whilst is used as a variant of *while*. Attention should also be drawn to *lest*
and *like*, which are particularly common in American English, and which in
British English are formal and informal respectively.
 Subordination can also be indicated by a **complex subordinating conjunction**, i.e. a linker consisting of more words than one:

(15)   You're as pale and drawn *as if* you just got out of a sickbed.

(16)   The apartment isn't mine, and *even if* it was, I couldn't pay for it.

(17)   *As soon as* he leaves the house, I start looking up at the ceiling for a hook.

(18)   The diagnosis is made harder if a child's gifts go unnoticed for a while, *so
        that* frustration reduces his or her academic performance.

Other complex subordinators which are common in English include *in case,
in (order) that, provided (that)* and *on condition (that)*.

3.10. Embedding and recursiveness

In many of the examples cited in the preceding sections we have seen that the
complex forms (groups, compound units, clauses) realizing sentence func-

tions contain internal functions which themselves are sometimes realized by complex forms, which then in turn require further analysis. Thus in an example like

(1)   Richard suspected *that Jack would tell Ursula and me if he got the chance.*

there are functions within the O:cl realized by all three complex form types: group-within-clause (*would tell*), compound unit-within-clause (*Ursula and me*), and clause-within-clause (*if he got the chance*). There are few restrictions on the constellation of form types within form types or on the number of constituent levels in a sentence.

Constellations of complex forms within complex forms are often referred to as **embedding**. Embedding (like coordination, cf. section 3.5) is **recursive** because in principle we can keep adding embedded constituents at any constituent level, as e.g. in:

(2)   Jack knew a young doctor who graduated from a university where the vice chancellor had decided to appoint a number of specialists who ...

Since embedded constituents are of the same form types as non-embedded constituents we can simply describe embedded constituents the way we do non-embedded constituents, and we thus already have the full system for describing sentences irrespective of length and complexity.

4. Clause types and utterance functions

4.1. Major types of clause

Clauses, as well as sentences, can be divided into **declarative, interrogative, imperative** and **exclamatory**:

Declarative clauses have the order of constituents described in the basic patterns in section 1.9 and typically express statements:

(1)   Richard inspected the book. (S P O)
(2)   The boys called her princess. (S P O Co)

Interrogative clauses typically express questions. They are subdivided into *wh*-**interrogative** and *yes-no* **interrogative** clauses. In *wh*-interrogative clauses the *wh*-constituent is in initial position. Thus the basic word order is retained if the interrogative pronoun realizes the subject:

(3)   *What*'s happening? (S P)
(4)   *Who* persuaded you? (S P O)

If the interrogative pronoun realizes any other function, this order is changed accordingly and we get subject-operator inversion (cf. section 7.2.1):

(5)   *Why* did you leave? (A P- S -P)

(6)   *What* do you mean? (O P- S - P)

In *yes-no* interrogative clauses there is always subject-operator inversion:

(7)   Is your attitude changing? (P- S -P)

(8)   Could you do me a favour? (P- S -P Oi Od)

Imperative clauses, which typically express directives or commands, have the same order as declarative clauses except that they are most often subjectless:

(9)   Shut the door. (P O)

(10)   Knock him unconscious. (P O Co)

The directive becomes more emphatic if it contains a subject:

(11)   You listen to me! (S P A)

Exclamatory clauses typically convey exclamations. To form an exclamatory clause, *how* or *what* is added to one of the functions and the extended constituent is placed in initial position. There is no inversion:

(12)   What a big crowd turned up! (S P)
       (cf. *A big crowd turned up*)

(13)   What a load of rubbish you're saying. (O S P)
       (cf. *You're saying a load of rubbish*)

(14)   How delightful it is. (C S P)
       (cf. *It is delightful*)

4.2. Communicative functions

In the previous section we examined various **form types** of clause. These types were defined primarily on the basis of constituent order, but we also mentioned their typical use: statement, question, directive and exclamation. These uses are called **communicative functions** (or **illocutionary values**). The four main communicative functions are defined as follows:

Statements give information:

(1)   John was quiet.

Questions seek information:

(2)   Was John quiet?

Directives instruct the hearer to perform some action or to behave in a certain way:

(3)   Be quiet!

Exclamations indicate emotional reaction (surprise, disapproval, pleasure, etc.):

(4)   How quiet John was!

In addition to these major types, it is sometimes necessary also to operate with the following:

Performatives, which actually perform the situation stated. Performatives contain verbs like PRONOUNCE, PROMISE, SWEAR and SENTENCE in the present tense and a first person (singular or plural) subject:

(5)   I (hereby) pronounce you man and wife.

(6)   We (hereby) promise to support James.

Optatives (from a Latin word meaning 'wish'), which express a wish or a benediction/malediction:

(7)   If only I were you.

(8)   God save the Queen.

(9)   May you rot in hell.

4.3. The forms of communicative functions

The communicative functions introduced in the previous section may be realized not just by clauses but also by the other form types (group, compound unit and single words), as in the following examples:

Statements

(1)	James left Brisbane yesterday	(cl)
(2)	In London.	(g)
(3)	John and Sarah.	(cu)
(4)	Yes.	(intj)

Questions

(5)	Will you join me tonight?	(cl)
(6)	From whom?	(g)
(7)	When and where?	(cu)
(8)	Why?	(adv)

Directives

(9)	Listen to me.	(cl)
(10)	After him!	(g)
(11)	Smile and be happy!	(cu)
(12)	Down!	(adv)

Exclamations

(13)	She can't mean that!	(cl)
(14)	Good Lord!	(g)
(15)	Blood and sand!	(cu)
(16)	Wow!	(intj)

As these examples demonstrate, form types smaller than the sentence or clause may serve complete communicative functions.

It is important not to confuse the function terms and the terms for the major clause types identified: statement versus declarative, question versus interrogative, directive versus imperative, and exclamations versus exclamative. Even at clause level, there is no one-to-one relation between them. Thus, though declarative clauses tend to express statements and interrogative clauses tend to express questions, etc., this is by no means always the case. Communicative functions are not clear-cut categories allowing a rigid classification of language units. They in fact vary in strength and intensity from language unit to language unit, and they may blend with each other, and with other functions. Consider e.g. questions. Questions can be asked more or less explicitly, with more or less subtlety, according to the form employed; compare:

(17a)   Did John write this book?

(17b)   John did not write this book, did he?

(17c)   John wrote this book, didn't he?

(17d)   John wrote this book, did he?

(17e)   John wrote this book?

(17f)   I do not know if John wrote this book.

(17g)   John wrote this book. ('Actually I do not know, it is my tentative guess, correct me if I am wrong, am I right so far?')

All of these (even (17f,g)) may be construed as questions and, in appropriate contexts, should be classified as such, but the 'illocutionary force' with which the speaker or writer puts the question varies considerably, the a-example being the most directly inquisitive, the f- and g-examples virtually pure statements and the others different blends of statement and question.

The fact that communicative functions are interrelated is also clear from the following examples:

(18a)   Close the window.

(18b)   Close the window, will you?

(18c)   Do you mind closing the window?

(18d)   Could you possibly close the window?

(18e)   Gee, it is cold in here!

(18f)   According to the building regulation, this window should remain closed at all times.

(18g)   The window is open.

All of these can be construed as directives, but like the questions in (17), some are more subtle than others. The imperative a-example is the most unambiguous directive of the set. The imperative b-example is slightly modified by the interrogative tag *will you?*. The *yes-no* questions in (18c,d) both express a request beyond a simple *yes-* or *no*-answer. The e-example has the form of an exclamation and expresses a fairly indirect request: it is left to the listener to conclude that the closing of the window is desired by the speaker. The last two examples have the typical form of statements but clearly may be spoken in order to make the hearer close the window.

5. Missing constituents, ellipsis and pro-forms

5.1. The zero convention

In sentence analysis, one occasionally gets a sense of **missing constituents**. An example of this is: *Ann became president and Jack vice-president*. This sentence is a 'short version' of *Ann became president and Jack became vice-president*. To avoid repetition of *became* we may well use the short version. When a constituent goes missing in this way, it is customary to talk of **ellipsis**. Ellipsis is a common device for abbreviating sentences and serves to avoid redundancy and repetition.

One way to deal with ellipsis in our sentence analysis is to incorporate the appropriate function label in the 'place' of the missing constituent and to have the function 'realized' by a **zero form** (represented by the symbol Ø) to indicate the lack of formal expression. This approach allows us to treat the sequence *Jack vice-president* as a clause consisting of a subject noun (*Jack*), a predicator that is missing (P:Ø) and a complement noun (*vice-president*).

Here are some other examples of missing forms (indicated by Ø):

(1)   We parked Ildiko's car behind Sandor's Ø.

(2)   She told me Ø she wanted to return.

(3)   Francis never received the letter Ø Ildiko sent from Rome.

In example (1), the speaker again suppresses repetition of a constituent (*car*). This can be shown by analysing the missing constituent as H:Ø. Note that if in this example we do not operate with a missing form, the analysis cannot show the parallel functions of *Ildiko's* (DEP:n) and *Sandor's* (DEP:n): without a head *Sandor's* cannot be a dependent. In example (2), there is no suppression of repetition: here the explicit marker of the subclause, the subordinator conjunction *that*, has been left out (SUB:Ø). In the linguistic context of the example (*She told me ...*), this does not, however, change the status of the clause, which is still an object subclause. Finally, in example (3) the relative pronoun *that* or *which* has been left out (O:Ø). Notice here that the zero convention makes it possible to supply an 'object' to the predicator verb *sent*, which is quite obviously used in a transitive sense and thus can be expected to have an object (cf. *Ildiko sent a letter from Rome*).

The picture that emerges from the examples provided above is that the zero convention is a useful tool which captures the intuition that one or more constituents are missing. In each case the missing constituent can be **retrieved** without this resulting in a change of the meaning or of the overall syntactic organization of the sentence. And in some cases the use of a zero constituent in the place where the missing form is felt to belong helps to clarify the relations between the constituents of the sentence.

5.2. Types of ellipsis

By examining the nature of retrievability we can distinguish several types of ellipsis. Missing forms can often be retrieved from **the text** itself. Thus, in *Ann became president and Jack Ø vice-president* the missing predicator in the second conjoint clause is retrievable from within the same sentence, more specifically from *became* in the first conjoint clause. Ellipsis with this kind of retrievability is called **intrasentential textual ellipsis**.

In addition to intrasentential textual ellipsis there are cases of missing forms that can only be retrieved textually from outside the sentence, i.e. from other sentences in the text. Consider the following examples:

(1)   Speaker A: Bill came at eight.
        Speaker B: Susan Ø already at seven.

(2)   Speaker A: I thought you were in a biology department.
        Speaker B: I was Ø.

We can argue here that the predicator *came* in (1) and the adverbial *in a biology department* in (2) have been omitted by Speaker B. In both (1) and (2) the missing constituent is easily recoverable from the preceding linguistic context. This is referred to as **extrasentential textual ellipsis**, i.e. textual ellipsis with extrasentential retrievability. Such ellipsis is not restricted to examples of communicative turn-taking:

(3)   Quite frankly, I left this morning. Ø Couldn't stand the noise.

The missing subject in the last sentence can be retrieved as *I* from the preceding sentence.

Textual ellipsis, whether intra- or extrasentential, can be described more specifically as **anaphoric** (i.e. Ø stands for something further back in the text) or **cataphoric** (i.e. Ø stands for something further on in the text). Examples like *Ann became president and Jack Ø vice-president* and (1) to (3) display anaphoric ellipsis. Cataphoric ellipsis is rare. Arguably we have it in examples like *Jack's Ø is a beautiful voice* and *She handed me the red Ø and the yellow box.*

Retrievability is not always textual, as in the examples discussed above. In some cases the part omitted from a simple sentence is recoverable only from the situational context:

(4)   Told you so.
(5)   See you later.

In the absence of a clarifying linguistic context it is impossible to say whether it is *I* and *I'll* or *We* and *We'll* which are missing. In a specific situational context, however, the hearer will often be able to determine precisely what is missing, so in examples of this type it seems warranted to operate with **situational ellipsis**.

In other cases, the retrievability of a constituent is dependent on our grammatical knowledge of the relationships between the constituents in the sentence rather than on the context. An example of this is *She told me Ø she wanted to return*, where the SUB:conj *that* is retrievable on the basis of our knowledge of the subordinate status of the finite clause *she wanted to return* in relation to the clause *She told me*. Similarly, in examples like:

(6)   Serves you right.
(7)   Anything the matter?

the hearer is capable of inferring the missing words too, not because of the situational context or the presence of any specific constituent elsewhere in the text, but because he or she knows that the utterances are in free variation with *It serves you right* and *Is anything the matter?*

Ellipsis, whether textual or non-textual, can be further described in terms of the position in the clause of the missing constituent(s). In examples like *Ø Serves you right* and *Ø Couldn't stand the noise*, we have **initial ellipsis**. In constructions like *Ann became president and Jack Ø vice-president* and *Susan Ø already at seven*, **medial ellipsis** is involved. Medial ellipsis is typically the result of suppressed repetition. Finally, there is **terminal ellipsis** in examples like *I was Ø* and *We parked Ildiko's car behind Sandor's Ø*. In this position, too, ellipsis is usually the result of suppressed repetition.

5.3. Pro-forms

Ellipsis is not the only way of achieving economy of expression. Consider the following examples:

(1)   {My little sister} saw *herself* in the mirror.

(2)   They arrested {Jeremy Soames}, *who* was on his honeymoon.

(3)   When {Jill's mother} asked for {a new film for the camera}, I gave *her one*.

The italicized constituents in these examples are **pro-forms**, more specifically pronouns, representing other constituents in the sentences, viz. those appearing in curly brackets. In (1) the reflexive pronoun *herself* represents *My little sister*, in (2) the relative pronoun *who* represents *Jeremy Soames*, and in (3) the personal pronoun *her* represents *Jill's mother* and the indefinite pronoun *one* represents *a new film for the camera*. In all four cases, the pronouns are light constituents standing proxy for heavier constituents in the linguistic context. Like ellipsis, the use of pro-forms ensures economy of expression: rather than repeating a heavy constituent we use a light pro-form.

Most pro-forms present no difficulty with respect to sentence analysis. In the examples above, each pronoun assumes an easily identifiable function: *herself* is O:pro, *who* is S:pro, *her* is Oi:pro and *one* is Od:pro.

Certain pro-forms may represent larger chunks of material in the linguistic context:

(4)   He's a friendly dog called Poulidor, but {he's now got so old that he's gone stone deaf}. Both Oliver and I find *this* terribly sad.

(5)   Deny *it* though he might, {he dumped his wife in Paris}.

Here the pro-forms represent a whole clause, *this* anaphorically and *it* cataphorically. Again the analysis is fairly straightforward: both pro-forms are O:pro. There is a tradition for calling items like *this* and *it* pronouns even in cases where they represent larger constituents, such as clauses.

Sometimes pro-forms represent less clearly identifiable constituents:

(6)   He may decide to join us next week, but I don't think *so*.

(7)   Speaker A: Will he join us next week?
        Speaker B: I hope *not*.

In (6) the adverb *so* represents the preceding clause but with an appropriate change of operator: ... *but I don't think he will join us next week*. In (7), the adverb *not* represents the whole of the preceding clause but changes it into a negative statement: ... *I hope he will not join us next week*. The proposed analysis of both items is O:adv.

Consider next the following examples:

(8)   I would like to go to Rome. *So would* my wife.

(9)   He cannot withdraw at this point. *Nor can* she.

(10)   My father didn't like Jenny, and *neither did* my mother.

Here there are complex pro-forms consisting of an adverb (*so, neither, nor*) plus an operator (either a repeated operator or a form of DO). In each example, the combination as a whole represents a **predicate**:

(8')   ... My wife *would like to go to Rome too.*

(9')   ... She *cannot withdraw at this point, either.*

(10') ... and my mother *didn't like Jenny, either.*

In such cases, the adverb stands proxy for a **predication**, i.e. a predicate minus the operator (e.g. *like to go to Rome too*).

Finally, it may be noted that it is not always easy to decide whether an example shows ellipsis or the use of proforms:

(11)   For years he wanted to *win the race* and he finally *did.*

(12)   Speaker A: *Will* he *propose marriage to her?*
       Speaker B: Well, he *may.*

In these examples, the operator (*did, may*) either serves as a pro-form representing a whole predicate (*won the race* and *may propose marriage to her*) or is left stranded after ellipsis of the predication (*win the race, propose marriage to her*). Similarly, in an example like *We parked Ildiko's car behind Sandor's* (cf. section 5.1), an alternative to saying that there is ellipsis of *car* after *Sandor's* is to regard *Sandor's* as a pro-form for *Sandor's car.*

6. Vocatives, interjections and dislocation

This section briefly examines three types of constituent which, like disjuncts and conjuncts (cf. section 2.7), are rather peripheral to sentence structure and often marked as such by punctuation. These are **vocatives**, **interjections** and **dislocated** constituents.

The term **vocative** refers to an expression used to address the hearer. In English a vocative is expressed by a separate **proper** or **common noun** (e.g. *Brenda* and *sir*) or a noun group (e.g. *my darling*) placed initially, medially or finally:

(1)   *Brenda*, I could do with a glass of sherry.

(2)   We are certainly, *sir*, treating the death as suspicious.

(3)   You must trust me, *my darling*.

A vocative may also be realized by the personal pronoun *you* or by a group containing this word. Except in informal expressions like *you guys* and *you chaps*, this type of address is usually rude:

(4)   *You (there)*, I need some service right away.

Moreover, in those cases where several people are addressed, the pronouns *all*, *everybody*, *everyone* may be used, and if the speaker wishes to catch the attention of any member of a group, he can use *somebody* or *someone*:

(5)   Clap your hands, *everybody*.
(6)   Answer the phone, *somebody*.

Vocatives have a number of different subfunctions. In the first place, they may be used to initiate an act of communication, and when used for this purpose they are naturally enough placed initially. Secondly, it is common practice for speakers to ensure that this act of communication is continued by interspersing their text with references to the listener. Thirdly, vocatives have various emotive functions. Their use has an implicitly positive effect which has been described as 'stroking', but they may also be descriptively positive (*darling*, *dearest John*, etc.) or negative (*clumsy clot*, *you idiot*, etc.). Finally, vocatives may signal respect for the addressee and are often required by rules of etiquette (*Your Majesty*, *Mr President*, *professor*, *sir*).

In imperative sentences it is sometimes difficult to separate **vocatives** from **subjects**. The reason for this is that imperative sentences are inherently vocative, either expressing or, more typically, assuming a second person singular or plural subject *you*, representing the listener(s) or reader(s). The difficulty of distinguishing between imperative subjects and vocatives can be illustrated by the following examples:

(7)   Everybody clap your hands.
(8)   John and Peter stand over there.

Traditionally, such sentences are held to contain third person subjects, but as they are synonymous with sentences with final vocatives (*Clap your hands, everybody*, etc.), it is reasonable to assume that they involve vocatives rather than subjects and are used to catch the attention of the intended receiver of the directive. In this view, the subject of imperative sentences is always implied or explicit *you*, cf. the presence of the possessive form *your* in (7) and the possibility of adding **tag questions** with *you*:

(9)   Somebody answer the phone, will you?

In some respects, vocatives are similar to **interjections**, i.e. to the class of words which includes emotive words like *oh*, *ugh*, *mm*, etc. and which is here assumed to include also 'reaction signals' like *yes*, *no*, *well* and greetings like *hi* and *hello*. Traditionally, interjections are defined as words which do not enter into syntactic relations, and in many cases they do indeed seem to constitute separate utterances:

(10)   Oh, I see.   (Oh + I see)
(11)   Yes, I know   (Yes + I know)

In these examples, the interjection serves as an exclamation and the following clause serves as a statement.

   In informal speech a nominal is sometimes **dislocated** to the periphery of a sentence and replaced by a corresponding pronoun. Here are first some examples with **right-dislocation**, i.e. where the dislocated nominal is added as a tag at the end of the clause (to the right):

(12)   *She*'s an excellent pianist, *your sister-in-law*.
(13)   I can't stand *him, that friend of yours*.

In such sentences – which are characteristic of spontaneous discourse – the nominal tag amplifies the message and serves to ensure that the entity referred to by the pronoun is correctly identified by the hearer. **Left-dislocation** (i.e. where the dislocated nominal appears as an initial tag to the left of the clause) is less common:

(14)   *Your sister-in-law*, *she*'s an excellent pianist.
(15)   *That friend of yours*, I simply can't stand *him*.

Left-dislocation is used in informal speech to ensure identification before embarking on the construction of the clause.

PART II

The purpose of Part II is to describe a number of syntactic and semantic characteristics of English: constituent order (including inversion and the position and order of optional adverbials), situation types, participant roles, voice, polarity, concord and complex sentences.

7. Constituent order

As pointed out in sections 1.7 to 1.9, the typical sentence structures in declarative statements (without optional adverbials) are:

Structure	Examples
S P	Nothing happened.
S P A	He squeezed between two motor-cars.
S P O	You must persuade her.
S P Cs	She proved surprisingly uncooperative.
S P Oi Od	They bought my daughter a new bike.
S P O Co	He had knocked two opponents totally senseless.
S P O A	We must put some flesh on your bones.

In an account of constituent order in English, it is a convenient descriptive device to take one's point of departure in these patterns and describe other orderings as the result of **movement** of constituents, or the **insertion** of optional adverbials. For example, in a complex-transitive sentence like:

(1)   On the table he put the book. (A S P O)

the adverbial can be regarded as having moved from the designated A position of the regular S P O A structure (*He put the book on the table*) to a position before the subject for reasons of style or focus.

In a sentence like:

(2)   So Richard was again sleeping heavily in my room. (A S P- A -P A A)

four optional adverbials have been inserted in various positions in the basic intransitive S P structure in order to supply further information.

In this chapter we shall examine the rules which seem to govern constituent order. Central questions which have to be considered are 'What does constituent order signal communicatively?', 'What motivates a change of constituent order from the basic structures identified?' and 'Into what positions are adverbials inserted and what is their sequential order?'.

7.1. Functions of constituent order

In English, constituent order has three different functions: 1) to signal grammatical relations; 2) to signal illocutionary value; and 3) to signal information structure. In the following I shall briefly explain and exemplify these functions.

Grammatical relations. Constituent order is highly revealing of grammatical relations in the sense that the relative position of a constituent gives us a reliable clue about its status as e.g. subject, direct object or indirect object. As the basic sentence structures show, obligatory sentence functions have characteristic positions. Thus for example in a sentence like:

(1)   England gave Sweden Norway. (S P Oi Od)

(which refers to the historical situation right after the Napoleonic wars), *England* is subject (because it precedes the predicator), *Sweden* is indirect object and *Norway* direct object (because they follow the predicator, with the indirect object normally preceding the direct object). We thus interpret *England* to be the agent (the giver), *Sweden* the beneficiary (the recipient) and *Norway* the affected (the country given away). If we change the order (as in *Norway gave Sweden England*), we change the grammatical relations of the three constituents (*Norway* is now subject, *Sweden* indirect object and *England* direct object) and, as a result, we change the meaning of the sentence as a whole.

Illocutionary value. As we saw in section 4.1, we can change a declarative sentence into an interrogative or exclamatory one by changing the order of constituents:

declarative	S P C	Greg is a jerk.
interrogative	P S C	Is Greg a jerk?
	P- S -P C	Has Greg been a jerk?
	C P S	What is Greg?
exclamatory	C S P	What a jerk Greg is!

Although there is no strict one-to-one relation between sentence type and illocutionary value (cf. section 4.3), it is generally true to say that the different constituent orders characteristic of the different sentence types guide the listener towards different illocutionary values. Thus the straight constituent order S P C in *Greg is a jerk* will guide the listener towards the value 'statement' whereas the changed P- S - P C order in *Has Greg been a jerk?* will guide the listener towards the value 'question'. Note also that by leaving the subject out altogether, we may signal 'directive' as in the following imperative sentence:

imperative   P C   Be a jerk.

Information structure. Often the constituent order of a sentence is a result of the way the speaker presents the information. As noted in section 2.8, sentences can be divided into subject and predicate, where the subject expresses the topic and the predicate the comment of the sentence. The topic is often associated with **given information** whereas the comment is associated with **new information**. This can be illustrated by an example like *The letter is from your mother*, in which the subject and topic *The letter* is given information (i.e. assumed to be known) and the predicate and comment *is from your mother* is new information and in the centre of the speaker's communicative interest. The tendency to place new and important information at the end of the sentence is called the principle of **end-focus**. Related to the principle of end-focus is the principle of **end-weight**. According to this principle there is a tendency, wherever possible, to place heavy (i.e. long) constituents last. Compare the following examples:

(1)   The court pronounced *the woman* not guilty. (S P O Co)

(2)   The court pronounced not guilty *the woman who had been charged with the murder*. (S P Co O)

In example (1) there is the expected S P O Co order, where the object complement follows the object. In example (2) this order is reversed so that the object follows the object complement. The reason for that is that the object in (2) is much heavier than the complement and therefore allowed to move to the end of the sentence. When a heavy constituent is moved to the end of a sentence according to the principle of end-weight, it automatically receives end-focus. Thus in (1) there is end-focus on the object complement whereas in (2) there is end-focus on the object. The **postponement** of a constituent for reasons of information structure is called **focalization**. Here are some other examples of focalization:

(3)   I just saw on television *how some Indian people started a shop and put the old grocery on the corner out of business*. (S A P A O)

(4)   The rumour spread *that the King had been beheaded*. (S- P -S)

In (3) a heavy object is placed in final position after the adverbial (*on television*), and in (4) the dependent clause in the subject moves to final position after the verb, thus creating discontinuity. Extraposition of subject or object (cf. sections 2.2 and 2.3) is a special case of focalization:

(5)   It worries me *that the children have not returned*. (Sp P O Sr)

(6)   I find it a challenge *writing this report for the UN*. (S P Op Co Or)

Such examples clearly show the principle of end-weight at work, compare:

(5')   *That the children have not returned* worries me. (S P O)
(6')   I find *writing this report for the UN* a challenge. (S P O Co)

Under the heading of information structure there is another way to change the basic constituent order, also resulting in the highlighting of a constituent. A constituent which normally is in non-initial position (i.e. an object, a complement or an adverbial) can be moved to initial position, in which case the speaker highlights it as the topic of the sentence. Such **fronting** of a constituent is called **topicalization**. Examples:

(7)   *That story* I will tell you some other time. (O S P A)
(8)   *Chris Waddle* his name is. (C S P)
(9)   *On the table* he put the hat. (A S P O)

Most frequently the function of topicalization is to create a link, or **cohesion**, to the preceding context. One possible way to relate to the preceding context is to provide a 'contrast'. Thus, example (9) may be uttered to express a contrast between *On the table* and other locations in the context. But cohesion is often non-contrastive, as in the following example, where the fronted object pronoun *This* simply refers back to the preceding clause:

(10)   He knew what he liked and Lily didn't conform to the specifications. *This* he
        knew with a certainty as absolute as his knowledge that the food he served
        from the 'tourist' menu was rubbish.

To recapitulate: constituent order is used to signal grammatical relations (subject, object, etc.), to indicate illocutionary value (by marking type of sentence: declarative, interrogative, etc.) and to structure a message informationally (by means of topicalization and focalization).

7.2. Inversion

The term **inversion** refers to the reversal of the order of constituents. Although the term could have been used about the reversal of the order of **any** constituents, many grammarians restrict the use of the term to the reversal of subject and predicator.

A distinction should be drawn between subject-operator inversion (sometimes referred to as partial inversion) and full subject-predicator inversion. **Subject-operator inversion** is usually obligatory and involves the movement of the operator to a position in front of the subject:

(1)   Only with difficulty *could* Lily *have explained* her conduct to her parents.
       (cf. *Lily could have explained her conduct to her parents*)

(2)   *Have* they ever *sailed* a Wayfarer before?
       (cf. *They have sailed a Wayfarer before*)

If there is no operator in the predicator of the basic pattern (e.g. *After a while he noticed something peculiar*), DO is inserted as a dummy operator:

(3)   Only after a while *did* he *notice* something peculiar.

Where the predicator consists of only the primary verb BE, there is no DO-support and the whole predicator is moved:

(4)   *Are* you mad? (cf. *You are mad*)

The same applies to HAVE in conservative BrE:

(5)   *Have* you any doubt about his guilt?

In AmE, and increasingly in BrE, there is DO-support:

(6)   *Do* you *have* any doubt about his guilt?

Outside formal language, and especially in BrE, we also find HAVE *got*:

(7)   *Have* you *got* any doubt about his guilt?

Full subject-predicator inversion is often optional and involves the movement of the whole predicator to a position before the subject:

(8)   In rhyme and rhythm *resides* a certain magic power. (A P S)
(9)   Here *comes* the milkman. (A P S)

In sentences with BE (and occasionally in sentences with HAVE) as the only verb, it is difficult to distinguish between subject-operator inversion and full subject-predicator inversion, for in both cases the full predicator precedes the subject:

(10)   *Is* he comfortable? (P S C)
(11)   Here *is* my brother. (A P S)

Example (10) is an instance of subject-operator inversion (corresponding to e.g. *Has he been comfortable*), while example (11) is an instance of full subject-predicator inversion (corresponding to *Here comes my brother*). In other words, reversal of a subject and BE is treated as subject-operator inversion in those cases where such inversion occurs with other verbs.

7.2.1. Subject-operator inversion

Subject-operator inversion is used under two well-defined conditions: (1) to signal illocutionary value, and (2) in connection with a special opening constituent. More specifically we find subject-operator inversion of **the first type** in (i) interrogative clauses, (ii) certain expressions of wishes/maledictions, (iii) certain conditional clauses, and (iv) certain imperative clauses. Here are some examples and further comments:

(i.a) *Yes-no* interrogative clauses:

(1)   Could you live without me?
(2)   Did they let him go?

There is also subject-operator inversion in *yes-no* interrogative clauses used as exclamations:

(3)   Isn't she lovely!

(i.b) Tag-questions (i.e. questions added on to sentences for emphasis, consisting of only an operator and a subject, with or without the negative marker *not*):

(4)   You could always tell him the truth, *couldn't you*?
(5)   Tom didn't like Jenny a lot, *did he*?

(i.c) *Wh*-interrogative clauses in which the *wh*-word is not (part of) the subject:

(6)   What do you mean, the police?
(7)   Why are you always making such a fuss about your brother?

When the *wh*-word is (part of) the subject, there is straight subject-operator order:

(8)   Who signed me up for orienteering?
(9)   Which of the two teams came in first?

(ii) Wishes and maledictions expressed with MAY:

(10)   Please God, may it have been instantly.
(11)   May she rot in hell.

(iii) Formal expressions of conditional commitment with *had, should* or *were* as operator and without subordinating conjunction (i.e. without *if, unless, in case*, etc.):

(12)   *Had* I known this, I would never have accepted the offer.
(13)   *Should* he do that, I will crucify him.
(14)   The total output would be much worse *were* it not for the winter crop.

(iv) Negative imperative clauses with an expressed subject:

(15)   Don't you let him force you back.
(16)   Don't you listen to him.

The second type of subject-operator inversion is triggered by a special initial constituent (and is therefore often referred to as **attraction inversion**). It is found in:

(i) Sentences beginning with a topicalized negative or restrictive constituent other than the subject:

(17)   *Rarely* have I set eyes on such a stunning beauty.
(18)   *Not another pound* will you get from me.
(19)   *Only after a while* did he notice that his mother was crying.

If a negative word does not apply to the entire clause but only locally to the constituent in which it occurs, there is straight subject-predicator order:

(20)   Not long ago my mother turned eighty.

In spoken English, subject-operator inversion after a negative opener is particularly common in clauses beginning with one of the adverbial pro-forms NEITHER and NOR (cf. section 5.3):

(21)   I didn't turn up and *neither* did my wife.
(22)   Speaker A: I can't swim.   Speaker B: *Nor* can I.

(ii) In clauses beginning with the adverbial pro-form SO (cf. the use of NEITHER and NOR above):

(23)   I turned up and *so* did my wife.
(24)   Speaker A: I can swim.   Speaker B: *So* can I.

(iii) Sentences beginning with a topicalized, discontinuous SO or SUCH construction which ends in a *that*-clause:

(25)   *So much* did he eat *that he was almost sick.* (O- P- S -P -O)
(26)   *Such* was the heat *that she was unable to finish the recital.* (C- P S -C)

(iv) In formal-style subclauses which express comparison and begin with the subordinating conjunctions *as* or *than*:

(27)   Crabs were fresh and plentiful in the market at the moment, white vegetable was good, *as* were Holland beans.
(28)   Alice knew Peter far better *than* did most of her classmates.

Occasionally subject-operator inversion is found with other openers:

(29)   *Well* do I know that you hate me.
(30)   *Much rather* would I be dead.
(31)   *Thus* did a lovely evening end.

7.2.2. Full inversion

Full inversion is a matter of information structure. We find it most often in connection with topicalization (fronting), especially to avoid end-focus on a semantically light predicator or for reasons of end-weight.

We find full inversion **after a topicalized adverbial** in the following cases:

(i) In literary-style intransitive constructions with an initial adverbial of place (or more rarely of time):

(1)   *On the walls* were pictures of half-naked women and colourful landscapes.

(2)   *At his side* sat a black Alsatian dog.

(3)   *Now* comes the time we have been waiting for so long

In such examples, topicalization typically serves the purpose of establishing narrative continuity, and the verb is semantically light (e.g. BE, APPEAR, HANG, LIE, SIT, STAND, etc).

(ii) In informal short intransitive sentences beginning with one of the adverbs of place HERE and THERE:

(4)   Here comes the bus.

(5)   There goes the last bus.

(iii) In intransitive sentences beginning with a directional adverb like DOWN, UP, ALONG, IN and OUT:

(6)   Out darted a mouse.

(7)   Up went the prices once again.

The verbs in such vivid constructions typically express movement, e.g. COME, DART, FALL, FLY, GO, JUMP.

Related to sentences with fronted adverbials are constructions with a **topicalized predication** consisting of a present or past participle plus subsequent sentence functions (typically adverbials or objects), as in the present sentence as well as the following literary examples:

(8)   *Sandwiched between the Chinese restaurants* was the Curry Mahal.

(9)   *Awaiting them* were a tray of sandwiches, two bottles of wine, the director in uniform, and, to top it all off, an exceptionally beautiful girl.

This kind of construction is frequent also in journalism:

(10)   *Also killed in the shoot-out* were three teenagers from the Bronx.

The italicized predications in these sentences could alternatively be interpreted as initial adverbials. This interpretation is supported by the fact that BE is sometimes replaced by a full verb, as in (11), and by the fact that in less formal style we can insert *there* as a provisional subject (in which case there is therefore no inversion), as in (12):

(11)   Awaiting them *stood* a group of heavily armed soldiers. (A P S)

(12)   Heaped on the lectern near the window *there* were religious books and sheets of paper covered with writing. (A Sp P Sr)

We find full inversion **after a topicalized complement**:

(i) for reasons of end-weight:

(13)   Strange indeed was *her urge to tell everybody what she thought of them*.

(ii) in constructions which express comparison with the preceding text (typically in connection with BE):

(14)   A course in trigonometry may be useful enough, but *far more useful* would be a refresher course in elementary maths.

(15)   Grammar is undoubtedly relevant, but *equally relevant* are recent approaches to language learning.

We find full inversion **after a topicalized object** in cases where the object is reported speech. The inversion in the reporting clause is optional and can usually only take place if the subject is realized by a nominal constituent and there is no indirect object or adverbial present:

(16)   'Eh?' said the driver / the driver said.

Examples of inversion with an adverbial present are stylistically marked:

(17)   'Oh no!' said the pot *to the pan*.

If the subject is realized by a pronoun, there is usually no inversion:

(18)   'This is madness,' he said / *said he.

In earlier stages of English, inversion of pronoun and verb of saying was common, and thus has an archaic, poetic or even comical ring to it:

(19)   'Tis madness,' quoth he.

In everyday conversation, inversion is not uncommon in cases like:

(20)   Speaker A: 'Jack can do it.'
        Speaker B: 'Says who!'

(21)   Speaker A: 'John's wife can run a mile in four minutes.'
        Speaker B: 'Yeah, says he!'

In both cases the pronoun is fully stressed, and the construction conveys a tone of disbelief, contempt or derision.

In journalism there is occasionally inversion in initial reporting clauses, in accordance with the principle of end-weight:

(22)   Explained Clay Mulford, the national group's general counsel: 'We don't want to be held responsible for every action they take.' (P S O)

7.3. Constituent order in subclauses

Basically, the constituent order of subclauses is the same as in main clauses but note that it often includes an initial subordinator:

(1)   I told them *that* my wife gave the old man my umbrella.

The rules for inversion also often applies to subclauses, e.g.:

(2)   I was appalled to think *that never in my life would I have an opportunity to stride down a gangplank in a panama hat and a white suit.*

(3)   I was relieved to see *that under the bridge ran a small creek.*

However, there are some notable characteristics about constituent order in subclauses:

(i) In **relative subclauses**, the relative constituent (i.e. the one realized by or containing the relative pronoun or Ø) is always topicalized irrespective of its clause function:

(4)   This house, *which I bought last year*, is beyond repair. (O S P)

If the relative pronoun is a prepositional complement in an adverbial group, either the whole constituent or just the relative pronoun is topicalized. In the latter case the adverbial group is discontinuous, cf.:

(5a)   I called the editor *to whom you posted the book.* (A S P O)
(5b)   I called the editor *who/whom/that/Ø you posted the book to.* (A- S P O -A)

(ii) In **wh-interrogative subclauses**, the function realized by or containing the *wh*-word is always topicalized, as in corresponding main clauses (cf. section 4.1). But unlike *wh*-interrogative main clauses, *wh*-interrogative subclauses have straight S P order:

(6)   I fail to see *what you mean.* (O S P)
(7)   Tell me *what your name is.* (C S P)
(8)   I don't understand *how you can say that.* (A S P O)

If the interrogative pronoun is a prepositional complement in an adverbial group, either the whole constituent or just the relative pronoun is topicalized. In the latter case the adverbial group is discontinuous, cf.:

(9)   I would like to know *to whom I should post the manuscript.* (A S P O)
(10)   I would like to know *who(m) I should post the manuscript to.* (A- S P O -A)

(iii) In subordinate *yes-no* **interrogative clauses**, which begin with one of the subordinating conjunctions *if* or *whether*, there is no fronting of objects, complements or adverbials, nor is there inversion of subject and operator as in main-clause *yes-no* questions (see section 7.2.1 above):

(11)   He asks *if they think the weather will stay fine.* (SUB S P O)
        (cf. *Do they think the weather will stay fine?*)

(12)   I wonder *whether I hurt her feelings.* (SUB S P O)
        (cf. *Did I hurt her feelings?*)

(iv) As noted in section 7.2.1, there is sometimes partial inversion in sub-clauses to signal **conditional commitment**:

(13)   *Had I known this,* I would never have accepted the offer.

or as a result of attraction to a clause-initial constituent:

(14)   Alice is far more intelligent *than are most of her classmates.*

(v) Occasionally, in so-called **concessive clauses** with one of the conjunctions *as, if, that,* or *though,* we find topicalization of a complement (as in example (15)) or of a full predication (as in example (16)). The fronted element(s) precede(s) the subordinating conjunction:

(15)   *Confused* though he is, he manages well. (cf. *Though he is confused ...*)

(16)   I knew it for an aspect of my inheritance that I could never root out, *deny it though I might.* (cf. ..., *though I might deny it.*)

7.4. Position and order of adverbials

In this chapter we have so far been concerned with the position and order of obligatory sentence functions, especially in terms of deviation from the basic sentence structures defined in sections 1.7 to 1.9. We shall now examine the position and order of optional adverbials, i.e. the one major function type not included in our list of sentence structures.

   Let us begin with the possible positions of optional adverbials. In finite clauses we distinguish three main positions: **initial** (I), **medial** (M) and **terminal** (T), as in the following examples:

(1)   *Quite frankly,* she gave him every excuse.
(2)   Owen *substantially* improved my abilities as a student.
(3)   The Voice had not been idle *for the summer.*

Each of these main positions needs closer examination.

7.4.1. Initial position

I-position is always before the subject (or the predicator plus subject in inverted constructions) but after conjunctions and fronted constituents, if any:

(1)   *Quite frankly*, did she give him any excuse?
(2)   I admire her because, *quite frankly*, she gave him every excuse.
(3)   He loved her and, *quite frankly*, she gave him every excuse.
(4)   This solution, *obviously*, she would never accept.

7.4.2. Medial position

Any adverbial which follows the subject but precedes the head verb of the predicator is said to be in M-position. This definition accommodates three more specific M-positions:

(i) Central-M. This position is the **unmarked** (i.e. usual, neutral) position immediately after the operator (also if the operator is primary verb BE serving as full verb, as in example (2)):

(1)   Owen had *substantially* improved my abilities as a student.
(2)   Keith was *always* happy.

Central-M is the position taken up by the clause negator NOT:

(3)   Owen did *not* improve my abilities as a student.
(4)   Owen could *not* improve my abilities as a student.

In negative interrogative constructions, NOT is contracted across the subject to pre-subject position in spoken and informal written English; compare:

(5)   Had*n't* Owen improved my abilities as a student?
(6)   Had Owen *not* improved my abilities as a student?

If there is no operator but only a full verb in P, central-M position is simply between subject and predicator:

(7)   Keith *never* wanted her soul.

(ii) Pre-M. This position is always immediately before the operator. In BrE (unlike AmE), pre-M position is often **marked** (i.e. less usual, more special) and requires primary stress on the operator:

(8)   Owen *substantially* `did improve my abilities as a student.
(9)   Jane *never* `was fond of her sister.

Pre-M position is common in elliptical clauses with an operator representing a full predicate:

(10)   I miss you, darling, I *really* do.
(11)   You know that I fancy you, I *always* have.

(iii) Post-M. Certain adverbs, such as manner and degree adjuncts, which relate more closely to the head verb than to the operator, typically immediately precede the head verb. Often this results in central-M position:

(12)   Keith (had) *completely* recovered from the accident.

(13)   She was *seriously* crippled by the blow.

However, in strings with more auxiliaries than the operator, such adverbs stick with the head verb instead of remaining in central-M position. The position they take up between a nonfinite auxiliary and the head verb is called post-M:

(14)   She may be *secretly* supporting their cause.

(15)   He may not have been *completely* recovering from the accident.

7.4.3. Terminal position

T-position is the position of obligatory adverbials in S P A and S P O A constructions (as in e.g. *I stayed with my parents*) and of optional adverbials which follow objects, complements and obligatory adverbials, or intransitive predicators:

(1)   She gave me a quick kiss *on the cheek.*

(2)   Her parents got very upset *when they saw us together*.

(3)   I put the gun in my pocket *as casually as I could.*

(4)   He smoked *incessantly.*

We sometimes encounter cases where the optional adverbial follows the predicator but precedes an object, a complement or an obligatory adverbial (typically for reasons of end-weight):

(5)   Many subscribers to NLLT experienced *four times a year* excitement of a sort that the arrival of a scholarly journal in one's mailbox rarely occasions.

(6)   His parents seemed *often* very dependent on his support.

(7)   I put the gun *casually* in my pocket.

The position taken up by the italicized adverbials in these examples is called **pre-T**. Pre-T, which is the position after P but before other obligatory constituents, is primarily to be thought of as a marked alternative to T-position (as in (5)) or to central-M position (as in (6) and (7)).

7.4.4. Positions in nonfinite clauses

Adverbial positions in nonfinite clauses correspond to those in finite clauses with three important exceptions:

(i) There is **no genuine I-position**. Although superficially adverbials do occur initially in nonfinite clauses, they never actually precede the subject:

(1)   *Always* feeling guilty, she mostly kept to herself.

(2)   *Obviously* having difficulty reading the book, he watched television instead.

When a subject is present in a nonfinite clause, it precedes such adverbials:

(3)   Sarah *always* feeling guilty, I did not want to tell her what had happened.

Moreover, for clausal negation, NOT - the characteristic central-M adverbial - immediately **precedes** the first verb in the predicator, even BE:

(4)   *Not* feeling comfortable at all, he gave her a ring.

(5)   *Not* being happy with this decision, he quit.

It is therefore more appropriate to classify the adverbials in all these examples as central-M adverbials than to classify them as I-adverbials.

(ii) There is **neutralization between pre-M and central-M**. Since there is no operator in nonfinite clauses, by definition there can be no pre-M adverbials, either. However, on analogy with finite predicators, adverbials are often placed after the first auxiliary in nonfinite predicators. We thus find unmarked adverbials both before and after the first auxiliary of a nonfinite predicator; compare the following examples:

(6a)   With Jack *always* being shadowed, we endanger the whole operation.

(6b)   With Jack being *always* shadowed, we endanger the whole operation.

We classify *always* as a central-M adverbial in the a-example and as a post-M adverbial in the b-example, but the difference between the two positions is not as clearly felt as in finite clauses.

(iii) There is **a special M-position** between infinitive marker and infinitive. An adverbial in this position creates the so-called **split infinitive**:

(7)   For me to *suddenly* resign my job is unthinkable.

(8)   She has tried to *consciously* stop worrying.

The split infinitive is felt by many to be not only marked but in fact unacceptable. Despite widespread prejudice against it, this construction type is by no means rare.

7.4.5. Factors governing the distribution of adverbials

There are few hard-and-fast rules for the distribution of adverbials in the positions defined in sections 7.4.1 to 7.4.4 above, especially because many adverbials are mobile. Thus, except for the negation NOT and a few other adverbs (typically adverbs of time and frequency) such as ALWAYS, EVER,

OFTEN, NEVER, RARELY, REALLY, HARDLY (which are nearly always located in central-M position, at least in BrE), it is more appropriate to speak of certain factors contributing to the speaker/writer's location of adverbials:

(i) Form and relative weight. The form of the adverbial is the major factor determining the position it assumes in the clause. Statistical analyses have shown that **long** adverbials (clauses and long groups) tend to occur in I- and especially T-position (for reasons of end-weight) rather than in M-position:

(1)   *Knowing that Keith would be elsewhere*, I staked out the Black Cross.

(2)   One of the black guys was staring at me *with either affection or contempt*.

Short adverbials are more evenly distributed in the three main positions:

(3)   I cried all the time, *actually*.

(4)   *Actually* I cried all the time.

(5)   I *actually* cried all the time.

Long parenthetical adverbials occasionally occur in central- or even pre-M position:

(6)   Keith, *in my mind*, blew/had blown all his chances.

M-position is especially rare for weighty adverbials if the subject is an unstressed personal pronoun, compare:

(7)   Guy, *feeling no closer to life than to death*, pressed on.

(8)   *I, *knowing that Keith would be elsewhere*, staked out the Black Cross.

(ii) Textual and contextual cohesion. T-position is for many adverbials, especially long ones, the most unmarked position, i.e. the position they take up unless there is some reason for taking up a different position. (Con)textual cohesion (i.e. the binding together of sentences in a coherent text or, in speech, the use of utterances in particular contexts) is one such reason for appearing in I-position rather than T-position. As with other clause functions, adverbials appearing initially either receive special highlighting (as a fronted constituent) or establish a link to the context or preceding text, thus forming part of what is 'given' background information (cf. section 7.1):

(9)   Sometimes, when he stumbled into her bedsit in the small hours, Analiese was alone. *On other occasions* he surprised her in bed with famous people.

(10)   When Analiese gave herself to you, she would give herself utterly, and probably wouldn't ring the house. *In this last particular alone*, appearances were deceptive.

Not surprisingly, I-position is thus the 'natural' (but not the only) position for adverbials serving more particularly as **conjuncts** (cf. section 2.7):

(11)   *Besides*, Keith generally preferred short girls.

(12)   *To conclude*, I'll never have dealings with Telstra again.

(iii) Scope. By the 'scope' of an adverbial is meant the extent of its semantic relations to other constituents or to the context. The scope of an adverbial may be just one other constituent, typically the predicator, as in (13), or it may be a whole sentence, as in (14):

(13)   He walked *briskly* down the road.

(14)   *To tell the truth*, he was limping when he got up off the basketball court.

There is in language a general tendency for the scope of constituents to be determined by their position: in I-position the scope is typically broader than in M- and T-position, and in M-position it is typically narrower than in T-position. Compare for example:

(15a)   *Clearly* he saw her.

(15b)   He saw her *clearly*.

(16a)   *Quite frankly* he told me about the affair.

(16b)   He told me *quite frankly* about the affair.

Here the adverbials in the a-examples are disjuncts with sentential scope ('It was clear that he saw her' and 'I am telling you quite frankly that he told me about the affair'), while the adverbials in the b-examples are likely to be interpreted as manner adjuncts with predicator scope. As in these examples, adverbials in I-position tend to have wider scope than adverbials in M- or T-position. For the broadening of scope in T-position, see section 7.4.6 below.

(iv) Semantic clarity. Consider the following examples:

(17a)   In Paris he decided to study art.

(17b)   He decided to study art in Paris.

While (17a) conveys the information that someone decided to study art and that this decision was made in Paris, (17b) is likely to be interpreted to mean that the studying of art was to take place in Paris: *in Paris* seems to locate the 'studying' rather than the 'decision-taking'. But strictly speaking, (17b) could mean the same as (17a) and is thus ambiguous. Syntactically, the difference between the two readings of (17b) hinges on whether or not *in Paris* belongs as an adverbial to the object clause *to study art*. In (17a), the adverbial is unambiguously a matrix clause function. To ensure an unambiguous reading, the speaker or writer may thus decide to place the adverbial in I-position. Here are some examples where semantic clarity dictates a reversal of the normal O A order:

(18)   She herself interviewed *with hurtful disdain* the student I had turned down.

(19)   He urged *secretly* that she be dismissed.

In these examples, the only alternative to pre-T position, if the intended meaning is to be preserved, is M- or I-position, not T-position, which would drastically alter the meaning of the sentence.

(v) Style. While other clause functions are relatively fixed in the basic sentence structures, optional adverbials often move around more freely and thus lend themselves to stylistic variation as a means to break up a monotonous repetition of a sentence pattern or to achieve a more balanced and easy-going flow of narration.

An important stylistic factor is **avoidance of heavy adverbial clusters**. There is a natural tendency for adverbial clustering in T-position in accordance with the general principle of end-weight. However, the possibility of placing adverbials in other positions makes it possible to avoid too heavy clusters in one position and to create more evenly balanced constructions:

(20)   *On the fifth day* the sun burst through *again inexorably*.

(21)   *In excellent fettle, in the pink or the blue of boyish good health during their absence*, Marmaduke sickened *dramatically within a few hours of their return*.

Avoidance of clustering in a particular M-position may lead to utilization of different M-positions; compare:

(22a)   The key-note address was *certainly elegantly* delivered by David.

(22b)   The key-note address *certainly* was *elegantly* delivered by David.

In negative clauses, where NOT occupies central-M position, disjuncts are often shifted into pre-M position:

(23)   She *probably* has *not* seen David yet.

(24)   Keith *obviously* will *not* listen to you.

7.4.6. Relative position of adverbials

When adverbials appear in clusters, as they frequently do at I-position (for extensive backgrounding) and especially at T-position (in accordance with the general principle of end-weight), the question of sequential order becomes relevant. Again there are no hard-and-fast rules but rather a number of general tendencies.:

(i) Form/relative weight. There is a tendency for short adverbials to precede long adverbials. Single words thus often precede groups, and groups often precede clauses:

(1)   [In excellent fettle], [in the pink or the blue of boyish good health during their absence], Marmaduke sickened [dramatically] [within a few hours of their return].

(2)   [Twenty minutes later], [as he strode back up the beach], the wind threw everything it had at him.

(ii) Scope. From the point of view of scope, the sequence disjuncts-conjuncts-adjuncts would be most natural in I-position, as in:

(3)   [Unfortunately], [however], [last night] the old lady declined to see me.

Disjuncts tend to precede adjuncts in I-position but inversion is possible – especially if the disjunct serves as a parenthetical insertion; compare:

(4a)   [To be quite honest], [last night] he vowed never to see her again.
(4b)   [Last night], [to be quite honest], he vowed never to see her again.

There is more vacillation in the ordering of conjuncts and adjuncts:

(5a)   [However], [last night], he vowed never to see her again.
(5b)   [Last night], [however], he vowed never to see her again.

In T-position adjuncts generally precede disjuncts and conjuncts (which are rarer in T- position and often felt to be added as parenthetical afterthoughts):

(6)   Keith left the pub [a bit later], [unfortunately].
(7)   Trish called her [twice], [though].

Sequences of all three types of adverbial (adjunct-conjunct-disjunct) are possible in T-position but rare:

(8)   She didn't like him [much] [anyway], [to be frank].

In a sequence of adjuncts in T-position, those with narrow predicator scope precede those with broader predication or sentence scope:

(9)   Hope kissed him [passionately] [on the cheek].
(10)   Keith will react [violently] [if we press him too hard].

(iii) Semantic considerations. Adverbials in clusters often supplement each other progressively so that each new adverbial in the sequence offers further elaboration or specification:

(11)   [On the front passenger seat], [under the elegant rag of a white silk scarf], lies a heavy car-tool.

Sometimes adverbials seem to be in a completely random order, simply enumerating different aspects:

(12)   A couple of mornings a month, [stiff with pride], [deafened with aspirin], [reckless with Bloody Marys], Nicola would adumbrate serious reform.

Many grammarians have pointed to the sequence manner-place-time-others:

(13)   She played [beautifully] [at the concert] [last night] [even if she hadn't had time to practice].

There is considerable variation, however:

(14)   He whispered the same words [at night] [in the hotel] [with that strange accent of his].

(15)   He called her [at three o'clock in the morning] [from the Black Cross].

In M-position time and frequency adjuncts usually precede manner adjuncts:

(16)   He had [never] [knowingly] drunk a glass of wine.

(17)   She had [often] [secretly] admired Keith.

Similarly short manner adjuncts tend to precede obligatory adverbials:

(18)   I put the gun [casually] [in my pocket].

8. Situations and participants

Language allows us to talk about all the goings-on, dealings, emotions, perceptions, attitudes, etc. that are part of everyday human lives. With language we also identify things, and we classify, characterize and relate them. In this book, the term **situation** is used as a cover term for the many different meanings that sentences express. For example, by saying *Jack fixed the old motorbike*, the speaker informs the hearer of an instance of 'fixing' (expressed by *fixed*) in which there are two **participants**: someone who does the fixing (*Jack*) and something that is affected by this, i.e. something that gets fixed (*the old motorbike*). These components make up a total meaning, a proposition expressing 'the situation of Jack fixing the old motorbike'.

8.1. Actionality: dynamic versus stative situations

A sentence such as *The old man painted the wall* shares a number of features with the situation of 'Jack fixing the old motorbike' mentioned in the previous section: in both cases there is a participant doing something to another participant with a certain result (the motorbike gets fixed and the wall gets painted) and both situations endure over time before they reach a natural endpoint. For this reason they belong, at some level of classification, to the same **type of situation** despite the fact that they obviously differ with respect to all the more specific characteristics. Turning now to an example like *Ottawa is the capital of Canada*, it is clear that here there is no participant doing something to another participant. Nor is there any natural endpoint or result of an activity. Rather, the example expresses a relation between two (referentially identical) 'participants': one (*Ottawa*) is characterized in terms of the other (*the capital of Canada*). By looking at a large number of sentences, it is possible to classify the situations they express (real-world, hypothetical or fictional) in situation types on the basis of our conception of their differences and similarities. The study of situations expressed by sentences is called the study of **actionality**. The different types of situation that can be recognized are described in terms of the **action category**. As will be seen, the action category is relevant to several areas within English grammar (such as the active/passive distinction and the use of the progressive verb form).

The primary actional distinction is that between **dynamic** and **stative**. A dynamic situation requires a continual input of energy and typically involves change while a stative situation requires no input of energy and remains the same. A dynamic situation 'happens' or 'takes place' while a state 'exists' or is 'true' of someone or something. The situations of 'Jack fixing the old motorbike' and 'The old man painting the wall' are both dynamic whereas the situation of 'Ottawa being the capital of Canada' is stative.

8.2. Subtypes of dynamic situations

There is, strictly speaking, no end to the number of subtypes of dynamic and stative situations that may be identified for the action category. However, some subtypes are more important than others in the description of the English verb. The most important dynamic ones are considered first:

Punctual situations have little or no extension in time and hence no internal structure. The situation referred to by e.g. *He suddenly switched from Spanish to English* is punctual in this sense. Other examples: *She hit me hard on the nose / Stephen dropped the gun*. Beginnings and endings are also punctual situations, e.g. *He started running* and *He stopped talking*.

Telic situations are conceived of as durative (i.e. as having extension over time) leading up to and including a natural terminal point beyond which no further progression is possible or relevant, and without which the situation is not fully completed. The situations of 'Jack fixing the old motorbike' and 'The old man painting the wall' (described above), as well as the situation referred to by e.g. *The student wrote an article about the split infinitive*, are telic. The term 'telic' is based on Greek *télos* 'goal, end'.

Directed situations progress towards a natural terminal point but do not in fact include this point. The situation referred to by e.g. *Sally was building a small garden shed* is directed in this sense: the 'building' activity is directed towards a point of completion but this point is outside the situation expressed by the sentence, not inside as in the case of telic situations. Other examples: *The girl was catching up with the rest of us / He slowly approached the door / She tried to solve the problem.*

Self-contained situations are durative situations conceived of as not having, or being directed towards, any natural point of completion. In other words, they may be terminated at any time without this affecting their completeness. Self-contained situations are the least dynamic and the most stative of the dynamic situation types because, although they may describe energetic activity, they do not imply change. Examples: *James and George were sailing along the coast / We were celebrating Stephanie's birthday at my uncle's place / We discussed their predicament at the last meeting.*

Iterative situations consist of a number of identical, or similar, consecutively realized subsituations. The situation referred to by *Jack was knocking at Sally's door* is thus complex: it consists of a number of knocks. Other examples: *Someone was tapping me on the shoulder / The telephone was ringing / Roger kept calling me.*

To fully understand the nature of actional subtypes, it is essential to make a distinction between 'real situations' and situations as conceived by the speaker', i.e. between objective facts and the subjective way that we think of these objective facts or choose to think of them in a particular context. Actional distinctions are largely subjective. Thus, for example, the situation expressed by an example like *The bus stopped for a red light* is probably best classified as punctual from the point of view of the action category (because we tend to conceive of 'stopping' as a punctual situation), but, strictly speaking, it is not punctual in the real world (because here it involves braking and slowing down to a complete halt). Consider also:

(1)   Jack was reading the report when I got back last night.
(2)   Jack was reading when I got back last night.

Whether one chooses to refer to a situation of 'reading' as directed (as in (1)) or as self-contained (as in (2)) may have very little to do with the objective reality of the situation, which may well be the same. What matters is what the speaker wishes to make of this situation in his message to the listener.

8.3. Subtypes of stative situations

Stative situations, which are almost always **relations** of some sort, can be subclassified in this way:

Intensive relations. An intensive relation involves either a description of an entity in terms of another (for identificatory or classificatory purposes) or an assignment of a property to an entity (characterization). The situations referred to by *Ottawa is the capital of Canada* and *Victoria is beautiful* are both intensive relations. Other examples: *They were in high spirits / Joan is the small girl talking to Bob over there / She seemed very unhappy.*

Extensive relations. An extensive relation is a physical state, condition, location, position or possession obtaining for an entity. The situation referred to by e.g. *The village lies in a dark valley* is an extensive relation in which the village is specified with respect to location. The situation referred to by an example like *Ildiko has a red Mercedes Benz* is an extensive relation between a person and a thing in terms of possession. Other examples: *This factory belongs to Mr Hardcastle / The key is in the top drawer / This box contains all his private papers.*

Attitudes. An attitude is a psychological state (opinion, belief, love, hatred, liking, need, knowledge, supposition, etc.). The situation referred to by e.g. *George believes in God* is an attitude in this sense. Other examples: *I appreciate all her help / She hates all the fuss / Everybody knows the truth about Jim / Nobody likes me / They wanted it all.*

Perceptions. A perception is a sense relation (visual, auditory, etc.). The situation referred to by e.g. *I saw her clearly from my bedroom* is a perception, more specifically a visual sense relation. Other examples: *Charles heard her cries in the distance / She sensed a certain uneasiness on his part / I felt her damp hair against my skin.*

Habits. A habit is the product of a (dynamic or stative) situation occurring so regularly that it is conceived of as characteristic of someone or something. The situations referred to by e.g. *John teaches linguistics* and *Sally smokes* are not dynamic instances of teaching and smoking, respectively (though such instances are implied), but rather characterizations of John and Sally, cf. *John is a teacher of linguistics* and *Sally is a smoker*. The term 'habit' should be understood in a broad sense as including not only personal habits (like *Roger plays the guitar, Victoria would call me every day before breakfast*) but also 'universal truths' (e.g. *The sun rises in the east*) and 'ability' (e.g. *Vera speaks Italian*). Like iterativity, habituality is situationally complex, often implying a dynamic input.

Of the situations classified as stative above, intensive and extensive relations are the most stative. The fact that attitudes and especially perceptions are often temporary and/or involve a human participant makes them somewhat more dynamic in character. And as we have seen, habits often presuppose dynamic substitutions.

8.4. General participant roles

The study of the number and kinds of participants that may be associated with verbs is called the study of **valency**. Together with action, valency may contribute to a better understanding of the semantics of sentences.

First a distinction is drawn between those participant roles which are involved in dynamic situations and those which are involved in stative situations. The typical dynamic situation involves a **DOER** and a **DONE-TO**, i.e. someone/something bringing the situation about and someone/something passively affected by the situation. In *Jack fixed the old motorbike*, the subject *Jack* is the DOER and the object *the old motorbike* is the DONE-TO (it gets fixed). In *The landslide killed the old man*, similarly, *the landslide* is the DOER and *the old man* is the DONE-TO (he gets killed). In addition to these very general primary participants, there are a number of relevant **EXTRAS**. For example, in *Roger teased the rat with a stick*, the subject *Roger* is the DOER, the object *the rat* is the DONE-TO (it gets teased) and the adverbial *with a stick* is an EXTRA, indicating more specifically the instrument with which Roger brings about the situation.

By contrast, the typical stative situation, being a relation rather than a going-on, involves a **SPECIFIER** and a **SPECIFIED**. A SPECIFIER determines the nature of the state (relation) in conjunction with the predicator, and a SPECIFIED is someone/something for whom/which the state exists or is true. In *Jack is in London*, *Jack* is SPECIFIED with respect to the locational SPECIFIER *in London*. In *The girl is exceptionally clever*, *the girl* is SPECIFIED with respect to the qualitative SPECIFIER *exceptionally clever*. Like dynamic situations, states may involve various **EXTRAS**. For example, in *Jack was in London last week*, the adverbial *last week* is an EXTRA providing a temporal restriction of the extensive relation.

The very general roles proposed here are syntactically based in the following sense. In active declarative sentences, the DOER or the SPECIFIED always occupies subject position, the DONE-TO always occupies object position and the SPECIFIER always occupies object, adverbial or complement position.

8.5. Specific participant roles

It is sometimes useful to operate also with a system of more specific roles based on the following two distinctions: **dynamic** vs. **stative** and **volitional** vs. **non-volitional**. The possible combinations of the values in these distinctions yield the following four more specific versions of DOER and SPECIFIED:

AGENT represents the volitional (typically human) instigator of a dynamic situation (cf. *Jack fixed the old motorbike*).

CAUSE represents the non-volitional (typically non-human) entity bringing about a dynamic situation (cf. *The landslide killed the old man*).

CONTROLLER represents the volitional (typically human) participant for whom a state obtains for so long as the controller keeps it that way (e.g. *John keeps a gun in the cupboard / Sally wants some ice cream / Roger is in London / Mick Jones is a university professor / John teaches linguistics*).

HOLDER represents the non-volitional (typically but not inevitably non-human) participant for whom/which the state obtains (e.g. *The village lies in a dark valley / The jar contained some milk / Victoria is beautiful / The sun rises in the east*).

Schematically the central system of specific roles looks like this:

	Dynamic	*Stative*
Volitional	AGENT	CONTROLLER
Non-volitional	CAUSE	HOLDER

To this central system of specific roles we can add the following:

AFFECTED represents people or entities crucially involved in, or affected by, a dynamic situation (e.g. *Jack fixed the old motorbike / The old man painted the wall / Somebody had beat him up*) or passively forming part of the state description in extensive relations, attitudes, perceptions and habits (e.g. *John keeps a gun in the cupboard / Sally wants some icecream / I saw her clearly from my bedroom / Roger collects stamps*).

BENEFICIARY represents people or entities for whose sake the dynamic situation is brought about (e.g. *Roger bought Sally an expensive necklace / Mother baked us a chocolate cake / He told his parents a pack of lies*).

INSTRUMENT represents entities or means (typically non-human) used to bring about a dynamic situation (e.g. *Roger peeled the potatoes with his pocket-knife / Sally travelled by train*).

In addition, it is often useful to extend the notion of 'participant role' to more general semantic meanings like the following:

ATTRIBUTE represents three stative subroles: characterization (as in *Victoria is beautiful*), identification (as in *Bill Clinton is the fellow in the corner*) and classification (as in *Mick Jones is a university professor*).

RESULT represents an entity created by the situation (as in *He dug a hole*) or a change of state (*She became a raving lunatic / He got very upset*).

8.6. A few points in connection with participant roles

In the previous sections there have been many examples of how constituents can be described in terms of general and specific participant roles. This section offers a few additional notes:

(i) Interpretation of roles. Constituents are sometimes open to alternative role interpretations. For example, a sentence like *Sally ruined my marriage* is ambiguous, or simply vague, between a DOER AGENT reading and a DOER CAUSE reading of the subject noun. And in *He fell to the ground*, the subject could be interpreted as either DOER AGENT (if the referent of *He* falls intentionally) or DOER AFFECTED (if the referent of *He* falls unintentionally). Similarly with sentences like *The shop was closed*, in which the subject is either SPECIFIED HOLDER or DONE-TO AFFECTED, depending on whether the situation expressed is interpreted as stative or dynamic.

(ii) Presentation vs. 'reality'. Participant roles may change according to the nature of the situation specified by the lexical verb even if the reality of the situation remains more or less the same, which indicates that participant roles are often a question of the speaker's presentation of situations; compare:

(1a)   [Mr Wilson]^{CONTROLLER} owns [this house]^{AFFECTED}.

(1b)   [This house]^{HOLDER} belongs to [Mr Wilson]^{AFFECTED}.

In the first example, *Mr Wilson* is the SPECIFIED CONTROLLER of the 'state of owning' and *this house* is SPECIFIER AFFECTED. In the second example, the same reality is presented differently: with *This house* as the SPECIFIED HOLDER of the 'state of belonging to' and with *Mr. Wilson* as SPECIFIER AFFECTED.

(iii) Double roles. In some examples, the subject receives a double role analysis as the result of intransitive verbs being used as copula verbs:

(2)   He was born a slave. (= ' When he was born, he was (already) a slave')

(3)   He returned a new man. (= 'When he returned, he was a new man')

In (2) the subject is both AFFECTED (in relation to the basically intransitive predicator) and HOLDER (in relation to the imposed complement

ATTRIBUTE). In (3) the subject is both AGENT and HOLDER (or CON-
TROLLER).

When the adverbial in the S P O A sentence pattern has the semantic
function of ATTRIBUTE, the object receives double analysis:

(4)   [Clinton]^{AGENT} described [the case]$^{AFFECTED+HOLDER}$ [as serious]^{ATTRIBUTE}.

Here *the case* is affected in relation to the predicator but at the same time
there is an intensive relation between *the case* and *as serious*. The analysis of
the case as also HOLDER and of *as serious* as ATTRIBUTE captures this
intensive relation. Similarly in the S P O C pattern, where there is a
secondary, intensive relation between object and complement. When the
main situation expressed is dynamic, the subject is prototypically AGENT or
CAUSE, the object is twice AFFECTED and the complement is RESULT:

(5)   [Tyson]^{AGENT} knocked [Bruno]$^{AFFECTED+AFFECTED}$ [unconscious]^{RESULT}.
(6)   [He]^{AGENT} pronounced [us]$^{AFFECTED+AFFECTED}$ [man and wife]^{RESULT}.

The analysis of the object as AFFECTED+AFFECTED reflects the fact that
it is affected both in relation to the situation expressed by P (in e.g. *Tyson
knocked Bruno unconscious*, 'something happened to Bruno') and in relation
to the implied change of state ('Bruno became unconscious').

(iv) Role suppression. In English there is a tendency for fusion between the
predicator and one or more of the subsequent constituents. When a
constituent is very closely fused with the predicator, both constituents may
lose some of their semantic independence. In turn, this may affect the
assignment of semantic roles, not only to the fused constituent itself, but also
to other constituents in the sentence. Consider first an example like:

(7)   I caught sight of her.

Here it would be counter-intuitive to assign a separate participant role to
sight: Rather, it would be reasonable to analyse *caught sight of* as a kind of
complex predicator (= 'sighted') and simply analyse *her* as AFFECTED
object.

The S P O and S P O O patterns are especially prone to fusion between
predicator and direct object when the predicator is realized by semantically
general verbs like GIVE, TAKE, DO, HAVE, MAKE. The effect on the S P O
pattern is to make it 'semantically intransitive':

(8)   They had an argument. (cf. *They argued*)
(9)   She made a complaint. (cf. *She complained*)

The effect on the S P O O pattern is to turn it into a 'semantically monotransitive' construction. GIVE is especially frequent in this pattern:

(10) She gave her daughter a smack/nudge/bath/kiss. (cf. *She smacked/nudged/ bathed/kissed her daughter*)

(11) I paid my mother a visit. (cf. *I visited my mother*)

As a result, the semantic function of the indirect object is in such cases not BENEFICIARY but AFFECTED.

(v) Role embodiment. Finally, mention should be made of cases where the predicator is realized by a lexical verb embodying an INSTRUMENT:

(12) The assassin *knifed* the President.

(13) He *mouthed* the insult behind her back.

9. Voice: active versus passive

Most of the examples looked at so far are in **the active voice**. A sentence in **the passive voice** is a sentence in which the predicator contains a form of the auxiliary BE followed by the past participle of the main verb and in which the subject form typically performs the participant role DONE-TO (see section 8.4):

(1) The county prosecutor *was* finally *prodded* into action.

The terms 'active' and 'passive' are based on the semantic function performed by the subject form in sentences describing dynamic situations. While this form denotes the active participant (DOER) in an active sentence like *Our boss will kill me*, it denotes the passive participant (DONE-TO) in a passive sentence like *Our boss was killed in a plane crash*.

In passive sentences the DOER may be specified by a prepositional *by*-group:

(2) No public explanation was offered *by the Hazelton police*.

A passive sentence containing a DOER *by*-group is roughly synonymous with the corresponding active sentence. Thus, example (2) means more or less the same as *The Hazelton police offered no public explanation*.

Each of the four transitive patterns found in active declarative sentences (cf. section 1.9) has a passive counterpart:

S P O → S P (A)

(3a) Her fellow passengers might have saved her.

(3b) She might have been saved (by her fellow passengers).

S P Oi Od → S P Od (A)

(4a) The police gave the butler a reward.

(4b) The butler was given a reward (by the police).

S P O Co → S P Cs (A)

(5a)   The judge ruled him mentally unfit.
(5b)   He was ruled mentally unfit (by the judge).

S P O A → S P A (A):

(6a)   The robbers placed them on their backs.
(6b)   They were placed on their backs (by the robbers).

As an alternative to example (4b), *A reward was given to the butler* (S P A) is far commoner than *A reward was given the butler* (S P Oi).
    Examples like the following:

(7)   The bed has been slept in.
(8)   Their house hasn't been lived in for a long time.

are exceptional in being passive sentences matched by **intransitive** active sentences. For example, the nearest active parallel of (7) is *Someone has slept in the bed*, which can only be classified as an S P A construction. In such cases, the subject of the passive sentence corresponds not to an object but to the prepositional complement in the adverbial of the active sentence. In passive examples like (7) and (8), the preposition is left **stranded** (i.e. without a complement), cf. section 3.3.
    Active transitive sentences referring to states are normally unmatched by passive sentences:

(9)   Ildiko has a red Mercedes Benz. (extensive relation)
(10)   She hates all the fuss. (attitude)
(11)   I felt her damp hair against my skin. (perception)
(12)   Roger collects stamps. (habit)

Occasionally, however, we find passive expressions of attitudes and perceptions (i.e. the least stative of the stative subtypes, cf. section 8.3):

(13)   She is feared and resented for her outspokenness.
(14)   A shot was heard in the dark.

9.1. Functions of the passive

The passive provides a systematic means of choosing another participant than DOER as starting-point for the message without departing from subject-first constituent order. In other words, the use of the passive vs. active voice in English is largely determined by the way the speaker wishes to organize her message, i.e. is to do with information structure. In a passive sentence like *Celtic were beaten by Arsenal*, where the participant AFFECTED DONE-TO is placed initially, it is this participant (*Celtic*) and not AGENT

DOER (*Arsenal*) which constitutes the speaker's communicative point of departure. A main reason for choosing the passive voice is thus **topicalization**: *Celtic were beaten by Arsenal* differs from the corresponding active sentence in that it is a statement about Celtic, not Arsenal.

As pointed out in section 7.1 the organization of a message often reflects a division between **given and new information**, and the choice of the passive may also be due to a wish to proceed from given information:

(1)   *The front of the car* was crushed like an accordion by a big boulder.

The passive may also be selected to obtain **end-focus** and/or **end-weight**:

(2)   The last cup final was won *by Newcastle.* (end-focus)
(3)   The hearing was undercut *by Edward's refusal to testify and Thiel's obvious reluctance to provide jurors with information.* (end-focus and end-weight)

Another main reason for selecting the passive voice is **to avoid mentioning the DOER** participating in the situation described. This is illustrated by the following example, which simultaneously illustrates topicalization in that it is a text about a specific person:

(4)   Evander Jones is a war veteran, *was awarded* a Purple Heart, honorably *discharged* at the end of the war. Nine years ago he *was convicted* of first-degree murder in a drugstore holdup and *sentenced* to death.

By means of the passive the speaker is at liberty not to provide information which has to be provided in active sentences. As the DOER is often unknown, irrelevant, unimportant or can be inferred from the linguistic or situational context, this makes the passive an extremely useful construction. In (4) it saves the sender the trouble of specifying who awarded Evander Jones a Purple Heart, discharged him, convicted him and sentenced him.

The passive may be selected in order to **retain the same subject** in coordinated predicates:

(5)   He demanded to speak to her but was refused.
(6)   The case received a good deal of publicity locally and was taken up immediately by the state branch of the ACLU.

Finally it should be mentioned that passives may be motivated by a wish on the part of the speaker to **avoid self-reference** and come across impersonally:

(7)   Enough has been said above about the implications of the Faculty's announcement for the future of our Ph.D. programme.

In scientific English, where it is typically what happens which is of interest rather than who makes it happen, passive constructions (without DOER *by-*

groups) tend to be more frequent than in other registers of English. This usage can be illustrated by the following example:

(8)   Food *is put* in jars, the jars and their contents *are heated* to a temperature which *is maintained* long enough to ensure that all viruses *are destroyed*.

9.2. Voice restrictions

Because of the highly regular formation of active and passive sentences, it has often been assumed that there is a fixed, automatic correspondence between them. However, this view of the voice category is too simplistic. A number of important restrictions apply:

(i) Combinations of **two nonfinite forms of BE** are awkward. Sentences like *The cat must be chasing the mouse* and *The cat has been chasing the mouse* are therefore not normally passivized (*?The mouse must be being chased by the cat, ?The mouse has been being chased by the cat*).

(ii) In **imperative sentences,** passivization is found only in fixed expressions like *Please be seated* and in those cases where the hearer is ordered or advised to avoid becoming the target of an action, as in *Don't be taken in by that scoundrel.*

(iii) If the object is **cognate** (i.e. if the object head noun is derived from the verb preceding it, as in *live a good life* and *sleep the sleep of the just*), the passive voice is normally ruled out.

(iv) Fused P O constructions like *take a bath* and *have a smoke* (cf. section 8.6) have no passive counterparts.

(v) If there is **coreference between subject and object,** the passive voice is usually excluded. For example, sentences with **reflexive** or **reciprocal** object pronouns, as in *He shot himself* and *We hate each other*, respectively, have no passive counterparts.

(vi) Owing to the principle of end-weight, active sentences with **clausal objects** are only very occasionally passivized, as e.g. *That he is clever is known by all his friends and colleagues.* Only by means of extraposition – which secures end-weight – is it possible to match an example like *The public believe that there will be an election* with a passive: *It is believed by the public that there will be an election.*

(vii) When the predicator of an active sentence is realized by a **reciprocal verb,** such as MARRY and RESEMBLE (e.g. *Penny married Paul*), there is usually no corresponding passive sentence.

(viii) In most **passive sentences without a DOER *by*-group**, there is no specific corresponding active sentence. In *The county prosecutor was finally prodded into action*, for example, we do not know what form the subject of the corresponding active sentence is realized by (*somebody? something? people in the community?*).

(ix) BE *born* is a fixed passive expression with no active counterpart: e.g. *Shakespeare was born in 1564.*

9.3. Nonfinite passives

The following are examples of **nonfinite passives**:

(1)   What the boy had done now – or failed to do – Lee hoped not *to be told.*
(2)   A few days after *being released* from jail he disappeared.
(3)   *Having been criticized* by his superiors he decided to quit.
(4)   *To have been rejected* so suddenly really hurt.

As appears from (1) through (4), nonfinite passive verb groups are either **infinitive** or *-ing* **participle** constructions, or combinations.

In nonfinite passives the BE form is occasionally dropped:

(5)   Lydia knew herself *watched.*
(6)   We saw Denmark *beaten* by Spain.

This type of construction – in which *being* could be inserted at the beginning of the nonfinite predicator – is restricted to those cases where the finite predicator is realized by a small group of verbs, such as KNOW, SEE, WATCH, HEAR and WANT. Attention should also be drawn to passives without BE like the following:

(7)   *Considered* unqualified for the job, she was asked to leave on the spot.

Note that *being* could be inserted here as well. Participle *-ed* clauses are not invariably passive. For example, the subclause of a sentence like *Escaped from prison, the convict immediately contacted his old partners in crime* is clearly active (*Escaped = Having escaped*).

9.4. GET-passives

A GET-passive is a colloquial passive where GET replaces BE:

(1)   Dreyfus *got hit* on the head with a rake.
(2)   Denmark *got beaten* by Spain.

A GET-passive typically serves to indicate that the referent of the subject form passes from one state to another and thus has resultative meaning.

Consequently, there are many instances where GET cannot replace BE, e.g. *A public hearing was held* and *Through the spring they were often seen together in Yewville*.

GET-passives differ from BE-passives in that an element of initiative or responsibility is often ascribed to the referent of the subject form, as illustrated by *Malcolm got promoted/arrested*. GET-passives like *The jug got broken* in which the referent of the subject form is non-human are therefore relatively rare. Note in this connection the possibility of using GET-passives in the imperative: *Get lost! / Get (yourself) invited to the meeting*.

In some contexts, the GET-passive has the advantage over the BE-passive that it is unambiguously dynamic: examples like *The jug got broken* and *They got married* refer to dynamic situations only, while *The jug was broken* and *They were married* can refer either to dynamic situations or states (for further discussion, see section 9.6 below).

9.5. Notional 'passives'

A fairly large class of verbs called **middle verbs** appear not only in normal active and passive sentences (such as *Somebody opened the door* and *The door was opened*) but also in **intransitive active sentences** with the AFFECTED participant as topicalized subject: *The door opened*. As this is semantically similar to the (syntactic) passive, it is sometimes termed the **notional passive**. *The door opened* differs from *The door was opened* in that the participant chosen as starting-point for the message is not DONE-TO but DOER. By means of the intransitive construction the speaker presents the situation as if the subject is DOER while at the same time being aware that it cannot perform the action referred to of its own accord. What is similar to the two constructions, though, is that the specific participant role performed by the subject is AFFECTED. Although the semantics of the two constructions is not the same, they are most probably going to be understood in terms of similar situations.

The intransitive use of middle verbs in examples like *The door won't lock*, *Sugar dissolves in water*, *The shop has closed* and *This stanza doesn't scan* is lexically restricted, but the class of middle verbs in English is by no means a small one. In addition to verbs like OPEN, CLOSE, LOCK, BREAK, CRACK, SHATTER and WIDEN, there are verbs relating to cooking like BAKE, BOIL, COOK, FRY and ROAST (e.g. *The eggs are frying*) and verbs which combine with a few specific subject forms only, like FIRE, SHOW and SOUND (e.g. *The pistol fired*, *Her fatigue showed* and *The bugle sounded*). Some middle verbs are nearly always accompanied by adverbials expressing manner:

(1)   Julia Roberts photographs *well*. (= is photogenic)

(2)   This loaf doesn't cut *easily*.

Note next the use in conservative BrE of BE *drowned* and BE *burned*:

(3)   Shelley was drowned.

(4)   The house was burnt down.

Without an explicit or implicit agent, these are more or less synonymous with the now more frequent active middle-verb construction *Shelley drowned* and *The house burnt down*: in both the active and the passive construction the subject is AFFECTED (by water or by fire).

Note finally that there is vacillation between passive and active form with passive meaning in nonfinite predicators after the main verbs BE, NEED, DESERVE and WANT, cf. e.g. *There is no time to lose / to be lost, It needs doing / to be done, She deserves punishing / to be punished* and *Your aspidistra wants watering / to be watered*. In examples with REQUIRE and BEAR like *My car requires servicing* and *This does not bear repeating*, only the active form is possible although the active form here also has passive meaning.

9.6. Passives versus adjectival non-passives

Sentences containing a form of BE followed by an *-ed* participle are not invariably passive:

(1)   I *am* not *accustomed* to being interrupted.

(2)   All these people are *educated* and very reliable.

(3)   My heart *was* so *swollen* with feeling I could not reply.

Here BE is not an auxiliary but a main verb, and the *-ed* participle form does not realize the main verb but (part of) the subject complement. The situations described are stative, and the participles are to be interpreted as **adjectives**.

In some cases like *The ship was sunk* and *His cheeks were sunken*, the difference between passive and active is signalled formally: *sunk* is the head verb in P while *sunken* is C:adj. But more often than not there is no formal difference, as in e.g. *The jug was broken*, which is ambiguous between a dynamic passive S P reading and a stative active S P C reading.

Adjectival *-ed* forms differ from passive participles in a number of ways:

(i) They may be used after verbs other than BE, such as SEEM and BECOME.

(ii) They often accept intensifiers like VERY, RATHER, etc.

(iii) They may be coordinated with a true adjective.

The sentence pattern encountered in an example like *The case is complicated* is thus S P C, not S P:

(i)   The case *seems/is becoming* complicated.
(ii)   The case is *very* complicated.
(iii)   The case is *awkward and complicated*.

On the other hand, a sentence like *Three of the passengers were saved* is passive, for here the *-ed* form has none of the properties listed above.

While the distinction between passives and adjectival non-passives is basically clear, it should not be overlooked that borderline cases do exist, such as e.g. *The students were amused/annoyed/embarrassed by my dirty jokes*. The existence of the corresponding active construction *My dirty jokes amused/annoyed/embarrassed the students* points towards a passive analysis. On the other hand, the possibility of replacing *were* by *seemed* and of premodifying the participle with an intensifying adverb (e.g. *quite amused*) seems to indicate that the *-ed* forms are adjectival non-passives instead.

10. Polarity

10.1 Standard negation and rules of contraction

Consider the difference between the following examples:

(1)   Jack has apologized for being late again.
(2)   Jack has not apologized for being late again.

While example (1) is a **positive** sentence, example (2) is a **negative** sentence. The distinction between positive and negative is one of **polarity**. Semantically, a negative sentence differs from a corresponding positive sentence in stating the fact that the situation expressed by the positive sentence does not hold.

In its **standard** version, negation is signalled by placing the optional adjunct NOT after the operator, as in example (2). If there is no operator in the corresponding positive sentence, as in *Sanctions challenge vital interests*, the dummy operator DO is inserted before NOT in the negative sentence:

(3)   Sanctions do not challenge vital interests.

In informal English, there is typically **NOT-contraction** with the preceding operator. In that case it is pronounced /nt/ and written *n't*:

(4)   They *shouldn't* blame us.
(5)   I *didn't* know much about Rwanda.

When contracted with CAN, it should be added, NOT can also be written as *not* and pronounced – without stress – as /nɒt/:

(6)   Without autonomy, we *can't/cannot* be a truly free and democratic society.

The only auxiliary with which NOT may not be freely contracted is MAY. The contracted form *mayn't* does not occur in AmE, and in BrE it is extremely rare.

In cases where the operator is BE, HAVE or WILL an alternative to NOT contraction is **operator-contraction** to the subject, in which case NOT is obligatorily stressed; compare:

(7)   It isn't true / It's 'not `true.
(8)   She hasn't resigned yet / She's 'not re`signed yet.
(9)   He won't be missed much / He'll 'not be `missed much.

While DO and the modal auxiliaries (except WILL) permit only NOT-contraction, the verb form *am* permits only operator-contraction, as in *I'm not sorry* and *I'm not studying*. In non-standard English, particularly non-standard AmE, the contracted form *ain't* is used for *am, are, is* or *has/have* + NOT, for example in *I/she/you/they ain't sorry* and *I/she/you/they ain't finished yet*. Finally it should be mentioned that the contracted form *aren't* may be used in BrE not only with 2nd person singular or with plural subjects as in *You aren't the only survivor* and *They aren't here* but also with 1st person singular subjects. This use is restricted to negative questions, though, and is particularly common in tag questions: *I'm your wife, aren't I?*

10.2. Domain of negation: global versus local

In examples with standard negation, the **domain** of negation is **global** in the sense that the unit regarded as negative is the clause as a whole. All the examples offered in the previous section have global negation. When the unit regarded as negative is not the full clause but only a part of it, negation is **local**. In order to separate global from local negation, the **tag-question test** can be used. It is a characteristic of a sentence with global negation that it permits a positive rather than a negative tag question:

(1)   Paul didn't apologize for being late, *did he?*
(2)   They shouldn't blame us, *should they?*

Conversely, a sentence with local negation (or with no negation at all) permits a negative rather than a positive tag question:

(3)   Sarah gave us not less than $10 each, *didn't she?*
(4)   Simpson pleaded not guilty, *didn't he?*

Often local negation is expressed by other means than NOT. In examples like the following negation operates within the limits of the word by means of a **negative prefix**:

(5)   These distinctions were virtually *non*existent before the mid-17th century.

(6)   He was very *un*happy about his work.

Local negation with negative elements other than NOT or prefixes can be illustrated by examples like these:

(7)   We'll have your roof fixed in *no* time.

(8)   A hundred pounds for that room is *nothing* short of robbery.

Global and local negation may cooccur:

(9)   You can*'t not* come tomorrow. (= 'You are not at liberty to stay away')

(10)   *Not* long ago, Jane did *not* attend morning prayer.

The combination of local negation expressed by NOT and local negation expressed by a negative prefix is, well, not infrequent (particularly in connection with adjectives or adverbs):

(11)   Our new therapy is a *not in*significant step in the right direction.

(12)   *Not in*frequently there is torrential rain on this part of the coast.

Note finally that the domain of negation is also local in sentences like *I hope not* and *I'm afraid not* in which NOT is an object proform representing a negative subclause (e.g. *I hope that Norway isn't winning*). Such sentences are used in reply to questions (e.g. *Is Norway winning?*).

10.3. Syntactic field of negation: clausal versus limited

Global negation is not an exclusive property of standard negation. For example, we find it not only in a sentence like *The earthquake didn't cause any casualties* but also in a sentence without standard negation like *The earthquake caused no casualties*. That this is so appears from the fact that the second of these examples, like the first, selects a positive tag question:

(1)   The earthquake caused no casualties, *did it?*

While *The earthquake caused no casualties* thus resembles *The earthquake didn't cause any casualties* in having global negation, it differs from it with respect to **syntactic field**.

   While the domain of negation concerns the overall polarity of clauses, syntactic field concerns **the syntactic material actually negated**. In an example with standard global negation like *The earthquake didn't cause any casualties* the syntactic field of negation is **clausal**. However, in an example like *The earthquake caused no casualties*, the syntactic material actually negated is not the entire clause (as it is in all cases of standard negation) but only the object. Here, then, though the negation is global, the syntactic field of negation is not clausal but **limited**.

Negation of a sentence function frequently leads to global negation, i.e. although the syntactic field of negation is limited, the speaker presents and the hearer understands such a sentence as negative as a whole. In an S P O O sentence like *They gave us the tickets* the participants involved are AGENT (the subject), BENEFICIARY (the indirect object) and AFFECTED (the direct object). Now if one of these sentence functions is negated, as it is in *None of them gave us the tickets*, *They gave none of us the tickets* and *They gave us no tickets*, a participant is eliminated. The situation described by the sentence as a whole therefore has not taken place. For that reason the hearer understands the sentence to be negative.

Global domain combined with limited syntactic field is found in sentences with subjects, objects, complements and adverbials containing **negative or negated quantifiers, adverbs and pronouns** (e.g. *no, nothing, nobody, no one, none, neither, never, nowhere* or words like *one, many, much, all* and *every* preceded by NOT):

(2)   My mother noticed *nothing* of this.

(3)   *Nobody*'s perfect.

(4)   *Neither* of us said anything.

(5)   Alan Clark has *never* concealed his philandering ways.

(6)   *Not one / Not many* of the students will pass the exam.

Though the syntactic field of negation is here limited to subjects, objects or complements, the sentences become globally negative all the same.

Global but limited negation is preferred to standard negation in a number of idiomatic cases, in existential sentences and sentences with HAVE in the sense of 'possess':

(7)   It's no wonder.

(8)   There's no claret in the decanter.

(9)   We have no cash.

Global quantifier negation may cooccur with (global) standard negation:

(10)   Nobody didn't know the answer.

(11)   Not many of the students didn't pass the exam.

Here both the negative elements are operative, so although (10) and (11) as a whole are negative sentences, their meanings are roughly similar to those of *Everybody knew the answer* and *Most of the students passed the exam*. This type of genuine 'double negation' is also found in an example like *They don't owe me nothing* (= 'They owe me something') and should be distinguished from the one found outside Standard English, where there is **negative concord** and where the extra negative adds nothing to the meaning of the sentence apart from emphasis (*They don't owe me nothing* = *They don't owe me anything*).

The different types of negation examined so far are summarized in table 1:

	DOMAIN		FIELD	
		clausal (standard)		*You can't come tomorrow*
	global			
		limited:		
			a) S	*No man is an island*
			b) Od	*My mother noticed nothing*
Negation			c) Oi	*They gave none of us the tickets*
			d) C	*She's no one of importance*
			e) A	*At no point did they surrender*
	local:	a) negative prefixes		*This clause is nonrestrictive*
		b) *not*		*Not long ago Marion turned eighty*
		c) other negative elements		*We'll have your roof fixed in no time*

Table 1: Types of negation

10.4. Semantic scope of negation: complete versus incomplete

So far negation has been discussed in terms of the overall polarity of clauses (domain of negation) and the syntactic material actually negated (syntactic field of negation). In this section we take a closer look at what parts of a clause are affected semantically by negation, i.e. are within the **semantic scope** of negation. Consider first examples like the following:

(1)   Fortunately the earthquake didn't cause casualties.
(2)   Fortunately the earthquake caused no casualties.

Despite the fact that the negation is here global in both these examples, it has no semantic influence over the part of the meaning referred to by *Fortunately*. To cope with examples of this type, we need the concept of semantic scope is needed. The semantic scope of negation may be either **complete** or **incomplete**. While it is incomplete in examples like (1) and (2) in that the meaning described by *fortunately* is unaffected by negation, it is complete in examples like the next ones:

(3)   At first the earthquake didn't cause casualties.
(4)   At first the earthquake caused no casualties.

Here, then, the part of the meaning described by *At first* is inside the semantic scope of negation.

In locally negated examples, domain and field and scope all go together. This can be illustrated by an example like *Simpson pleads not guilty*, which has local domain, limited field and incomplete scope.

In examples of global negation, the semantic scope of negation is incomplete in connection with:

(i) Disjuncts and conjuncts:

(5)   Sanctions don't challenge vital interests, *unfortunately*.

(6)   Sanctions don't challenge vital interests, *however*.

These examples can be paraphrased 'Unfortunately/However it is not the case that sanctions challenge vital interests'.

(ii) Some optional adjuncts (especially adjuncts of reason or purpose):

(7)   *For those reasons*, Bill didn't write the book.

(8)   Jane *deliberately* didn't kill Bob.

These examples express the fact that there were reasons why Bill did not write the book and that Jane's not killing Bob was deliberate. However, all obligatory and most optional adjuncts are in fact inside the semantic scope of negation:

(9)   Jack didn't place the figures *in the right order*.

(10)   This bottle isn't labelled *very clearly*.

Note that in examples where an obligatory or optional adjunct is inside the semantic scope of negation, what is negated is the situation in conjunction with the adverbial, not the situation described without the adverbial. This means that in example (9) Jack did place the figures but not in the right order and in (10) the bottle is in fact labelled, but not very clearly. One gets a sense of the difference in semantic scope by comparing example (8) with *Jane didn't kill Bob deliberately*, which makes clear that Jane did kill Bob.

(iii) Some modal auxiliaries (such as e.g. MAY used in the sense of 'be perhaps likely to'):

(11)   She *may* not understand your decision.

This sentence can be paraphrased as 'It is perhaps likely to be the case that she does not understand your decision'. If MAY is used in the sense of 'be allowed to', it normally stands inside the scope of negation. For example, a sentence like *You may not borrow my car* can be paraphrased as 'It is not the case that you are allowed to borrow my car'

(iv) Indefinite non-specific quantified subjects:

(12)   *Many arrows* didn't hit the target.

(13)   *Two goals* weren't scored by Michael Laudrup.

There is a sense in which the subject is here excluded from the semantic scope of negation. Thus the fact that many arrows didn't hit the target does not exclude the possibility that many (other) arrows **did** hit the target. Similarly, the fact that two goals were not scored by Michael Laudrup does not exclude the possibility that Michael Laudrup **did** score two (other) goals.

10.5. Overview

Negation is without doubt a highly complicated topic. In tackling the analysis of negation in specific sentences, the following three-stage approach is recommended:

(i) Determine whether the domain of negation is global or local by using the tag-question test.

(ii) Then find out whether the syntactic field of negation is limited to a specific sentence function or is clausal.

(iii) Finally ascertain whether the semantic scope of negation is complete or incomplete by seeing if all the semantic material encoded in the sentence is influenced by negation or not.

When applied to a sentence like *Fortunately the earthquake caused no casualties*, this approach will demonstrate that the domain of negation is global, that the syntactic field of negation is limited to the object and that the semantic scope of negation is incomplete in that the meaning expressed by the first word is unaffected by negation.

Here is an overview of the possible combinations of domain, field and scope:

> *The earthquake didn't cause casualties*
>
> domain   └──────────────────────────────┘
> field   └────────────────────────────┘
> scope   └──────────────────────────────┘

> *Fortunately the earthquake didn't cause casualties*
>
> domain   └─────────────────────────────────┘
> field   └──────────────────────────────────┘
> scope   └──────────────────────────┘

The earthquake caused no casualties

domain	└────────────────────────────────┘
field	└──────────┘
scope	└────────────────────────────────┘

Fortunately the earthquake caused no casualties

domain	└──────────────────────────────────────┘
field	└──────────┘
scope	└────────────────────────────┘

Simpson pleads not guilty

domain	└──────────┘
field	└──────────┘
scope	└──────────┘

10.6. Polarity in non-declarative sentences

In *yes-no* **interrogative sentences** there is negation if the speaker's expectation with respect to positive-negative is not neutral but positive:

(1)   Isn't your attitude changing?

(2)   Didn't they prove uncooperative?

Here the speaker seeks information but at the same time indicates that she expects the state of affairs referred to to hold ('Tell me if I'm right in assuming that your attitude is changing/that they proved uncooperative').

In *wh*-**interrogative sentences** the speaker's assumption is positive in positive constructions, as in e.g. *Who persuaded you?* ('Someone persuaded you. Who was it?'), and negative in negative constructions, as in e.g. *Who didn't arrive on time?* ('Someone didn't arrive on time. Who was it?'), especially in sentences with *why* (e.g. *Why don't you live in London?*). In some cases a *wh*-interrogative sentence has no negative counterpart, e.g. *Whatever put that idea into your head?*

Negative imperative sentences are formed by placing *don't* before the main verb, also when this is BE:

(3)   Don't knock him unconscious.

(4)   Don't be afraid.

Note in passing that BE only accepts DO-support in negative imperatives like (4) and in emphatic imperatives like the following:

(5)   Do be nice to him.

A *you*-subject may be used in imperative sentences to add an element of emotional involvement. This is possible in negative imperatives as well:

(6)   Don't you knock him unconscious.

Here the presence of *you* makes the message come across as a threat.

Exclamatory sentences differ from other sentence types in not normally being capable of negation. For example *How beautiful she doesn't look! is not grammatical in any context. On the other hand a negative exclamatory sentence like *How cleverly she doesn't stop speaking!* cannot be ruled out in a context where the person talked about tries to retain the upper hand in a debate. The illocutionary value 'exclamation' is often expressed by negative sentences, but these nearly always belong to other sentence types, particularly the interrogative one. This can be illustrated by examples like *Wasn't she lovely!* and *Isn't he English!*, the communicative function of which, despite the interrogative form, is not to seek information but to indicate an emotional reaction.

11. Subject-predicator concord

By **concord** is understood agreement in form between different constituents. In noun groups like *this girl* and *these girls*, for example, the pronoun and the noun agree with respect to **number**: *this* and *girl* are both singular and *these* and *girls* are both plural. Concord involves not only number but also other grammatical categories. In a sentence like *I'm sorry* there is agreement between the pronoun realizing the subject and the verb realizing the predicator not only with respect to number (singular) but also with respect to **person** (first). Concord may be **internal** in the sense that the co-occurrence restrictions it imposes involve the realization of group constituents (as in *this girl/these girls*) or **external** in that it involves the realization of different sentence functions (e.g. of subject and predicator in *I'm sorry*). This chapter examines the external concord between subject and predicator.

11.1. The basic rule

There is concord between subject and predicator when the latter contains a present form of a full verb or of one of the primary verbs BE, HAVE and DO. The **-s form** of the finite verb is used if the subject is realized by a singular nominal or third person singular pronominal:

(1)   France *has* always relished its "special role" in Africa.
(2)   She *does*n't know much about Rwanda.

(3)   This consideration *has* led France to play gendarme in Africa.

(4)   The stated objective *seems* laudable.

Otherwise the *-Ø* **form** of the verb is used:

(5)   France and England *have* always disagreed on this point.

(6)   They *do*n't know much about Rwanda.

(7)   These considerations *have* led France to play gendarme in Africa.

(8)   The stated objectives *seem* laudable.

This basic rule does not apply to sentences with modal auxiliaries (e.g. *The stated objective(s) may seem laudable*). In those cases where the predicator is realized by a form of BE, concord involves not only the present form but also the past form: if the subject is realized by a singular nominal, the first person singular pronoun *I* or a third person singular pronominal, the verb form selected is *was* (e.g. *Escape was easier than before / I was clearly an embarrassment on that visit / Nothing of this was said to me*). Otherwise, the form selected is *were*. In the present form of BE, furthermore, there are not two but three distinctions: *am* is selected if the subject realization is *I*, *is* if it is in the third person singular, and *are* in all other cases. In the following account of concord, *are* and *were* are to be regarded as the present and past *-Ø* form of BE.

    Though the basic rule of concord is quite simple, concord problems arise for three main reasons: 1) in some cases it is not obvious whether the form realizing the subject (or the head of the subject group) is **singular or plural**; 2) syntactic concord may be overruled by so-called **notional concord**; 3) the rule of concord may be broken because there are nouns between the subject head noun and the predicator whose number differs from that of the subject head – a side-tracking factor referred to as **attraction**.

11.2. Singular or plural subject realization?

Let us first investigate subject-predicator concord in a number of cases where the subject realization is not clearly marked as either singular or plural:

A) Identical singular and plural form. Normally, the noun realizing the (head of the) subject (group) is marked inflectionally as singular or plural by means of *-Ø* and *-s* respectively (e.g. *car/cars*). In some nouns, however, there is no such inflectional distinction:

(1)   The *sheep ignore/ignores* the dogs.

Other nouns behaving like *sheep* are *counsel, craft, deer, cod, means, series, (gas)works, headquarters*, etc., see section 14.4.1 below.

B) Subjects realized by number-invariable nouns. Some nouns are invariably singular **or** plural, such as e.g. *furniture*, *peace* and *poverty*, which are always singular (and treated as such from the point of view of concord), and *scissors*, *jeans* and *the Alps*, which are always plural (and treated as such from the point of view of concord). There are two kinds of number-invariable nouns which pose special problems in connection with concord:

(i) Nouns with 'plural form' used as singular nouns, such as names of sciences and subjects like *mathematics* and *phonetics*, diseases like *measles* and *mumps*, games like *billiards* and *darts*, and the individual mass noun *news*. These select the *-s* form of the verb. Nouns ending in *-ics* occasionally select the *-Ø* form when they refer to 'manifestation' or 'activity' rather than 'subject' (cf. *Mathematics is boring* versus *His mathematics are poor*).

(ii) Nouns with 'singular form' used as plural nouns, such as those referring to a collection of entities like *cattle, police, clergy, livestock, vermin*, etc. These select the *-Ø* form of the verb.

C) Subjects realized by compound units (see also section 11.3.E below). If the conjoints are plural, the *-Ø* form is selected: *The boys and girls are now with their parents / The boys or the girls are on duty now*. If the conjunction is **and** and the conjoints are realized by singular (pro)nominals, the compound unit selects the *-Ø* form of the verb, i.e. counts as plural: *Bradbury and his partner bear a heavy responsibility*. If the conjunction is **or**, on the other hand, concord is usually determined by the last conjoint: *Bradbury or his partner bears a heavy responsibility / Bradbury or his partners are likely to want a settlement*. Constructions with **both ... and** and **either ... or** behave like constructions with *and* and *or* respectively.

A compound unit with singular conjoints has singular concord when coordinated by **neither ... nor**: *Neither Bradbury nor his partner bears a heavy responsibility*. In informal language plural concord cannot be ruled out here.

D) Coordinated adjectival modification. If the subject is realized by a group in which the noun is premodified by a **coordinated adjective construction** with *and*, the *-Ø* form of the verb is selected if the speaker has a plurality in mind:

(2)   Primary and secondary education *require* more skilled teachers.

If the speaker does not regard the situation in this way, however, she will select the *-s* form of the verb:

(3)   Secondary and tertiary education *needs* support from the government.

E) Subjects realized by clauses. Clausal subjects, whether finite or non-finite, count as singular:

(4)   That I have done a thing like that *bothers* me night and day.

(5)   To have done a thing like that *bothers* me night and day.

Note that subjects realized by what is traditionally referred to as an **independent relative clause** (see section 15.3.3 [B.c]) take the *-Ø* form of the verb in the matrix clause if the *wh*-element determines a plural noun:

(6)   What friends he has *live* abroad.

(7)   Whatever guests you invite *are* welcome.

In S P C sentences in which the subject is realized by an independent relative clause with *what* and in which the complement has plural meaning, there tends to be plural rather than singular subject-predicator concord:

(8)   What is required now *are (is)* food, drink and good company.

F) Subjects realized by pronouns. The following overview is divided into the various subclasses of pronouns:

(i) The **personal pronouns** *I*, *he*, *she*, and *it* are singular, *we* and *they* are plural, and *you* is used in both the singular and the plural.

(ii) Demonstrative *this* and *that* are singular, *these* and *those* are plural.

(iii) When realizing a subject, the **interrogative pronouns *what*, *which*** and ***who*** take singular concord even if the context implies a plural meaning. This can be illustrated by an example like *Who is going to help her. Her parents? Her friends?* If followed by an *of-* or *among*-construction, *which* and *who* take singular or plural concord depending on the intended meaning, e.g. *Which of the boys is/are going to help her?*

(iv) The **relative pronouns** *who*, *which* and *that* are singular or plural depending on what they refer to: *The soldiers, who were brave, ran forward* vs. *The soldier, who was brave, ran forward*. When **what** is used as a subject in an independent relative clause (cf. section 15.3.3 [B.c]), it usually takes singular concord but may occasionally take plural concord if the speaker has a clear plurality in mind (cf. also example (8) above):

(9)   What *is (are)* required now are food, drink and good company.

(v) Concord in sentences with a **provisional subject** realized by *there* is determined by the number of the real subject: *There's a fly in my soup / There are good reasons for this*. In colloquial language, however, there is singular concord also in those cases where the real subject is realized by a plural form (e.g. *There's many Danes who dislike European integration*).

(vi) If (the head of) a subject is realized by one of the following **indefinite pronouns**, there is singular concord: *somebody, anybody, everybody,* *nobody*, the corresponding pronouns ending in *-one* or *-thing*, as well as *one* and *each*. Examples: *Nobody knows / Everyone seems happy enough / Something is burning / One was better than the other*.

Either and **neither** prefer singular concord, for example in *(N)either seems qualified for the job*, but when postmodified by an **of-group** in which the dependent is realized by a plural construction, it is often the *-Ø* form of the verb which is selected, particularly in the case of *neither* (*Neither of the applicants seem qualified*). With non-textual reference to persons, **none** prefers plural concord, as in *None are so deaf as those that will not hear*. When postmodified by a preposition group containing a plural (pro)noun – as it typically is – *none* selects the *-s* form of the verb in formal BrE and the *-Ø* form in American and informal BrE. This is the case both when the pronoun group refers to persons (e.g. *None of the applicants seem(s) qualified*) and to a plurality of nonpersonal entities (e.g. *None of your suggestions seem(s) useful*). Under these conditions **some** and **all** always have plural concord (*Some/All of the applicants seem qualified; Some/All of your suggestions seem useful*), and when these pronouns realize a subject on their own, plural concord is obligatory in the case of personal reference too (*Some like it hot / All accept your proposal*). With reference to something non-countable, **none**, **some** and **all** select the *-s* form, e.g. *Some (of the cheese) has been left in the fridge*. When *all* means 'everything', it takes the *-s* form, even if a plurality is implied (e.g. *All is lost now / All we need now is doctors*).

11.3. Notional concord

Sometimes what determines the selection of verb form is the notional number of the subject rather than its grammatical number. This is known as **notional concord**. Some common cases of notional concord include:

A) Collective nouns. A collective noun is a number-inflecting noun whose singular form can be interpreted in two different ways: a) as referring to a single unit; or b) as referring to a collection of individuals. Examples: AUDIENCE, BAND, CHORUS, CLASS, COMMITTEE, COMPANY, CROWD, DEPARTMENT, FAMILY, FIRM, GOVERNMENT, HERD, JURY, MAJORITY, OPPOSITION, etc. In BrE, in addition to the normal rules of concord, the speaker or writer may choose the *-Ø* form of the verb in connection with the singular form of a collective noun, thus inviting the receiver to interpret the referent of the noun in terms of individuals rather than as a unit:

(1)   The audience *were* impressed by his performance.
(2)   My family rather *like* to stay in Sydney.

The intended meaning of a collective noun in the singular form is reflected not only in the form of the verb but also in the selection of related pronouns, whether personal, possessive, reflexive or relative (e.g. *it* vs. *they*, *its* vs. *their*, *itself* vs. *themselves* and *which/that* vs. *who*):

(3)   The orchestra *are* playing poorly tonight, for *they* haven't been rehearsing.

(4)   The jury *seem* to be disagreeing among *themselves*.

Sometimes the coreferential pronouns *they* and *their* are used instead of *it* and *its* even in those cases where a collective noun selects the *-s* form:

(5)   The company *needs* a new managing director for *their* Paris branch.

Conversely, the relative pronoun selected may be *which* or *that* rather than *who* in those cases where the collective noun group selects the *-Ø* form:

(6)   The crowd *which/that has* gathered at the entrance *keep* shouting slogans and throwing stones.

The 'good language' requires consistency across all the relevant elements in the sentence, but inconsistency (as in (5) and (6)) is by no means uncommon.

In AmE, the *-s* form of the verb is almost always selected if the noun group contains a collective noun in the singular.

Proper nouns referring to **companies, organizations, institutions** etc. like *Ford*, *Leyland* and *UNESCO* are, strictly speaking, not collective nouns in the sense described above as they do not inflect for number. However, in BrE, they resemble such nouns in permitting selection of the *-Ø* form of the verb for the purpose of expressing collective plural meaning (e.g. *Toyota have decided to launch yet another advertising campaign*). Singular names of **sports teams** very occasionally select the *-s* form of the verb, but in an overwhelming majority of cases they take plural concord, as in *Arsenal are playing Tottenham on Sunday* (in AmE only: *Arsenal is playing Tottenham on Sunday*).

B) Plural expressions of quantity and measure may select the *-s* form of the verb:

(7a)   The first six months *was* spent in India.

(8a)   Two pints of milk *has* always been sufficient.

In such examples the referent of the subject is described as a unit rather than as a plurality. While plural expressions of quantity or measure very often select the *-s* form, the speaker may also prefer to focus on the separate members of the set referred to and thus observe the rule of syntactic concord:

(7b)   The first six months *were* spent in India.

(8b)   Two pints of milk *have* always been sufficient.

C) Plural proper nouns. Geographical proper nouns in the plural form like *the Andes, the Alps* and *the Hebrides* select the -Ø form. With some geographical plural nouns, however, the speaker has a choice between the -Ø form and the -*s* form and can in this way focus on a set as a unit or on the separate members of a set. To these nouns belong *the Netherlands, the Midlands* and *Kew Gardens*:

(9)   The Midlands *reflects* the same picture of poverty and misery.

(10)   The Midlands *attract* surprisingly many tourists.

The United States nearly always selects the -*s* form of the verb, and so does *the United Nations*.

Titles of **books, plays**, etc. select the -s form of the verb if they are regarded as names, i.e. are used as proper nouns: *'The Three Musketeers' is undoubtedly Dumas' best known work / 'Ghosts' was produced last night at the National Theatre / My Canterbury Tales is on the table*. But if they are used to describe a literary production as consisting of a number of separate parts, it is usually the -Ø form of the verb which is selected: *The Canterbury Tales contain several bawdy stories*. Names of **companies, institutions, etc. in the plural form** behave like collective nouns with respect to subject-predicator concord: *British Airways expect(s) still more customers next year*.

D) Plural 'fact' expressions. We also find notional concord in:

(11)   Many cars on the roads *means* many traffic accidents.

Behind the plural expression there appears to lie a singular concept which explains the selection of the -*s* form of the verb. Reference is made to a **fact** or **circumstance**, and the meaning of the plural subject expression can therefore be captured by the paraphrase 'The fact that there is/are x'.

Plural 'fact' expressions are particularly common in sentences where the predicator is realized by MEAN (or related verbs like ENTAIL, IMPLY, INVOLVE), but we find it in sentences with other verbs as well:

(12)   High production costs *prevents* reasonable consumer prices.

E) Compound units with *and*. If the referent of such a compound unit is regarded as constituting a unit, the -*s* form of the verb is used:

(13)   Bed and breakfast *is* provided at fifteen pounds.

Notional concord of this type is found with compound units referring to meals (*bacon and eggs, fish and chips*), drinks (*gin and tonic, whisky and soda, rum and cola*), pubs (*the Spade and Becket, the Fox and Goose*) and with other established expressions such as *board and lodging, trial and error* and *the Stars and Stripes*. Names of companies, etc. (e.g. *Harland and Wolff*), behave like collective nouns.

If a compound unit with *and* is used to refer to one person or thing only, it is naturally enough the *-s* form of the verb which is selected:

(14)   My colleague and friend, Ian Mackay, *has* just published another book.

11.4. Attraction

We speak of **attraction** when a form other than the one we would normally expect to determine concord exerts decisive influence on the form of the verb. Typically, in the case of subject groups, such a distracting form intervenes between the head of the subject and the predicator, and the longer the distance between the subject head and the predicator, the more likely it is that the speaker will let this form determine the form of the verb. In examples like the ones mentioned in section 11.2 (vi) (e.g. *Neither of the applicants seem qualified*), attraction can hardly be considered incorrect. But in (real) examples like the following – which are characteristic of unplanned dis-course and not uncommon – it is generally considered incorrect:

(1)   *The situation in Bosnian mountain areas and forests now *seem* critical.

(2)   *The systematic study of grammar, phonetics, semantics and linguistics *are* generally considered indispensable to students of a foreign language.

Another type of attraction is found in sentences in which a subject complement is realized by a plural form:

(3)   Markoff's material *were* 20,000 letters comprised in the first chapter and the first 16 sonnets of the second chapter ...

Attraction of the type illustrated by (3) is generally considered incorrect.

12. The complex sentence

12.1. Definition and classifications

A complex sentence is a sentence in which at least one sentence function is realized by a subclause:

(1)   *To see her falling in love* hurts. (S:cl)

(2)   The question is *whether she wants him back.* (C:cl)

(3)   We must assume *that elsewhere all hell is being let loose.* (O:cl)

(4)   Lucy spent that summer *writing letters of application.* (A:cl)

Complex sentences should be distinguished from sentences containing complex groups in which a head or dependent is realized clausally:

(5)   The residents *living in the house* avoided her like a leper. (DEP:cl in S:g)

(6)   His *giving me this note* is an act of defiance. (H:cl in S:g)

Formally, subclauses may be divided into **finite clauses, nonfinite clauses** and **verbless clauses**:

(7)   Jack said *that he would come*. (finite)
(8)   She wanted *to leave her husband*. (nonfinite)
(9)   *When in Rome*, do as the Romans do. (verbless)

The reason why *When in Rome* is regarded as a clause is that it contains constituents that can be appropriately analysed only in terms of clause functions: a SUB:conj (*When*) and an A:g (*in Rome*).

Finite subclauses are often initiated by *that* (**that-clauses**), Ø or some other conjunction, by a relative pronoun (**relative clauses**) or by an interrogative pronoun (**interrogative clauses**):

(10)   She discovered *that they were listening with apparent interest*. (*that*-clause)
(11)   He didn't call her, *which really bothered me*. (relative clause)
(12)   I've discovered *who my real friends are*. (wh-interrogative)

Yes-no interrogative subclauses are signalled by *if* or *whether*:

(13)   *Whether your plan will succeed* remains to be seen. (*yes-no* interrogative clause)

Nonfinite clauses may be divided into *-ing participle clauses* (also referred to as present participle clauses), *-en participle clauses* (or past participle clauses), *to-infinitive clauses* and *bare infinitive clauses*, cf. the following examples, respectively:

(14)   *Going home that evening*, I stopped at the chemist's for some razor blades.
(15)   The soldiers were silent *unless spoken to by the passengers*.
(16)   I was only trying *to forestall alarm and despondency*.
(17)   All I did was *ask them round for drinks*.

According to **syntactic function**, subclauses realizing sentence functions can be subdivided into:

subject clauses:

(18)   *That you dislike him* is only too obvious.

direct object clauses:

(19)   Police believe *that the shooter was a professional*. (Od)

indirect object clauses:

(20)   She gave *going to France* a good deal of thought. (Oi)

subject complement clauses:

(21)   To see her is *to love her*. (Cs)

object complement clauses:

(22)   I would call that *casting pearls before swine*. (Co)

adverbial clauses:

(23)   He was doing the dishes *when suddenly the phone rang*. (A)

The first five types are traditionally referred to as **nominal clauses**, because the sentence functions involved are typically realized by nominals. **Adverbial** clauses are often further subclassified according to their semantics:

(24)   *When independent publications were finally legalized*, dozens of new titles sprang up. (time)

(25)   You can sit *where you like*. (place)

(26)   I left my wife *because I realized I had made an awful mistake*. (reason)

(27)   Shortly after the shooting, anonymous callers telephoned TV stations *to warn that more police officials would be harmed*. (purpose)

(28)   *Though my car is quite old*, it's still in running order. (concession)

(29)   Ronald knelt down, *his hands behind his back*. (attendant circumstance)

(30)   I'll write it *if somebody wants it*. (condition)

12.2. Additional points

A number of points should be noted in connection with the classifications of clauses presented above:

(i) Complex sentences and sentences with complex groups are sometimes semantically very similar; compare:

(1a)   *Him being Jewish* makes no difference.

(1b)   *His being Jewish* makes no difference.

(2a)   I remember *John telling me that story*.

(2b)   I remember *John's telling me that story*.

(1a) contains a subject clause in a complex sentence, whereas (1b) has a subject group with a head clause (*being Jewish*) determined by a dependent noun/pronoun (*His*). In (2a) and (2b) the same distinction can be seen in object position. The difference between the two competing constructions is very slight: in the a-examples *Him/John* has subject status in the subclause and is more in the centre of the speaker's interest than in the b-examples, where *His/John's* has subordinate syntactic status (DEP) in relation to *being Jewish / telling me that story*. Note, however, that the genitive construction may be chosen to avoid the potential ambiguity of the other construction, cf.:

(3a)   There was no complaint about *the Judge's summing up.*
(3b)   There was no complaint about *the Judge summing up.*

The italicized part of example (3b) is here ambiguous between a clause reading (which is similar to the reading of (1a) and (2a) and close in meaning to (3a)) and a group reading where *summing up* is a dependent intended to define which judge the speaker refers to (= 'the one who summed up').

(ii) It is sometimes difficult to distinguish between **interrogative *what*-clauses** and **independent relative *what*-clauses** (cf. section 15.3.3 [B.c]). For example, a sentence like *What he said was unclear* is ambiguous in written English in that it can mean either 'That which he said was lacking in clarity' (*What* = relative) or 'I didn't get what he was trying to say' (*What* = interrogative). In spoken English, this example is unambiguous, for here *what* is unstressed if the subject clause is relative and is pronounced with nuclear stress if the subject clause is interrogative. Syntactically, independent relative *what*-clauses realizing a subject differ from interrogative *what*-clauses performing this sentence function in that they select the plural form of the verb if *what* determines a noun in the plural:

(4)   *What enemies he has* have left the department. (independent relative)
(5)   *What enemies he has* is hard to tell. (interrogative)

Furthermore, independent relative clauses in which *what* determines a noun differ from interrogative *what*-clauses of this type in that they may be followed by *few* and *little*. For example, *few* can be inserted after *what* in (4) but not in (5), and *little* can be inserted after *what* in *What money he has will soon be spent* (relative) but not in *What money he has is hard to tell* (interrogative). Semantically, interrogative *wh*-clauses differ from independent relative clauses in that there is an element of 'unknown information'.

   As in the case of subject clauses, it is sometimes difficult to tell whether an object clause is realized by an independent relative *what*-clause or an interrogative *what*-clause. Thus *He asked me what I expected* is ambiguous – not only in written but also in spoken English – in that it can mean either 'He asked me that which I expected' or 'He asked me "What do you expect?"'.

12.3. Clausal complementation

As previous examples have shown, there is a great variety in clause types realizing object, adverbial and complement function. The term **clausal complementation** refers to what type(s) of clause specific verbs require in these three functions. Verbs vary considerably with respect to what forms of clausal complementation they take. For example, AVOID requires an *-ing* clause and ANSWER a *that*-clause:

(1)   I avoided drinking wine.
         (*I avoided to drink wine / *I avoided that I drank wine)
(2)   She answered that she joined the party.
         (*She answered to join the party / *She answered joining the party)

WANT may take an object *to*-infinitive clause, in some cases a participle clause, but not a *that*-clause:

(3a)   I want you to leave at once.
         (*I want that you leave at once)
(3b)   I don't want you arriving late.
(3c)   I want it done now.

Other verbs that allow of more than one type of clausal complementation:

(4a)   I believe him (to be) guilty of murder.
(4b)   I believe that he is guilty of murder.
(5a)   She liked to swim in the morning.
(5b)   She liked swimming in the morning.

In these examples there is very little semantic difference between the options. In other cases, there is a clear difference of meaning:

(6a)   I remembered to post the letter. (= 'I did not neglect to post it')
(6b)   I remembered posting the letter. (= 'I looked back on the event')
(7a)   She tried to close the window (but it was stuck).
(7b)   She tried closing the window (but there was still too much noise).

Note that different types of clausal complementation sometimes assume different sentence functions, resulting in an even clearer difference of meaning:

(8a)   Jack stopped to examine the results. (S P A)
(8b)   Jack stopped examining the results. (S P O)
(9a)   Sally went on to discuss the children. (S P A)
(9b)   Sally went on discussing the children. (S P O)

Two types of object clause should receive special attention:

(i) the so-called **accusative with infinitive**, which is an infinitive clause with a nominal or pronominal subject:

(10)   I wanted *him to leave at once*. (*to*-infinitive clause)
(11)   We watched *the sun set behind the mountains*. (bare infinitive clause)

When a personal pronoun is used as the subject of the infinitive clause, as in (10), the objective case is used (in Latin grammar the objective case is called the 'accusative' case, hence the name 'accusative with infinitive'). An example like *She left him to do the shopping* is ambiguous between an interpretation in terms of an accusative with infinitive (= she left it to him to do the shopping', i.e. where *him* has subject function in relation to *to do*) and an interpretation in terms of an O + A sequence (= she left him in order to do the shopping', i.e. with *him* as O:pro and *to do the shopping* as A:cl with the subject of the matrix clause as the implicit subject of *to do*).

(ii) the **accusative with participle**, which is a (present or past) participle clause with a nominal or pronominal subject:

(12)   I want *this reported to the police*. (past participle clause)

(13)   She saw *them laughing together*. (present participle clause)

After certain verbs of perception (such as SEE and HEAR) there is a distinction between **bare infinitive** and **present participle** constructions which is semantically very similar to the distinction between progressive and nonprogressive forms: e.g. example (13) versus *She saw them laugh together*. In such examples the difference is one of external situational focus (the infinitive) and internal situational focus (the present participle), cf. section 13.3.6.

As verbal complementation is primarily a matter of information about individual verbs, the reader should consult a reliable dictionary for more specific advice.

12.4. Discontinuous subject clauses

Corresponding to some active accusative with infinitive/participle constructions (see above), there are passive **nominative with infinitive/participle** constructions, compare:

(1a)   The judge believed *him to be guilty*. (accusative with infinitive)

(1b)   *He* was believed *to be guilty*. (nominative with infinitive)

(2a)   They heard *the girl screaming*. (accusative with participle)

(2b)   *The girl* was heard *screaming*. (nominative with participle)

While the subclauses in (1a) and (2a) are continuous object clauses, the subclauses in (1b) and (2b) are **discontinuous subject clauses**.

Discontinuous subject clauses are also found with the verbs APPEAR, HAPPEN and SEEM, compare:

(3a)   It (so) happens *that I know him well*.

(3b)   *I* happen *to know him well*.

(4a)   It seems *that John takes his job too much to heart*.

(4b)   *John* seems *to take his job too much to heart*.

(5a)   It appears *that Alfred is hungry*.

(5b)   *Alfred* appears *to be hungry.*

The a-examples here contain extraposed real subject *that*-clauses, while the b-examples contain discontinuous infinitive subject clauses. The subject of such subclauses is sometimes said to have been **raised** into the subject position in the matrix clause.

   Discontinuous subject clauses are also found in sentences with complements realized by adjectives like DIFFICULT, HARD, EASY, SIMPLE, NICE, WONDERFUL, compare:

(6a)   It was hard *to believe his explanation.*

(6b)   *His explanation* was hard *to believe.*

(7a)   It is easy *to please my parents.*

(7b)   *My parents* are easy *to please.*

(8a)   It is wonderful *to work with her.*

(8b)   *She* is wonderful *to work with.*

The extraposed real subject infinitive clauses in the a-examples correspond to the discontinuous subject infinitive clauses in the b-examples. The raising here involves the object (in (6b) and (7b)) or the prepositional complement (in (8b)) rather than the subject of the subclause. Nevertheless, raised pronouns (as in (8b)) are in subjective case rather than objective case because they take up the position normally reserved for the subject of the matrix.

   Note finally that nominative with infinitive constructions are sometimes unmatched by accusative with infinitive constructions:

(9)   *Kiri* is said *to be very rich.*
      (cf. **They say Kiri to be very rich*)

(10)   *She* is rumoured *to have shot him.*
      (cf. **They rumoured her to have shot him*)

12.5. The subject function in subclauses

Finite subclauses always contain a subject:

(1)   I thought that *I had made an awful mistake.*

(2)   Please give me a call *when you get back.*

Nonfinite and verbless clauses may also have their own subject:

(3)   *Our chairman being away on holiday*, there is nothing we can do right now.

(4)   Ronald knelt down, *his hands behind his back.*

Nonfinite and verbless **adverbial** clauses like (3) and (4) which have a subject and are not introduced by a subordinating conjunction are traditionally called **absolute clauses**.

As we saw in the preceding section, infinitive object clauses may have a nominal or pronominal subject (as in e.g. *I wanted him to leave at once*). When such a subject is left out, the implied or 'understood' subject is normally the overt subject of the matrix:

(5)   I wanted *to leave at once.* (implied subject of *to leave* = *I*)

Continuous infinitive subject clauses do not normally contain a subject (for discontinuous subject clauses, see section 12.4 above):

(6)   *To step down now* would be frowned upon by everybody.

In such clauses, an AGENT (or another participant with subject-potential in a corresponding finite clause) may be expressed by an initial adverbial group with the preposition *for* as head:

(7)   *For Rita to step down now* would be frowned upon by everybody.

Many nonfinite or verbless adverbial clauses do not contain an overt subject. In such subclauses, the implied or 'understood' subject is again normally the overt subject of the superordinate clause:

(8)   *Keeping a nervous eye on passing traffic*, many wondered out loud which of them would be next. (implied subject of *Keeping* = *many*)

(9)   The family enrolled in courses *to attain enlightenment.* (implied subject of *to attain* = *The family*)

As illustrated by the next examples, however, this is not always so:

(10)   *Putting it mildly*, you have caused us some inconvenience.

(11)   *When dining in the restaurant*, a jacket and tie are required.

(12)   *Keeping a nervous eye on passing traffic*, it suddenly occurred to me that my own family might be next.

In cases like these it is customary to speak of **unattached participles** (or **dangling participles**). In general, an unattached participle is acceptable if it serves as predicator in a disjunct (as in example (10)) or if the implied subject is a generic pronoun or *it* as a prop word (as in examples (11) and (12), respectively). Examples where the participle is attached to a function in the matrix clause other than the subject should be avoided but are not uncommon if that function is more 'relatable' to the participle than the subject. Thus (13) is not as unacceptable as (14):

(13)   ?*Known primarily as the author of 'Changing Places' and 'Small World'*, many consider Lodge a humourist and writer of campus novels.

(14)   *Known primarily as the author of 'Changing Places' and 'Small World'*, my brother considers Lodge a humourist and writer of campus novels.

The subject of the matrix in (13) (*many*) has a general, plural meaning incompatible with the implied specific, singular subject of the participle, and this leads the listener to relate the participle correctly with the singular, specific object *Lodge*. Not so in (14), where *my brother* is sufficiently relatable to the participle to be wrongly interpreted as its implied subject.

12.6. Conditional clauses

A conditional sentence contains a subclause, realized as an adverbial, which expresses some condition for the speaker's message in the matrix:

(1)   *If we are attacked*, we will defend ourselves.

(2)   You will sleep better *if you get a new mattress*.

Conditional subclauses typically begin with *if* or with a semantically related conjunction: *in case*, *supposing (that)*, *assuming (that)*, *on condition (that)*, *unless* (= 'if not'):

(3)   *In case we are attacked*, we will defend ourselves.

Conditional subclauses are sometimes signalled by subject-operator inversion (cf. section 7.2.1):

(4)   *Had he been convicted of theft*, he would have had to resign.

The situation expressed by a conditional clause is often temporally and/or causally linked to the situation expressed by the matrix, as in the examples offered above. Sometimes the relationship between the two situations is one of inference:

(5)   *If today is Friday*, he is here already.

or simply one of relevance:

(6)   There's a beer in the fridge, *if you feel like one*.

(7)   You may see her at once, *if you like*.

A conditional subclause can also serve as a pure disjunct, expressing the speaker's comment on the form or content of the matrix:

(8)   He's very very busy tonight, *if you know what I mean*.

(9)   They couldn't have chosen a better woman for the job, *if I may say so*.

In conditional sentences expressing temporally or causally linked situations, there are certain typical patterns of verb forms in the matrix and the subclause:

(i) A simple present predicator in the subclause is coupled with a present future predicator (i.e. *will* + infinitive) or with a modal verb (e.g. *may*) plus infinitive in the matrix:

(10)   If she *asks* him, he *will be* angry.

(11)   You *may sleep* better if you *get* a new mattress.

In such examples, the condition laid down by the subclause is **factual**, or neutral, in the sense that it is a completely open question whether the situation expressed by the subclause will turn out to materialize or not.

(ii) A simple past predicator in the subclause is coupled with a past future predicator (*would* + infinitive) or with a past modal form (e.g. *might* or *could*) followed by an infinitive in the matrix:

(12)   If she *asked* him, he *would be* angry.

(13)   She *could win* this case if Roger *testified.*

In such examples, the condition laid down by the subclause is more **hypothetical**. The situation expressed by the subclause is presented as more unlikely to take place.

(iii) A past perfect predicator in the subclause is coupled with a past future perfect (i.e. *would have* + past participle) or by a past modal form like *might* or *could* followed by a perfect infinitive in the matrix:

(14)   If she *had asked* him, he *would have been* angry.

(15)   She *might have won* this case, if Roger *had testified.*

Here the condition laid down by the subclause is normally interpreted as **counterfactual**. The opportunity for the realization of the situation expressed by the subclause is presented as having passed.

    Note finally that conditional sentences are not always declarative but may be **interrogative, imperative** or **exclamatory**:

(16)   What happens *if the Queen turns out to be a foreigner*?

(17)   *If that's all you've got to say,* let's go home right away.

(18)   How wonderful it would be *if that's true*!

12.7. Clausally realized disjuncts

There are three major types of clausally realized adverbial with disjunct subfunction: comment clauses, tag questions and sentential relative clauses.

(i) Comment clauses, which are particularly common in speech, add a parenthetic comment to the content of the matrix, as in:

(1)   That's outrageous, *I agree.*

(2)   It's private, *you see.*

They are typically markers of **linguistic interaction**, as shown by the fact that their subject is in most cases realized by a 1st or 2nd person pronoun (referring to the speaker and the hearer). Commonly occurring examples are *I'm sure, I'm afraid, I admit, I gather, I dare say* and *you see, you know, mind you, you must admit.* Many comment clauses are stereotyped fillers which are inserted into running speech in order to establish informal contact with the hearer. When the subject is realized by *I*, their function is to inform the hearer of the speaker's degree of certainty (e.g. *I know / I suppose*) or of her emotional attitude to the content of the matrix clause (e.g. *I'm happy/sorry to say*). When the subject is realized by *you*, the function of comment clauses is typically to catch or keep the hearer's attention or to request her agreement (e.g. *you see / you must admit*). There are also subjectless comment clauses, such as the following *to*-infinitive clause and *-ing* participle clause:

(3)   *To be honest*, I haven't seen her since last Christmas.

(4)   There are 200 students in the auditorium, *roughly speaking.*

(ii) Tag questions. Like comment clauses, tag questions are characteristic of the spoken language and mark linguistic interaction in that they signal a questioning attitude. A tag question consists of a subject pronoun preceded by a primary verb or modal auxiliary (*has she, did you, can't we, isn't it,* etc.). It is tagged on to a declarative, imperative or exclamatory matrix:

(5)   This has been the tendency, hasn't it?

(6)   Shut the door, will you?

(7)   How well she sings, doesn't she!

The subject of a tag question represents the subject of the matrix clause (in imperative sentences the understood subject form *you*), and in declarative and exclamatory sentences the finite verb form of the matrix clause is repeated in the tag question (if it is an operator) or is replaced by a form of DO (if it is a full verb).

Declarative sentences ending in tag questions are normally characterized by **reversed polarity**: if the declarative sentence is positive, the tag is negative (as in *This has been the tendency, hasn't it?*), and vice versa (as in *This hasn't been the tendency, has it?*). The effect of the construction is to seek confirmation of the content of the matrix (this effect is stronger if the tag question is pronounced with rising intonation than with falling intonation).

If both the matrix and the tag are positive, the matrix expresses an inference and the confirmation-seeking element of the tag is weakened:

(8)   So she's a Roman Catholic, is she?

(iii) Sentential relative clauses. A sentential relative clause refers back to the preceding clause, from which it is separated by intonation or – in writing – punctuation (comma, dash or sometimes full stop). It nearly always begins with the relative pronoun *which*:

(9)   The twins don't look alike, *which puzzles me*.
(10)   The terrorists have claimed responsibility for the bomb blast, *which is exactly what we've been expecting*.

In such examples, *which* has demonstrative-like meaning (= 'and this'). Occasionally a sentential relative clause refers to just the predication of the preceding clause:

(11)   She commutes between Boston and New York, which I wouldn't do.

The examples examined so far show **anaphoric** sentential relative constructions, i.e. constructions referring backwards. Occasionally there are **cataphoric** (i.e. forward-referring) cases with *what*, as in the following examples, where the two types are juxtaposed:

(12)   She was late, *which* was bad, but *what* was worse, she didn't apologize.

Which is used cataphorically after a coordinating conjunction from which it is separated by means of a comma or some other device clearly marking the relative clause as a parenthetical insertion:

(13)   Change of meaning may also be effected, by means of figurative language, or, *which* is a similar process, the use of a concrete term for an abstract conception.

12.8. Transferred negation

In complex sentences negation is sometimes **transferred** to the matrix clause from a subclause where it belongs semantically. The matrix clause verbs which permit such transferred negation are **verbs of opinion** like BELIEVE, EXPECT, IMAGINE, SUPPOSE, THINK and **verbs of perception** like APPEAR, SEEM, FEEL/LOOK/SOUND *as if*:

(1a)   I don't believe/think it's raining any longer.
(2a)   I don't expect/imagine/suppose I'll pass the exam.
(3a)   They didn't appear/seem to be convinced by the argument.
(4a)   It doesn't look/sound as if Major knows the answer to this.

These examples should be compared with the following, in which the negative element is placed where it belongs semantically:

(1b)   I believe/think it's not raining any longer.
(2b)   I expect/imagine/suppose I won't pass the exam.

(3b)   They appeared/seemed not to be convinced by the argument.

(4b)   It looks/sounds as if Major doesn't know the answer to this.

The a-examples are more or less synonymous with the b-examples, but more informal. The verb HOPE does not allow transferred negation:

(5a)   I hope she won't be there.

(5b)   *I don't hope she will be there.

Consequently, NOT rather than an expression with SO is used as a pro-form representing the subclause (cf. section 5.3):

(6)   Speaker A: Will he join us next week?
       Speaker B: I hope not / *I don't hope so

With the verb THINK, both options are available (with the SO expression as the more common):

(7)   Speaker A: Will she win the election?
       Speaker B: I think not / I don't think so.

12.9. Cleft sentences

Compare the following expressions:

(1)   The poor quality of your work worries me.

(2)   It is the poor quality of your work that worries me.

(1) is a straightforward S P O sentence. The sentence in (2) presents practically the same information, but in a syntactically different way: it is a so-called **cleft sentence**. A cleft sentence is a sentence in which a constituent singled out for **emphatic identification** is placed as a subject complement between provisional subject *it* + BE and a subclause realizing the remainder of the corresponding simple sentence as the real, extraposed subject. The term 'cleft' refers to the fact that a constituent is picked out for **focalization**, thereby dividing ('cleaving') the original sentence into two parts. Typically, the second of these, the subclause (such as *that worries me*), expresses given information and is pronounced without prosodic prominence, whereas the focalized element in the matrix clause (such as *the poor quality of your work*) expresses new information in relation to the subclause and is pronounced with nuclear stress. By means of the cleft construction not only subjects but also objects, complements, adverbials and even prepositional complements may be focalized:

(3)   It was Russell that/who met Keynes in Cambridge.

(4)   It was her mother (that) I saw.

(5)   It is president of the board (that) she has become.

(6)   It was in Sydney (that) she regained control of the situation.

(7)   It is her last novel (that) I'm interested in.

Sometimes the subclause is omitted from a cleft sentence if its content is clear from the context, as in *It wasn't me* instead of *It wasn't me who broke the window* in reply to a question like *Who broke the window?*

The subclause in a cleft sentence resembles a **restrictive relative clause** (cf. section 15.3.3 [A]) in that it is not separated prosodically or orthographically from its antecedent (i.e. the element it refers back to), and in that there is often a preference for *that* or Ø instead of *who* and *which* (except when the relative pronoun serves as subject).

Consider now sentences like the following:

(8)   *What worries me* is the poor quality of your work.
       (cf. *The poor quality of your work worries me*)

(9)   *What she did* was (to) tell me off in public.
       (cf. *She told me off in public*)

Such sentences are called **pseudo-cleft sentences**. A pseudo-cleft sentence typically consists of a subject realized by an **independent relative what-clause** (cf. section 15.3.3 [B.c]) followed by BE and a subject complement. A pseudo-cleft sentence topicalizes a whole clause in which one constituent – provisionally represented by *what* – is left to be specified (focalized) by the subject complement. There are two main types of pseudo-cleft sentence: those in which *what* provisionally represents a **participant** of the situation expressed by the *what*-clause (as in (8)) and those in which *what* provisionally represents a type of **situation** (as in (9)). Thus, for example, in (8) the pseudo-cleft sentence is used to identify the DOER of the situation, as expressed by the original **subject** (*the poor quality of your work*), whereas in (9) it is used to identify the type of situation brought about by a DOER, as expressed by the original **predication** (the 'telling me off in public').

Note finally that the *what*-clause may serve as subject complement rather than as subject:

(10)   The poor quality of your work is *what worries me*.

Here the *what*-clause receives unmarked end-focus and the subject expresses given rather than new information. The difference between (10) and *The poor quality of your work worries me* is that while the latter is a 'neutral' presentation of the information contained in the sentence, (10) assumes as background knowledge that 'something worries me'. The difference between (10) and the pseudo-cleft sentence in (8) is the status of 'the poor quality of your work' as given or new information.

PART III

Part III examines major group types with respect to their use and internal constituency: verbals (chapter 13), nominals (chapter 14), pronominals (chapter 15), adjectivals and adverbals (chapter 16).

13. Verbals

13.1. Introduction

Verbals typically describe types of **situation** (e.g. 'fixing', 'running', 'smiling'), and in this respect they differ from e.g. nominals and pronominals, which normally express the **participants** involved in situations. In an example like *Jim gave us the wrong tickets*, the verb *gave* expresses a past time situation of 'giving', i.e. a situation where somebody (the AGENT) hands over something (the AFFECTED) to somebody (the BENEFICIARY), and the three noun groups are used to specify these participant roles. Describing the nature of a situation is a composite function involving a number of categories, such as tense, aspect, action, mood and modality. In this chapter we examine how verbals enable speakers to describe situations.

13.1.1. Verb forms

In section 2.1 a number of distinctions and terms were introduced (such as full versus auxiliary verbs, modal versus primary auxiliaries, finite versus nonfinite, operator, infinitive, present and past participles). In this section I shall elaborate a little on the inflectional forms that most lexical verbs in English have: the **base form**, the **-s form**, the **-ing form** and the **-ed form**. A verb like FISH, for example, has the forms *fish, fishes, fishing, fished*. A lexical verb is considered morphologically **regular** if both the past form and the past participle are formed by adding the suffix *-ed* to the base form.

In many **irregular verbs** the past participle differs from the past form in ending in *-en*, as illustrated by verbs like TAKE (*took - taken*) and BEAT (*beat - beaten*). For this reason – and in order to have separate terms for the two forms – the past participle is referred to as the **-en form**.

Irregular verbs may have five, four or three inflectional forms. This can be illustrated by respectively DRIVE (*drive - drives - driving - drove - driven*), HANG (*hang - hangs - hanging - hung (- hung)*) and PUT (*put - puts - putting (- put - put)*). The verb BE is idiosyncratic in having eight distinct forms (*be - am/are/is - being - was/were - been*).

There are about 200 irregular verbs in English. For an overview of the inflectional morphology of irregular verbs the reader is referred to good dictionaries of English, such as *Oxford Advanced Learner's Dictionary*.

The **base form** is used in present indicative constructions (except in the 3rd person singular), imperative constructions, subjunctive constructions and infinitive constructions (for the terms 'indicative' and 'subjunctive', see section 13.4). Examples: *I wash my hands in Pears soap / Wash your hands / I insist that he wash his hands / I would like to wash my hands*. The **-s form** is used in 3rd person singular present indicative constructions (*He washes his hands in Pears soap*). The **-ing form** is used in progressive constructions and in participle constructions (*She is washing her hands / He hates washing his hands*). The basic function of the **-ed form** is to express pastness in indicative constructions (as in *I washed my hands this morning* and *I took a shower*). The **-en form**, finally, is used in perfect and the passive forms (e.g. *I've washed my hands / I have already taken a shower / The crops were washed away / The case was taken far too seriously*) and in participle constructions (e.g. *Taken to its logical extreme, this proposal could backfire / That finished, they all disappeared*).

13.1.2. Semi-auxiliaries

Most verbs are very clearly either **full verbs** (like SAY and LAUGH) or **auxilaries** (like MAY and MUST). Full verbs are typically predicators, or heads in predicators, whereas auxiliaries are dependents. And while full verbs take DO-support in *yes-no* interrogative sentences or when negated (e.g. *Did she laugh? / She didn't laugh*), auxiliaries do not (e.g. *Must she laugh? / She mustn't laugh*), cf. section 2.1. The **primary verbs** BE, HAVE and DO are special in that they regularly serve as both full verbs and auxiliaries. But a number of other verbs too are difficult to classify unambiguously as either auxiliaries or full verbs because they share properties with both subclasses. They are called **semi-auxiliaries** and include OUGHT (*to*), USED (*to*), NEED, DARE, BE (*to*), HAVE (*to*), BE GOING (*to*), KEEP, GET and others.

(I) OUGHT (*to*), which is close in meaning to SHOULD (cf. section 13.5.5), is like a modal auxiliary in that it does not take the *-s* form (e.g. *She ought/*oughts to leave soon*), and it requires no DO-support in negative and interrogative sentences or in tag questions (e.g. *You oughtn't to have said that / Ought I to see a doctor? / We ought to go, oughtn't we?*). However, elsewhere OUGHT takes DO as a pro-form, e.g. *You ought to go and so does your wife*. Another reason why OUGHT can be excluded from the class of central auxiliaries is that like full verbs (such as e.g. WANT) it is separated from a following infinitive by *to* (cf. *He ought to go / He wants to go*).

(ii) USED (*to*), which expresses past states or (discontinued) habits, is sometimes found without D O-support in negative and interrogative constructions (*He used not to work late hours / Used she to smoke?*), or even in tag questions (*They used to smoke, use(d)n't they?*). More commonly, however, USED TO takes DO-support (*He didn't use to work late hours / Did she use to smoke? / They used to smoke, didn't they?*). In other types of construction USED TO behaves like a full verb in taking DO as a pro-form (e.g. *He used to smoke a pipe, and so did she*). Like OUGHT, USED is always separated from a following infinitive by *to*. In writing, the 'd' is sometimes retained in connection with DO-support (*... didn't used to ... / Did ... used to ...?*) though this is generally considered incorrect.

(iii) DARE and **NEED** show three characteristics when used as auxiliaries: a) there is no DO-support; b) the following infinitive is a bare infinitive; c) there is no -*s* form in the present; compare *Dad need not be told* (where *need* is an auxiliary with an association of 'requirement' attached to the circumstances) with *Dad does not need to be told* (where *need* is a full verb with an association of 'requirement' attached to the subject). Blends of the two uses are not unusual for DARE: e.g. *They do not dare ask for more money* (where there is DO-support but the following infinitive is bare) and *He dares not try to contact the authorities* (where DARE takes the third person singular -*s* suffix but is negated by NOT and followed by the bare infinitive).

(iv) HAVE followed by *to* is close in meaning to MUST (cf. section 13.5.4) and behaves like HAVE as a primary verb: in conservative BrE it is occasionally found without DO-support in interrogative or negative declarative sentences: e.g. *Have you to go now? / I haven't to go to church today.* In AmE HAVE *to* always takes DO-support in such constructions, and in BrE the normal expression is with DO-support or, more colloquially, with *got*: e.g. *Do you have to go now? / You haven't got to go now.*

(v) KEEP and **GET** behave syntactically and morphologically like full verbs (i.e. they take DO-support and appear regularly in the -*s* form) but they often function as dependents in predicators. As mentioned in section 9.4, GET is used as a passive auxiliary instead of BE (e.g. *He got run over yesterday*), and KEEP is used instead of BE in a special progressive construction expressing 'persistent progression or iteration': e.g. *She kept laughing / They kept knocking at the door.* KEEP and GET are sometimes called **catenative** verbs because they are chained together with other full verbs but with a subordinate status.

(vi) BE *(to)*, BE *about (to)* and BE *going (to)* are alternative expressions to the WILL future and will therefore be dealt with in section 13.3.3.

13.1.3. The external relations of verbals

Finite verbals always function as P:

(1)   He *had* always *loved* Rosemary.

but may in that capacity be coordinated, in which case they are CJTs within the P function:

(2)   Roger *bought* and *sold* companies.

Nonfinite verbals also function as P and CJT within P:

(3)   *Having* always *loved* Rosemary, he moved to Falmer.
(4)   She let Roger *buy* and *sell* companies.

but they may assume other clause functions:

(5)   *To love* is more important than to work. (S)
(6)   To negotiate at this point would be *to surrender*. (C)
(7)   I do not want *to go*. (O)
(8)   He stopped *to smoke*. (A)

In the following examples the italicized verb serves as DEP:

(9)   By *leaving* he indicated his dissatisfaction with the negotiations.
(10)   There was a *dancing* girl on the stage.

Most verbals realizing other functions than P still have P potential in full nonfinite clauses realizing the same functions in the main clause, e.g.:

(5')   *To love her* is more important than to work.
(8')   He stopped *to smoke a cigar*.
(9')   By *leaving the meeting* he indicated his dissatisfaction with the negotiations.

13.1.4. The internal structure of verbals

The structure of finite verbals is determined by a number of **ordered choices** in relation to a full verb. Each choice affects the form of the verbal:

1) present or past:	± *-ed*
2) modal or non-modal:	± modal verb
3) perfect or nonperfect:	± HAVE + *-en* form
4) progressive or nonprogressive:	± BE + *-ing* form
5) active or passive:	± BE + *-en* form

The linear order of elements in a **finite verbal** looks like this:

1st choice	2nd choice	3rd choice	4th choice	5th choice	full verb
present past	± modality	± perfect	± progressive	voice	

±-ed   +   (e.g. MAY)   +   (HAVE -en)   +   (BE -ing)   +   (BE -en)   +   V

Normally there is a maximum of three auxiliaries in a verbal. Each auxiliary determines the inflectional form of the following verb (whether a full verb or an auxiliary). A modal is followed by a base form, perfect HAVE by an *-en* form, progressive BE by an *-ing* form and passive BE by an *-en* form: e.g. *may call/take, has called/taken, is calling/taking* and *is called/taken*. Here are some more examples with an illustration of their construction (the arrows show how each choice determines the form of the following verb chosen):

+ -ed   +   (Ø)   +   (HAVE -en)   +   (BE -ing)   +   (BE -en)   +   V
                        had   taken

- -ed   +   (MAY)   +   (HAVE -en)   +   (BE -ing)   +   (BE -en)   +   V
              may   have   been   dancing

+ -ed   +   (CAN)   +   (HAVE -en)   +   (BE -ing)   +   (BE -en)   +   V
              could   have   been   broken

In **nonfinite** verbals there are no modal auxiliaries, such auxiliaries having only finite forms. In other words, in forming infinitival or participial verbals, the first two choices are skipped. The remaining choices have the same linear order but are restricted by two principles: a) English does not allow two consecutive *-ing* forms (such as *being singing*), and b) two consecutive forms of BE are normally avoided (?*to have been being examined*). Thus apart from the three basic nonfinite forms (infinitives, present and past participles) we find the following nonfinite verb groups:

Participial verbals:

having V *-en*	having examined/broken
having been V*-ing*	having been examining/breaking
having been V*-en*	having been examined/broken
being V*-en*	being examined/broken

Infinitival verbals:

(to) be V*-ing*	(to) be examining/breaking
(to) be V*-en*	(to) be examined/broken
(to) have V*-en*	(to) have examined/broken
(to) have been V*-ing*	(to) have been examining/breaking
(to) have been V*-en*	(to) have been examined/broken

Here are some real examples:

(1)   Palme accused him of *having made* "contact with American spies".
(2)   Her arm was in a sling but showed no signs of *having been damaged*.
(3)   He appears *to be working for the Russians*.
(4)   The meeting seemed *to have been planned* by the CIA.

13.2. Complex predicators

13.2.1. Phrasal verbs

All the predicators looked at so far have consisted of verbs only. This and the following sections examine predicators that are somewhat more complex in that they consist not only of verbs but also of items from other word classes. These items have become so closely related with the full verb that they are felt to make up an integrated unit of expression with it. We turn first to predicators in which the full verb is fused with a following adverb, the so-called **phrasal verb**:

(1)   Thor *turned down* the generous offer.
       (cf. *Thor rejected the generous offer*)
(2)   Julia *called up* Simon.
       (cf. *Julia phoned Simon*)
(3)   Cassandra *gave in* eventually.
       (cf. *Cassandra surrendered/yielded eventually*)

In the clearest cases of phrasal predicators, the verb and the adverb are fused semantically: the meaning is not simply a composite of the meaning of the verb and the meaning of the adverb but rather derived in a fairly unpredictable way. Neither verb nor adverb seems to retain the meaning they usually have when used more independently.

There are several characteristic features of adverbs in phrasal verbs: a) they are typically drawn from a fairly small set of mono- or disyllabic adverbs (ABOUT, ACROSS, DOWN, IN, OFF, ON, OUT, OVER, UP, etc.); b) outside the phrasal construction they have general locative (spatial or directional) meaning; c) they are capable of serving also as prepositions (e.g. *up the chimney, down the street, in a bad mood*); and d) they receive primary stress.

One syntactic characteristic of adverbs in phrasal predicators is that, unlike many other adverbs, their position is relatively fixed. In **intransitive phrasal predicators**, the adverb always immediately follows the full verb (as in example (3) above). In **transitive constructions** with a nominal direct object, the adverb may occur before or after the object with no semantic difference:

(1a)   Thor *turned down* the generous offer.
(1b)   Thor *turned* the generous offer *down*.

If the object is an unstressed pronoun, the adverb follows the object:

(1c)   Thor *turned* it *down*.
(1d)   *Thor *turned down* it.

Transitive phrasal constructions allow of pronominal question form with *who* or *what* like other S P O constructions (see section 2.3):

(1e)   What *did* Thor *turn down*?   (the generous offer)

13.2.2. Prepositional verbs

Predicators containing a full verb followed by a preposition with which it forms a formal and/or semantic unit are called **prepositional verbs**:

(1)   Miranda *waited on* the Wilson family.
       (cf. *Miranda served the Wilson family*)
(2)   Alfred's wife always *stood by* Jack.
       (cf. *Alfred's wife always supported Jack*)
(3)   Stephen *took after* his father.
       (cf. *Stephen resembled his father*)

These can be compared with clauses where an ordinary predicator is clearly followed by an adverbial realized by a prepositional phrase:

(4)   Miranda *waited* on the corner.
(5)   Alfred's wife always *stood* by the fireplace.
(6)   This is what Stephen *took* after his divorce.

Unlike phrasal predicators, prepositional predicators are always transitive, taking a direct object. This object is sometimes referred to as a 'prepositional object'. Like 'ordinary' S P O constructions, sentences with prepositional predicators allow pronominal question forms with *who* or *what*:

(1a)   Who(m) *did* Miranda *wait on*?   (the Wilson family)

Unlike adverbs in phrasal constructions, prepositions in prepositional predicators are normally unstressed and are always in pre-object position:

(1b)   *Miranda *waited* the Wilson family *on*.

In some cases the verb and the preposition are not fused semantically but typically 'go together':

(7)   Julia often *looked at* the picture.

(8)   As always, I *dealt with* his request at once.

The italicized constructions here are regarded as prepositional verbs by some grammarians. On the same count, the following constructions could be viewed as **ditransitive** prepositional predicators:

(9)   The incident *reminded* me *of* her warning.

(10)   The countess *supplied* him *with* opium.

13.2.3. Phrasal-prepositional verbs

Sometimes there is fusion between a verb and both an adverb and a preposition, as in the following examples:

(1)   Cassandra *looked down on* the nurses.
        (cf. *Cassandra despised the nurses*)

(2)   She *came up with* a solution in no time.
        (cf. *She found a solution in no time*)

(3)   He no longer *put up with* her whims.
        (cf. *He no longer tolerated her whims*)

The order of constituents in such constructions is always: verb + adverb + preposition. To qualify as a **phrasal-prepositional verb**, there should be some fusion between all three elements with a new derived meaning; compare examples (1) to (3) with the following, where the adverb and the preposition are more independent of the verb, and all three elements actually retain their original lexical meaning:

(4)   From the tower one could *look* down on the roof of Julia's house.

(5)   After a couple of minutes the diver *came* up with an interesting shell.

(6)   Did you read the notice he *put* up with yellow tape?

Arguably, the following are 'ditransitive' phrasal-prepositional constructions:

(7)   Stephen always *took* her infidelity *out on* me.

(8)   They *put* her behaviour *down to* lack of confidence.

Both monotransitive and ditransitive phrasal-prepositional constructions pass the *wh*-question test for objecthood like ordinary S P O constructions:

(1a)   Who *did* Cassandra *look down on?*   (the nurses)

(8a)   What *did* they *put* her behaviour *down to?*   (lack of confidence)

13.2.4. Other complex predicators

A number of expressions, largely of an idiomatic nature, seem to involve other combinations of words in predicators. Here are some of them:

v + adj	e.g. CUT *short,* FORCE *open,* PUT *straight,* RUB *dry,* BREAK *even;*
v + n (+ prep)	e.g. TAKE *place,* BRING *home,* MAKE *amends (for),* GIVE *offence (to),* PAY *heed (to),* PAY *attention (to),* TAKE *care (of),* LOSE *touch (with),* CATCH *sight of,* GIVE *rise to;*
v + v (+ prep)	e.g. MAKE *do with,* GET *rid of,* HAVE *done with,* BE *going to;*
others	BE *on the point of,* BE *about to.*

Semantically it makes sense to treat such expressions in terms of complex predicators: for example, PAY *attention to* corresponds to HEED and BE *on the point of leaving* can be viewed as a special form of the verb LEAVE, just like the progressive form in *She was leaving.* But it is problematic to determine the internal structure of such fixed or idiomatic expressions: how does one determine the H - DEP relationships in *paid attention to* and *was on the point of leaving?* What exactly is the head of the construction in expressions like MAKE *do with,* GET *rid of* and BE *going to?* The fixed lexical nature of these expressions makes it hard to think of internal relations and hence to analyse their constituent structure.

13.3. Tense and aspect

13.3.1. Introduction

Tense and aspect are closely related categories in that both of them concern the presentation of situations. **Tense** is defined as grammatically expressed assignment to situations of **location in time** and can be illustrated by examples like *Linda lives in Stockholm* and *Linda lived in Stockholm.* In using the inflection *-s* in the first of these, the speaker instructs the hearer to identify a situation that applies at the moment the utterance is made, and in using the inflection *-ed* in the second to identify a situation that applies before this moment. **Aspect** is defined as grammatically expressed assignment of **situational focus** and can be illustrated by examples like *It was snowing in Stockholm* and *It snowed in Stockholm*. In using the progressive form *was snowing* in the first of these, the speaker instructs the hearer to select an internal focus, i.e. to adopt an **in medias res** perspective and view the situation as unfolding. In using the simple form *snowed* in the second example, the speaker instructs the hearer to select an external focus, i.e. to view the situation from without, as a complete unit.

In English, tense and aspect are tightly interwoven and will therefore be treated together in terms of a fused tense-aspect system. This system involves the first four choices determining the internal structure of verbals (cf. section 13.1.4):

1) present or past	± *-ed*
2) future or nonfuture	± WILL
3) perfect or nonperfect	± HAVE + *-en* form
4) progressive or nonprogressive	± BE + *-ing* form

The first distinction is marked inflectionally (as in *happens : happened* and *has : had*) and is **deictic** (in that the temporal meanings involved are understood in relation to the time of the utterance). The other three distinctions are relative to the first, deictic one. The future is signalled by the modal verb WILL (used without modal meaning, such as 'intention') and the nonfuture by the absence of this auxiliary, as in *will happen : happens* and *would happen : happened*. The perfect is signalled by a form of the auxiliary HAVE followed by a past participle and the nonperfect by the absence of this combination, as illustrated by *has happened : happens* and *had happened : happened*. The progressive is signalled by a form of the auxiliary BE followed by a present participle and the nonprogressive by the absence of this combination, as illustrated by *is happening : happens* and *was happening : happened*.

The choices of the system are made in the order in which they are presented (i.e. the choice between e.g. perfect/nonperfect is made after the choices present/past and future/nonfuture). As there are four binary distinctions, the speaker has at his disposal a total of **sixteen** tense-aspect forms:

the present	*happens*
the past	*happened*
the present future	*will happen*
the past future	*would happen*
the present perfect	*has happened*
the past perfect	*had happened*

the present future perfect	*will have happened*
the past future perfect	*would have happened*
the present progressive	*is happening*
the past progressive	*was happening*
the present future progressive	*will be happening*
the past future progressive	*would be happening*
the present perfect progressive	*has been happening*
the past perfect progressive	*had been happening*
the present future perfect progressive	*will have been happening*
the past future perfect progressive	*would have been happening*

These forms are first examined in relation to their basic, or primary, uses (sections 13.3.2 to 13.3.9), and then in relation to their uses in **indirect speech** (section 13.3.10), in **narration** (section 13.3.11) and in **modal expressions** (sections 13.3.12-13).

13.3.2. Deictic forms: present and past

Basically, **the present** instructs the hearer to identify the situation referred to as present in relation to **the moment of speech** and **the past** to identify the situation as past in relation to this moment.

The use of the **simple past** can be illustrated by the following examples:

(1)   A luxury jet yesterday *brought* Imelda Marcos to New York.

(2)   The election *got* off to a lacklustre start at a relatively low-key rally.

In using the past, the speaker signals that he has **a particular past time** in mind. This particular time may be expressed by an adverbial which functions as an anchor (cf. *yesterday* in example (1)), or it may be an element of the wider context (as in example (2)). If the speaker has no particular past time in mind, the present perfect is used instead (e.g. *John has resigned*).

Unlike the simple past, the **simple present** is restricted by the actionality of the situation expressed (cf. sections 8.1 to 8.3). It is used more specifically to express present **states**, such as attitudes, intensive and extensive relations:

(3)   George *hates* all the fuss.

(4)   They *are* in high spirits.

(5)   This factory *belongs* to Mr Hardcastle.

The simple present is also used to express habitual situations, including:

(i) universal conditions (e.g. eternal and mathematical truths):

(6)   Water *boils* at 100 degrees centigrade.

(7)   The sun *sets* in the west.

(ii) personal habits, i.e. constructions which describe a settled manner of human (or animal) behaviour:

(8)   Sally *buys* her clothes at Marks & Spencer's.

(9)   She *cycles* to work.

(iii) present ability:

(10)   Evelyn *speaks* Russian.

(11)   Jim *runs* a mile in less than 6 minutes.

The use of the simple present to express present dynamic situations is fairly restricted: it is found only in (broadcast) commentaries, demonstrations, special exclamatory sentences and performatives, i.e. constructions supplementing a visual experience and/or referring to highly regulated, ritualized or ordered events:

(12)   Wright *passes* the ball to Bergkamp. (commentary)

(13)   I now *remove* the moss and *top* up the pot with compost. (demonstration)

(14)   Here *comes* the bride! (exclamation)

(15)   I *promise* to be back by ten. (performative)

Apart from such cases, dynamic situations taking place at the moment of speech require description by means of the present progressive (e.g. *Right now Jack is writing a report to his boss*).

The simple present is used to express a **present plan** to engage in a **future** situation when the time is anchored by means of an adverbial:

(16)   She *flies* to Sydney *next week*.

The simple present is also used more generally about the future in subclauses initiated by *when, as soon as, if, unless*, etc. expressing time or condition:

(17)   I will leave *when/as soon as/if* Roger *comes*.

The predicator of the matrix is in such cases typically in the present future.

The simple present is used 'instead' of the present perfect in connection with HEAR, SAY and TELL to express 'present rumour':

(18)   I *hear* he's quite a one for the girls.

(19)   Peter *tells* me you're going to the States.

The simple present is used 'instead' of the simple past in the so-called **dramatic present** (or historic present) to make the description of a past situation more vivid:

(20)   We proceeded along the main road. Up the road we *enter* the courtyard of a run-down palazzo.

13.3.3. Future forms

The **present future** instructs the hearer to **look ahead** at a situation from a **present viewpoint**. The meaning of the present future is thus 'it applies now that something is ahead':

(1)   In a day or two – father – you *will feel* yourself again.

(2)   Oh dear ... whatever *will* the Bishop *say*?

Unlike the past, the present future does not require any expressed or implied anchor. While a past time anchor is required to understand a sentence like *She regretted the decision*, no future time anchor is necessary for the understanding of *She'll regret the decision*.

The WILL found in present future forms differs from modal-volitional WILL in expressing time exclusively. Unlike examples (1) and (2), an example with volitional WILL like *I will gladly help you* expresses not only futurity but also willingness. Another property of present future WILL is that a sentence in which it occurs describes the future as if it were certain. In this way future WILL differs from modal verbs more generally. Syntactically, future WILL differs from volitional WILL in occurring in passive sentences, progressive sentences and before HAVE + V + -*ed*:

(3)   I *will be brought* back in disgrace.

(4)   We*'ll be throwing* a party.

(5)   By tomorrow, I*'ll* no doubt *have finished* sorting out the first replies.

Furthermore, future WILL differs from volitional WILL in not normally occurring in conditional or temporal subclauses. In an example like *If you'll be patient for a few minutes more, I'll have finished*, we thus find modal WILL in the subclause and future WILL in the matrix clause.

In formal BrE, SHALL is used instead of temporal WILL to form the present future in sentences with 1st person pronoun subjects, as in *I feel I shall never get over it* and *We shall never be as we were*. This SHALL can readily be replaced by WILL.

Futurity can also be expressed by BE *going to*, BE *about to* and BE *to*, all of which signal more specific meanings than WILL. **BE *going to*** is very close in meaning to the present future but often expresses 'present cause or determination' in addition to future meaning. Thus, for example, if the clouds are gathering, it would be appropriate to say *I think it is going to rain*. **BE *about to*** is used to describe the imminent future, as in *She's about to join the navy*, and **BE *to*** is used to express a situation that is arranged or destined to happen in the (present or past) future: e.g. *I am to see the principal tomorrow / He was to die young*. The construction may also serve as a directive (an order or a command): e.g. *This telephone is to be disconnected by tomorrow*.

The **past future** instructs the hearer to **look ahead** from a **past viewpoint**; in other words, its meaning is 'It applied then that something was ahead'. This use is found in **subclauses** of sentences with matrix clause verbs of thinking, believing, feeling or knowing (cf. section 13.3.10 on 'backshifting'):

(6)   I expected it *would take* us three hours to reach the summit, but now I realize I was too optimistic.

The past future is common in **matrix clauses** of **conditional sentences**, i.e. in examples like *If she asked him, he would be angry*. Here the matrix clause does not describe a past time situation but a hypothetical situation that is dependent on the truth of the situation described by the subclause and which is temporally ahead of this (cf. section 12.6).

13.3.4. Perfect forms

The **present perfect** instructs the hearer to **look back** at a situation from a **present viewpoint**. The meaning of the perfect is thus 'It applies now that something is anterior in time':

(1)   It*'s become* part of the folklore.
(2)   I *have called* her several times this month.
(3)   I*'ve been* in Copenhagen since last week.

The present perfect normally implies a present **result** of a past situation (as in (1)), the **repetition** of a situation in a period of time leading up to the present (as in (2)), or present **continuation** of a situation that began in the past (as in (3)). The actionality of the full verb is typically dynamic in the first two cases and stative in the last.

Unlike the past, the present perfect does not require any expressed or implied anchor, but it often combines with time adverbials (as in (2) and (3) above). In this connection, the following should be noted:

(i) The present perfect may combine with adverbials referring to a time which includes or leads up to the moment of speech, e.g. *now, up to now, so far, already, yet* and *since 1958*. Such adverbials do not normally combine with the simple past; but exceptions to this rule are found in AmE, as illustrated by *Did the children come home yet?* (BrE: *Have the children come home yet?*).

(ii) The present perfect does not combine with adverbials referring to a past time separated from the moment of speech, such as *yesterday, a year ago* and *the other day*. Such adverbials are typically used in connection with the past.

(iii) Adverbials which are neutral with respect to the time distinctions specified in (i) and (ii) – e.g. *for five years, recently* and *this morning* – are used in connection with the present perfect or with the simple past, depending on the time perspective intended by the speaker. When they are used in sentences in the past, the time described is divorced from the moment of speech (e.g. *I saw her this morning*, spoken in the late morning, afternoon or evening of the same day). In sentences where they combine with the present perfect, on the other hand, no such separation from the moment of speech is signalled (e.g. *I've seen her this morning*, spoken in the morning of the same day).

(iv) ALWAYS, EVER and **NEVER** are special in sometimes allowing either the present perfect or the simple past with little or no difference of meaning:

(4)   Jim *was always* a man of honour / Jim *has always been* a man of honour.

(5)   *Did* you *ever hear* of incest / *Have* you *ever heard* of incest?

(6)   I *never saw* such a crowd / I *have never seen* such a crowd.

With these adverbials the simple past is perhaps slightly more intense or vivid. It is especially frequent in AmE.

In many cases a past situation may equally well be described by a sentence in the present perfect and a sentence in the simple past. If the speaker's focus is the present time result or continuation of this situation, she will use the present perfect. If her focus is on the past situation itself, she will use the simple past. This can be illustrated by *I have made that point in the telegram* and *I made that point in the telegram*.

The **past perfect** instructs the hearer to **look back** at a situation from a **past viewpoint**. The meaning of the past perfect is thus 'It applied at a past time that something was anterior in time':

(7)   When she arrived, I *had* already *sent* Jim away.

(8)   Well, a few hours earlier I *had gone* off to church.

Here sending Jim away and going off to church are represented as anterior to the past time the hearer is instructed to reckon with.

The past perfect competes with the simple past in clauses beginning with *after*, such as *After we (had) parked, I peeped through a flap in the tent and saw it all*. As *after* unequivocally places the situation described in the matrix clause as subsequent to that described by the subclause, the past perfect can here be replaced by the simple past without loss of information. A similar vacillation is found in matrix clauses containing an adverbial introduced by *before*: *I (had) read the novel before I visited my sister*.

Note finally perfect-like constructions like the following with BE rather than HAVE:

(9)   The guests *are gone*.

The difference between this sentence and an ordinary perfect (*The guests have gone*) is slight: (11) expresses pure stative meaning ('they are not here') whereas the example with HAVE expresses this state as a result of the prior situation of 'going'.

13.3.5. Future perfect forms

The **present future perfect** is semantically complex and not very frequent. It instructs the hearer to **look ahead** to a future time from a **present viewpoint**, and then to **look back** at a situation from that future time:

(1)   The committee *will have finished* its work on April 30th.

(2)   If you could be patient for a few minutes more, I'*ll have found* her for you.

By means of the first of these sentences the speaker instructs the hearer that right now there is ahead of him a time in relation to which the committee's finishing of their work is anterior. Here the time from which the hearer is instructed to look back is specified by means of the adverbial *on April 30th*.

In temporal subclauses, future anterior situations are expressed by the present perfect rather than by the present future perfect, compare:

(3)   I'*ll have finished* when you come. (present future perfect in matrix)

(4)   When you *have finished* I'll leave. (present perfect in subclause)

The **past future perfect** basically instructs the hearer **to look ahead** to a later time from a **past-time viewpoint**, and then to **look back** at a situation from that later time. Outside conditional sentences the past future perfect is relatively rare:

(5)   I remember being convinced that she *would have finished* the book before the first of April.

(6)   I was hoping his fit of rage *would have culminated* soon.

The use of the past future perfect in conditional sentences, e.g. *If she had asked him, he would have been angry*, was dealt with in section 12.6.

13.3.6. Progressive forms: introduction

The progressive form serves the purpose of presenting a situation as being in progress, i.e. with an **internal focus**. In using a nonprogressive form, the speaker presents a situation as a fact, or a complete unit, i.e. with an **external focus**. This distinction concerns the **aspect category**. Examples:

(1)   It *was raining* in Dublin.

(2)   It *rained* in Dublin.

While (1) describes only the middle phase of the situation, i.e. adopts an 'in medias res' perspective excluding both the initial and the terminal phase, (2) describes the situation without concern for its internal phases.

In accounting for progressive forms the most important factor to take into consideration apart from aspect is **actionality** (see chapter 8): the use of the progressive is often dependent on the type of situation the speaker wishes to express. In addition to aspectual and actional meaning, there is often a strong element of **situation time**: progressive situations are typically viewed as **temporary**. The following more specific points should be noted:

(i) As progression entails an input of energy, the progressive is normally used only in sentences whose actionality is **dynamic**. For example, sentences like *Ottawa is the capital of Canada* (intensive relation), *The village lies in a dark valley* (extensive relation) and *George believes in God* (attitude) could not be changed to corresponding sentences in the progressive. Certain verbs have a strong potential for expressing stative meaning, such as BE, BELIEVE, BELONG, CONTAIN, KNOW, MEAN, POSSESS and OWN, and these do not normally take kindly to the progressive form:

(3)   He *possessed/*was possessing* a certain wildness.

(4)   This bottle *contains/*is containing* two pints of milk.

(5)   In those days I *knew/*was knowing* him well, of course.

When such verbs are used dynamically to denote progression or a change of state, they are of course compatible with the progressive form:

(6)   He said it with that smug look that *had been possessing* him lately.

(7)   The jug seemed *to be containing* less water as the experiment progressed.

Note also examples like *Sally was being silly* and *You're being pigheaded* where the main verb involved is BE. These differ from *Sally was silly* and *You're pigheaded* (both intensive) in describing a dynamic situation, i.e. *being* here means approximately 'acting' or 'behaving'. In such cases temporariness is a strong additional meaning. With some verbs temporariness is the dominant motivation for choosing the progressive, e.g. *Peter is/was living in London*, which differs from *Peter lives/lived in London* (extensive) in expressing non-permanent residence. Note finally that though e.g. *My back aches* and *The wound itches* can be changed to *My back is aching* and *The wound is itching*, the situation described is no longer viewed as purely stative (perception) but as more dynamic (self-contained) and intensive.

(ii) The progressive is not normally used to express **punctual** situations, for punctual situations have no internal structure and therefore cannot progress. Verbs with a strong potential for expressing punctual meaning, such as

ARRIVE, DIE, DROP, HIT, KICK, KNOCK, POP, SLAM, SNATCH, SWITCH, START, STOP, STRIKE, TAP, etc. may appear in the progressive but then express either **direction** or **iteration**:

(8a)   The truck stopped for a red light. (punctual)
(8b)   The truck was stopping for a red light. (direction)
(9a)   A door slammed behind me. (punctual)
(9b)   A door was slamming behind me. (iterative)

However, the progressive may express a punctual situation as strictly **simultaneous** with another situation expressed in the sentence:

(10)   She entered the room *just as* the clock *was striking* one.

(iii) The progressive is not normally used to express **telic** situations, for the terminal point characterizing telic situations (cf. section 8.2) falls outside the internal focus of the progressive. Thus nonprogressive forms expressing telic situations alternate with progressive forms expressing **directed** situations:

(11a)   Sally *built* a small garden shed. (telic)
(11b)   Sally *was building* a small garden shed. (directed)
(12a)   Walter *moved* to the door, still talking. (telic)
(12b)   Walter *was moving* to the door, still talking. (directed)

In presenting the situation of 'building' and 'moving' with an internal focus (as in the b-examples), the speaker eliminates the completion of the situation from the reference of the verbal, i.e. she merely describes a situation progressing **towards** its natural conclusion or termination. With an external focus (as in the a-examples) the situation reaches its completion.

(iv) Both the progressive and the nonprogressive are used to express **self-contained** situations:

(13a)   They *walked* along the beach, arm in arm.
(13b)   They *were walking* along the beach, arm in arm.
(14a)   We *celebrated* Stephanie's birthday at my uncle's.
(14b)   We *were celebrating* Stephanie's birthday at my uncle's.

In such pairs of examples, it is the same (self-contained) situation which is described but in slightly different ways (external vs. internal focus). The difference is one of pure aspect. In the other pairs of examples examined so far, the difference is one of both aspect and action.

(v) Verbs like STAND, SIT, LIE, HOLD, KEEP, OCCUPY, SLEEP, STAY, WAIT, WEAR, which have a clear stative potential, are often used to refer to **temporary** posture or conditions: e.g. *He waited for her in the library / She wore her mother's wedding dress.* In connection with subjects referring to volitional agents more or less 'in command' of what is going on, such situations are in a grey zone between dynamic and stative and are therefore best classified as self-contained (i.e. the most stative of the dynamic subsituations). Like other self-contained situations, they often permit expression by both the progressive and nonprogressive verb forms with only a slight difference of aspectual meaning (cf. *He was waiting for her in the library / She was wearing her mother's wedding dress*).

Here is an overview of some of the characteristic aspectual and actional meanings associated with pairs of nonprogressive and progressive forms:

Nonprogressive <-> Progressive

Aspect

| external focus | <-> internal focus |

Action		Examples
stative	<-> dynamic	*Roger is silly* *Roger is being silly*
punctual	<-> iterative	*A door slammed behind him* *A door was slamming behind him*
punctual	<-> directed	*She caught up with the others* *She was catching up with the others*
telic	<-> directed	*She built a new garden shed* *She was building a new garden shed*
self-contained	<-> self-contained	*They walked along the beach* *They were walking along the beach*

Note finally that in sentences with **directed** actionality the progressive may be used to describe a future (posterior) situation – usually under the control of the person referred to by the subject form – which is in preparation at the time identified by the form of BE:

(14a)   Linda *is moving* to France tomorrow.

(14b)   Linda *was moving* to France the following day.

In these examples the adverbial informs the hearer that the speaker has a situation ahead in mind; but even in the absence of such adverbials a sentence in the progressive may be used intentionally to describe a posterior situation which is in preparation at the time identified. Depending on the larger linguistic and/or situational context examples like *Linda is moving to France* and *Linda was moving to France* may thus describe a situation that is in progress at the time identified or which is ahead of it.

13.3.7. Present and past progressive forms

The **present progressive** instructs the hearer to look at a situation progressing at the moment of communication. The meaning of the present progressive is thus 'It applies now that a situation is in progress', as in *Federal authorities are investigating allegations of currency violations.*

While the simple present is often used to express present habitual meaning (including universal conditions, personal habits and ability, cf. section 13.3.2), the present progressive is typically used to express a specific dynamic situation taking place at the moment of speech, cf.:

(1a)   The sun *sets* in the west.
(1b)   The sun *is setting* in the west.
(2a)   Sally *buys* clothes at Marks & Spencer's.
(2b)   Sally *is buying* clothes at Marks & Spencer's.

If the simple present is replaced by the present progressive in a sentence describing a **personal habit**, as in (2a-b), there are two possibilities: either the habitual meaning disappears and a situation is presented as being in progress at the moment of speech, or the habitual meaning is retained but with the difference that it is a **temporary habit** which is now described. Temporary habitual meaning is present also in a sentence like *I'm walking to work this week.* It should be added that the temporary implication of the habitual progressive may be cancelled by adverbials expressing all-inclusive time like ALWAYS and FOREVER, as illustrated by *She's always/forever asking silly questions.* Such constructions often express annoyance.

The **past progressive** instructs the hearer to look at a situation progressing at a past time. The meaning of the past progressive is thus 'It applied at a past time that a situation was in progress', as in:

(3)   I thought he *was* simply *babbling*, but suddenly he got up and left.
(4)   Since it *was snowing*, I went with her in the direction of the Praga Bridge.

In complex sentences a past progressive form in one clause may have the effect of **framing** a punctual or telic situation described by a simple past form in another clause:

(5)   When Ann *returned*, Jim *was painting* the view from their hotel window.
(6)   While she *was eating*, a new customer *entered* the restaurant.

Here the situation described by the matrix clause in (5) and the subclause in (6) are presented as being in progress at the time when the situations described by the subclause in (5) and the matrix clause in (6) took place. Note that if the nonprogressive had been used in the matrix clause of (5), the painting of the view would be subsequent to Ann's return. If the situation expressed by the simple form is self-contained, the framing effect of the progressive is weakened to mere simultaneity:

(7)   While she *was eating*, I *looked* at the other customers.

In such cases, the simple form can often be replaced by the progressive form (*While she was eating, I was looking at the other customers*). The difference between the two expressions is slight and only involves a choice between a neutral external focus and a more marked internal focus.

13.3.8. Future progressive forms

The **present future progressive** basically instructs the hearer to look ahead from a present viewpoint to a situation progressing at a future time, as in:

(1)   We*'ll be travelling* by boat.

But the present future progressive is often used to express pure future time, as in *They will be leaving in half an hour*, which is very close in meaning to *They will leave in half an hour* and *They are leaving in half an hour*. In some cases the present future progressive may be preferred to the present future because WILL + V may – out of context – be ambiguous:

(2)   I*'ll keep* watch for you.
(3)   I*'ll be keeping* watch for you.

Here WILL in (2) may be either volitional or purely temporal, and only by means of the context is the hearer able to determine whether the communicative function of the sentence is a promise or a descriptive statement. In (3), WILL can only be understood to be purely temporal.

In using the **past future progressive** the speaker instructs the hearer to look ahead from a past viewpoint to a situation progressing at a later time:

(4)   I knew that before long she *would be asking* payment for my meals.

The past future progressive also occurs in the matrix clause of conditional sentences, i.e. in examples of the type *I'd be wandering around alone if it weren't for Sonya*. Here the matrix clause does not express a past future time but a hypothetical situation (cf. section 12.6).

13.3.9. Perfect and future perfect progressive forms

The **present perfect progressive** instructs the hearer to look back from a present viewpoint at a situation progressing towards the present:

(1)   *Has* Father *been talking* to you?

(2)   Minna, they tell me you*'ve been looking* for me.

Like the present perfect, the present perfect progressive does not combine with adverbials which exclude the moment of speech, such as *yesterday, a year ago* and *the other day* (see section 13.3.4).

   The **past perfect progressive** instructs the hearer to look back from a past viewpoint at a situation progressing towards the past viewpoint:

(3)   Then the thing I *had been dreading* happened.

(4)   One of the writers *had been hanging* around Edusha.

The future perfect progressive forms are semantically highly complex, so not surprisingly they are rarely encountered. The **present future perfect progressive** instructs the hearer to look ahead from a present viewpoint to a future time towards which an anterior situation is progressing:

(5)   The committee *will have been negotiating* the treaty for two months soon.

The **past future perfect progressive** is primarily used to express counter-factual situations in progress in conditional sentences (cf. section 12.6):

(6)   He *would have been reading* my letters if I had given him the chance.

In non-conditional sentences, the past future perfect progressive is used with inferential meaning (signalling probability, cf. section 13.3.12 on modal usage):

(7)   On his arrival she *would have been milking* the cow.

13.3.10. Tense-aspect in indirect speech

Indirect speech is basically the reporting of what an original speaker said. This is normally accompanied by changes of tense-aspect, person and other deictic elements (such as place references and demonstratives), as in:

(1)   Peter said that *his* commanding officer *would regard that* as cowardice.

If this sentence is compared with its direct speech counterpart *Peter said, "My commanding officer will regard this as cowardice"*, it can be seen that the past future form *would regard* is a **backshifted** version of *will regard*. Backshifting is common not only with reported speech (in connection with verbs like SAY and TELL) but also with reported thought and feeling (in connection with verbs like KNOW, THINK and FEEL).

Backshifting of tense-aspect in indirect speech is not obligatory, as demonstrated by the acceptability of *Peter said that his commanding officer will regard this as cowardice*. But it is more neutral than lack of backshifting, so if a verb of saying is in the past, the verbs in the following subclauses are normally past forms too (past, past perfect, past future or past future perfect).

Backshifting in indirect speech affects the first tense-aspect choice (present vs. past). If the original construction contained a present form, the possible backshifts can be summed up in this way:

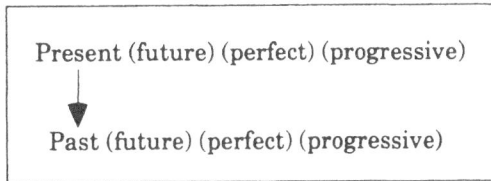

Present (future) (perfect) (progressive)

↓

Past (future) (perfect) (progressive)

This system yields specific shifts like:

Present	→	Past
Present perfect	→	Past perfect
Present future perfect	→	Past future perfect
Present future progressive	→	Past future progressive
etc.		

The result of these shifts can be illustrated by the following examples:

(2)   The counsellor said that blood was thicker than water.

(3)   Mary said she hadn't been to the States since 1972.

(4)   He said he would have finished sorting out the first replies next Friday.

(5)   The contractor told me they would be working again next week.

If the original construction contained a past form, the possible backshifts can be summed up in this way:

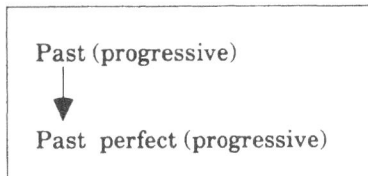

Past (progressive)

↓

Past perfect (progressive)

This system yields the following specific shifts:

Past	→	Past perfect
Past progressive	→	Past perfect progressive

The result of these two shifts can be illustrated by the following examples:

(6)   Mary told me she had gone to California last year.

(7)   Jim claimed that he had been staying at the Park Lodge over Christmas.

In indirect speech a past perfect form may thus represent either a backshifted past form or a backshifted present perfect, so the hearer has to work out which of the two types of backshifting is involved. Note also that, as there is no verb form available for the backshifting of a past perfect form, a sentence like the following is – out of context – ambiguous:

(8)   Peter told me that when the second half began Rush had scored two goals.

Here *had scored* may be either a backshifted version of *scored* or an unshifted past perfect (i.e. either *"When the second half began Rush scored two goals"* or *"When the second half began Rush had scored two goals"*.
    The reporting clause is sometimes left out, or parenthesized. This is called **free** or **implicit indirect speech**, cf.:

(9)   Would she be able to recognize this interpretation of herself, he wondered?

(10)   'So what time did the train leave tomorrow morning?'

In (10) the speaker enquires about the listener's conversation with a third party (e.g. *'So what time did he say the train left tomorrow morning?'*).

13.3.11. Tense-aspect in narration

In narration it is typically the **past verb forms** (past, past perfect, past future, past future perfect, progressive as well as nonprogressive) which are used, even in stories about imaginary present or future events. In using the past, the writer describes not a past time situation but an **imaginary situation at the stage reached** in the narration. Compare the following examples:

(1)   'I *climbed* the steep dune yesterday, now it's your turn.'

(2)   He *climbed* the steep dune before him hurriedly, not taking the time to remove his shoes and socks. His panting under the effort of running uphill *seemed* delicious to him; it *was* the taste of his renewed youth.

In the spoken utterance in (1), the situation of 'climbing' is mentally distant for the hearer, who is instructed to identify a past situation. In the written piece of fiction in (2), the writer creates, or introduces, an imaginary situation of climbing at the stage reached in the narration, simply by writing it. The 'climbing' thus becomes mentally present for the reader, who is invited to 'witness', or envisage, the situation at this particular point in the narration. More technically, the difference is that the past form is deictic in (1) while it is non-deictic in (2): the interpretation of the form in (2) is not dependent on the reader's awareness of the moment of communication (the writing of the novel). Thus in (2) but not in (1), we can replace the past forms by present forms with little or no difference of meaning:

(2')   He *climbs* the steep dune before him hurriedly, not taking the time to remove his shoes and socks. His panting under the effort of running uphill *seems* delicious to him; it *is* the taste of his renewed youth.

The difference between the present and the past in literary narrative is that the present has a more dramatic potential (cf. section 13.3.2 on the dramatic present), representing a calculated stylistic choice on the part of the writer.

In narration the **past perfect** and the **past future** forms instruct the reader to look back and ahead, respectively, from the stage reached in the narration:

(3)   He was sitting beside his radio set which he *had* just *switched* off. It was late at night. He *had listened* to a symphony concert ... Now all was silent.

(4)   Ready to weep he prepared himself for bed. He *would* not *sleep*.

In using the **past future perfect** the writer instructs the reader to look back from a later point in the narration:

(5)   Five days later Mrs Blair *would have left* her husband.

Similarly, in a present-form narrative, the reader may be instructed by present perfect and present future forms to look back/ahead from the stage reached:

(6)   A window smashes in one of the small bedrooms; the cause is Henry, who *has put* his left arm through and down, and *slashed* it savagely on the glass.

(7)   What is happening upstairs is something Howard *will hear* about later.

Outside fiction, we cannot normally use the simple present form to refer to a specific, strictly present dynamic situation (cf. section 13.3.2):

(8a)   *'He *opens* his packsack'.

(9a)   *'He *takes* off his shoes and socks'.

Here only the progressive is possible. But in fiction the simple present is not nearly as constrained. For the examples in (8a) and (9a) to become acceptable we only have to imagine a fictional context, such as a stage direction or simply a piece of narration:

(8b)   After a while David says 'Well children, time to break out the grass'. *He opens his packsack* and gropes around inside.

(9b)   The two little girls go with him, then slip out of their shoes. *Paul takes off his shoes and socks*, rolls up his trousers like an elderly tripper at the seaside.

Outside fiction, such simple forms have a more general habitual meaning:

(8c)   He *always opens* his packsack to check its contents.

(9c)   When going to bed, Paul *usually takes* off his shoes and socks.

Note finally that in narration the framing effect of the progressive (cf. section 13.3.7) typically serves the purpose of describing the **background** against which a number of consecutive events described by clauses in the simple past (or present) are recounted:

(10)   At twelve o'clock sharp I *left* my flat. The sun *was shining* and people *were sunning* themselves on benches in the park. I *unlocked* the car, *fastened* the seat belt, *started* the engine and *drove* to the first intersection. On the pavements pedestrians *were strolling* along. Suddenly an idea *occurred* to me.

Here each nonprogressive form makes the plot advance, while the progressive forms are used to describe a situation that is simultaneous with that described by the preceding nonprogressive form.

13.3.12. Modal uses of past tense-aspect forms

Modality involves non-factuality. There are two major types of modal meaning: **probability** (comprising logical possibility and necessity, hypothetical meaning, beliefs and predictability) and **desirability** (comprising permission, obligation and volition). This is illustrated by the modal verb MAY, which is used to judge the probability of a situation in *The economy may get worse* and to express permission in *May I come in?* The type of modality which concerns probability is termed **epistemic** while that which concerns desirability is termed **deontic**. In English all the tense-aspect forms except the simple present, the present progressive and the present perfect can be used modally. In the following account of these modal uses, tense-aspect usage in conditional sentences will be disregarded, for that has already been dealt with, cf. section 12.6.

Let us consider first the modal use of the **past** and the **past perfect** forms (progressive as well as nonprogressive). As in conditional clauses these forms can be used for the expression of hypothetical meaning, i.e. epistemically, in object clauses and adverbial comparative clauses:

(1)   I wish I *knew* the answer to that.
(2)   I wish I *had known* the answer to that.
(3)   He talks as if he *was writing* a doctoral dissertation on the subject.
(4)   He talks as if he *had read* the entire literature on this subject.

In (1) and (3) the subclauses express a counterfactual situation in present time; and in (2) and (4) they express a counterfactual situation at a past time.

The past is also used for the expression of (deontic) tentativeness and politeness:

(5)   *Could* you *do* me a favour?
(6)   We *were wondering* if we can expect to see you down here any time.

The use of past forms in these examples makes the request less direct – and therefore easier to turn down – than if the present had been used.

In expressions like *It's time we left* and *It's time you went to bed*, the past is used deontically about that which is considered appropriate or necessary for the subject to do.

13.3.13. Modal uses of WILL

WILL is special in that it has both temporal and modal meanings. On the one hand it is often used for the expression of temporal 'aheadness' in the tense-aspect system, as we have seen. But on the other hand, it is also used frequently with modal meanings and, like the modal auxiliaries more generally, it appears in the second slot in the structure of the verb group (cf. sections 13.1.4 and 13.3.1). However, since future meaning is the prevailing element of WILL even in its modal uses, it is here treated as a tense-aspect auxiliary with certain modal uses, rather than a modal auxiliary with certain temporal uses. In other words, WILL is dealt with here rather than in section 13.5 on modal verbs.

Future (perfect) (progressive) forms can be used both epistemically and deontically. The deontic use can be exemplified by:

(1)   You *will do* as I say at once.

(2)   You *will drop* me by the cathedral in Léon.

(3)   You *will be studying* hard in your room when I return.

The future forms here present an order in a non-negotiable way as a future fact, and this makes it impolite and condescending.

The future forms are used epistemically for the expression of nonfuture predictability. The following examples express **specific predictability**:

(4)   They *will be* home at this time of day.

(5)   They *will be watching* telly now.

(6)   It was midnight. The President *would have finished* the letter now.

The future forms may also express **habitual predictability**:

(7)   She *will sit* there for hours doing nothing.

(8)   Occasionally a tradesman's cart *would rattle* round the corner.

(9)   Every afternoon between 4 and 6 he*'ll be preparing* dinner.

Finally, the present future – but not the complex present future forms – may be used to express **general predictability**:

(10)   Oil *will float* on water.

(11)   Sugar *will dissolve* in water.

Semantically, such present future sentences are closely related to sentences in the present expressing a universal statement, like *Water boils at 100 degrees centigrade* (see section 13.3.2).

When WILL with this sense is stressed, general predictability becomes an **inevitability** and approaches the meaning of strong volition (see below):

(12)   Boys *'will be* boys.

Examples like the following illustrate the **volitional use of WILL**:

(13)   I think today I*'ll* stick to cheese.
(14)   I *will* never leave you, father.
(15)   *Will* you come with me, Sancho?
(16)   If she*'ll* wait in the study, I can see her in a minute.

Here the present form *will* is used in **factual statements** about willingness or intention, but at the same time it has futurity as a constant secondary meaning.

WILL is occasionally used for what has been termed **strong volition**:

(17)   He *'will* go swimming in dangerous waters.

When used for this purpose, i.e. in the sense of 'insist on', WILL is obligatorily stressed and cannot be contracted to *'ll*.

The past form is used with non-past meaning for the expression of **weakened volition**, often in polite requests:

(18)   *Would* you pay us in cash, please?
(19)   We *would* like to sit down soon.

Volitional *would* is also used without past time meaning in **hypothetical conditional sentences** and in **indirect speech** (sections 12.6 and 13.3.10):

(20)   If you did that, I *would* bash in your brains.
(21)   My wife said she *would* phone us after dinner.

Here it seems clear that *would* serves the purpose of expressing not only aheadness but also intention.

13.4. Mood

Mood in English is traditionally regarded as an inflectional verbal category with three members which can be used to define sentence/clause types according to how their meaning relates to reality: the **indicative** (which has -*s* in the 3rd person singular of the present, and which basically expresses something real or factual), the **imperative** (which is realized by Ø and expresses something which needs to be made real) and the **subjunctive** (which is also realized by Ø but which expresses something less factual):

(1)   Somebody *opens* the door (all the time). (indicative)

(2)   Somebody *open* the door (will you?). (imperative)

(3)   I suggest that somebody *open* the door. (subjunctive)

The indicative comprises (positive and negative) statements and questions, and the imperative comprises directives. The communicative function of the subjunctive mood is less homogeneous, however. In an example like (3) it appears to be directive like the imperative, in *God save the Queen* it expresses a wish and in *Lest anyone worry we're sinking, let me reassure you we're not* it describes a hypothetical situation.

So far, this grammar has dealt predominantly with sentences in the indicative mood. There now follows an examination of the imperative and subjunctive moods.

13.4.1. The imperative

In using the imperative the speaker typically issues a **directive** to the hearer to behave in a specific way. Directives may be divided into a number of different functional subtypes, e.g.:

(1)   Shut up. (command)

(2)   Sit down, please. (request)

(3)   Wash hair and rinse carefully. (instruction)

(4)   Don't buy that brand if you can get others. (advice)

(5)   Take as many sweets as you like. (permission)

(6)   Give us this day our daily bread. (prayer)

Which of these subtypes of directive a sentence in the imperative mood expresses is dependent on the linguistic and/or situational context. A marker like *please* informs the hearer that an imperative probably functions as a request, and if the speaker's relation to the hearer is that of a superior to his subordinate, an imperative is likely to be understood as a command.

While the function of an imperative is typically directive, this is not invariably the case. In sentences like *Sleep well* and *Have a good time* it is used for the expression of a wish, and here it is clearly non-directive.

The imperative shows no present/past distinction (and is therefore perhaps best considered nonfinite). Nor does it interact with the other choices in the tense-aspect system though its combination with the progressive cannot be ruled out entirely. The imperative is also highly restricted with respect to voice. Thus imperative passives are only found in stock expressions like *Be seated* and in constructions directing the hearer to avoid becoming the target (DONE-TO) of an action, as in the following negative imperative passive:

(7)   *Don't be taken in* by that scoundrel.

A special type of imperative which is very common has LET as its verb followed by *us* (optionally contracted to *let's*):

(8)   *Let's* go to the theatre.
(9)   *Let's* not be petty-minded.

Here the directive is aimed not only at the hearer but simultaneously at the speaker, and thus expresses a **mutual proposal**. However, as the following examples show, LET can also be used as an ordinary directive:

(10)   Just *let* him try.
(11)   *Let* AB be equal to BA.

Prohibitive imperatives are expressed by *don't* + V:

(12)   *Don't buy* that brand if you can get others.

The auxiliary DO is also used in emphatic imperatives:

(13)   *Do help* yourself to some more wine.

Even BE gets DO-support in such constructions, cf. *Don't be late, Do be careful*. The negative of *let's* is *let's not* (e.g. *Let's not be petty-minded*), though in BrE *don't lets* is possible as well (*Don't let's waste more time*). When unaccompanied by *us*, LET requires DO-support (e.g. *Don't let him fool you*).

Imperatives are typically subjectless (cf. section 4.1), but where a contrast needs to be expressed, or emphatic displeasure, they contain the subject *you*:

(14)   You *take* the wine and I'll take the hamper.
(15)   You *mind* your own business.

13.4.2. The subjunctive

The subjunctive has both epistemic and deontic uses in English. What is common to these uses is non-factuality.

The **epistemic subjunctive** is used to express hypothetical meaning in conditional, comparative and concessive clauses. Outside formal language the only instance of this is the use of *were* in combination with 1st or 3rd person singular subjects:

(1)   The task would be difficult if the old party *were* suddenly to reappear.
(2)   Kinglake would have rung if the plane *were*n't on its way.

In BrE *was* is used in everyday language instead of subjunctive *were* in conditional clauses, except in the fixed expression *If I were you*. Subjunctive *were* is also found along with *had* and *should* in the type of conditional clause signalled not by a subordinating conjunction but by inversion (see section 7.2.1) and in comparative and concessive clauses:

(3)   The total output would be much worse *were* it not for the winter crop.

(4)   It was as though no one else *were* there.

(5)   Even if it *were* expedient I couldn't say what came before what.

In those cases where the situation described by a concessive clause is not hypothetical but factual, *was* is naturally enough used instead of *were*, as in *Even if he was exceedingly well-off, I never considered marrying him.*

In formal style, subjunctive *were* is used in *that*-clauses (with or without *that*) for the expression of wishful or hypothetical speculation (thus typically in object clauses after the verbs WISH and SUPPOSE):

(6)   I wish I *were* famous.

(7)   Suppose a pretty high-school girl *were* to come forward with the solution.

Subjunctive *be* is very formal. It is found primarily (but not exclusively) in conditional and concessive clauses:

(8)   If any vehicle *be* found parked on these premises, it shall be towed away at the expense of the vehicle's owner.

(9)   They did not approve of Atkinson who, *be* he a brewer in name, actually committed the indignity of conducting trial marshings and fermentations.

The subjunctive is used more frequently in AmE than in BrE. One example illustrating this is its use after the conjunction *lest*:

(10)   But *lest* it *appear* that I am always dishing it out, let me tell you the full story, Miss Rose.

The **deontic subjunctive** is used for the expression of **wishes** in set expressions like *God save the Queen*, *Long live Trotsky* and *Heaven forbid*. The subjunctive is also used deontically for the expression of **compulsion** in *that*-clauses after verbs, adjectives or nouns expressing demand, resolution, recommendation, or the like. This so-called **mandative subjunctive** is standard practice in AmE:

(11)

$$
\text{I} \begin{bmatrix} \text{demand} \\ \text{insist} \\ \text{suggest} \\ \text{move} \end{bmatrix} \text{that Smith} \begin{bmatrix} \text{be fired} \\ \text{leave at once} \end{bmatrix}
$$

(12)

$$\text{I support the} \begin{bmatrix} \text{demand} \\ \text{suggestion} \\ \text{proposal} \end{bmatrix} \text{that Smith} \begin{bmatrix} \text{be fired} \\ \text{leave at once} \end{bmatrix}$$

(13)

$$\text{It is} \begin{bmatrix} \text{essential} \\ \text{necessary} \\ \text{important} \end{bmatrix} \text{that Smith} \begin{bmatrix} \text{be fired} \\ \text{leave at once} \end{bmatrix}$$

In BrE, on the other hand, compulsion may also be expressed by *should* + V in *that*-clauses (e.g. *I suggest that Smith should leave at once*).

A third deontic use of the subjunctive is the expression of **concessive** meaning in frozen examples like these:

(14)   *Be* that as it may, we'll still finish on time.

(15)   *Come* what may, we'll proceed in the same way.

(16)   *Suffice* it to say that he's totally incompetent.

13.5. Modality

13.5.1. Introduction

As pointed out in section 13.3.12, modality primarily involves two kinds of **non-factuality**: **epistemic** and **deontic**. In producing epistemically modalized utterances like *Perhaps Colonel Gaddafi is dead* and *Colonel Gaddafi may be dead* – which are qualified by *perhaps* and *may* respectively – the speaker expresses that a certain situation is conceivably real. And in producing a deontically modalized utterance like *She ought to be in bed* – qualified by OUGHT – she expresses that a certain situation is desirable. With categorical (non-modal) utterances like *Colonel Gaddafi is dead* and *She is in bed*, on the other hand, the speaker describes situations which she considers factual.

In English, modality may be expressed **lexically** in a number of different ways. This can be illustrated by examples like the following:

(1)   *Hopefully* this is enough. (deontic adverb)

(2)   She is *likely* to lose. (epistemic adjective)

(3)   I *permit* you to smoke. (deontic verb)

As we have already seen, modality can also be expressed grammatically by means of the mood category (cf. section 13.4) and by means of tense-aspect forms, especially forms of WILL (cf. sections 13.3.12 and 13.3.13). In addition to these means, modality can be expressed by forms of the modal auxiliaries CAN, MAY, MUST and SHALL. The expression of modality by modal auxiliaries can be illustrated by epistemic examples like the following:

(4)   She may/can't/must be right.

Here the finite verb forms signal a qualification whereby the speaker operates with alternatives to factual meaning: 'I consider it possible/impossible/ necessary that she is right'.

Modality is often expressed by highly regular **collocations** of modal verbs and certain adverbs:

(5)   They *can't possibly* be playing tennis.

(6)   It *may well* be a back-formation.

Though the modal verb and the adverb in such combinations usually express the same kind of modality (e.g. epistemic modality), their combination is not a matter of pleonastic reiteration of the same modal meaning but rather a stylistically powerful, synergetic means of expression.

However, modal auxiliaries do not always express modality:

(7)   Linford *can* run 100 yards in nine seconds.

Here CAN is used in a factual statement about ability.

Modal verbs differ from other verbs in having no infinitive and participle forms, and no third-person singular -*s* form in the present. Furthermore, the past forms are typically used not to instruct the hearer to identify a past-time situation but to express a weaker degree of modality, or a different kind of modality, than the present forms:

(8)   She *might* be right.

(9)   *Could* she be right?

These differ from *She may be right* and *Can she be right?* only in that the degree of epistemic possibility expressed is relatively weak. To stress the individual nature of the present and past forms of modal verbs, we use small capitals for both (e.g. SHALL/SHOULD) in our discussion below.

13.5.2. MAY/MIGHT

MAY is used both epistemically and deontically. When used **epistemically**, MAY expresses **uncertain possibility**:

(1)   That *may* be the best light I'll ever appear in, to them.

(2)   She *may* have a solution to our problem.

MAY is used **deontically** to express **permission**:

(3)   *May* I speak to you for a moment?

(4)   You *may* enter now.

MAY (as well as MIGHT) is epistemic, not deontic, when followed by a perfect and/or progressive form: *Jones may be leaving / Jones may have left / Jones may have been leaving*.

MAY is also used deontically to express **wishes** and **maledictions** (in sentences with subject-operator inversion, see section 7.2.1):

(5)   Please God, *may* it have been instantly.

(6)   *May* it choke him.

In **interrogative sentences**, epistemic MAY is virtually ruled out. Here uncertain possibility is expressed by CAN, as illustrated by *Can it be true?* and *Can spring be far behind?* (which should be compared with corresponding declarative sentences like *It may be true* and *Spring may be far behind*). Deontic MAY, on the other hand, is used as readily in interrogative sentences as in declarative sentences.

In **negative sentences**, the semantic scope of negation excludes epistemic MAY but normally includes deontic MAY:

(7)   They *may* not have gone very far.
        (= 'It is **possible** that they have **not** gone very far')

(8)   You *may* not borrow my car.
        (= 'You are **not permitted** to borrow my car')

If the speaker wishes to describe a situation as 'not possible' rather than 'possible ... not', she can do so by means of epistemic CAN followed by NOT:

(9)   They *can't* have gone very far.
        (= 'It is **not possible** that they have gone very far')

MIGHT is not used with past-time meaning, but adds **tentativeness** to MAY. Epistemic MIGHT thus expresses weaker possibility than MAY:

(10)   That woman *might* attack you.

(11)   What you suggest *might* be regarded as a recipe for folly and madness.

MIGHT is used as a backshifted version of both epistemic and deontic MAY:

(12)   She said the time *might* come in my generation when the educational system itself was mixed.

(13)   Father said we *might* leave the table.

MIGHT is used deontically with non-past meaning for the expression of a more tentative or polite request:

(14)   *Might* I ask you to do me a favour?

This use of MIGHT is rare and characteristically restricted to questions and wishes (e.g. *If only I might be allowed to see him*).

13.5.3. CAN/COULD

There are three uses of CAN/COULD: epistemic, non-modal and deontic.

(i) Epistemic uses: CAN is used epistemically to express **possibility** in interrogative sentences (and thus performs the same function as MAY in declarative sentences):

(1)   But *can* she be right? (cf. *She may be right*)
(2)   How *can* this be irrelevant? (cf. *This may be irrelevant*)

CAN is normally epistemic in interrogative and negative declarative sentences when followed by a perfect or progressive form:

(3)   *Can* she *be staying* at the Park Lodge?
(4)   They *can't have left* the hotel already.

CAN is also used epistemically in negative declarative sentences when followed by BE:

(5)   You *can't be* serious.
(6)   They *can't be* in London yet.

Negative sentences like (4) to (6) describe the situation as 'not possible', i.e. the semantic scope of NOT extends over the entire sentence and thus includes the modal verb. Epistemic CAN is avoided in positive declarative sentences, even when followed by a perfect or progressive form. Instead MAY is used:

(7)   She may/*can have been jealous.
(8)   They may/*can be studying in the library.

Epistemic **COULD** conveys **non-past tentative possibility** and is thus close in meaning to MIGHT, but while MIGHT is used about **uncertain** possibility, COULD is used about **actual** possibility. Epistemic COULD is found in declarative as well as interrogative sentences:

(9)   He's not much here but he *could* arrive.
(10)   They *could* have left the stuff behind.
(11)   But *could* she be right?

Epistemic COULD is also used without past time meaning in conditional sentences and in indirect speech:

(12)   If we instructed him carefully, Jones *could* be the right man for the job.
(13)   She asked me if it *could* be due to fear.

(ii) Non-modal uses: CAN is often used to express 'possibility' non-modally, i.e. not as the speaker's qualification of a statement but as deriving from an **inherent capacity** of the subject. This use of CAN is common in positive declarative sentences:

(14)   The exit *can* be blocked.

(15)   He *can* be jealous.

These examples differ from corresponding examples with MAY in expressing possible manifestations of some characteristic of the subject rather than the speaker's uncertainty as to what is possibly the case. This meaning of CAN is often realized more specifically as **the subject's ability** in connection with dynamic situations and perceptions

(16)   Linford *can* run 100 yards in nine seconds.

(17)   She *can* speak seven languages.

(18)   I *can* see/hear him very clearly now.

COULD is used regularly about **past time capacity and general ability**:

(19)   He *could* be very jealous in those days.

(20)   Already as a girl she *could* speak seven languages.

The use of COULD to refer to a single past instance of ability is possible only in negative sentences:

(21)   We *couldn't/*could* catch the bus.

For single past instances of ability in positive sentences other expressions are used, e.g.:

(22)   We *managed* to catch the bus.

(23)   They *were able to* move the stuff in less than half an hour.

(iii) Deontic uses: like MAY, CAN is used to express **permission**:

(24)   *Can* I stay out as long as I wish, Mum?

(25)   You *can* smoke in this part of the canteen area.

CAN is often more informal than MAY (as in (24)) or used about 'impersonal permission' (as in (25), which expresses permission indirectly by informing the hearer that the rules allow smoking).

Deontic CAN is sometimes used for the expression of **offers, requests** and **orders**:

(26)   I *can* help you, if you like.

(27)   *Can* I get you anything?

(28)   *Can* I talk to you for a minute?

(29)   'Young man,' I say, 'you *can* just get up and leave this table.'

The deontic use of CAN to express permission in negative sentences is illustrated by:

(30)   You *can't* stay with her.

Here – as in the case of epistemic *can't* – the semantic scope of NOT extends over the entire sentence
    Unlike MIGHT, COULD is freely used to express **past time permission**:

(31)   In the late sixties we *could* do pretty much as we pleased.

But COULD is also used with non-past meaning:

(32)   You *could* easily sleep here tonight.

(33)   *Could* I have a word with you?

The past form makes a permission **tentative**, and in interrogative sentences like (33) a request for it will therefore be felt to be **polite**.

13.5.4. MUST

MUST has both epistemic and deontic uses:

(i) MUST is used **epistemically** to indicate that a certain situation is **necessarily real** and that this can be inferred from a set of facts. The modality involved here is thus a combination of **necessity** and **deduction**:

(1)   I expect she hates me, why shouldn't she, she *must* be sore as hell.

(2)   She *must* care a lot for him.

MUST is usually epistemic when followed by a statively used verb, as in the examples above, or a perfect or progressive form: *She must be travelling with Jim again / They must have left separately / He must have been dozing off.*
    Apart from positive declarative sentences (as in (1) and (2) above), we find epistemic MUST in *wh*-**interrogative sentences**:

(3)   What *must* it have been like in the Middle Ages, I wonder?

In *yes-no* **interrogative sentences**, on the other hand, MUST is very rare. Normally, epistemic necessity is here expressed by NEED:

(4)   *Need* this suggestion have any party political implications?

In **negative declarative sentences**, epistemic MUST is not used. Here, too, necessity is expressed by NEED:

(5)   It *needn't* affect the incidence of local taxation.

What sentences of this type express is that the situation described is 'not necessarily real', i.e. the semantic scope of NOT extends over the entire sentence and thus includes the necessity modal.

(ii) MUST is used **deontically** to express **compulsion**:

(6)   If the Labour Party disagrees with that assessment, it *must* give its reasons.

(7)   Your friends will be going and you *must* go with them.

When *you* is subject, as in (7), MUST is directive in meaning. In sentences where the subject is in the first person, the speaker appeals to herself, i.e. *I/we must* has the meaning of self-admonishment:

(8)   I *must* tell them that some other time, it's a separate story.

(9)   We *must* go round to Tim's place, at once, all of us.

Deontic examples of MUST in **interrogative sentences**:

(10)   *Must* I go back to school so soon?

(11)   But why *must* I sit here?

In *yes-no* **interrogative sentences** like (10), the speaker asks the hearer to decide a course of action for her. In *wh*-**interrogative sentences** like (11) the hearer is asked to explain the particular reason, place, time or identity of a directive. In some interrogative sentences with MUST where the subject is in the second person, the speaker indicates annoyance with the hearer:

(12)   *Must* you discuss all the time?

In interrogative sentences, compulsion may also be expressed by sentences with NEED, especially in *yes-no* questions:

(13)   *Need* I stay at home tonight?

The following examples illustrate the deontic use of MUST in **negative declarative sentences**:

(14)   You *mustn't* think that I don't understand your feelings, my dear.

(15)   You *mustn't* take me for an old fool with his head in the clouds.

In sentences of this type, the semantic scope of negation excludes the modal (e.g. (15) = 'it is **compulsory** that you do **not** take me for an old fool ...'). If the speaker wishes to describe a situation as 'not compulsory', i.e. with compulsion within the semantic scope of negation, she must select NEED:

(16)   And you *needn't* glare at me like that.

The semantic contrast between deontic MUST and NEED in negative sentences can thus be illustrated by examples like *You mustn't reply* (compulsory-not) and *You needn't reply* (not-compulsory).

A frequent alternative to MUST for the expression of epistemic necessity or deontic compulsion is HAVE TO:

(17)   There must/has to be a way out. (epistemic)

(18)   You must/have to do it at once. (deontic)

13.5.5. SHALL/SHOULD

Compared with the other modals **SHALL** is very rare, particularly in AmE. It is used **deontically** to express the speaker's **commitment** in declarative sentences with second or third person subjects (SHALL with first person subjects being a formal, infrequent substitute for the future form WILL):

(1)   You *shall* have your car back by Friday.

(2)   Our children *shan't* ever bother you again.

This use of SHALL is somewhat old-fashioned, and WILL is often used as a natural alternative, although it does not commit the speaker to the same degree as SHALL.

SHALL is also used deontically to express **weak compulsion**, though only in **interrogative sentences** with first person subjects:

(3)   *Shall* we go to the theatre?

(4)   Where *shall* I put it?

The meaning signalled by *Shall I/we* is here 'Do you want me/us to ...?' – a meaning more commonly expressed by *Would you like (me/us) to* or *Should I/we*, particularly in AmE.

In **declarative sentences**, the use of SHALL for deontic compulsion is only found with third person subjects to denote what is **legally mandatory**:

(5)   The tenant *shall* quietly possess and enjoy the premises during the tenancy without any interruption from the Landlord.

SHALL is never used epistemically.

SHOULD has both epistemic and deontic uses:

(i) When SHOULD is used **epistemically**, the speaker indicates that she expects the situation described to be real but does not feel absolutely certain, for example because the facts upon which her deduction is made may not be complete. The use of SHOULD to indicate such **tentative certainty** or **weakened necessity** can be illustrated by examples like:

(6)   They *should* have reached their destination by now.

(7)   You *should* be seeing my family tomorrow.

The epistemic use of SHOULD in **negative sentences** is illustrated by:

(8)   It *shouldn't* be difficult to get out.

Here the semantic scope of NOT excludes the necessity modal: the speaker expresses tentative certainty about 'it not being difficult to get out'.

SHOULD is common in the matrix of **conditional sentences**:

(9)   If you press that button, the engine *should* start.

and in conditional subclauses (with inversion) (see section 7.2.1):

(10)   *Should* you happen to be passing, do drop in.

A special use of epistemic SHOULD is found in examples like:

(11)   Well, it surprises me that Eileen *should* be surprised.
(12)   I can't think why he *should* have been angry.

SHOULD is here used for the expression of **report**, i.e. to signal that the speaker passes on something he has heard about and the truth of which he is therefore not committed to.

(ii) Deontic SHOULD is used with **non-past meaning** for the expression of **weakened compulsion**. What is indicated in this way is often no more than a **suggestion**:

(13)   Perhaps we *should* pay his mother a visit.
(14)   Etiquette demands that I *should* invite him.

As illustrated by (14), one context in which SHOULD of compulsion occurs is *that*-clauses after verbs, adjectives or nouns expressing demand, resolution, recommendation and the like (see the discussion in section 13.4.2 of the mandative subjunctive, which also occurs in this context).

The deontic use of SHOULD in **negative sentences** is illustrated by:

(15)   It shouldn't be supposed that Stone identifies with Socrates in any overt way.

Here the semantic scope of NOT excludes the modal: 'It is weakly compulsory not to suppose ....'.

Apart from the fact that it expresses compulsion tentatively, deontic SHOULD often differs from deontic MUST in indicating that the situation described is **morally desirable**:

(16)   A man shouldn't leave his home. Or he'll become a wanderer, a lost soul.

The meaning expressed by SHOULD – whether epistemic or deontic – can also be expressed by the semi-auxiliary OUGHT TO:

(17)   They should/ought to have arrived by now. (epistemic)
(18)   We should/ought to declare war on them right away. (deontic)

14. Nominals

14.1. Introduction

While verbals typically express types of situation, nominals typically express the **participants** involved in situations, e.g. AGENT, AFFECTED or INSTRU-MENT. The main communicative function of nominals is thus to code meaning as **things** (or 'entities') in a broad sense (concrete as well as abstract, animate as well as inanimate). This function is very composite, involving many different communicative subfunctions, such as determination and modification. This chapter examines the ways in which nominals enable the speaker to 'talk about things'.

14.1.1. The external relations of nominals

Nominals may assume the following functions:

S	*The restaurant* was crowded.
Od	I was drinking *vintage champagne.*
Oi	I finally told *Jack's wife* my little secret.
Cs	Most of the diners were *tourists.*
Co	We elected Irene *our first female director.*
A	*This time* the bastards won't get away with it.

In addition, nominals may serve as dependents (e.g. in noun, preposition and adjective groups) and as conjoints in compound units:

DEP	These *solar energy* schemes were proposed by *my boss.*
	The figure was *ten inches* tall.
CJT	*The organist* and *the photographer* were hired.

Note also that nominals may serve a number of communicative functions on their own, e.g. *Christ!* (exclamation) and *A book?* (question).

14.1.2. The internal structure of noun groups

By definition, nouns assume head function in noun groups. Dependents appear in either **pre-head** or **post-head** position. The following is an initial approximation to the structural potential of noun groups:

pre-H dependents	H	post-H dependents

Typical pre-H dependents include:

(i) articles (as in *a bed / an enemy / the boat*);

(ii) possessive pronouns and nominals in the genitive (as in *her book / my speech / John's pen / the old professor's office / my sister's new book*);

(iii) demonstrative, interrogative and relative pronouns (as in *this girl / those plays / which book / whose idea / what students*);

(iv) indefinite pronouns and quantifiers (as in *some sugar / any woman / no entry / every word / neither statement / many proposals / all the letters*);

(v) adjectivals (as in *excellent teachers / solar energy / a very interesting idea / a most original exhibition*);

(vi) present and past participles (as in *a dancing girl / rising prices / returned goods / a defeated enemy*);

(vii) nominals (as in *a development plan / university students / a civil rights movement / a fifth Middle East war*).

Occasionally we find the following as pre-H dependents:

(viii) adverbs (as in *the then king / the above examples / the in thing*);

(ix) complex group- and clause-like structures, the unity of which is usually marked by means of hyphenation (as in *a two-year-old boy / the latest Humphrey-for-President movement / a small, what-else-can-you-expect nod*).

As can be seen, pre-head dependents are usually determiners (as in *a bed / her book*) or modifiers (as in *excellent teachers / university students*).

Typical post-H dependents include:

(i) preposition groups (as in *a letter from my uncle / a rule of this kind / a town in Germany / a visit to my parents*);

(ii) relative clauses (as in *the letter which you wrote last night / John, who moved to Hove last year, / the film that you found so interesting*);

(iii) single or coordinated adjectivals (as in *the only stars visible / professors keen to take early retirement / the leaves, so soft and yellow.*);

(iv) nominals (as in *the meeting last night / the match next week / Jack Parker, my neighbour, / our new manager, the tall guy who just left, / the number six / my dear friend Richard*);

(v) present and past participles and participial clauses (as in *all the guests leaving / the prisoners deported / the colleagues remaining behind / some of the cars tested last month*);

(vi) infinitive groups or infinitive clauses (as in *any attempt <u>to move</u> / the decision <u>to break up the party</u>*);

(vii) non-relative *that*-clauses (as in *the fact <u>that she wants to leave</u> / the idea <u>that I should marry her</u> / the hope <u>that someone will step in and rescue her</u>*);

(viii) adverbals (as in *the meeting <u>inside</u> / the book <u>here</u> / the road <u>back</u>*).

As these examples show, the most common relationships between head and post-head dependent are modification (as in *a letter from my uncle*) and complementation (as in *any attempt to move*), cf. section 3.2. But it is also possible to find what may be referred to as **elaboratives**, i.e. dependents which enter an identity relation to the head but at the same time elaborate on the content of the head: *Jack Parker, my neighbour,* → 'Jack Parker = my neighbour', *the number six* → 'the number = six'. In some constructions with clausal elaboratives, the head noun serves primarily as a means to nominalize the content of the dependent clause: *the fact that she wants to leave* → 'the fact = she wants to leave', *the idea that I should marry her* → 'the idea = I should marry her'. In such constructions the head noun is always abstract (other examples: ANSWER, BELIEF, CHANCE, CLAIM, NEWS, POSSIBIL-ITY, PROPOSAL, SUGGESTION).

Post-head parenthetical dependents, i.e. dependents which are separated from the head by means of intonation or commas, are called **appositional** (e.g. *Jack Parker, <u>my neighbour,</u> / John, <u>who moved to Hove last year,</u>*).

14.1.3. The functional structure of nominals

Nominals enable speakers to code what they want to talk about **as things** with the degree of specificity required for their communicative purposes: speakers encode meaning in nominals in the shape of things and listeners decode such constituents accordingly. Nominals are used for a variety of more specific communicative functions, such as to **identify** specific things:

(1)   *The restaurant* was crowded.

(2)   *The bastards* won't get away with it.

or to **mention** 'type of thing':

(3)   I told her I wanted *an apple*.

(4)   *Teachers who work overtime* must be very idealistic.

or to **describe** an already identified thing:

(5)   Most of the diners were *Japanese tourists*.

(6)   Rose is *a very good student*.

or to **specify** the 'situation' expressed by the verb in examples of syntactic and semantic fusion between predicator and object (cf. section 8.6):

(7)   The meeting took *place* yesterday. (*took place* = 'happened')

(8)   We caught *sight* of her. (*caught sight of* = 'saw', 'sighted')

In all these examples the italicized nominals code meaning as things, but the things coded are used for different communicative purposes.

To understand how nominals are used, it is important to examine the contribution of each constituent part of nominals to the overall function of expressing things. The following chart provides the point of departure for a description of the relationship between communicative function (shaded cells) and internal constituent structure (white cells):

expression of meaning as things		
pre-H	H	post-H

There are two regular communicative subfunctions of pre-head dependents: **determination** and **modification** (cf. section 3.2). These subfunctions can be thought of in terms of **zones** in the noun group arranged more specifically in the following order:

determination	modification	H	post-H

Determination is realized by articles, pronouns and genitive constructions, while modification is chiefly realized by adjectivals:

determination	modification	H	post-H
the	little	girl	with the shy smile
this	very dull	visit	to her parents
no	additional	staffing,	academic or secretarial,
my	best	student,	who left school early,
the	sudden	death	of my father

The communicative subfunction of the head of a noun group is to provide a close lexical match for the referent of the construction. The head thus represents the referent as a member of a **category** of the things, persons, etc. In e.g. *the little girl with the shy smile*, the head noun *girl* categorizes the person referred to as a girl (rather than as e.g. a woman, a boy or a man). The functional nucleus of the noun group is thus **categorization**:

determination	modification	categorization	post-H

Post-head dependents are used for a variety of communicative functions: determination, modification, categorization and complementation (see section 3.2). Thus, for example, in *the sudden death of my father*, the post-head dependent *of my father* is determinative in conjunction with the definite article (cf. *my father's sudden death*, where *my father's* is pre-head determination). In *the little girl with the shy smile*, the post-head preposition group *with the shy smile* is clearly a modifier on a par with *little*, describing the head noun *girl*. In *no additional staffing, academic or secretarial*, the post-head compound unit *academic or secretarial* offers a subcategorization of the head noun *staff*. And finally, in *this very dull visit to her parents*, the post-head preposition group *to her parents* serves as complementation to the head noun *visit*. These many post-head functions do not often co-occur and therefore do not represent well-established zones. This account thus operates simply with one post-head **multi-functional** zone:

determination	modification	categorization	(multi-functional)

One important communicative function – related mainly, but not exclusively, to the head and pre-head constituents – is **quantification**. It is natural that quantification should play a central role: when we talk about things it is often essential to signal their quantity. In any discussion of quantification, a distinction must be drawn between **countable** and **non-countable** things. Countable things are things that are thought of as something we can count: cars, houses, books, records, etc. Non-countable things are things that are thought of as masses of some sort and which we do not usually count (though there are other ways of measuring them): water, flour, sand, sugar, etc. Countable things are indivisible while non-countable things are divisible in the following sense: we can divide water into parts, each part still being water, but a car cannot be divided into parts and each part be regarded as a car by itself. The singular/plural distinction in nouns referring to countable entities (e.g. *boy/boys, girl/girls, man/men, woman/women*, etc.) is at the very heart of quantification but by no means the only way of expressing this communicative subfunction (which also involves non-countable concepts: one can talk about more or less water, flour, sand, sugar, etc.). Here are some examples:

(9)   *These ten books* are far too expensive.
(10)   *A short meeting* took place last night.
(11)   She complained about *my numerous girlfriends*.
(12)   *Some students* seem to think that life is a bowl of cherries.
(13)   It took *little effort* to finish the job.
(14)   *Students in great numbers* have cancelled their participation.

As these examples show, quantification is often expressed in connection with determination (*These, A, Some*) and categorization (singular *meeting* and plural *books, girlfriends, students*) but sometimes also in connection with modification (*short, numerous, ten, little, in great numbers*).

The following chart summarizes our discussion so far of the functional structure of the nominal:

expression of meaning as things			
quantification			
determination	modification	categorization	(multi-functional)

The rest of this chapter is devoted to a discussion of categorization (in section 14.2), determination (in section 14.3) and quantification (in section 14.4). Modification will be examined more closely in chapter 16 on adjectivals.

14.2. Categorization

14.2.1. What's in a head?

The central categorizing unit in the noun group is the head. As has been seen, the head typically consists of just a noun. However, there are cases where two or more root forms that function independently in other circumstances seem to constitute a single lexical item as head, a **compound**:

(1)   We are now approaching the *airport*.
(2)   She simply adored her *mother-in-law*.
(3)   Have you met our new *dancing master*?
(4)   He takes a professional interest in the human *nervous system*.

In writing, the unitary status of these items is sometimes indicated by absence of an empty space or by hyphenation, as in (1) and (2). In speech, compounds consisting of two elements typically take main stress on their first element, i.e. they are pronounced with so-called **unitary stress**. Thus *'dancing ,master* (= master of dancing) contrasts with the syntactic group *,dancing 'master* (= master engaged in dancing), and the first element of *'nervous ,system* contrasts with the first element in the group *,nervous 'girls*. Sometimes, as in *French teacher*, stress is criterial for the classification of a word as either a noun or an adjective: with unitary stress on the first element (*'French ,teacher*), *French* is a noun forming a part of a compound with the meaning 'teacher of French'; with main stress on the second element (*,French 'teacher*), it is a premodifying adjective denoting the nationality of the referent of the head noun.

It is sometimes convenient to treat orthographically complex units as heads because they are fixed collocations, often resisting internal analysis, e.g. **names**, **titles**, and combinations of titles and names:

(5)   *Randi White*, our new headmaster, had also been busy.

(6)   Christie's *"Ten Little Niggers"* is a detective story with no detective.

(7)   My dear *Professor White*, what can I do for you?

Note also the following phrases, which, superficially, seem to consist of a noun plus a postmodifying adjective (typically of French origin): *court martial, heir apparent, Secretary General, devil incarnate, body politic, Poet Laureate, president elect*, etc. Unlike most other combinations of nouns and adjectives, these collocations are syntactically fixed and receive main stress on the adjective. It seems most appropriate to view them as compounds.

Disregarding the problem posed by compounds, heads in noun groups are fairly easy to identify. Thus when noun groups function as subject, the number of the head (singular or plural) governs subject-predicator concord:

(8a)   A *cup* of coffee *is* surely more expensive than a cup of tea.

(8b)   Two *cups* of coffee *are* surely more expensive than two cups of tea.

While this criterion is in general very reliable – even in cases where the head is not necessarily the most important word – there are occasionally factors (such as e.g. attraction, cf. section 11.4) which interfere with this neat regular pattern. One phenomenon in particular requires mention here: sometimes what looks like, and may well be analysed as, the **syntactic head** does not in fact determine subject-predicator concord directly, cf.:

(9)   A *lot* of milk *was* needed.

(10)   A *lot* of eggs *were* needed.

In these examples concord seems to be governed by a part of the post-head constituent (*milk* and *eggs*, respectively). If the criterion of subject-predicator concord being governed by the head of the subject noun group is adhered to, *a lot of* has to be analysed as a pre-head constituent (e.g. a quantifier on a par with *many* and *much*), which is syntactically awkward. A similar problem is posed by phrases like *plenty of, lots of, the rest of, the remainder of, a number of*. The term **number-transparent** is sometimes used for these expressions: they let the number of the whole nominal be determined by what is syntactically part of a post-head constituent, thus in effect assuming number according to group-internal context.

Number-transparency sometimes affects determiner use in constructions with *kind of* or *sort of*: e.g. *these sort of theories, those sort of people*, etc.

The noun NUMBER itself is number-transparent when it has a quantifying meaning (typically with the indefinite article, as in e.g. *a number of students were present*). When it is used about a particular number **as a number** it behaves like other nouns (typically with the definite article as in e.g. *the number of students enrolled has gone up a bit since we last talked*).

14.2.2. Gender

In English most nouns with human or animate referents are **common gender** in that they refer equally well to male and female members of the class: e.g. DRIVER, DOCTOR, EDITOR, FOOL, FRIEND, HELPER, INMATE, MUSIC-IAN, NEIGHBOUR, READER, STUDENT, TEACHER, etc.

In some cases, English has one term for female referents, another for male referents and a third for referents of either sex, e.g.:

FATHER	MOTHER	PARENT
SON	DAUGHTER	CHILD
BOY	GIRL	CHILD
KING	QUEEN	MONARCH
BROTHER	SISTER	SIBLING
RAM	EWE	SHEEP
STALLION	MARE	HORSE

The male/female distinction is often expressed by unrelated words, as in the trios above (cf. also UNCLE/AUNT, GENTLEMAN/LADY, MONK/NUN, BACHELOR/SPINSTER, etc.). Occasionally, however, the distinction is expressed morphologically (with -*ess* as the most common suffix), e.g.:

HERO	HEROINE
ACTOR	ACTRESS
LION	LIONESS

MASTER	MISTRESS
GOD	GODDESS

In these examples, the male term is basic and the female term derived. There are few exceptions to this dominant pattern:

WIDOWER	WIDOW
BRIDEGROOM	BRIDE

In some cases of related male and female terms, the male term may be used as a unisex term, especially in contexts where the male/female distinction is irrelevant:

LION	LIONESS
TIGER	TIGRESS
JEW	JEWESS

In such cases, the male term is actually semantically unmarked while the female term is semantically marked (positively female). This means that the male term is only explicitly masculine when there is an overt contrast involved (as in e.g. *I saw both a lion and a lioness*). Otherwise, the male term has unisex reference (as in e.g. *He shot three lions the other day*). In the following examples, the female is the unmarked term, having either feminine or unisex reference, while the male term is explicitly masculine:

DRAKE	DUCK
GANDER	GOOSE
DRONE	BEE

The male term MAN is special in denoting either 'mankind' in general (thus including women, as in e.g. *All men are equal*) or simply 'male members of the human race' (as in *Men are generally taller than women* and *These men are exceptionally tall*).

When MAN forms a part of a compound, it sometimes denotes male (as in MANSERVANT, BUSINESSMAN, DOORMAN), sometimes it has unisex reference (as in MANSLAUGHTER, SPOKESMAN, STATESMAN, CHAIR-MAN). But there is a tendency to avoid using MAN compounds about women: CHAIRPERSON, STATESWOMAN, SPOKESWOMAN.

In addition to MAN and WOMAN, MALE and FEMALE are often used to specify sex in neutral nouns: *male/female reader*, *male/female driver*, etc. Note also: *gentleman friend, lady friend, boy friend, girl friend, maid-servant*.

Note finally that special compounds are sometimes used of animals to specify sex: COCK-PHEASANT / HEN-PHEASANT, JACKASS / JENNY-ASS, BILLY-GOAT / NANNY-GOAT, TOM-CAT / TABBY-CAT.

14.2.3. Types of nouns and referents

It is important, first of all, to clarify the terms **referent** and **reference**. Both terms are used in a fairly broad sense: referent about the thing coded in an expression and reference about the communicative function of establishing something as a referent. Thus, for example, when a speaker says *I bought a new car yesterday*, the car that she bought is the referent and *a new car* is a referring expression, and the link between them is one of reference. In other words, 'referent' refers to the nature of the thing expressed, 'reference' to how language is used to actually encode things.

Central to the notion of categorization are the following main kinds of referents: **unique**, **generic** and **class-member** referents. Though, from a strictly objective point of view, every thing in the world is unique in some sense, human beings tend to classify things sharing one or more similarities as belonging to the same **type** or **class**. Thus apart from persons or entities that are recognized as unique (such as Peter Schmeichel, Paris, Spain, etc.), there are cars, bikes, books, trees, etc. Every car is, strictly speaking, unique and yet the noun CAR can be used to refer to a fascinating range of vehicles. Any particular car is thus a member of the class of things which may be appropriately referred to by the noun CAR. Most of the examples offered so far in this chapter are examples of class-member referents in this sense: the (head) noun is used to refer to one or more particular things that may be conceived as members of a class of things which may be appropriately referred to by using the noun. For example, in an expression like *I found the dissertation in the top drawer*, the referent of the direct object *the dissertation* may be understood as 'a (specific) member of the class of things appropriately termed *dissertation*'; and in an expression like *I want an apple, please*, the referent of *an apple* may be understood as 'a (non-specific) member of the class of things appropriately termed *apple*'. Whether specific or non-specific, the referent is viewed as an instance of a more general **kind** or **type** of thing (dissertations, apples).

Significantly, instead of referring to individual class members, one can choose to refer to the kind or type in question as such: e.g. *The lion is no longer common in this part of India* and *Children need a lot of attention*. Here *The lion* refers to a kind of animal, a species (in contrast to an example like *Jack killed the lion with his spear*, which refers to a particular member of the class of lions), and *Children* refers to the whole class of children (in contrast to *The children missed their parents after only a few hours*, which refers to a group of particular children). In both cases we have a so-called generic referent.

Corresponding to the semantic distinction between unique referents and non-unique (generic or class-member) referents there is the form distinction between **proper nouns** and **common nouns**. Proper nouns are capitalized, and with their central function – that of naming – they are fairly restricted with respect to determination and quantification: *Mary, Sweden, London, the Hebrides, *a Mary, *the Sweden, *some Londons, *these Hebrides*. Common nouns, by contrast, are fairly unrestricted with respect to determination and quantification: *a/the/these/some train/trains, a/the/these/some pencil/pencils*, etc. The distinction between generic and class-member referents is also grammatically relevant. It is not, however, reflected in different classes of nouns but, as we shall see, in the use of determiners.

There is no strict one-to-one correspondence between unique referents and proper nouns, on the one hand, and between non-unique referents and common nouns on the other. We may distinguish between **proper nouns** and **names**. Proper nouns are typically, though far from inevitably, used as names (e.g. *Jack, Germany*, etc.). But names may consist, wholly or partially, of common nouns: e.g. *High Street, Congress, the Copenhagen Business School, London Bridge, Mother, Uncle*, etc. And when not used simply for naming, proper nouns are far more unrestricted with respect to determination and quantification:

(1)   He can be a real *Sylvester Stallone* sometimes.

(2)   It was good fun to watch all the young *Peter Schmeichels* practising.

In these examples, the proper noun expressions *all the young Peter Schmeichels* and *a real Sylvester Stallone* have class-member referents rather than unique referents, assigning to their referents certain ambitions, qualities, status or behaviour that we associate with the bearer of the name.

14.2.4. Countability

The referents of common nouns are subject to a further distinction between **countable** and **non-countable**. Nouns whose referents are conceived of as something individualized which can be counted are called **count nouns** whereas nouns whose referents are conceived of as something unindividualized which we cannot count (or simply do not count) are called **mass nouns**. Here are some examples of count nouns: BOOK, WINDOW, CAR, PENCIL, HOUSE, IDEA, FRIEND, etc. And here are some examples of mass nouns: WATER, SAND, BUTTER, MILK, RICE, MONEY, FURNITURE, ADVICE, NEWS, etc. The possible referents of most of these are obviously non-countable but, strictly speaking, e.g. rice and money are countable. In English, however, the nouns RICE and MONEY are mass nouns by convention.

Count nouns allow of quantification in terms of the singular/plural distinction (e.g. *book/books, window/windows,* etc.) and are thus compatible with pronominal determiners and quantifiers like *some, more, many, few, several,* etc. and incompatible with *much* and *less: many ideas, few movements, *much computers, ?less schools* (the not infrequent use of *less* in connection with count nouns, as in *less schools, less problems,* etc., is generally considered colloquial). Mass nouns, by contrast, allow of direct quantification only in terms of pronominal determiners and quantifiers: the singular/plural distinction does not apply to mass nouns. They are compatible with *much, less, little, some* and *more* but not with *many, several, few* and *one* or with the indefinite article *a(n): much water, less wine, little sand, *few furniture / *a furniture / *many furnitures.*

However, mass nouns, whether concrete or abstract, may be quantified more indirectly in **partitive *of*-constructions** preceded by a quantified count-noun: *two pints of bitter, a cup of coffee, many bottles of wine, few bowls of rice, several slices of bread, an acre of land, a word of advice, a fit of passion, an attack of pneumonia,* etc. In some such partitive expressions there is a very close relation between the head count noun and the quantified mass noun: *a suit of armour, a tankard of beer, a sheet of paper, a clove of garlic; a stroke of luck, a pang of remorse, a flash of lightning.* Note that count nouns may be quantified in a similar fashion: *a page of a book,* etc. Very similar to **quantity partition** is **quality partition** as in *a new kind of butter* and *a new generation of computers.*

It is important to note that the distinction between count nouns and mass nouns is somewhat blurred, grammatically speaking. Many nouns are used equally well as count nouns (for bounded entities) and mass nouns (for unbounded material or concept), e.g. STONE, COCONUT and CONVICTION:

(1a)   He found *three stones.*

(1b)   The figure was of *stone.*

(2a)   There were *coconuts* everywhere on the beach.

(2b)   The worshippers bought *coconut* and flowers for their offerings.

(3a)   He acted in accordance with his *convictions.*

(3b)   It appeared to be the result of blind *conviction.*

Many nouns that primarily behave like count nouns are sometimes used the way mass nouns are used, and vice versa:

(4)   Everything was grimy under a low ceiling of grey *cloud.*

(5)   One black sock had sagged to reveal a section of bare *leg.*

(6)   There was enough *moon* now to silver the minarets outside.

(7)   This is actually *an* excellent *wine.*

(8)   He imports *several coffees* from Africa.

(9)   Over the years she did me *many kindnesses*.

(10)   *Two coffees*, please.

When typical count nouns, such as CLOUD, LEG and MOON, are used like mass nouns (as in (4) to (6)), the speaker or writer emphasizes the **material**, **character** or **concept** of the referent rather than simply the referent as a bounded entity (thus e.g. *moon* in (6) gets very close in meaning to MOONLIGHT). Conversely, when typical mass nouns are used like count nouns, as in (7) to (10), the expression either has **sub-generic reference**, i.e. it denotes a subclass of a class, as in (7) and (8) (*an excellent wine = an excellent kind of wine, several coffees = several kinds of coffee*), or it denotes **instances** or **realizations** of the non-countable entity (*many kindnesses = e.g. many acts of kindness, two coffees = two cups of coffee*) as in (9) and (10).

The concept of countability does not usually apply to proper nouns functioning as **names**: they are neither count nouns nor mass nouns. Though names are either formally singular (e.g. *John Wilson, London, France*) or, less often, formally plural (e.g. *the Hebrides, General Motors*), we do not immediately conceive of their referents as countable, or even quantifiable. However, like count nouns, names typically have individualized referents. With a more extensive function than simply naming, proper nouns readily accept quantification: *all the young Peter Schmeichels, a real Sylvester Stallone*, etc. But there are also examples of proper nouns retaining their status as names despite the association of countability:

(11)   Have you invited *the Wilsons* to stay with us?

(12)   Is there *a Sarah Mortimer* staying at this hotel?

Here *the Wilsons* means 'the Wilson family' and *a Sarah Mortimer* means 'a certain Sarah Mortimer or 'someone called Sarah Mortimer'. In both cases there is a clear sense of uniqueness despite the explicit quantification. Consider finally examples like:

(13)   *How many Peters* are there in this department?

(14)   We play badminton on *Mondays*.

Here the proper noun expressions *Peters* and *Mondays* have referents actually called 'Peter' and 'Monday', respectively (and thus differ from the proper noun expressions *Peter Schmeichels* and *a real Sylvester Stallone*). Such examples combine classmembership and uniqueness by referring to 'unique but recurring phenomena'. What these examples also show is that there is a grey zone between common nouns and proper nouns, and that this affects the question of countability.

14.3. Determination

14.3.1. Types of determiner

Determiners are used to signal the kind of reference involved in the expression of a nominal. There are four main subcategories of determination:

(i) Definite determination. There are four form types realizing definite determination: a) the definite article *the* (as in *the* doctor, *the* bright girls); b) the demonstrative pronouns *this, that, these, those* (as in *this* bicycle, *those* bastards); c) the possessive pronouns *my, your, his, her, its, our* and *their* (as in *my* wedding, *his* student days); and d) genitive nominals (as in *Jack's* truck, *my old father's* idea). To these types of definite determination we may add *such*, which is a demonstrative-like qualitative pronoun with subgeneric meaning: *such* misery, *such* students.

(ii) Indefinite determination. There are three form types expressing indefinite determination: a) the indefinite article *a(n)* (as in *a* new hall, *an* arrogant journalist); b) zero (Ø) (as in _ professors, _ sugar); c) the indefinite pronouns *any, no, each, every, either, neither, some* (as in *any* suggestion, *no* joy, *either* way, *some* girl(s)). To these indefinite determiners we may add *one* as an emphatic alternative to the indefinite article and *another*, which combines the indefinite article *an* and the modifier *other* (cf. the definite counterpart, which is in two words: *the other*).

(iii) Interrogative determination. Interrogative determination is used to form a question about the head. There are three interrogative pronouns which may serve a determinative function: *which, what* and *whose* (as in *Which* book do you prefer? / *What* colour did she suggest? / *Whose* key is this?).

(iv) Relative determination. *Which, what* and *whose* may also serve as relative determiners (as in Her visitor left at four o'clock, by *which* time the FBI had already arrived / He enjoyed *what* wine was left / The boy *whose* bike was stolen knocked on my door). In addition one finds emphatic *whichever* and *whatever* (as in Whichever book you choose I am sure your parents will approve / Whatever solution he comes up with she will support him). Relative determination by *which* and *whose* is used to relate the head to a preceding constituent, while *What(ever)* and *whichever* are **independent** of other constituents (cf. section 15.3.3 [B.c])).

14.3.2. Co-occurring determiners: pre- and postdeterminers

Determiners are normally in complementary distribution: the selection of one precludes the selection of another. There are, however, certain exceptions:

(i) *such* may precede the indefinite article plus singular count noun (as in *such a fool*, *such a good idea*);

(ii) *what*, too, may precede the indefinite article plus singular count noun to form an exclamative expression (as in *What a fool! / What a good idea!*);

(iii) possessive pronouns and genitive constructions may be followed by *every* plus a singular count noun as an emphatic alternative to an expression with the quantifier *all* plus a plural count noun (compare *the old man's every move / all the old man's moves*, *her every wish / all her wishes*);

(iv) *such* occasionally follows a determinative indefinite pronoun (as in *no such luck*, *any such move*, *each such development*, *some such problem*);

(v) in elevated, rhetorical speech, possessive pronouns sometimes follow demonstrative pronouns (as in e.g. *On this his last day in office he visited his predecessor*). One possible analysis of this kind of construction, however, is to say that the possessive pronoun specifies the demonstrative pronoun non-restrictively.

The following chart summarizes the possible collocations of determiners:

DETERMINERS: pre- central post-			EXAMPLES
such *what*	indefinite article		*such a fool* *what a fool*
	genitive constructions possessive pronouns	*every*	*Jack's every move* *her every wish*
	indefinite pronouns	*such*	*any such luck*
	(demonstrative pronouns)	(possessive pronouns)	*(this his last day)*

What and *such* are **predeterminers** when they precede the indefinite article and *every*, *such* and possessive pronouns are **postdeterminers** when they follow other determiners. All other determiners are **central determiners**.

14.3.3. Determiners and quantifiers

Determiners are inextricably linked up with **quantifiers**. Thus, obviously, demonstrative pronouns are either singular (*this, that*) or plural (*these, those*) in concord with the head noun, and the indefinite article (as well as its emphatic alternative *one*) is used only with singular count nouns (in contrast to Ø, which is used with plural count nouns and with mass nouns). Also the indefinite determiners *any, no, each, every, either, neither, some* have a more or less clear association of quantification about them: in some of their central uses they add different nuances of quantifying meaning to the basic indefinite class-member or mass referents of the noun group as a whole. Of the indefinite determiners, *no* and *some* are the ones with the clearest association of quantification: *no* means 'absence of quantity' and *some* means 'indefinite, undefined amount or number of'. At the same time, however, *no* and *some* are clear determiners. When followed by e.g. a singular count noun, *no* is the negative form of the indefinite article (= *'not a(n)'*); compare:

(1)   There is *a pen* in the top drawer / There is *no pen* in the top drawer.

When followed by e.g. a plural count noun, *some* is the plural equivalent of the indefinite article in noun groups with class-member reference; compare:

(2)   I met *a professor* in London / I met *some professors* in London.

Some thus supplements Ø, which in connection with plural count nouns often signals generic reference; compare:

(3)   *Professors* like poetry / *Some professors* like poetry.

While *any, no, each, every, either, neither* and *some* are primarily determiners with an association of quantification, other indefinite pronouns and numerals are primarily quantifiers with an association of determination: e.g. *both, all, half, one, many, five, second*, etc. Note that unlike the indefinite pronouns listed as determiners above, all these items are compatible with both definite and indefinite reference: *both girls / both the girls; all cars / all the cars; half a bottle / half the bottle; one case / the one case; many books / the many books; five calls / the five calls; the second attempt / a second attempt.* While many of these items may occur in constructions without genuine determiners, they can all co-occur with central determiners. Like predeterminers, the following quantifiers may precede central determiners:

(i) Both, all, half: these three quantifiers may precede definite central determiners (the definite article, demonstrative pronouns and genitive/possessive constructions). They can also function as heads in pronoun groups with a very similar meaning; compare: *all the soldiers / all of the soldiers; half the money / half of the money; both these solutions / both of these* *solutions*. Unlike the two others, *half* may precede the indefinite article in connection with head nouns expressing quantity or measurement: *half a pound, half a mile, half a pint, half an inch.*

(ii) Multipliers: *double, twice, three times*, etc. may precede definite central determiners (just like *both, all* and *half*): *double the average, twice his income, three times this amount*. In expressions of frequency where the head noun expresses a standard against which the frequency is determined, *once, twice* and expressions with *times* (e.g. *three times*) may precede the indefinite article or the indefinite pronouns *every* or *each*: *once a week, twice each month, three times every fortnight.*

(iii) Fractions: *two-thirds, one-fifth*, etc. may precede the definite article (e.g. *two-thirds the amount*) or serve as group heads followed by an *of*-construction (e.g. *two-thirds of his salary*).

Many quantifiers may follow central determiners: **cardinal numbers** (*his one objection / these two claims*), **ordinal numbers and other ordinals** (*her second car / the next meeting*), as well as certain other items (*the many problems / John's few attempts*); for further discussion see section 16.2.3.

14.3.4. Referential orientation

There are two ways in which it is relevant to speak of **types of reference** (as distinct from types of referents, cf. section 14.2.3): a) types relating to the question of 'referential orientation' of referring expressions (i.e. the question of where to look for a referent), and b) types relating to the relationship between referring expression and type of referent (e.g. 'definite specific reference' = reference to a specific referent by means of a definite nominal). In this section the former typology is examined, the latter being left to the discussion of the use of the articles in sections 14.3.5-7.

Two main referential orientations can be distinguished. There is often reference to something mentioned elsewhere in the (spoken or written) text: this is called **textual (or endophoric) reference** (note that 'text' and 'textual' are to be understood to include not only written language but also spoken language). But there can also be reference to something in the extralinguistic, non-textual context, i.e. something in some real or fictional world: we call that **non-textual (or exophoric) reference**. Examples of non-textual reference:

(1)   Will you pass *the salt*, please.
(2)   There's *an apple* in the basket.
(3)   Hurry up, or you will run into *their security guard*.

(4)   *The sun* set about half an hour later.

These examples are perfectly well-formed even if there is no other mention of the referents in the preceding or following text. The context may be very **specific**, as in (1) to (3), where the referent is close by and can be manipulated in one way or another, or it may be very general, as in (4), where the referent is a natural phenomenon on which human existence depends, and thus actually part of any context if only very implicitly.

There are two main types of textual reference: **anaphoric** and **cataphoric** reference. Anaphoric reference is **backward** reference to a preceding textual unit (called the **antecedent**), whereas cataphoric reference is **forward** reference to a following unit (there is no appropriate traditional name for this unit, but let us call it **postcedent**). Here are some examples of textual reference (in which the antecedent/postcedent is indicated in curly brackets):

(5)   {A man} and a woman entered. *The man* was wearing a tie.

(6)   If *the movement* is to preserve its appeal, {radical feminism} must realize that the ideological climate has changed.

Textual reference, both anaphoric and cataphoric, may or may not cut across the sentence boundary: in example (6) the relation is **intrasentential**, in example (5) it is **extrasentential**.

Anaphoric reference is **repetitive** if the head noun of the referring group is identical with the head noun of the antecedent, otherwise it is **non-repetitive**. Thus while (5) above is an example of repetitive anaphoric reference, the following sentences are examples of non-repetitive anaphoric reference:

(7)   {A man and a woman} were sitting on the bench; *the couple* seemed to be very much in love.

(8)   For several weeks I avoided {Roger}. I couldn't bear to see his gleeful face. God, how I hated *the bastard*.

Cataphoric reference is always non-repetitive (cf. example (6)).

Non-repetitive anaphoric reference is either **direct** or **indirect** (repetitive reference is always direct). The examples looked at so far are instances of direct reference in the sense that the expression under analysis establishes (repetitively or non-repetitively) exactly the same entity as the antecedent. With indirect reference, the expression establishes a referent which is related to, but not identical with, the antecedent. The antecedent provides a background against which the existence of the referent of the expression under analysis may be recognized or accepted, as in:

(9)   It was {a wide ditch}, and when they crept up to *the edge* and looked into it they could see it was also deep, and there were many rocks at *the bottom*.

The italicized noun groups are examples of indirect anaphoric reference with *a very wide ditch* as the antecedent: *the edge* and *the bottom* are to be understood precisely as 'the edge of the ditch' and 'the bottom of the ditch', respectively.

The following chart summarizes the types of reference identified above in connection with referential orientation:

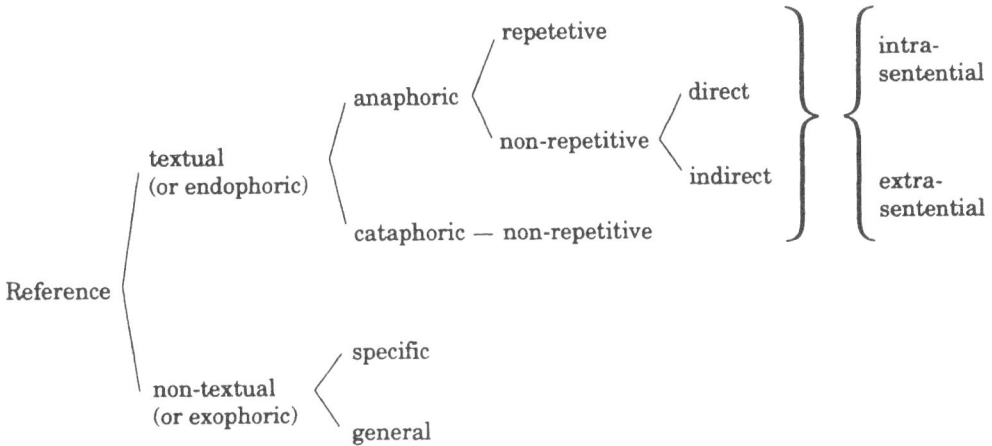

```
                                                repetetive                        intra-
                                anaphoric                         direct          sentential
                 textual                        non-repetitive
                 (or endophoric)                                  indirect        extra-
                                                                                  sentential
                                cataphoric — non-repetitive

Reference

                                specific
                 non-textual
                 (or exophoric)
                                general
```

14.3.5. The definite article

The definite article is a central determiner which typically singles out or delimits the referent of the noun group relative to the communicative context. It has the following more specific uses:

A) Definite specific reference. In its most central use, the definite article is used by the speaker in connection with common nouns to indicate that he expects the listener to be able to single out a particular referent, typically on the basis of a **shared familiarity**. For example, if someone says: *Have you seen the kettle?*, the speaker signals that he expects the kettle in question to be familiar to the listener. If the speaker thinks that the listener may not know about the kettle, he will use the indefinite article: *Have you seen a kettle around here somewhere?* If the speaker thinks that the listener has some knowledge of the possible referents of the noun KETTLE but not enough to recognize the particular kettle in question, he will supply what information he deems necessary for the listener to do so. In other words, he will **establish** a shared familiarity, e.g.:

(1)   Have you seen the kettle *that I borrowed from Sally*?
(2)   Have you seen the kettle *with the broken handle*?
(3)   Have you seen the *new* kettle?

In other words, by using the definite article the speaker signals that he will provide the listener with enough information to figure out what the speaker is talking about. The degree of precision with which the listener is expected by the speaker to recognize the referent may vary contextually. In some cases, the definite article merely signals a plea for the listener's acceptance of the existence of a particular referent. For example, in a case like *It turned out that John had been to the same school as Max*, the speaker expects no more of the listener than her ready acceptance of the existence of a particular school to which both John and Max used to go. Similarly, in an example like *The winner of the race will receive $1,000*, though at present there is no specific referent of the subject group, the definite article indicates that at some point there will be.

Definite specific reference is possible with all four main kinds of nouns (common count singular, common count plural, common mass, proper):

(4)   Dan argued that Owen truly adored *the school*.

(5)   *The girls next door* were doing their homework.

(6)   She passed him *the sugar*.

(7)   I want *the two Peters* in this class to report to Mr Wilson.

Characteristically, definite specific reference picks the referent out as one or more particular members of a class (as in examples (4), (5) and (7)) or as particular, limited 'sub-mass' (as in example (6)). In each case, however, there is a clear implication that, **in context**, the referent is unique (if the noun is singular) or all-inclusive (if the noun is plural). Thus in the context of example (4) there is only one school to which the expression *the school* may apply and in the context of example (5), all and only the girls next door are included in the referent of *The girls next door*.

Reference to specific limitations or specific bounded instances of non-countable entities such as e.g. 'love', 'life', 'nature', 'goodness', 'tyranny', 'art', 'materialism', 'mud', 'water', 'rice' etc. requires the definite article; compare:

(8)   He studied *architecture* / He studied *the architecture of the Roman Empire*.

(9)   *Life* is sweet / *The new life she gave me* was so exciting.

Non-specific limitation of a generic referent is often possible without the definite article, as in:

(8')   He studied *Roman architecture*.

The result of such limitation is sub-generic reference: in (8') the referent 'Roman architecture' is a subtype of 'architecture'.

B) Generic reference. In the singular, generic expressions may take the definite article:

(10) He took a professional interest in *the diesel engine.*

(11) *The funnel-web spider* is common in New South Wales.

To use a singular count noun representatively for the whole class or kind in this way is somewhat more formal than to use indefinite plural expressions (e.g. *diesel engines, funnel-web spiders*). With musical instruments and dances, however, the definite singular noun group is the usual expression:

(12) She plays *the guitar* and *the lute.*

(13) Jack absolutely hates to dance *the foxtrot.*

In the plural, generic reference is typically indefinite: *diesel engines* ('all engines'). Normally the definite article is used only when there is reference to national or ethnic groups (e.g. *the Russians, the Europeans, the Blacks,* etc.).

C) **Unique reference.** Since names have unique referents, they usually lack the definite article (*Jack, London, France, Europe, Carlsberg,* etc.). There are, however, a number of exceptions to this rule:

(i) Some geographical names, especially plural names of regions, archipelagos and mountain ranges, take the definite article: e.g. *the Hague, the Tyrol, the Sahara, the Ukraine; the Americas, the Orkneys, the Alps.* The same applies to names of seas, rivers and canals: *the Pacific, the Atlantic, the Thames, the Nile, the Suez Canal,* etc. The article is dropped in a river name if it is part of the name of a town (as in *Newcastle-on-Tyne*) or if it is part of an enumeration (as in *a network of canals, connecting Humber, Severn, Mersey and Thames*).

(ii) Names of hotels, restaurants, clubs, cinemas, theatres, major buildings, journals, newspapers and ships often require the definite article: *the Imperial, the Hungry Monk, the Savoy, the Taj Mahal, The Times, the Estonia,* etc.

(iii) Some titles of persons: *the Queen of Denmark, the Reverend Roger Smith, the President of the United States, the Marquess of Salisbury,* etc.

(iv) Proper nouns used as names may take the definite article if they are modified to express a certain aspect or version of the referent: *the young Churchill* (= 'Churchill as a young man' / 'Churchill Junior' **or** 'Churchill, who was a young man' (depending on *young* being restrictive or non-restrictive)), *the real Spain, the famous Mick Jagger,* etc. Expression like *the young Churchill* and *the famous Mick Jagger* may also be interpreted to refer restrictively to particular bearers of these names in contrast to other bearers of the same name, e.g. someone called Churchill who is not young and someone called Mick Jagger who is not famous. The article may be dropped if the group assumes the status of a new name (as in *Merry Old England*) or if the adjective is non-restrictive (especially in journalism):

(14)   The fall is that of *famed Niagara*, the roar awe-inspiring.

(15)   When Jess Conrad kissed *11-year-old Susan, pretty Yvonne Bell* broke down.

(v) Proper nouns used for specific, limited (typically restrictively modified) class-member reference:

(16)   Stockholm is *the Venice of the North*.

(17)   I would like to speak to *the two Peters in this class*.

In the first example, the name *Venice* is used qualitatively about a referent with another name. In (17), *Peters* is used quantitatively about specific members of the class of people called 'Peter'.

(vi) Note in particular the use of the definite article in connection with the names of weekdays, months, annual events, etc. Without the definite article, such nouns are used **deictically**, i.e. in relation to the 'here and now' of the speaker, whereas with the definite article, they are used in relation to some other point of time relevant in the context; compare:

(18)   I will see you on *(next) Monday*.

(19)   I will see you on *the (following) Monday*.

(20)   She fell in love with him *last August*.

(21)   She fell in love with him *the following August*.

Without the article, such nouns have unique referents, with the article they have definite specific class-member referents.

D) The emphatic definite article. Note finally the emphatic use of the definite article (pronounced /ði:/) to denote that the referent deserves the description provided by the group in the highest degree:

(22)   She is *the* expert on computational linguistics.

14.3.6. The indefinite article

The indefinite article *a(n)* is a central determiner and thus usually precedes any modifiers in the noun group (as in e.g. *an unassimilated Canadian*). There is, however, attraction of modifiers to pre-determiner position by HOW(EVER), AS and SO in examples like the following:

(1)   *However beautiful a woman* she is, she does not fool me.

(2)   He may not be *as competent a doctor* as Bill.

(3)   I cannot resist *so nice a proposition*.

Attraction is also possible (with little or no difference of meaning) when modifiers appear in conjunction with the degree adverbs TOO and NO LESS:

(4)   Sandra is *a too critical reader* / Sandra is *too critical a reader*.

Adverbs like QUITE and RATHER are often found in pre-determiner position relating to all of what follows in the noun group rather than simply serving as a dependent of a modifier; compare:

(5)   Joe is *a quite/rather competent sailor* / Joe is *quite/rather a competent sailor.*

The indefinite article has a number of determinative uses:

A) Unmarked determination: class-member reference. Basically, the indefinite article is used by the speaker in connection with singular count nouns with class-member referents to indicate that she does not expect the listener to be familiar with a particular referent of the noun group:

(6)   She was wearing *an enormous kimono.*

(7)   He was stepped on by *an elephant* while his father was buying cigarettes?

In each case, the noun group containing the indefinite article refers to a member of the class of things potentially referred to by the head noun: for example, *an elephant* refers to a member of the class of elephants.

Once the speaker or writer has introduced a referent by an indefinite noun group, enough familiarity has been established to warrant the use of the definite article in subsequent noun groups with the same referent:

(8)   'You were stepped on by *an elephant* while your father was buying cigarettes?', Farrokh asked ... The doctor didn't believe he could fix what *the elephant* had done.

B) Description in terms of class-membership. Noun groups containing the indefinite article are frequent as complements, as well as after *as* or *for* and as appositional elaboratives, serving as descriptions of the referent of other constituents (e.g. the subject or the object) in terms of class-membership:

(9)   Mr. Garg was *a regular customer.*

(10)   They called him *a damned fool.*

(11)   Vinod refused to see himself as *a "servant".*

(12)   I took him *for a criminal.*

(13)   She fell in love with Max Jones, *a real-estate agent from Minnesota.*

C) Indefinite specific vs. indefinite non-specific reference. Most of the examples offered so far in this section are examples of **indefinite specific reference**: in each case a particular referent answering the description of the noun group is picked out specifically. Thus in example (8) above, *an elephant* does not simply refer to a random member of the class of elephants, but to a particular member. When an indefinite noun group does not refer to a particular member but to potentially any member of the class, we speak of **indefinite non-specific reference**. Here are some examples of indefinite non-specific reference (with indefinite specific counterparts in parentheses):

(14)   I would like *an apple*, please. (cf. *He gave me an apple*)

(15)   Are we likely to see *a viper* here? (cf. *We saw a viper here yesterday*)

Here the indefinite article approaches the meaning of 'any': any entity answering the description of the head is a potential referent. Some noun groups are ambiguous between a specific and a non-specific reading:

(16)   Sally wants to marry *a Norwegian who is rich*.

The noun group *a Norwegian who is rich* either refers to a particular person, a rich Norwegian (specific reference), or it marks anyone who is a rich Norwegian as a potential future husband (non-specific reference).

D) The indefinite article in generic-like expressions. Moving one step further away from indefinite specific reference, the indefinite article is used to denote 'typical class-member', cf. the following examples:

(17)   *An elephant* is a very dangerous animal.

(18)   *A linguist* is someone who studies languages.

The indefinite article here has a generic-like function. It is more informal and less contrastive than the definite article in generic expressions (e.g. *The elephant is a very dangerous animal*).

E) Count nouns with little association of class-membership. The indefinite article is sometimes used in idiomatic expressions with little association of class-membership:

(19)   I have *a mind* to tell him exactly what I mean.

(20)   I did it with *a view* to being useful.

Note also constructions like *He gave a nod* and *They had an argument*, where there is fusion between predicator and direct object (cf. section 8.6).

F) The indefinite article and mass nouns. As a general rule, mass nouns do not take the indefinite article. When unmodified, they typically appear without article (generic use, as in *Sugar is more expensive than rice*) or with quantifiers like SOME (e.g. *Could I have some water, please*). However, the indefinite article is used in connection with mass nouns to denote '**subtype** of the non-countable entity' (especially in noun groups containing restrictive modification as in example (21)) or 'instances' of the non-countable entity (as in example (22)):

(21)   This is actually *an excellent wine*.

(22)   He ordered *a beer* and *a coffee*.

If the referent is an abstract concept and this concept is restricted by the meaning of one or more modifiers, the indefinite article is used for indefinite expression (cf. our discussion of the use of the definite article in similar contexts in section 14.3.5):

(23)   She showed *a loyalty* towards her master *which I could not match.*

G) The indefinite article and proper nouns. The indefinite article is occasionally used with proper nouns to denote class-membership, as in:

(24)   Dr. Aziz said, 'Have you heard about Dr. Dev?' Farrokh wondered, Which
        Dr. Dev? There was *a Dr. Dev* who was a cardiologist, there was another
        Dev who was an anesthesiologist – there are a bunch of Devs, he thought.

In this example, the referents actually belong to a class of people bearing the name provided by the proper noun. But proper names may also be used with the indefinite article for members of a class of people simply sharing some quality with the bearer of the name or being of the same standard, as in:

(25)   This country has never produced *a Shakespeare* or *a Picasso.*

The indefinite article (as well as emphatic *one*) is sometimes used in connection with a proper name to indicate that the bearer of the name is unknown to the speaker or assumed by the speaker to be unknown by the listener:

(26)   Is there *a Sarah Mortimer* staying at this hotel?
(27)   In the cupboard I found a pretty volume, the work of *one William Canton.*

Groups containing a modified proper noun preceded by the indefinite article typically indicate that the bearer of the name is in a temporary state:

(28)   "I hope it won't be another 50 years before we can celebrate like this again,"
        joked *a high-spirited Bing Crosby.*

H) The indefinite article as a basis of quantification. As a marker of singular meaning, the indefinite article lends itself to quantified expressions involving a standard against which something is measured or counted:

(29)   They made love twice *a day.*
(30)   It costs $45 *a pound.*

The indefinite article here approaches *each* (or *per*) in meaning.

14.3.7. Zero determination

A distinction must be drawn between **zero determiner**, which is associated with indefiniteness, and **no determiner**. Names take no determiner rather than zero determiner because they have unique (and thus inherently definite) reference, as in *Farrokh and Julia were sharing a bath together.* Note in this connection the lack of determiner in connection with count nouns expressing family relations: *Uncle will join Mom and Dad in a moment.* This applies also to vocatives like the following: *How are you this morning, <u>Professor</u>? / Come on, <u>Darling</u> / See you there, <u>mate</u>.*

Let us turn now to the uses of zero determination:

A) Indefinite class-member reference. Zero (or *some*) is regularly used in connection with plural count nouns for indefinite specific or non-specific class-member reference (corresponding to the use of the indefinite article plus singular count noun):

(1)   I was going to buy (*some*) *clothes*. (cf. *I was going to buy a hat*)
(2)   She wore *bells* on her ankles. (cf. *She wore a bell on her left ankle*)

This use of plural nouns with zero determiner is compatible with modification and/or quantification:

(3)   They wore *navy-blue shorts and kneesocks*, too – and *black shoes*.
(4)   She dances with *two beautiful peacocks*.

B) Indefinite mass reference. Zero is also used in connection with mass nouns for indefinite specific or non-specific reference to non-countable entities and concepts:

(5)   Danny poured *hot water* over the peas.
(6)   It contained *some whitish stuff – curdled milk* or *flour* and *water*.
(7)   Martin would be kept in *perpetual darkness*.

Non-specific reference to non-countable entities and concepts, as in the last example, have a generic potential (cf. subsection C below).

Note that names for diseases are usually non-countable and take zero determiner: e.g. CANCER, PNEUMONIA, CLAMYDIA, etc.:

(8)   He suffers from *cancer*.
(9)   Her child had *pneumonia*.

C) Generic reference. Zero is used in connection with plural count nouns and with mass nouns for indefinite non-specific reference. In general contexts with no explicit or implicit limitation on the referent, the expression may assume a generic meaning, referring to all the members of a class (e.g. all 'cars', 'tigers', 'trees') or to a general concept (such as e.g. 'love', 'art', 'life'):

(10)   *Elephants* are dangerous animals.
(11)   *Trachoma* is one of the leading causes of *blindness* in the world.
(12)   *Time* is still a mystery to *science*.

Unlike other count nouns MAN and WOMAN take zero article in generic expressions, the former sometimes in the sense of 'mankind' (though this is often avoided to escape accusations of sexism):

(13)   The temperament of *man*, either male or female, cannot help falling down before and worshipping this sacrificial note.

(14)   It was *man* who ended the Cold War in case you didn't notice. It wasn't weaponry, or technology, or armies or campaigns.

(15)   The nineteenth century was an age where *woman*, not *man*, was sacred; and where you could buy a thirteen-year-old girl for a few shillings.

Count nouns occasionally serve as generic terms for academic subjects, sports and activities:

(16)   Mary studied *dance* as well as *film*.

(17)   All he is interested in is playing *football*.

D) Generic-like expressions in specific contexts. Abstract and concrete mass nouns, as well as plural count nouns, are sometimes used in a generic-like way in contexts that are so specific that the meaning is close to definite specific expressions:

(18)   *(Our) sources* say he was once a paid informer for the FBI.

(19)   *(The) traffic* had to be diverted because *(the) roads* were flooded.

Note particularly the use of certain general count nouns like CONDITIONS, MATTERS, EVENTS, THINGS, etc., without determiner even in rather specific contexts:

(20)   *Conditions* were hopeless.

(21)   Don't make *matters* worse.

E) Other uses of zero. In a number of cases there is a certain vacillation over the choice between the articles and zero determination:

(i) Count nouns take zero article rather than the indefinite article when they are used as complements, as appositional elaboratives, and after *as* and *for* for unique reference rather than class membership: *Bill Clinton became president of the United States / She was elected chairman of the Equal Rights Committee*, etc. Note further fronted complements in concessive and conditional subclauses:

(22)   But *pious man* that Reverend Jackson was, he was also a father whose children needed a mother.

(23)   This fault – if *fault* it is – is an amiable one.

The indefinite article is also sometimes left out to create an emphasis on different aspects or (changing) 'character' or 'quality' of the referent described, especially in constructions with *as*, after the verb TURN, and in connection with *kind of* and *sort of*:

(24)   As *American*, the writer distrusted Europe; as *writer*, he envied us.

(25)   He had turned *spy.*

(26)   What *sort of man* would do such a thing!

(ii) Count nouns are sometimes used like mass nouns to emphasize the material, character or concept of the referent rather than simply the referent as an individual entity (cf. also section 14.2.4), in which case they take zero article: *The scrapyard was full of smashed car / He is impervious to argument / She was incapable of plotting murder.* Note especially the frequent absence of determination after *kind of* and *sort of: What kind of car is this / Any sort of knife will do,* etc.

(iii) Count nouns are used without determination in a great many standard expressions for typical recurring activities, events and conditions:

•   locatives with an emphasis on the function of the place rather than its location: e.g. *be in* or *go to bed/church/school/prison/college;*

•   transport and communication: e.g. *go/travel/come by bus/train /car, send by post/satellite;*

•   meals: e.g. *When is dinner? Do come for lunch tomorrow;*

•   time expressions: *summer, autumn, morning, evening; at dawn, by night, in winter.*

As many of the examples show, the absence of an article is especially frequent in preposition groups.

(iv) Count nouns are often used without a determiner in compound units even if the individual noun would require an article:

(27)   As he spoke, he cupped his hand near the bony fusion of *ankle* and *foot,* which the beggar awkwardly rested on the heel.

(28)   We could say that they are *brother* and *sister,* that one looks after the other.

A similar phenomenon is observed in fixed adverbial collocations and idiomatic expressions like: *hand in hand, side by side, mile after mile,* etc.

(v) Nouns with zero determination often occur in fixed expressions, especially verb + noun collocations (such as *catch sight of, take place, make use of, make contact with, take pains, take care, cast anchor,* etc.) and in preposition groups (such as *at ease, at pains, in mind, in proportion to, at first glance, off balance, for sale, in need of, in style, by hand, by surprise, on holiday, peace of mind, out of character, in support of, in fear that, at high speed, in case, by means of, in charge of).*

14.3.8. The genitive

The genitive construction is first and foremost a central definite determiner used to express a relation between two referents: that of **the genitive construction** itself and that of **the head of the group**. This relation is often, but by no means always, one of possession, as in e.g. *the old man's hat*. This example refers to a particular hat (and is thus much closer in meaning to *the hat* than to *a hat*). At the same time it indicates that the hat belongs in some sense to the referent of *the old man*. In its central function, the genitive construction is called **the specifying genitive**.

In writing, the genitive case is formed by adding *'s* to singular nouns or (certain indefinite) pronouns and to irregular plural nouns that do not end in *-s*: *father's, Jack's; somebody's, nobody's; women's, children's*. The genitive of plural nouns ending in *-s* is formed by simply adding the apostrophe: *boys', writers'*. There are few exceptions to these rules: foreign, especially Greek names of more than one syllable ending in *-es* take only the apostrophe: *Socrates', Xerxes'*. With names, English as well as foreign, ending in *-s* pronounced /z/, usage varies: *Lyons'* or *Lyons's*, /laɪənz/ or /laɪənzɪz/.

Though the genitive marker is added simply to nouns (or certain pronouns), the genitive construction potentially contains a whole noun group or compound unit: cf. *women's (disinclination)* vs. *the old women's (disinclination)* and *Jack's (humour)* vs. *Jack and Jill's (humour)*. Sometimes the genitive marker is not added to the head of the group contained in the genitive construction but to a post-head dependent:

> the King *of Sweden*'s (decision)
> somebody *else*'s (friend)
> the girl *who lives next door*'s (bike)

There is an obvious relationship between genitive constructions and possessive pronouns: compare *the old man's hat* and *his hat*. By and large possessive pronouns are used like genitive constructions. Thus much of what we have to say about the use of genitive constructions applies also to possessive pronouns (for some of the differences see section 15.2.2 [A]). Let us turn now to some of the important features of the genitive.

A) Syntactic functions of the genitive. Although the genitive construction is basically a central definite determiner (**the specifying genitive**), it has other important uses. It may serve as a premodifier, entering a compound-like relationship with the head of the group:

(1)   She lives in a quaint old *shepherd's* cottage. (not 'the cottage of a quaint old shepherd' but 'a quaint old cottage of a certain kind')

(2)   He took a *doctor's* degree. (i.e. 'a special kind of degree')
(3)   She bought some *children's* shoes. (i.e. 'some shoes for children')

The premodifying genitive, which is called **the classifying genitive**, differs from the specifying genitive phonologically in having unitary stress on its first element and syntactically in being inseparable from the head of the group. Semantically the classifying genitive denotes 'kind' or 'type'. Note that we cannot insert e.g. an adjective between the genitive and the head and still preserve the status of the genitive as a classifying genitive: cf. *some children's expensive shoes / some expensive children's shoes*. Groups containing a classifying genitive may have indefinite reference (as in the examples above).

Consider next the **autonomous genitive**. The autonomous genitive is a specifying genitive construction which does not relate to an overt head but rather by itself assumes an external function like that of a group:

(4)   I parked my car behind *Jack's*.
(5)   Jennifer's hat is more expensive than *her mother's*.
(6)   *George's* is the only voice she is likely to recognize.

In these examples, the head is **ellipted** because it is contextually clear (*Jack's = Jack's car, her mother's = her mother's hat, George's = George's voice*). The autonomous genitive also occurs in expressions referring to homes, buildings, institutions, businesses and other places, in which case it is often referred to as the **local genitive**:

(7)   I met her at *my uncle's*.
(8)   I got these rolls at *the baker's*.
(9)   He has been to London often but never actually seen *St Paul's*.

Finally the autonomous genitive may appear in a postmodifying *of*-construction with a quantifying, partitive meaning ('of several'). This genitive is called **the post-genitive**; examples:

(10)   He introduced me to some friends of *my neighbour's*.
(11)   Jack borrowed a picture of *my sister's*.

The post-genitive, which provides an indefinite alternative to the specifying genitive (cf. *my neighbour's friends, his sister's raincoat*), is compatible with a head noun determined by the definite article or a demonstrative pronoun when followed by a restrictive relative clause: *the/that/this unfortunate student of Otto Jespersen's who failed the grammar exam*. The partitive content becomes especially clear when we consider similar constructions with the uninflected noun:

(12)   Jack borrowed a picture of *my sister*.

(13)   He was a student of *Otto Jespersen.*

(14)   He introduced me to some friends of *my neighbour.*

There is in these examples no partitive meaning but rather a relation defined by the head of the group directed towards the complement of *of* (i.e. 'Jack borrowed a picture representing my sister', 'he studied Otto Jespersen', ' he introduced me to some people who consider themselves to be friends'). Nouns incapable of expressing such a unidirectional relation do not appear in this kind of construction: *He wore a raincoat of my sister.*

In examples containing demonstrative pronouns like:

(15)   Now tell me something about *that/this brother of Stephanie's.*

the partitive association is replaced by an association of the speaker's (approving or disapproving) interest in the referent.

Here is an overview of the syntactic functions of the genitive:

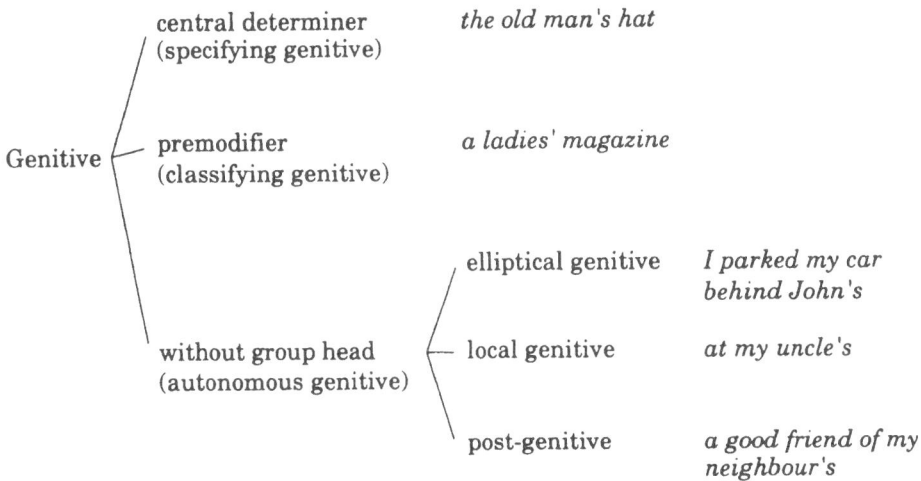

Genitive		
central determiner (specifying genitive)		*the old man's hat*
premodifier (classifying genitive)		*a ladies' magazine*
without group head (autonomous genitive)	elliptical genitive	*I parked my car behind John's*
	local genitive	*at my uncle's*
	post-genitive	*a good friend of my neighbour's*

The rest of this section is devoted to the specifying genitive.

B) The semantics of the specifying genitive. The specifying genitive is traditionally said to express possession in a broad sense: *the doctor's right hand, his wife's only other reading material.* In an example like *the girl's bathtub at the Hotel Bardez*, the bathtub is more likely to belong to the hotel than to the girl; and in *John's bike*, John may or may not be the owner of the bike (the bike could simply be one that John is riding).

The fact is that in many cases, there is simply just **some unspecified relation** between the referent of the genitive construction and the referent of the group as a whole. This has led to various classifications of the specifying genitive on a semantic basis. Apart from the possessive genitive, we get e.g. the **genitive of origin** (as in *Jack's letter* 'the letter is from Jack'), the **genitive of attribute** (as in *Nancy's irritation* 'Nancy is irritated'), etc. Two distinct kinds of genitive have attracted special attention: the so-called **subjective genitive** and the so-called **objective genitive**. These genitives are relevant in connection with verbal nouns, such as ESTIMATION, DELIVERY, EMBRACE, RIDICULE, etc., to which we can assign potential participant roles usually associated with syntactic 'subject' and/or 'object' function.

In the following examples, the specifying genitive is a subjective genitive in the sense that the referent of the genitive construction is the DOER of an (explicit or implicit) situational referent of the group as a whole:

(16)   In *Dr. Daruwalla's estimation*, the Jesuits were intellectually crafty and sly.

(17)   Dr. Daruwalla sat shivering in *Julia's embrace*.

When the head of the group is a nonfinite clause, the referent of the subjective genitive is either the active DOER/SPECIFIED or the passive DONE-TO of the situation expressed by the clause:

(18)   *Jenny's neglecting to write that letter* upset John. (Jenny = DOER)

(19)   *Jack's being so considerate lately* made her suspicious. (Jack = SPECIFIED*)*

(20)   *Jenny's getting pushed over the edge* was an accident. (Jenny = DONE-TO)

While the subjective genitive is frequent, the objective genitive has rather restricted occurrence, the objective relation being often expressed more naturally by an *of*-construction:

(21)   Was there another clue to *Mr. Lal's murder*, or another threat to Dhar? (= 'the murder of Mr. Lal')

(22)   She relished the details of *old Jack's release*. (= 'the release of Jack')

In these examples, the referent of the genitive construction is semantically the DONE-TO.

C) The specifying genitive vs. the *of*-construction. The use of the genitive is somewhat restricted in the sense that many nouns do not normally occur in the genitive: it would be fairly unusual to say e.g. *the table's price, the house's roof, obedience's ramifications, his conversion's miracle*, etc. To express the intended meaning, we often use an entirely different syntactic construction: the definite article + head noun + an *of*-construction containing the referent to which the head is related (*the price of the table, the roof of the house, the ramifications of obedience, the miracle of his conversion*). In many cases, both expressions are possible with little or no difference of meaning: *Veronica Rose's offspring / the offspring of Veronica Rose, the* *girl's mutilated body / the mutilated body of the girl*, etc. Here are some guidelines for the use of these two competing constructions:

a) Semantic considerations. The greater an association of humanness, animacy and/or individuality, the more likely we are to be able to use a noun in the genitive. Thus names of persons and higher animals and count nouns referring to people usually take the genitive (e.g. *Jim's book, Fido's kennel; the girl's arm, the teacher's car*, etc.) while nouns referring to inanimate entities usually take the *of*-construction (e.g. *the colour of the wall, the other side of the coin, the result of this test*, etc.).

Geographical names, collective nouns, count nouns referring to institutions, regions, places, etc. are common in both constructions: *Goa's white beaches / the white beaches of Goa; my family's reputation / the reputation of my family, the clinic's name / the name of the clinic*; etc.

It is often claimed that more 'individuality' or 'focus of interest' is placed on an inanimate or non-human referent of a noun by using it in the genitive rather than in the *of*-construction in examples like *the bikini's bottom half, a lizard's eyes, the novel's title, the fire's friendly crackling, the envelope's shape and size*, etc. In practice such distinctions are hard to perceive.

Abstracts rarely take the genitive (*the significance of this concept, the beauty of this idea*, much rather than *this concept's significance, this idea's beauty*) unless personified or individualized (*nature's wonderful solution to that problem, life's many mysteries*).

As already noted above, the objective genitive is rarer than the possessive and the subjective genitive, being typical only in connection with names and nouns referring to persons (*John's defeat, the woman's release*).

Time and distance expressions often appear in the genitive: *within two or three weeks' time, at a yard's distance, a moment's reflection*, etc.

When a noun relates to one of the lexical items EDGE, END, SURFACE and SAKE as head of the noun group, we often get a genitive construction rather than an *of*-construction: *the water's edge, the journey's end, the lake's surface, for brevity's sake*, etc. In the case of WORTH only the genitive construction is possible: *his money's worth*.

Note finally idiomatic expressions like: *Not for the death of me / Not for the life of me / I don't like the look of that man*.

b) Formal considerations. Strings of genitives are often avoided (*Martin's heart's desire, my cousin's wife's first husband*). Strings of *of*-constructions are common even if somewhat clumsy (*many of the conclusions of the report*). Mixtures of the two constructions are often a happy compromise (*the first husband of my cousin's wife, many of the report's conclusions*).

Heavy genitive constructions are generally avoided in formal language, especially if the genitive marker can only be placed on a postmodifier (cf. *the man I met yesterday's wife / the wife of the man I met yesterday, the former division officer in this firm's secretary / the secretary of the former division officer in this firm*). Considerations of end-focus and end-weight are important in cases like *the former prime minister's daughter* vs. *the daughter of the former prime minister*.

Of-constructions are used in order to make it possible to attach a relative clause or participial construction directly to the head it modifies, cf.:

(23)   There is a characteristic 'double deprivation' in the lives of these children, who tend to deprive themselves further through ... (.. in these children's lives, who tend to ..)

Adjectives used with generic nominal referents, as in *the poor, the rich, the merely fanciful*, etc.) do not take the genitive case: **the poor's conditions / the conditions of the poor*, cf. section 16.4.1.

In cases where the genitive singular and plural are identical in sound (*friend's/friends', girl's/girls'*, etc.), the *of*-construction is sometimes used instead of the genitive plural to avoid ambiguity: *his friend's opinion / the opinion of his friends*. In writing, such plural genitives are common:

(24)   He awakened to the sound of the *skiers'* boots tramping on the snow.

14.4. Quantification: the number category

14.4.1. The formal singular/plural distinction

Number is a morphological category with the singular as the unmarked zero form and the plural as the morphologically marked *-s* form: *car/cars, girl/girls, book/books*, etc. For rules of spelling and pronunciation, as well as an overview of irregular and foreign plurals, see appendix A.2.

With certain count nouns there is **no formal difference** between the singular and the plural. This applies to:

• some animal names (*deer, grouse, plaice, salmon, sheep, snipe, trout*); others vacillate (*buffalo(es), antelope(s)*);

• nationality names in *-ese* (*Chinese, Japanese, Portuguese*) and *Swiss*;

• *craft* (= 'boat') and compounds containing *-craft* (*aircraft, spacecraft*); *counsel*; *offspring*;

• the following nouns denoting number, weight or measure: *head* (as in *five head of cattle*), *brace, yoke, gross, horsepower, hundredweight, stone*).

There is also no formal distinction between the singular and the plural of the following nouns ending in *-s*: *barracks, gallows, headquarters, innings, means* (= 'method(s)'), *series, species, works* (and compounds containing *-works*: *gasworks, waterworks*). When *means* means 'money' it is always plural. Unlike the nouns mentioned above, these *-s* nouns may be used as plurals (e.g. with respect to concord) even if they refer to a single entity: *Our old headquarters were abandoned.*

Some nouns are invariably either singular or plural, or at least restricted with respect to the singular/plural contrast. These are called **number-invariable nouns**. For example, as we have seen, mass nouns (like *kindness* and *wine*) are singular (unless they express 'instances' or 'kinds of' as in e.g. *kindnesses* and *wines*). The same applies to situation-referring *-ing* forms: cf. *Their dancing on the table is unlikely to please him* vs. *His writings have caused quite a scandal.* Names are either singular (such as *John, Denmark, the University of Sussex*) or, less often, plural (such as *the Hebrides, the Alps, General Motors*), but they are usually invariable with respect to quantification (for the use of proper nouns for class-member reference in examples like *the two Peters*, see sections 14.2.4 and 14.3.5). There are some more specific cases involving number-invariable nouns:

(i) Nouns with 'plural form' used as singular nouns. Several kinds of noun ending in *-s* fall under this heading:

• Nouns ending in *-ics* denoting a science or a subject: *acoustics, athletics, mathematics* (also *maths*), *linguistics, pragmatics*, etc. (e.g. *Pragmatics is a fascinating new subbranch of linguistics*). Note that *politics* may be treated as a plural noun if it denotes an individual's views (*His politics were becoming an embarrassment*). Similarly, *statistics* can be used more loosely about 'figures', in which case it contrasts with singular *statistic*.

• Nouns ending in *-s* denoting diseases are usually used as singular nouns: *mumps, shingles, rickets, measles*.

• Nouns ending in *-s* denoting games: *billiards, cards, darts, dominoes*, etc.

• *News* is always singular: *No news is good news, This news is very depressing*. The same applies to *shambles*: *The house is in a shambles*.

(ii) nouns with 'singular form' used as plural nouns. Under this heading we find nouns referring to composite entities like *cattle, clergy, police, poultry, vermin, people, crew, staff*. These nouns behave differently with respect to quantification:

• *Cattle* is compatible with large and/or imprecise numbers: *There were fifty/some cattle in the field, He bought hundreds of cattle / a thousand cattle* (but *?I saw three cattle* is unusual).

• *Clergy* and *police* accept precise quantification even in small numbers: *There were three clergy and 12 police present at the meeting.*

• *Poultry* and *vermin* do not usually allow of precise quantification: *a lot of poultry/vermin; *seven /*a hundred poultry/vermin.*

• *People, crew* and *staff* are 'internally countable' like *police: ten/several people/crew/staff.* Unlike *police,* however, they can be used as singular nouns with regular plural forms: e.g. *The Danes are a tough people / There are several English-speaking peoples.*

(iii) nouns with 'plural form' used as plural nouns. We here include:

• The so-called binary nouns (nouns referring to entities which consist of two equal parts, usually instruments or articles of dress): *binoculars, glasses, forceps, scissors, pliers, pincers, scales; jeans, pants, trousers, slacks, tights.* To indicate a number distinction, we here have to use partitive constructions like *a pair of / several pairs of glasses/scissors/ jeans/* etc.

• A number of nouns which regularly occur in the plural form with a meaning that has no obvious counterpart in the singular: *airs* (as in *to put on airs*), *brains* (*He has got brains*), *contents* (= that which is contained, as in *table of contents*), *colours* (as in e.g. *to join the colours*), *customs* (= import duties), *fireworks, funds, goods, looks* (as in *his good looks*), *media, oats, odds, outskirts, pains* (= 'care', as in *to take pains*), *premises* (= building, location), *remains, riches, spirits* (= strong liquour). Not all of these are found in the singular but when they are they have a different meaning: e.g. *content* (= 'that which is written or spoken', or about 'proportion', as in *the silver content of this spoon*), *custom* (= habit), *pain* (= physical suffering), *premise* (= hypothesis, part of a formal argument), *spirit* (= mind, soul); these singular nouns have regular plural forms which preserve the meaning of the singular.

Obviously related to this last group are the so-called **intensive plurals,** i.e. plurals with a distinct meaning which is, however, related to the concept of the corresponding singular mass or count noun: *apologies* (as in *She sent her apologies*), *fears* (*She felt grave fears for him*), *gardens* (e.g. *the botanical gardens*), *orders* (*She was under orders to kill her boss*), *regrets* (e.g. *He expressed his regrets*), *skies* (*the sunny skies of Italy*), *waters* (*the waters of the lake, the stormy waters of the Atlantic*), etc.

For discussion of **collective nouns,** see section 11.3 [A].

14.4.2. What is pluralized?

Usually there is no problem in identifying the relevant unit to pluralize in a noun group: it is, of course, the head noun. Thus we say e.g. *the two chaps from London*, not *the two chap from Londons*. In compound units with nouns as conjoints, each noun is normally pluralized if plural meaning is intended: e.g. *knives and forks*.

With compounds and noun + noun combinations, the plural suffix is usually added to the last element if it is a noun: *headmasters, toothpicks, city halls, state universities*, etc. Even if the final element is not a noun, we pluralize the last element if the compound is felt to be a regular unit: *bucketfuls, breakdowns, stowaways, knock-outs, break-ins*.

The first element of a hyphenated compound is pluralized in:

(i) Noun + preposition + noun combinations: *fathers-in-law, men-of-war, commanders-in-chief*, etc.

(ii) Noun + adverb combinations if the noun expresses the DOER: *lookers-on, passers-by, runners-up*. Note, however, also *goings-on*.

(iii) Noun + adjective combinations: *postmasters-general, poets-laureate*, etc. but there is often vacillation: *courts-martial/court-martials, attorneys-general/attorney-generals*.

Both elements in noun + noun combinations are pluralized in:

(i) Compounds where the first noun is *woman* or *man* (also *gentleman*) denoting the sex of the referent: *men-servants, women doctors, gentlemen thieves* (such examples contrast with *man-eaters, woman-haters*, etc.).

(ii) Certain formal titles: *Knights Templars, Lords Chancellors, Lords Justices*.

There is vacillation in combinations consisting of title + name: *the two Miss Smiths / the two Misses Smith*, the latter being the more formal variant.

14.4.3. The uses of the singular and the plural

In this section we shall briefly mention a number of specific rules for the use of the singular and the plural which do not follow automatically from any general characterization of the number distinction.

(i) The distributive plural. The distributive plural is common in constructions consisting of two or more premodifying adjectives and a head noun where the adjectives refer to separate entities, the head noun being often pluralized even if each adjective relates to a single entity only: *the sixteenth and seventeenth centuries, the English and French nations, the* *third and fourth chapters*, etc. The singular is sometimes used to avoid ambiguity, cf. *in this and the following chapter/chapters*.

The distributive plural is also found in constructions consisting of head noun + *of* + compound unit, as in *the reigns of Elizabeth and James, the ages of 14 and 18*. Similarly in reciprocal expressions, especially with verbs like CHANGE, SWAP, etc.: *He changed trains at Reading, The two women swapped husbands, They shook hands*. Note also individualizing expressions like *Bob and John took their hats off* (i.e. 'each his own hat'), *They ought to be having their bottoms kicked and their noses tweaked*.

(ii) Noun groups as modifiers. When noun groups function as modifiers or as parts of modifiers, the head noun is singular even if it would have been plural in the corresponding independent noun group; compare: *three pieces / three-piece suits; four courses / a four-course dinner; eight hours / the eight-hour day; ten years / a ten-year-old boy; six feet / a six foot tall boy*, etc. There is occasionally vacillation with single nouns serving as modifiers or first elements of compounds: *a wage(s) agreement, trouser(s) pocket*. The plural is used when it has a distinct meaning (cf. section 14.4.1 (iii)) and thus serves to avoid misunderstanding: *a customs officer, a goods train*.

(iii) Number and weight. The numbers *dozen, score, hundred, thousand, million* and *billion* are not pluralized when they are (part of) dependents or when, as heads, they are preceded by definite numerals (cardinal numbers):

(1)   two hundred bikes / *two hundreds bikes (but *hundreds of bikes / *two hundreds of bikes*)

(2)   a few thousand cars / *a few thousands cars (but *several thousands of cars / *four thousands of cars*)

(3)   How many bikes were there? – About two hundred / *two hundreds

(4)   Can you count to four thousand / *four thousands?

Foot and *pound* remain singular when followed by a numeral: *four foot two, five pound fifty*. Both the singular and the plural of *ton* is found when it serves as the head of the group: *two ton(s) of flour*.

(iv) Collectivizing. Many animal names have both singular and plural forms (e.g. *lion/lions, elephant/elephants, duck/ducks*, etc. When regarded as food or as prey, the singular is used with a collectivizing effect; compare: *They have shot several lion / We saw several lions in the park; We bagged three elephant that day / Three elephants came running towards us*.

15. Pronominals

15.1. Introduction

Like nominals, pronominals may be used to express the participants involved in situations. But while nominal constituents serve this communicative function by means of a strong lexical element (the noun) categorizing some entity, pronominal constituents do it without specific categorization, either deictically by determining the referent directly in relation to the communicative situation (e.g. *I* and *you*, which represent the speaker and hearer of the utterance, respectively) or more indirectly by representing referents already established by nominals in the linguistic context (e.g. *When Roger finally got hold of Rebecca, he did not even tell her about the deal*). In addition, pronominals often serve as determiners (as in e.g. *his* wish).

As will be recalled, a pronoun group is defined as a group with a pronoun as head (cf. section 3.1), as in *We in the English Department believe in tough grammar exams*. But pronoun groups are relatively rare: single pronouns easily represent whole noun groups (not just nouns, as the term 'pronoun' may lead one to believe), and hence do not often require group status:

(1)   *The gentleman staying in the room at the end of the corridor* hardly
        recognized *himself* in the mirror.

Here *himself* represents not only the head noun *gentleman* but the whole subject group *The gentleman staying in the room at the end of the corridor*. The main emphasis of this chapter is therefore on single pronouns.

15.1.1. Classification of pronouns

Here are the main types of pronoun:

personal:	*I/me, you, he/him, she/her, it, we/us, they/them*;
possessive:	*my/mine, your/yours, his, her/hers, its, our/ours, their/theirs*;
reflexive:	*myself, yourself, himself, herself, itself, ourselves, themselves*;
demonstrative:	*this/these, that/those*;
interrogative:	*who/whom, which, what; whoever, whichever, whatever; where, when, how, why*;
relative:	*who/whom, which, what, that, Ø; whoever, whichever, whatever; where, when, why*;

indefinite: *any/anybody/anyone/anything*
               every/everybody/everyone/everything
               no/nobody/no one/none/nothing
               some/somebody/someone/something
               all, each, both, either/neither, one/ones, other(s).

Personal, possessive and reflexive pronouns are grouped together as **central pronouns**: they are special in showing person distinctions and in being formally related (e.g. a possessive pronoun can be regarded as an inflectional case variant – the genitive – of a personal pronoun).

Interrogative and relative *where, when* and *why*, and interrogative *how*, are traditionally classified as adverbs rather than pro**nouns**. However, as the term 'pronoun' is often used more generally about pro-forms, it seems reasonable to include them in this chapter. As pro-forms they typically represent preposition groups (e.g. 'at what place', 'for what reason', etc.).

The use of pronominal *there* as a provisional subject was described in section 2.2.

15.1.2. The external relations of pronominals

Initially it is convenient to distinguish two main syntactic uses of pronouns: **autonomous** and **determinative**. Autonomous pronouns are either heads of pronoun groups (e.g. *someone I like, which of you*) or syntactically independent (as in *She gave me some*). Determinative pronouns serve as DEP (as in *her car, some people*). Some pronouns only have autonomous use (e.g. *he, somebody, there, who, it,* as in *He called somebody*). A few only have determinative use (*my, your, their, no,* as in *Their boss paid no attention to my efforts*). Many have both uses (e.g. *his, her, which, what, some, any, either,* as in *Some like it hot* vs. *Some guys like it hot*). Pronominal constituents may serve the following autonomous, external functions:

S   *We* tried eating out on the little balcony.
Sp   *There* was nothing we could do about it now.
Od   Jack shot *himself.*
Oi   *Whoever* did you give that book?
Op   I take *it* that you are going to resign.
Cs   Jane is *someone I regard very highly.*
Co   You can call me *that* again!
A   *Where* did you hide the doll?

In addition they may function autonomously as conjoints and as prepositional complements:

CJT   It was a row between *me* and *someone you don't know.*

DEP   The scheme was proposed by *those working in our department.*

Determinative use of pronominals is typically found in noun groups:

(1)   *Her smiles* lasted just a fraction of a second too long. (noun group)

(2)   *No teacher* likes *all his students*. (noun groups)

Occasionally pronouns serve as modifiers:

(3)   It cannot be *that* bad. (DEP in adjective group)

(4)   He *himself* cannot speak a word of French. (DEP in pronoun group)

15.1.3. The communicative function of pronominals

Pronominals serve two main communicative functions: **specification** (as in e.g. *his* decision, *this* mess, *every* step, *what* church, etc.) and **representation of 'things'** (e.g. *they, mine, herself, who, whatever, everybody, none* in examples like *They ignored mine, She hated herself*, etc.). It is tempting to relate these two communicative functions to the determinative and autonomous uses mentioned in section 15.1.2 above, but there is no simple one-to-one relationship. When serving as specifying determiners, pronouns still have a representational value, as in *his decision*, where *his* represents e.g. *Jack's*: the representational value is in such cases used to specify the head noun. And when used autonomously, pronouns still have a specifying value, as in *Sally often thought of Jack. God, how she hated him*, where both *She* and *him* have definite specific reference.

Given the representational value of pronouns, it is not surprising that the notions of reference and referent (cf. section 14.2.3) are relevant in any discussion of pronouns. Consider, for example:

(1)   I didn't know half the people *who* were there.

(2)   Not having a key to our new home in Mount Street, I had to knock at the door. Fiona opened *it*.

(3)   Before anyone could stop *her*, Zelda yelled out.

(4)   'Look at *this!*' [uttered by someone pointing at the mess in the kitchen]

(1) and (2) are examples of direct non-repetitive anaphoric textual reference: the antecedent of *who* is *the people* and the antecedent of *it* is *the door*. While there is intrasentential reference in (1), there is extrasentential reference in (2). In (3), *her* has non-repetitive cataphoric textual (more specifically intrasentential) reference to *Zelda*. Finally, in (4) *this* has non-textual deictic reference to a specific referent (the mess).

15.2. Central pronouns

15.2.1. Personal pronouns

The table below offers an overview of personal pronouns and the categories which apply to them:

NUMBER	PERSON	GENDER	CASE	
			subjective	objective
singular	1	-	*I*	*me*
	2	-	*you*	*you*
	3	masculine	*he*	*him*
		feminine	*she*	*her*
		neuter	*it*	*it*
plural	1	-	*we*	*us*
	2	-	*you*	*you*
	3	-	*they*	*them*

Four categories are relevant to the discussion of personal pronouns: **number, person, gender** and **case**. The first three also apply to the derivatives of personal pronouns: possessive and reflexive pronouns (see below).

A) Number. As with nominals, the pronominal number category comprises the members **singular** and **plural**. There is an important semantic difference between the nominal and pronominal number category: while e.g. the plural noun *cars* is the plural of the singular noun *car* in the sense that it simply denotes a plurality of entities denoted by the singular form, the plural central pronouns do not necessarily denote a plurality of entities denoted by the singular pronouns. Thus, for example, *we* is not in any obvious sense the plural of *I* (the pronoun denoting the speaker of the utterance): the plural pronoun does not normally denote a plurality of 'speakers' of the utterance (though in principle it may, e.g. in chants or petitions involving several individuals). Rather, *we* typically includes the speaker plus others associated with the speaker (potentially including the hearer(s)). Note also that in formal language *we* is sometimes used authoritatively about a singular speaker (e.g. the 'royal *we*', as in *We are not amused* for 'I am not amused', spoken by e.g. the Queen; or the 'editorial *we*', as in *We therefore propose* ... for 'I therefore propose ...', used by e.g. an author or public speaker).

Singular *you* represents the hearer: here an ordinary plural interpretation is more normal. Plural *you* easily represents a plurality of hearers. But it may also represent the hearer(s) **plus** others associated with the hearer(s).

The third-person plural *they* differs from the third-person singular pronouns in being gender-neutral: *they* may refer to a plurality of persons or things, and if it refers to persons it may refer to male groups, female groups or mixed groups. Increasingly, *they* and its derivatives are also used as gender-neutral terms referring anaphorically to a singular antecedent, as in *Everybody took their children along* (see subsection C on gender below).

B) Person. In conjunction with the number category, the person category has formal repercussions for subject-predicator concord in connection with the verb BE (cf. section 11.1). Referentially, the person category is a **deictic category**, the first person being defined in terms of the speaker of the expression (*I* referring to the speaker and *we* referring to the speaker plus others), the second person in terms of the hearer (either the hearer alone or the hearer plus others associated with him or her), and the third person in terms of referents not directly involved in the communicative act. Note the occasional use of *we* about the **hearer**, basically as an expression of solidarity but often with a humourous, ironic or condescending effect:

(1)   Good morning, Alma, how are *we* today?

(2)   What's this? Are *we* wearing an expensive new shirt this morning?

As we shall see in the paragraph below on the referential properties of personal pronouns, there are other extensions of the basic person system.

C) Gender. The gender category applies to the third-person singular personal pronouns only (plus derived possessive and reflexive forms). The basic system is as follows: masculine *he* is used for human males, feminine *she* for human females, and neuter (or non-personal) *it* elsewhere.

This basic system has a number of extensions. Pronominal gender terms are not simply a question of objective sex distinctions but often reflect the speaker's attitude towards the referent: *he* and *she* may thus be used about animals (e.g. domestic animals, as in *He always barked fiercely at strangers*), and especially *she* is used about other objects of human affection or concern (ships, cars, countries, etc., as in *She's a fine ship*). More generally we can say that *he* and *she* (plus derived forms) are used stylistically as a means of personification (as in e.g. *History has revised her verdict*). Conversely, the neuter term *it* is occasionally used about a baby (typically as a marker of dissociation, e.g. *It kept screaming all night*). Note in this connection the use of *it* vs. *he* or *she* in examples like the following:

(3)   Someone opened the door and entered. *It/*She* was my mother.

(4)   Jack was standing at the top of the stairs. *It/He* must be the captain.

While *it* is used in presentations of **identity** (as in the first example), *he* and *she* (and plural *they*) are used in sentences providing **further information**.

The traditional use of *he* (and *him* as well as the derived possessive pronoun *his* and reflexive pronoun *himself*) as an unmarked, neutral common gender term when the sex of the referent is unknown, irrelevant or meant to include both sexes, is still not uncommon although, increasingly, there is a tendency to avoid the sexist bias, compare:

(5)   The reader who works *his* way through this exposition will be rewarded.

(6)   Practically everybody in the place had fallen into the habit nowadays of looking cautiously over *his or her* shoulder before *he or she* spoke.

As (6) shows, there is no simple solution to the problem: compound units like *he or she* and *his or her* are not only cumbersome but, alas, give linear priority to the male term. The third person plural pronoun *they* (plus derived forms) is increasingly used as a common gender pro-form for singular referents, especially when the antecedent is an indefinite pronoun:

(7)   Everybody/Somebody/Nobody cheered when *they* heard the news.

These pronouns are grammatically singular (cf. e.g. *Everybody calls me Jack*) but have plural associations, thus inviting representation by a plural pronoun.

D) Case. Within the class of central pronouns the basic case system is as follows: there are three cases, the **subjective** – traditionally referred to as the 'nominative' – the **objective** – traditionally referred to as the 'accusative' – and the **possessive** – traditionally referred to as the 'genitive'. Possessive pronouns will be treated separately in section 15.2.2.

Generally, the subjective form is used only when the pronoun functions as the subject of **finite** predicators, the objective form elsewhere (e.g. as direct object or as subject of nonfinite predicators), e.g.:

(8)   *She* had chosen Wednesday for their flight.

(9)   Macon hadn't seen *her* since his son was born.

(10)   I want *her* to leave now.

Note, however, the use of the subjective form in discontinuous clauses like *He was hard to beat* (cf. section 12.4) and in absolute clauses like *She moved forward, he remaining behind* (cf. section 12.5).

As subject complement, the subjective case does occur but is generally felt to be (humourously) hypercorrect unless it is the antecedent of a following relative clause in which the relative pronoun serves as the subject of a finite predicator, compare:

(11)   'Who's there?' he called out. 'It is *I / me*,' she whispered.

(12)   Actually it is *she* who rings him.

Compound units pose special problems. A pronoun realizing a conjoint in a subject compound unit is often found in the objective case in very informal, spoken language, especially if it realizes the first conjoint:

(13)   'Meet us there and *me* and my friend will show you the photos.'

Conversely there is a tendency to use *I* instead of the more acceptable *me* as the last conjoint irrespective of the function of the compound unit:

(14)   Between *you and I*, there was some cheating. (DEP of preposition)

Sometimes, if subject function is implied, the subjective case is found even outside subject position, especially after *except*, *but*, *as* and *than*:

(15)   No one laughed but/except *he/him*.

(16)   Lena is much richer than *I/me*.

The objective case is here the unmarked choice, the subjective case being slightly formal or affected. Alternatively the speaker may add an operator:

(17)   Lena is much richer than *I am*.

E) Syntax. As light-weight constituents, personal pronominal subjects are not usually separated from the predicator by heavy adverbials:

(18)   Bob *a few minutes later* left the building.

(19)   *He *a few minutes later* left the building.

While nominals may precede or follow the adverb in a phrasal verb construction, unstressed pronouns always precede the adverb (cf. *I called him up* / *I called up him*). There are also restrictions on pronouns in connection with full inversion (cf. section 7.2.2), cf. e.g. *'This is an outrage,' said John* /*said he*). And, as pointed out in section 2.4, while nominal indirect objects always precede nominal direct objects, pronominal indirect objects may occasionally follow pronominal direct objects in BrE (e.g. *I gave it them*).

In compound units, the first person is in polite language realized as the last conjoint and the second person as the first conjoint: *he and I*, *you and me*, *you and he*, etc. In the third person singular, the masculine precedes the feminine – despite the obvious sexual bias: *he or she* rather than *she or he*.

Personal pronouns only take pre-head dependents in expressions like *Poor him*, *Clever you*, etc. and when used as nouns in examples like:

(20)   Is it *a he* or *a she*? (i.e. 'a male or female')

By contrast, they take a somewhat broader range of post-head dependents:

(21)   You *yourself* must have realized what was going on.

(22)   We *professors* must make a stand.

(23)   He *who stayed the longest* fell in love with my wife.

F) Reference. Generally first and second person singular and plural pronouns (*I, we, you* plus derivatives) have **non-textual deictic reference** to the participants of a communicative situation and others associated with them. Thus, *I* refers to the speaker, *we* refers to the speaker plus others, and *you* refers to the hearer or to the hearer plus others. By contrast, third person singular and plural pronouns (*he, she, it, they* plus derivatives) generally have **textual anaphoric reference**, referring back to a preceding constituent:

(24)   'You heard what {Fiona} was saying. *She* was in East Berlin long enough to develop strong feelings of friendship.'

(25)   {Her painting} was far better than I thought *it* would be.

As a referential pronoun, *it* may also have (part of) a preceding sentence or, more vaguely, the condition(s) expressed by the preceding linguistic context as its antecedent:

(26)   Being in love makes you liable to fall in love. People think *it* has to do with sex, that someone is not doing his duty in bed, or her duty in bed, but I think this is not the case. *It* has to do with the heart.

Here *it* is in competition with the demonstrative pronouns *this* and *that*.

Occasionally we come across **cataphoric textual reference** in subordinate adverbial clauses optionally placed in sentence-initial position:

(27)   Before anyone could stop *her*, {Zelda} yelled out.

Only rarely do we come across third person pronouns with **specific non-textual reference**:

(28)   'I'm not going with *her*, if that's what you think.' [child pointing at a nurse]

The number of people or things embraced by the plural pronouns *we, you* and *they* (plus derivatives) vary from expression to expression (*We raised our children in Birmingham / We Americans cherish our freedom of speech*). Sometimes they are used in a very general sense, somewhat abstracted from specific referents:

(29)   In the twentieth century *we* have come to take too many things for granted.

(30)   I have stopped smoking altogether. *You* never know what cigarettes will do to *you* in the long run.

(31)   Another thing this young chap does. He talks to himself in his room. *They* say these creative people can be a bit potty. But he's got bags of charm.

Despite the generic-like value of the pronouns in these examples of non-textual reference, *we* retains its basic speaker-inclusive meaning while *they* retains its speaker- and hearer-exclusive meaning ('those responsible or in the know'). In examples like (30), *you* is all-inclusive and not specifically hearer-oriented. The speaker uses it to avoid referring directly and bluntly to him- or herself. A more formal and impersonal alternative to general *you* is *one*:

(32)   *One* never knows what cigarettes will do to *one* in the long run.

After *as* and *than*, **non-referential** *it* is not used as a subject:

(33)   I shall act *as seems best.*

(34)   It was a book more rewarding *than at first sight might appear.*

If, however, the clause contains an infinitive lacking its object or complement, the subject is not omitted:

(35)   The translation is as removed from plain prose *as it is possible to be.*

(36)   He got more *than it is possible to get today.*

Note finally that *he* followed by a restrictive relative clause is sometimes used generically in the sense 'anyone':

(37)   *He* who betrays our country must be punished.

Such expressions are formal and have an old-fashioned ring to them by comparison with e.g. *those who* ...

15.2.2. Possessive pronouns

Possessive pronouns can be regarded as personal pronouns in the genitive case. There are two sets of possessive forms, **determinative** and **autonomous**, corresponding to the specifying and the autonomous nominal genitive (cf. section 14.3.8 [A]):

NUMBER	PERSON	GENDER	FUNCTION	
			DET	AUT
singular	1	-	*my*	*mine*
	2	-	*your*	*yours*
	3	masculine	*his*	*his*
		feminine	*her*	*hers*
		neuter	*its*	*(its)*
plural	1	-	*our*	*ours*
	2	-	*your*	*yours*
	3	-	*their*	*theirs*

Here are some examples showing the determinative and autonomous uses of possessive pronouns:

(1)   He tacked a note on the door of *his* little yellow house. (determinative use)

(2)   Most of the women were fastening *their* corsets. (determinative use)

(3)   There was not another stomach like *hers* on earth. (autonomous use)

(4)   He'd fucked up his own life, so he stole *mine*. (autonomous use)

Except for *mine* and *his*, the autonomous items are formed by adding the suffix *-s* to the determinative form. This suffix should not be confused with the apostrophe *s* (*'s*) suffix used in connection with nominal genitives such as *John's* (thus while *its* in *its colour* is a possessive pronoun, *it's* is the contracted form of *it is*). Note in this connection that *its* is rarely, if ever, used with autonomous function without the emphasizer OWN:

(5)   The cat knows that this dish is *its own*.

A) Possessive pronouns vs. *of*-constructions. Though generally the determinative possessive forms correspond to specifying nominal genitives (both constructions expressing definiteness, as in e.g. *the old man's hat* and *his hat*), determinative possessive pronouns have a wider distribution, covering much of the ground occupied by the *of*-construction as well as the specifying genitive in noun groups. Thus while we would normally have to say *the roof of the house* rather than *the house's roof*, we can only say *its roof*, not **the roof of it*. However, the *of*-construction is often used in connection with:

(i) expressions with little or no possessive meaning: *Let's stop this discussion – I quite frankly don't see <u>the point of it</u> / The kitchen was one big mess and in <u>the middle of it</u> was this young kid getting supper ready.*

(ii) fixed expressions: *the long and short of it / on the face of it / by the look of him / for the life of me / he soon got the knack of it*, etc.;

(iii) pronoun groups ending with a personal pronoun like *all of them / one of us / both of you / either of them*, etc.: *the feelings of either of them* rather than *either of their feelings*, which strictly speaking is ambiguous.

B) Possessive pronouns as post-genitives. Determinative possessive pronouns are definite determiners like nominal genitives. Indefinite reference can only be achieved by means of the post-genitive:

(6)   I met *a friend of his* the other day.

Like nominal post-genitives, pronominal ones typically have partitive meaning (*a friend of his* = *one of his friends*). Pronominal post-genitives behave like nominal ones with respect to determiner usage (cf. section 14.3.8

[A]). Note in this connection the lack of partitive association in groups with a demonstrative determiner expressing the speaker's (approving or disapproving) interest:

(7)   Stuart married *that boring little goodie-goodie wife of his.*

C) Possessive pronouns vs. the definite article. Generally the distinction between these two definite determiners is clear: the definite article signals definiteness only, possessive pronouns signal definiteness plus some relation between two referents (for example, *his wife* is not only definite but also expresses a relation between the referents of *wife* and *his*). In expressions referring to **parts of the body or clothes** associated with someone, possessive pronouns are used rather than the definite article: *He put his hand in his pocket.* But the definite article is in such cases often used:

(i) in detached, clinically objective expressions such as *How is the chest now?*

(ii) in preposition groups if the 'possessor' is represented as DONE-TO elsewhere in the clause:

(8)   I gave [him]^DONE-TO a little poke in *the* face with *my* head.

(9)   [Bob]^DONE-TO was hit right on *the* nose by Jack.

D) Possessive pronouns vs. personal pronouns. As shown in section 12.2, there is sometimes vacillation between possessive pronouns and the objective form of personal pronouns when followed by a clause:

(10)   It happened without *him/his* realising what was going on.

E) Possessive pronouns emphasized by OWN. Possessive pronouns can be emphasized by OWN, as in the following examples:

(11)   He apologised for going on so much about *his own* life.

This combination of pronoun and OWN can also be used autonomously, even in post-genitive constructions without partitive association. In such cases, however, the determinative form of the pronoun is retained:

(12)   I realized that the husky voice was *my own.*

(13)   She hasn't even got a car of *her own.*

15.2.3. Reflexive pronouns

In the first and second persons the reflexive pronouns are formed by adding the singular suffix *-self* or the plural suffix *-selves* to the determinative possessive pronoun. In the third person the suffixes are added to the objective form of the personal pronoun.

In addition to the reflexive pronouns listed in the table, *oneself* is used as the counterpart to *one* in its generic sense, cf. e.g. *One does not, on the whole, permit oneself to attend ceremonies to which one has not been invited.*

NUMBER	PERSON	GENDER	REFLEXIVE
singular	1	-	myself
	2	-	yourself
	3	masculine	himself
		feminine	herself
		neuter	itself
plural	1	-	ourselves
	2	-	yourselves
	3	-	themselves

There are three distinct uses of reflexive pronouns in English: a) **reflexive**, b) **emphatic dependent**, and c) **emphatic autonomous**.

A) Reflexive use. When used reflexively, the pronoun assumes one of the following functions: Od, Oi, Cs, CJT, DEP of a preposition, or S of nonfinite P, as in the following examples, respectively:

(1)   Porter just perched *himself* up in the attic window. (Od)
(2)   She bought *herself* a new Ferrari. (Oi)
(3)   Liz and Roger were not quite *themselves*. (Cs)
(4)   She blamed me and *herself* for what happened. (CJT in O:cu)
(5)   You see, I used to have this joke with *myself*. (DEP of preposition)
(6)   'You get out now,' I heard *myself* saying. (S of nonfinite P)

A defining feature of pronouns used reflexively, is the fact that they are **coreferential** with the subject of the clause within which they occur, as in (1) to (5). If the pronoun occurs as the subject of a nonfinite subclause, it is co-referential with the subject of the matrix clause, as in (6). If in a nonfinite subclause the pronoun assumes one of the other functions (e.g. object), it is coreferential with the explicit or implied subject of the subclause, as in (7) and (8), respectively:

(7)   I wanted [her to improve *herself*].
(8)   I wanted [to improve *myself*].

Some verbs always require reflexive objects. Such verbs are called **reflexive verbs**: e.g. ABSENT, BESTIR, INGRATIATE, PRIDE.

(9)   He obviously tried to ingratiate *himself* with his superiors.

Other verbs are used reflexively with a distinct meaning: e.g. APPLY, AVAIL, CONDUCT, EXERT.

(10)   I sometimes got better marks than him, but that was when he chose not to exert *himself*. (i.e. EXERT used in the sense 'to make a great effort', not 'to use' as in 'to exert one's influence')

Reflexivization is obligatory in most cases of coreferentiality. But there are notable exceptions. In an example like:

(11)   Jack loves only Jack.

the lack of reflexivization is a deliberate stylistic choice.

With some verbs, such as BEHAVE, DRESS, SHAVE, WASH, there is a choice between strictly intransitive use and transitive reflexive use with only a slight difference of meaning:

(12)   She began to dress (*herself*).

In preposition groups, the objective form of a personal pronoun is occasionally used instead of the corresponding reflexive pronoun, thus commonly in constructions expressing space or location:

(13)   He didn't seem to notice the decoration above *him*.
(14)   She closed the door behind *her*.

In some cases, the reflexive pronoun is used idiomatically while the personal pronoun is used in a concrete locational sense, compare:

(15)   They were beside *me*. (concrete location)
(16)   They were beside *themselves* with rage. (figurative meaning)

B) Emphatic dependent use. When used as emphatic dependents, reflexive pronouns add contrastive meaning to a (pro)nominal constituent:

(17)   They were treated by Miss Florence Nightingale *herself*.
(18)   He *himself* had never felt this way before.

Reflexive pronouns with emphatic dependent use receive primary stress and often appear in post-head position. But they also take up positions identified elsewhere as adverbial positions in the clause (cf. section 7.4):

(19a)   Helen would *herself* tell me the bad news. (central-M)
(19b)   Helen would tell me the bad news *herself*. (T)

C) Emphatic autonomous use. Finally, reflexive pronouns are used non-reflexively and autonomously as emphatic **alternatives** to the personal pronouns – typically after prepositions (especially *than, as, like, except* and *but*) or when serving as a CJT in a compound unit:

(20)   No one knew this better than *himself*.
(21)   She's about the same age as *myself*.
(22)   Everybody except *herself* laughed at the joke.
(23)   That topic was connected with the terminal row between Sally and *myself*.

The reflexive pronoun is here often used to avoid having to choose between the subjective and objective form of the personal pronoun (*than he / than him, as I / as me*, etc.).

15.3. Pronouns without a person distinction

15.3.1. Demonstrative pronouns

The demonstrative pronouns in English can be presented in terms of the two categories applying to them, **number** and **deixis**:

NUMBER DEIXIS	singular	plural
near	*this*	*these*
distant	*that*	*those*

To these four central demonstratives we can add the two locative adverbial demonstratives *here* and *there*.

Demonstratives are emphatic in nature. They have both determinative and autonomous uses:

(1)   At *that* exact moment they were both indoors. (determinative)
(2)   In *this* way, the name acquired a quasi-official status. (determinative)
(3)   *These* couldn't be her children. (autonomous)
(4)   He counted *those* who were late. (autonomous)

Demonstratives assume the usual range of external functions: S, Od, Oi, Cs, Co, CJT, and DEP of preposition. Here are some examples:

(5)   *That*'s normal, isn't it? (S)

(6)   Why am I telling you *this*? (Od)

(7)   I'm going to give *those who failed me* a little surprise. (Oi)

(8)   How did it ever come to *this*? (DEP of preposition)

Elsewhere, demonstratives normally serve as determiners (as in *that exact moment*, *this way*, etc.). But in connection with adjectives and quantifiers such as *much* and *many*, the singular demonstratives may serve also as degree adverbs, indicating a precise amount or measure:

(9)   I didn't give her *that much*.

(10)   The worm was *this long*.

Informally they serve as intensifiers without an association of precise degree:

(11)   The party wasn't *that bad*.

(12)   I was *that pleased!*

A) The number category. The singular pronouns *this* and *that* are used in connection with singular and uncountable concepts:

(13)   *This* is my favourite dish.

(14)   We have to use a little bit of *that* sugar.

These and *those* are used in connection with plural concepts:

(15)   They say *these* creative people can be a bit potty.

(16)   I want two of *these* and three of *those*.

Only the singular pronouns are used in connection with collective nouns like FAMILY, GOVERNMENT, etc.: *this family*, *that government*, etc., not **these family*, **those government*, etc. However, 'internally countable' nouns (see section 14.4.1) permit both singular and plural pronouns, depending on the intended meaning: *this people / these people*; *that crew / those crew*.

B) Reference to persons. When used determinatively, all four demonstratives are compatible with personal referents: *that girl*, *this woman*, *those neighbours*, *these composers*. When used autonomously, the singular forms are used only with personal referents in expressions serving as introductions or identification (in competition with *it*):

(17)   *This* is my wife.

(18)   *That* was my brother on the phone.

Elsewhere emphatic personal pronouns, not demonstrative pronouns, are used to refer deictically to singular personal referents:

(19)   'I'm not going with *her/*that*.'

The plural forms are used in these contexts too: *These are my neighbours / Those were two of my colleagues*. But in addition, *these* is occasionally used anaphorically in competition with *they* (as in *All her best friends were there and these never dare criticize her*), and *those* is used freely with personal reference when restrictively modified (as in *Those who want to continue, please raise your hands / Those in the know will surely keep it a secret*).

C) Deixis. Like the definite article, the demonstrative pronouns are markers of definiteness. But unlike the definite article, the demonstratives specify the referent as near or distant in relation to the speaker:

(20)   I want *these gloves*, not *those*.

(21)   Non-native language teacher, holding a book in his hand: 'Repeat after me: *This is a book.*'
Learner at the back: '*That is a book.*'
Language teacher: 'I said: *This is a book.*'
Learner: 'Well, let's just say: *It's a book.*'

This last example is from an authentic classroom situation, where the learner had a better intuitive understanding of the deictic nature of the demonstrative pronouns than the teacher. In both examples, the near pronouns *this* and *these* are used about what is near at hand in relation to the speaker, and the distant pronouns *that* and *those* are used about more distant referents.

The deixis of demonstratives operates not only on a spatial dimension but also on a temporal one:

(22)   How's life *these days*? / How *was* life back in *those days*?

This and *these* are used about present time and *that* and *those* about past time.

D) Related referential properties. When used with textual reference, the deictic nature of the demonstratives is often subdued. Both the near and the distant pronouns are used anaphorically in competition with *it*:

(23)   Oliver's {career}, if *that* isn't too grand a word for it, had made only a single movement, and that was downwards.

(24)   He's a friendly dog called Poulidor, but {he's now got so old that he's gone stone deaf}. Both Oliver and I find *this* terribly sad.

The difference between the near and the distant pronouns is in such cases very subtle. Often, as in (23) and (24), both variants are possible. The effect of using the distant pronouns is to direct the hearer's attention to something mentioned in the preceding linguistic context, while the effect of using the near pronouns is to 'update' something mentioned in what is technically the preceding linguistic context as part of the current linguistic context, with the immediacy of present relevance. In other words, with the distant pronouns, the hearer is guided backwards in the text, whereas with the near pronouns, the hearer is prompted to consider the antecedent as immediately present in the communicative situation.

In practice, though often interchangeable, the distant pronouns tend to be used with specific, clearly delimited antecedents while the near pronouns tend to be used with more general antecedents, often approaching a qualitative value like *such*, compare:

(25)   {Filthy old lecher, seducer of schoolgirls, abandoner of wife and child} ... A chap can't expect to get much of a hearing with *those* labels attached.

(26)   It was awful. It was a shouting match. I was just trying to be practical, trying to express something that I thought came out of my love for Oliver, and he got all jumpy and hostile. *These* things don't immediately go away, either.

Not surprisingly, the near pronouns rather than the distant pronouns are used **cataphorically**, often in contrast to an anaphoric distant pronoun:

(27)   Poor old Ollie, up to his mucous membrane in a tub of merde, how inspissated, how uncheerful ... No, actually *that*'s not what I think. What I think is *this*. {I love Gillian, she loves me}. *That*'s the starting-point ...

E) Uses without a deictic contrast. The deictic value of the demonstratives is sometimes replaced by an association of familiarity (plus approval or disapproval):

(28)   I wish him everything, *that* Stuart: health, hearth, happiness and herpes.

(29)   Perhaps he's ashamed of *this* girlfriend of his.

Idiomatically, demonstratives are used with little or no deictic value:

(30)   Oh, we talked about *this* and *that*.

(31)   *That*'s my big girl!

(32)   She finally left him, and *that*'s *that*.

The distant pronouns are used without a contrast to the near pronouns when followed by restrictive modification:

(33)   Let us agree upon the following generality: that *those who have inflicted marriage upon themselves* assume such rival guises alternately.

(34)   Roger was careful not to mention *that which everybody had already guessed.*

When followed by restrictive modification, *that* and *those* are in competition with *the one* and *the ones*:

(35)   Sam changes his chair for *that / the one* in which his uncle had been sitting.

(36)   The issues in 1960 are no longer *those / the ones* that existed in 1935.

In the singular, the expression with *that* is more formal than *the one*, while in the plural *those* is normal in expressions implying 'established category', *the ones* being somewhat colloquial

That and *those*, but not *this* and *these*, are used determinatively followed by a restrictively modified nominal head:

(37)   I even had time to give an ironic accent to *that* crappy bit of the service in which you promise to 'share' your worldly goods with your partner.

(38)   Oliver is one of *those* people who make more sense in a context.

The difference between the definite article and demonstrative pronoun in such constructions is that the latter implies not only definiteness but also 'established category'.

15.3.2. Interrogative pronouns

The central interrogative pronouns in English are:

who, whom, whose / which / what

To this list we can add the adverbial pro-forms *when, where, why* and *how* (which represent prepositional groups such as *at what time, in what place, for what reason* and *in what way*).

A) Syntax. Interrogative pronouns, whose primary function is to form *wh*-interrogative constructions, normally take up clause-initial position. In main clauses they trigger subject-operator inversion unless they serve as subjects:

(1)   *Who* did you meet? (O)

(2)   *What* is this? (Cs)

(3)   *Who* wants to go? (S)

Interrogative pronouns may take up terminal position when repeated (as in *Who is who?* and *He does not know which is which*), as well as in echo-questions (*You said WHAT?*).

There is no partial inversion in interrogative subclauses:

(4)   I asked her *who you met / what this was / where you live / who wanted to go*.

Note that in corresponding *yes-no* interrogative subclauses, *if* and *whether* serve as interrogative conjunctions:

(5)   I asked her if/whether you met her.

Autonomous interrogative pronouns are occasionally modified by specifying or intensifying expressions: *where in France, who on earth, why the hell*, etc. Intensification is often provided by adding *ever* to the pronoun: *whoever, whatever, wherever*, etc. *Which* is frequently followed by an *of*-construction:

Which of them did it? / Which of your friends are coming? Similarly, *who* may be followed by *among*: *Who among them knew what was going on?* Rhetorically, *who* may also be used with an *of*-construction, or even a relative clause: *Who of us would join the Republicans? / Who that has heard him can doubt his motives?*

The following interrogatives can serve not only autonomously but also as determiners: *whose, which* and *what*, as in e.g. *Whose car is this? / Which book do you prefer? / What strategies have you prepared?* Exclamatory *what* may serve as a predeterminer: *What a load of rubbish you are saying!* Only *how* can serve as a modifier: *How expensive is this car?*

B) Categories. Three categories are relevant to the description of interrogatives: **case** (*who* vs. *whom* vs. *whose*), **gender** (*who* vs. *what*) and what might be termed **interrogative scope** (*who* and *what* vs. *which*).

a) Case applies to the series *who, whom* and *whose*, the last two being inflectional variants of the first. While *whom* is an objective form like e.g. *him*, its distribution is different. It is obligatory only after a preposition in clause-initial position, a fairly formal construction: *To whom did you give the book?* Very colloquially, the subjective form does occur even after a preposition but only when the group appears as a complete utterance by itself (*To who?*) or in clause-final position (*Di shacked up with who?*). The reason we are unlikely to find *To who did you give the book* is that there is a stylistic clash: fronting of the whole preposition group is formal whilst the use of the subjective form *who* is informal. The objective form is used also as prepositional complement in discontinuous adverbials and as object: *Whom did you give the book to? / Whom did you call last night?*, but such constructions are felt to be somewhat cumbersome and formal.

The genitive form *whose* is used determinatively and autonomously like possessive pronouns: *Whose shoes are these? / Whose are these shoes?*

b) Gender. The gender distinction between personal and non-personal is relevant to the description of all the three central pronouns *who, which* and *what*. While *who* (and its case variants *whom* and *whose*) can be used only about personal referents, *which* is used about both personal and nonpersonal referents, cf. the following examples which show determinative and autonomous use, respectively:

(6)   *Which car/kid had disappeared?*

(7)   *Which of the cars/kids had disappeared?*

Determinative *what* is also used about both personal and non-personal referents:

(8)   *What cars/drivers will make it in time?*

Used autonomously, *what* is used about non-personal referents (but see subsection c below):

(9)   *What* did he say?

(10)   *What* went wrong?

c) Interrogative scope works on two dimensions: quantitative and qualitative selectivity. **Quantitative selectivity** affects the choice of pronoun in this way: if a question is general, not assuming a limited set of possible answers, *who* or *what* is chosen; if a question assumes a limited number of alternatives, *which* is chosen (with an implicit or explicit *of*-construction). Thus, for example, the difference between:

(11)   *Who* is Roger Wilkinson?

(12)   *Which (of them)* is Roger Wilkinson?

is that (12), unlike (11), requires a specific context with a limited number of potential bearers of the name Roger Wilkinson. Similarly, in:

(13)   *What books* do you like?

(14)   *Which (of these) books* do you like best?

the first question is completely open, while the second assumes discrimination within a limited set of books. One exception to the rule about *who* assuming general selectivity is when it is followed by *among*, resembling *which* followed by *of*:

(15)   *Who among them* would think up such a plan?

Sometimes *who* and *what* are used instead of *which* in contexts where, superficially, there seems to be a limited choice:

(16)   *What* would you like to do: go for a walk or make love to me?

(17)   *Who* did you call, John or Roger?

However, even in such cases, *who* and *what* retain their association of general selectivity, the specified alternatives serving more as examples of possible answers than as an imposed limitation.

The second dimension of interrogative scope, **qualitative selectivity**, distinguishes *what* from *who/whom* and *which*. The difference between them is often that *what* is used to query 'kind of referent' whereas *who/whom* and *which* are used to query 'identity of referent', compare:

(18a)   *Who* is your best friend? (Roger!)

(18b)   *What* is your best friend? (A university professor)

(19a)   *Which years* are leap years? (1952, 1956, 1960 ...)

(19b)   *What years* are leap years? (e.g. years in which February has 29 days)

In rhetorical questions, *who* is however used not so much about identity but about 'kind of referent':

(20)   *Who* would do this to her? (i.e. 'What kind of person would do this to her?')

15.3.3. Relative pronouns

The central interrogative pronouns serve also as the central relative pronouns:

>   who, whom, whose / which / what

To these we can add the conjunction-like *that*, the 'zero relative' Ø, the relative adjuncts *when, where, why* and *how* and the intensive *-ever* forms: *whoever, whichever, whatever*.

A) Syntax. Relative pronouns, unlike interrogative pronouns, characteristically serve a double purpose: they signal clausal subordination like subordinating conjunctions and at the same time they take on a clause function other than SUB in the subclause (e.g. subject or object), referring anaphorically to a constituent in the matrix:

(1)   You remember the case of {the craftsman} *who* chipped out a priest's hole for himself on the ship? (S)

(2)   {The second story}, *which* I pass on without comment, touches on more delicate matters. (O)

Autonomous function only: *who, whom, that, Ø, whoever* (as well as *when, where, why* and *how*), as in:

(3)   They arrested Jeremy Soames, *who* was on his honeymoon.

Determinative function only: *whose*, as in:

(4)   Why did God preserve this species, *whose creation* did not reflect particularly well on its creator?

Either autonomous or determinative function: *which(ever)* and *what(-ever)*; compare:

(5)   He used a gun *which* he had borrowed from a friend.

(6)   He used a gun, *which fact* bothered the rabbis.

Autonomous relatives may serve as S or Od (as in some of the examples above) or as Cs, Co, A or DEP in a preposition group, but usually not as Oi:

(7)   Roger wasn't quite the speaker *that* he used to be. (Cs)

(8)   He's a bit of a jerk, *which* some of the girls even call him to his face. (Co)

(9)   I met him in the gallery *where* we used to meet. (A)

(10)   Then came the day *Ø* we had been longing *for*. (DEP in preposition group)

Relatives always appear in clause-initial position, as in the examples above, or as part of a larger clause-initial constituent, e.g.:

(11)   We interviewed a great many applicants, *the majority of whom* we rejected.

Relative clauses are either **restrictive** or **non-restrictive**. Restrictive relative clauses help establish the referent of the antecedent, while non-restrictive ones offer additional information about the referent of the antecedent:

(12a)   The soldiers *who were brave* ran forward. (restrictive)
(12b)   The soldiers, *who were brave*, ran forward. (non-restrictive)

A restrictive relative clause is a DEP in relation to its antecedent, whereas a non-restrictive clause, which is always marked orthographically or intonationally as a separate information unit, is best analysed as an adverbial.

B) Categories. Relatives assume the **number** and **person** of the antecedent:

(13a)   The *soldiers* who *were* brave ran forward.
(13b)   The *soldier* who *was* brave ran forward.
(14)   *I* who *am* ... / *You* who *are* ... / *He* who *is* ..., etc.

a) The gender category accounts for the distinction between *who(m)* and *which*. As in the examples offered so far, *who(m)* is used with personal or personified antecedents (including e.g. pet animals, as in *Spotty, who was our first dog, followed little Jane everywhere*), while *which* is used with non-personal or depersonified antecedents (including sometimes small children, as in *She bore four children, one of which died in infancy*).

That and *Ø* are used with both personal and nonpersonal antecedents: *The woman that/Ø you met at my party is Jack's sister; The house that/Ø they built has never been insured.*

What is used with personal referents only in determinative use in examples like *She called what friends she had* ('she called the friends that she had') where the relative is used **independently** of an antecedent (see below).

Though basically non-personal, *which* is used about 'type or kind of person' when serving as complement in non-restrictive relative clauses:

(15)   They considered him a frightful bore, *which* he is. (Cs)
(16)   He's a bit of a jerk, *which* some of the girls even call him to his face. (Co)

Whose is used with personal antecedents (as in *I ran into Jack, whose car had just been stolen*), as well as with non-personal antecedents (as in *This is the palace whose demolition has been ordered by the King*).

b) The case category accounts for the distinction between *who, whom* and *whose*. The genitive form *whose* is used determinatively like the possessive pronouns and therefore never overlaps with *who* and *whom*, which are always autonomous. The objective form *whom* is obligatory after a preposition and generally the preferred form as object and as discontinuous DEP of a preposition, especially in non-restrictive relative clauses; while the subjective form *who* is used as subject and informally as object and DEP in a discontinuous preposition group; cf. the following examples:

(17)   The agent *to whom/*to who* I transferred all the money has disappeared.

(18)   Ian, *whom/who* I trusted with the money, has disappeared.

(19)   Ian, *whom/who* I transferred all the money *to*, has disappeared.

(20)   The agent *who/*whom* transferred all the money to me has disappeared.

c) Reference. One of the central functions of relative pronouns is to refer anaphorically to a particular constituent, such as (the head of) a group, as in the examples discussed so far. However, relative pronouns may also have **clausal referents** (i.e. serve as **sentential relatives**, cf. section 12.7 [iii]), *which* with anaphoric value and *what* with cataphoric value:

(21)   {She was late}, *which* was bad, but *what* was worse, {she didn't apologize}.

As a parenthetical insertion after a coordinating conjunction *which* very occasionally has a cataphoric-like value:

(22)   X is reduced to virtually nothing, and, *which* shouldn't bother us unduly at this point, {Y is left unaffected}.

Sentential *which* is commonly used as a determiner, especially in preposition groups: *..., which fact led her to state ... / ..., for which reason she decided ... / ..., in which case we will have to ...*

A distinction must be drawn between relatives with the normal textual (anaphoric or cataphoric) reference and the so-called **independent relatives** (see also section 12.2 [ii]). Independent relatives have non-textual reference and can be interpreted as a fusion of a relative and an antecedent. The following items can be used in this way: *what(ever), whoever, whichever, where(ever), when(ever), why, how*; cf.:

(23)   I gave her *what* was left.

(24)   *Whoever* fails to attend the meeting will be fired.

Independent relatives thus approach the value of a demonstrative or an indefinite pronoun followed by an anaphoric relative (i.e. 'that which', 'anyone who', etc.). *What*, unlike *whoever*, is also used determinatively with an association of 'small quantity':

(25)   I gave her *what oranges* we found.

(26)   She called *what friends* she had.

Independent *who(m)* is found only in idiomatic expressions like *Who delays pays* and with a very restricted set of verbs (CHOOSE, LIKE, PLEASE) as a very formal alternative to *whoever*: *You may marry whom/whoever you like.* The objective form *whomever* is not used, even as a prepositional complement: *You may give this book to whoever/*whomever you want.*

That is not used independently, except in rare expressions like *Stupid is that stupid says* and *Handsome is that handsome does.*

The relative adjuncts *when*, *where* and *why* can be used independently: *8 p.m. is (the time/moment) <u>when</u> you leave / This is (the place) <u>where</u> I was born / That was (the reason) <u>why</u> he left.* Relative *how* is always used independently: *This is (*the manner) how you operate the machine.*

C) **The choice of relative pronoun.** There are few hard and fast rules applying to the choice of relative pronoun. But the following overview will serve as a rough first approximation:

Restrictive clauses		
Function of pronoun	Choice of pronoun	Examples
S	who/which/that	*The man who/that remained* *The table which/that remained*
O or DEP of preposition placed finally	that/Ø/which	*The man that/Ø I saw* *The man that/Ø I glanced at* *The table which/that/Ø I saw* *The table which/that/Ø I glanced at*
DEP of preceding preposition	whom/which	*The man at whom I glanced* *The table at which I glanced*
C	that/Ø	*He is not the lover that/Ø he used to be*

Non-restrictive clauses		
Function of pronoun	Choice of pronoun	Examples
S	who/which	*Peter, who lives in Lancaster,* *Paris, which is the capital of France,*
O or DEP of preposition placed finally	who(m)/which	*Peter, who(m) I know well,* *Paris, which I know well,* *Peter, who(m) I glanced at,* *Paris, which I am fond of,*
DEP of preceding preposition	whom/which	*Peter, to whom I sent the contract,* *This room, from which the noise came,*
C	which	*They consider him a frightful bore, which he is*

Let us now look at some of the finer details in connection with the choice of relative pronoun:

a) After a preposition only *whom* and *which* are used. Continuous relativized preposition groups are fairly formal:

(27)   They chose the material according to the purpose *for which* it was intended.

(28)   She had lied to Charles, *to whom* her affair came as a nasty surprise.

b) As complement *which* is used in non-restrictive relative clauses and *that* or Ø in restrictive relative clauses, irrespective of the nature of the antecedent, as in *They consider him a frightful bore, which he is* and *He is not the lover that/Ø he used to be.*

In **other** functions, there is much more vacillation in the choice of pronoun, with the gender-neutral and light relatives *that* and Ø as common alternatives to *who(m)* and *which*, above all in restrictive relative clauses. In general, considerations of weight, rhythm, syntactic complexity and medium play an important role. Thus *that* and Ø are commoner a) when immediately following the head (pro)noun of the antecedent; b) when the relative clause is syntactically simple; and c) in informal, spoken language. For example, *that* is a more likely pronoun than *which* (or *who*) in:

(29)   You are right, by the way, to see the animals *that* fled as the nobler species.

By contrast we are not surprised to find *which* rather than *that* in:

(30)   They had mobile faces very similar to human beings *which* you could swear were about to utter speech.

c) As subject *who* and *which* are used in non-restrictive relative clauses. In restrictive relative clauses, *that* is sometimes chosen instead of *who* especially if the antecedent is modified/determined by a superlative or by *all, any, every, no* or *only*:

(31)   They were obliged to select *the best pair that* presented itself.

(32)   *Any student that* passes this exam will receive a scholarship.

As subject, *that* is a common choice instead of *which* in restrictive relative clauses. The difference between them is largely one of medium and style, the light pronoun being frequent in spoken, informal English, *which* in written, formal English:

(33)   In the version *that* has come down to you, the raven has a very small part.

(34)   On the list were several books which could only be studied in the library.

As a rule of thumb, Ø is not used as subject. Exceptions are a) constructions with zero for real subject in existential clauses with *there* as provisional subject; b) existential *there* sentences in colloquial speech; and c) very colloquial cleft sentences, as in the following examples respectively:

(35)   We quickly decided to lie about how many of us Ø there were.

(36)   There is someone here Ø wants to see you.

(37)   It was John Ø did it, not me!

d) As object or DEP in discontinuous preposition groups in non-restrictive relative clauses, we find *which* with non-personal antecedents and *whom* (or informal *who*) with personal antecedents. In restrictive relative clauses *that* and *Ø* are frequent alternatives to *who(m)* and *which*:

(38)   Here's the book *that/Ø* I got from my sister.

(39)   Here's the book *that/Ø* he keeps quoting *from*.

(40)   My sister helped the girl *that/Ø* we just met.

(41)   My sister helped the girl *that/Ø* I sent the book *to*.

With personal antecedents, *that* or *Ø* is often chosen to avoid the case problem of *who* vs. *whom*, both of which are also often felt to be somewhat cumbersome and, in the case of *whom*, formal. Thus the first example is clearly preferred to the second:

(42)   The man *that/Ø* I saw said it was all right to visit you this afternoon.

(43)   The man *who(m)* I saw said it was all right to visit you this afternoon.

e) As adverbials relative *when* and *where* may occur in both restrictive and non-restrictive clauses, relative dependent *why* only in restrictive clauses with REASON as antecedent. *How* is only used independently. In restrictive relative clauses, *when* and *why* are often replaced by *Ø* or *that*, *where* only occasionally so:

(44)   I am thinking of the time/morning *Ø/that* he had the ass keel-hauled.

(45)   The only reason *Ø/that* he didn't come was that he didn't want to be elected.

(46)   The place *Ø/that* we used to meet was unknown to my boss.

(47)   *The village *Ø/that* I was born lies in the Blue Mountains.

Relativized prepositional groups are often used instead of the proadverbials *when* and *where*:

(48)   My secretary noted the exact time *at which* the first meeting started.

(49)   The room *in which* the negotiations took place was next to my office.

f) A few extra points: Nonpersonal *all*, *everything* and *anything* are virtually always followed by *that* (or *Ø* outside subject function):

(50)   All *that* matters is that you get well.

(51)   Everything *Ø/that* he said made her very angry.

In subject function, *who* is normal after personal *all*, *everyone*, *anyone* and *someone*:

(52)   Anyone *who* knows anything about wood would have done the same.

(53)   I am looking for someone *who* can write up the report for us.

That instead of *which* is rare in non-restrictive relative clauses:

(54)   The ash trees retain their long and melancholy-looking seeds, *that* are sometimes called ash-keys.

Outside subject function Ø is often used in restrictive relative clauses if the subject is a personal pronoun:

(55)   The soldier Ø you killed was only a boy.

15.3.4. Indefinite pronouns

The following pronouns constitute the central system of indefinites:

every	*everyone*	*everybody*	*everything*	
some	*someone*	*somebody*	*something*	
any	*anyone*	*anybody*	*anything*	
no	*no one*	*nobody*	*nothing*	*none*

In addition, the following items will be briefly dealt with: a) **indefinite pro-adjuncts** such as *everywhere, sometimes, somehow*; b) *each* and *all*; c) the **dual pronouns** *both* and *(n)either*; and d) the **marginal pronoun** *one(s)*.

A) The central system. The four basic items *every, some, any* and *no* and their derivatives are distinguished in a number of ways.

a) Syntax. The derived forms function autonomously only (i.e. as group heads, S, Oi, Od, Cs, Co and prepositional complement); *every* and *no* serve as determiners only; and *some* and *any* have both functions:

(1)   *Everyone* laughed at *anything* he said.

(2)   *No* director has time to consider *every* script that comes his way.

(3)   *Some* projects did not get *any* funding at all.

(4)   While I got *some* of the money, my brothers hardly got *any*.

The more marginal items expressing place (*some-, any-, no-, else-, every-where*), time (*sometimes*) and manner (*somehow, anyhow*, AmE *someway*) typically (but not exclusively) serve as adverbials:

(5)   They *sometimes/somehow* let her down. (A)

When used autonomously, indefinite pronouns permit postmodification but not premodification or determination:

(6)   He was toying with *something dangerous*.

(7)   *Someone in Paris* leaked information to *some of his agents*.

But note that pre-head dependents qualifying the quantitative meaning are possible: *hardly anything, nearly everyone, virtually no one*, etc.

Derived indefinites are occasionally used as nouns and thus permit pre-H dependents:

(8)   Bond remarked on *the cute little nothing* she was wearing.

The *of*-construction is particularly frequent with *some, any* and *none* in partitive expressions:

(9)   I gave her *some of the money* but *none of the books*.

(10)   Have you read *any of John Irving's novels*?

With *something* and *nothing* the *of*-construction has qualitative rather than partitive meaning:

(11)   There is *something of the mad scientist* about him.

(12)   She had *nothing of her brother's charm*.

No and *any* may serve as dependents in comparative or comparative-like adjective and adverb groups:

(13)   Is her behaviour *any better* now?

(14)   In my view this is *no different*.

Note expressions with the positive form *good* (e.g. *Is he any good? / They are no good*) and *all/any/none* in comparative expressions with the definite article: *We didn't feel any the better for it / We felt none the wiser*.

None is used in connection with *too* + adjective/adverb and in expressions with *other*: *I was none too proud of what we had done / He was none other than the king himself*.

Something, nothing and *anything* approach adverb-like status in expressions like *He is something/nothing/not anything like his father*.

In colloquial AmE *some* and *any* may serve as degree adverbials: *Then she cried some, but that did not bother me any*.

b) Gender. Among the derivatives, the *-one* and *-body* forms are distinguished from the *-thing* forms in terms of the gender category (personal vs. non-personal). The basic forms *some* and *any*, as well as the derived form *none*, are used autonomously about both personal and non-personal referents:

Some/None of his cars/friends impressed me. All four basic forms are used determinatively in expressions with either personal or non-personal referents: e.g. *no sugar / no friend, some cars / some people*.

c) **Case and number**. The *-body* and *-one* forms behave like nouns with respect to case: they appear in the subjective case (as in the examples examined so far) and in the genitive case: *It is nobody's fault*. For discussion of number in relation to indefinite pronouns, see section 11.2 [F].

d) **General/restricted**. There is no well-established category to explain the distinction between the *-one* forms and the *-body* forms. Often the two are felt to be interchangeable: *Everybody/Everyone laughed when he fell*. The difference between them is subtle: the *-body* forms often imply a general context (as in e.g. *Nobody loves me*), whereas the *-one* forms imply a restricted context (e.g. *No one [i.e. no one present] agreed with me*).

e) **Universal/partitive**. The four series of central indefinite pronouns are classified in this way:

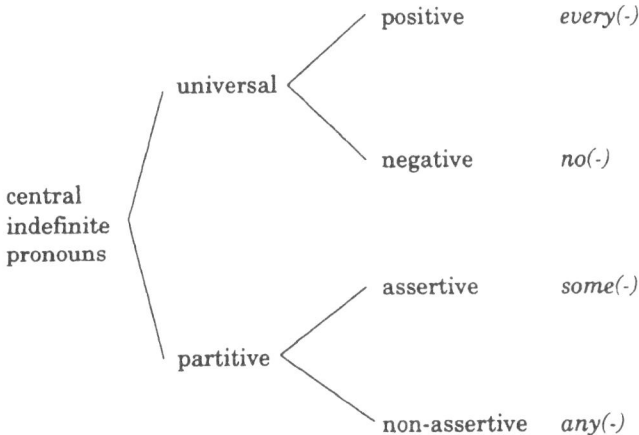

Universal pronouns are basically 'all or nothing' pronouns, while partitive pronouns indicate something in between. While the positive/negative distinction of universal pronouns is intuitively obvious, the assertive/non-assertive distinction of partitive pronouns requires some explanation. The assertive forms imply the existence of a referent whereas non-assertive forms do not. Thus, in positive statements, assertive forms are normal:

(15)   I found *some/*any* magazines in the drawer.
(16)   There was *someone/*anyone* in the kitchen.

Non-assertive forms are normal in questions and negative statements:

(17)   Was there *anyone* in the kitchen?

(18)   I didn't find *any* magazines in the drawer.

Non-assertive forms are frequent also in conditional clauses:

(19)   If you find *anything* in the drawer, please tell me at once.

However, non-assertive forms are sometimes used in positive statements with the implication that within the bounds specified there is **no limit** on the possible referent:

(20)   *Anyone* can beat him in chess.
(21)   He did absolutely *anything* he could think of.

Assertive forms are used in questions and conditional clauses with the implication that there is, or is likely to be, a particular referent:

(22)   Did *somebody* mess up your life?
(23)   If you see *someone* make a pass at her, call me at once.

f) Reference. When used as determiners, indefinite pronouns do not refer by themselves but obviously affect the referential properties of the head of the construction; cf. *every student* vs. *no student*.

   All the derived *-one*, *-body* and *-thing* forms have non-textual reference though their scope may be textually restricted by a modifier, as in *Someone in the English Department has complained*, or by another (intra- or extra-sentential) constituent, as in *When I visited University of Sussex last year, everyone was very helpful*.

   With autonomous *some*, *any* and *none*, textual restriction by means of an *of*-construction is particularly frequent:

(24)   *Some of my students* didn't want to attend *any of the courses*.
(25)   *None of my friends* could accept the proposal.

With plural meaning *some* and *none* are very occasionally used for non-textual reference without any form of textual restriction:

(26)   *None* are so deaf as those that will not hear.
(27)   *Some* will say that he did it for the money.

Autonomous *some*, *any* and *none* have textual, anaphoric reference in constructions like:

(28)   I offered them {some peanuts}. He didn't want *any* but she took *some*. She then asked for {some milk}, but there was *none* left in the fridge.

B) All. Like *every(-)* and *no(-)*, *all* is a universal pronoun. It is used autonomously (with or without postmodification) and (pre)determinatively about both personal and non-personal, singular and plural referents:

(29)   I hope *all* is well with you and your family.

(30)   *All* of us agreed to join him for dinner.

(31)   Did not Adam give the names to *all* the cattle?

(32)   I shall, in *all* humility, remain silent on the matter.

With non-textual reference, *all* is used idiomatically with a general meaning about non-personal referents (i.e. 'conditions'), as in (29). With personal or non-personal plural referents, non-textual *all* is normally replaced by *everyone/everybody* or *everything* unless there is a clear textual restriction on the potential referents, as e.g. in (30), where *all* is followed by an *of-*construction. With singular referents, *all* is used with non-countable meaning: *all humility, all milk, all life*, etc. *All* is used determinatively with geographical names conceived as collectives in constructions like *All Brighton were down at the beach.*

    All is also used as a post-head dependent:

(33)   I am tired of it *all*.

When the group functions as subject, postmodifying *all* is in the adverbial central-M position and thus potentially detached from its head:

(34)   They (have) *all* betrayed her.

All serves as a dependent of some adjectives, prepositions and adverbs:

(35)   Jack was *all* upset about the news.

(36)   She was *all* against my proposal.

(37)   The job was done *all* wrong.

Note finally the use of *all* in an expression like *She was all smiles* and fixed idiomatic collocations: *above all, after all, all in all, at all.*

C) Each is an individualizing universal pronoun used autonomously (if there is sufficient textual restriction) or determinatively about both personal and non-personal singular referents:

(38)   The two sisters smiled, *each* handing me a small envelope.

(39)   *Each* of the books was signed by the author.

(40)   I gave *each* car a thorough examination.

Unlike *all*, *each* is not used autonomously with non-textual reference unless there is some textual restriction, as in (38) and (39).

    Like *all* and *every(-)*, *each* refers to all members of a group. But there is a difference: *all* focuses on the group as a whole while *each* picks out the members of the group individually; *every(-)* shares some of the value of both *all* and *each*, referring to the individual members of the group collectively: *He told all of us / everyone / each of us the truth. Each* is thus near-synonymous with emphatic *every 'one* (which has the association of 'without exception'). *He told every 'one of us the truth*. Unlike *all* and *every(-)*, *each* is capable of referring to groups containing two members only (as in (38)).

Like *all*, *each* is also used as a post-head dependent:

(41)   We gave them *each* a big apple.

When the group serves as subject, postmodifying *each* is in the adverbial central-M position and thus potentially detached from its head:

(42)   They *each* took a big apple / They have *each* taken a big apple.

Unlike *all*, post-head *each* may appear also in terminal position:

(43)   We gave them a big apple *each*.
(44)   They took a big apple *each*.

D) The dual pronouns, which include *both* and *(n)either*, presuppose the existence of a class consisting of only two members.

a) Both is the dual counterpart to universal *all*. It is used autonomously (if there is sufficient textual restriction) or (pre)determinatively about both personal and non-personal referents:

(45)   Then the two girls turned up. *Both* wanted to see Ann about the funeral.
(46)   *Both* of the books were signed by the author.
(47)   *Both men* broke down on *both* occasions.

Like *all* and *each*, *both* is also used as a post-head dependent:

(48)   We gave them *both* a big apple.

When the group serves as subject, postmodifying *both* is in the adverbial central-M position and thus potentially detached from its head:

(49)   They (have) *both* understood what you are driving at.

b) (N)either. Positive *either* is the dual counterpart to *any*, while negative *neither* is the dual counterpart to *no/none*. The two pronouns are used autonomously (if there is sufficient textual restriction) or determinatively about both personal and non-personal referents:

(50)   Ann and Joan both played, but *neither* made a good impression.
(51)   He was quite happy to sign *either* of the books.
(52)   *Either* player can make the first move.

Either normally means 'one **or** the other of two group members', as in the examples above. In connection with nouns like SIDE and END however, it is sometimes used in an inclusive sense 'one **and** the other':

(53)   People were waiting at *either* side of the street.
(54)   There was a little candle at *either* end of the table.

E) One has a number of distinct functions:

(i) It is used determinatively or autonomously as a kind of emphatic indefinite article with singular numerical value in contrast to plural *some*, other cardinal numbers (*two, three ...*) and quantifiers like *several, many*, etc.:

(55)   The terrorists were going to execute *one* hostage an hour.

Its affinity with the indefinite article is obvious also in connection with proper names; compare: *I am looking for a/one Sarah Mortimer*. With contrastive stress it combines with the basic indefinite pronouns as an individualizing alternative to the *-one* compounds: *Every `one of them objected*.

(ii) As noted in section 15.2.1 [F], generic *one* (as well as its derivatives *one's* and *oneself*) is used as a formal alternative to *you*:

(56)   *One* never knows what cigarettes will do to *one* in the long run.

In AmE, this *one* may be referred anaphorically to by central pronouns:

(57)   *One* can't always trust *himself*, now can *he*?

(iii) *One* without determination refers in (somewhat formal) expressions to persons; here *one* approaches the meaning of 'someone':

(58)   She was never *one* to help her friends out of trouble.
(59)   He was *one* who would never forgive but who might forget.

One(s) is normal in definite singular or plural expressions about persons:

(60)   John was the *one* to consult on sentence analysis.
(61)   They are the *ones* who wouldn't let my sister alone last night.

Note in this connection the more or less fixed expressions: *the Holy One, the Evil One, the little/young ones*.

(iv) *One* is used anaphorically as a pro-form for a whole singular (pro)noun group (**g-replacive *one***):

(62)   When she asked for {a cigarette}, I gave her *one*.
(63)   Have you got {another film for this camera}? – Yes, there's *one* here.

(v) Singular *one* and plural *ones* are used as a pro-form for a singular or plural count noun rather than a whole group (**n-replacive *one***):

(64)   There were three {visitors}. The tall *one* with the glasses left early.
(65)   Some countries didn't welcome {journalists} and thought that white-skinned *ones* pretending interest in archaeological sites were British spies.

Note that n-replacive *one(s)* serves as a group head, allowing both pre- and postmodification, as well as determination.

N-replacive *one(s)* is naturally avoided when the antecedent is non-countable: *Old furniture is sometimes more expensive than new/*new one(s)*. It is also normally left out:

(i) after autonomous genitives/possessive pronouns and after *own: I much prefer her car to his / my own / my brother's.*

(ii) after numerals and quantifiers like *many, several, a few,* etc.: *They offered me five books of my own choice but I only took two / There were plenty of coins in the bag but he only gave her a few.*

There is vacillation in the following cases:

(i) in indefinite plural or definite singular or plural constructions with two parallel adjectives, *one* is often left out, especially in literary language, and especially if the adjectives express a natural contrast: *There were many Dutch politicians at the meeting but very few German (ones) / Everyone likes the old manager better than the new (one).*

(ii) after a comparative adjective *one* is often left out: *Two men entered the saloon. The younger (one) ordered a drink / This is not a good solution but can you think of a better (one)?*

(iii) after a superlative form *one* is often avoided outside distinctly colloquial speech: *Having examined the bottles very carefully, he selected the cheapest.*

(iv) after *another, other, last* and *next,* and after ordinals, *one* is optional but avoided in formal language: *If you miss the first news broadcast you can always watch the next one / I liked the first proposal better than the second.*

With some of the examples with the definite article, it is difficult to decide whether the adjective is used substantivally (cf. section 16.4) or is part of an elliptic construction.

N-replacive *one* is normally used:

(i) after the indefinite article + adjective in the positive form: *Having examined the many bottles very carefully, she selected a cheap one.* In distinctly literary language *one* is here sometimes dropped if the construction expresses a natural contrast.

(ii) to avoid syntactic ambiguity in cases where the modifier is a potential nominal head: *They were clearly human trails, not just the usual animal ones.*

(iii) after *only: Having examined the bottles very carefully, she selected the only one from Barossa Valley.*

16. Adjectivals and adverbals

Adjectivals and adverbals are closely related: a) both typically express **properties**; b) the category of **comparison** applies to both; and c) adverbs are often derived **morphologically** from adjectives (e.g. *blunt* → *bluntly*). The following sections deal first with adjectivals, focussing on three major problem areas: positional ordering (section 16.2), comparison (section 16.3) and the substantival use of adjectives (section 16.4). Much of what is said about adjectivals prepares the ground for the final section 16.5 on adverbals.

16.1. Preliminary discussion of adjectivals

16.1.1. Adjectives and adjective groups

Adjectivals are either single adjectives or groups with an adjective as head:

(1)   The *bitter* rivals spent a *long* time developing *very different* systems.

(2)   *French* women are *famous for their sensuality.*

(3)   He was *very fond of her parents.*

In adjective groups the head adjective accepts a pre-head dependent (as in *very different*) or a post-head dependent (as in *famous for their sensuality*) or both (as in *very fond of her parents*).

Pre-head dependents are predominantly adverbals (adverbs or adverb groups) modifying the adjective with respect to **degree**. Frequent degree adverbs found in this position are: VERY, MUCH, QUITE, EXTREMELY, RATHER, HIGHLY, REALLY, AS, SO, TOO, MORE, MOST, LESS, LEAST. But we also find pre-head nominals expressing **quantity**: *two years old / five feet tall / several miles long.*

Post-head dependents take the following forms: finite clauses (*certain that she will be there*), *to*-infinitive clauses (*eager to try it out*), *than*-clauses (*taller than she is*) and preposition groups (*capable of anything*). In addition we find the adverb ENOUGH in post-head position (*clever enough*). After WORTH we find post-head nominals and -*ing* clauses (*worth millions/doing again*). Post-head preposition groups and clauses usually express complementation rather than modification (cf. section 3.2). In some cases the presence of a post-head dependent is obligatory: *fond of her / bent on doing it / bound to accept* (cf. e.g. **He was fond*). In others the dependent is syntactically optional but if there is one, and if it is realized by a preposition group, the adjective often selects a certain preposition to the exclusion of others: *keen on, afraid of, similar to*, etc.

We often find **discontinuous dependents** in adjective groups, especially in connection with comparison:

(4)   Sally is *more* beautiful *than Jane.*

(5)   Sally is *as* calm *as she was yesterday.*

Here the post-head dependent is, strictly speaking, a post-head dependent of the adverb (*more/as*) rather than of the adjective.

The definite article is used as a pre-head dependent in connection with comparatives in correlative constructions like the following:

(6)   *The calmer* Sally appeared, *the angrier* Jack became.

Such constructions express a systematic relation between two changing properties. The definite article is also found in comparative adjectival or adverbal constructions preceded by *all*, *any* or *none*, e.g. *His explanation left me none the wiser / I hated her all the more because of the lies she told.*

16.1.2. Semantics

Adjectives express a large range of **properties in relation to things expressed by (pro)nominals**. These properties include subjective or emotional evaluation (NICE, GOOD, BEAUTIFUL), size (BIG, SMALL, LITTLE), shape (ROUND, SQUARE, FLAT), colour (RED, GREEN, GOLDEN, DARK, LIGHT), nationality (ENGLISH, CHINESE), age (OLD, YOUNG), material (WOODEN, SILVER, SILKY), category (REPUBLICAN, CONGRESSIONAL, SOLAR), etc. Many adjectives form pairs of opposites (antonyms): GOOD-BAD, TALL-SHORT, etc. A large number of adjectives do not enter a binary system but are systemically more complex (e.g. colour terms and nationality terms) or systemically indeterminate (such as ECONOMIC, RELIGIOUS, LINGUISTIC, INDUSTRIAL, etc.).

A number of terms are useful for the semantic description of adjectives:

(i) Gradable vs. non-gradable. Gradable adjectives (e.g. NICE, SENSIBLE, BAD, etc.) denote scalar properties and thus take degree adverbs like VERY and EXTREMELY and permit comparison (e.g. *very beautiful, nicer*). Non-gradable adjectives (e.g. ATOMIC, LINGUISTIC, MEDICAL, OWN, OTHER) denote categorial or determinative properties and are not normally compatible with intensification or comparison (**very linguistic*, *more atomic*, *owner*, *very other*). Some adjectives are gradable in one sense and non-gradable in another, cf. *a (very) popular politician / popular culture* and *a (more) civil young man / civil rights.*

(ii) Inherent vs. non-inherent. Inherent adjectives directly ascribe a property to the **referent** of the head they modify and may be used equally

well as pre-head modifiers and as subject complements, e.g. *a beautiful girl /
the girl is beautiful*; *a very angry man / the man is very angry*. Non-inherent
adjectives relate by way of association to the meaning of the **head noun**
rather than ascribing a property to the referent as such. Generally, non-
inherent adjectives cannot be used as subject complements. Thus, for
example, *an old friend* is not necessarily a friend who is old but someone
with whom one has had a friendship of long standing, and *a heavy sleeper* is
someone who sleeps heavily, not a sleeping person who is heavy. Other
examples are: *a complete idiot / foreign policy / animate nouns*.

(iii) Restrictive vs. non-restrictive. Dependent adjectives denoting properties which help the listener establish the referent of the head are called
restrictive adjectives. Thus, for example, *brave* is restrictive in *The brave
soldiers ran forward* if it singles out a subclass of soldiers in the context (i.e.
if only some of the soldiers, those who were brave, ran forward). If it
describes a property of all the soldiers present in that particular context, it is
non-restrictive (i.e. 'the soldiers, who were all brave, ran forward').

16.1.3. Morphology

Adjectives can be divided into several fairly distinct morphological classes.
There are, first of all, a number of **simple lexical stems**: GOOD, BAD, NICE,
BIG, LONG, OLD, YOUNG, FAIR, CLEVER, NOBLE, MELLOW, etc. But
many adjectives are morphologically more complex:

(i) denominal adjectives: e.g. BEAUTIFUL, RESTLESS, FRIENDLY, BOOR-
ISH, POETIC, HISTORICAL, HUMOROUS, CONSTITUTIONAL;

(ii) deverbal adjectives: e.g. CHARMING, DERIVED, DRUNKEN, REMARK-
ABLE, RESISTIBLE, RESTRICTIVE, DOMINANT.

In some cases, there is more than one derivation from a noun or verb
depending on the intended meaning: FRIENDLY/FRIENDLESS, WORRIED/
WORRYING, etc. In the case of denominal **adjectives ending in -ic or -ical**,
there is often little difference of meaning, e.g. POETIC/POETICAL. There is a
tendency for the adjective ending in *-ic* to denote 'category' and for the one
ending in *-ical* to be gradable and more descriptive in meaning. A good
example of this is ECONOMIC ('of economics') vs. ECONOMICAL ('careful
in spending money, time, etc.'). An important exception, where the relation is
exactly the opposite, is HISTORIC ('notable or memorable in history') vs.
HISTORICAL ('pertaining or belonging to history').

Many deverbal adjectives are **present or past participles**. Some of these
are fully adjectivalized (e.g. *a worried man / a fascinating event*) in the sense
that they behave like other typical adjectives (e.g. may be intensified by

VERY). Others preserve more of their verbal character: *a rarely/*very heard opera*; *rapidly/*very falling share prices.*

Usually adjectival past participles are **passive** in meaning: *the deported prisoners* (i.e. the prisoners were deported), *the invited relatives* (i.e. the relatives were invited), etc. Occasionally adjectival past participles have active meaning if they are derived from an intransitive verb denoting a change of state, e.g. *the escaped prisoners* (i.e. the prisoners had escaped), *the departed relatives* (i.e. the relatives had departed). Some participles allow of both a passive and an active reading, depending on the nature of the head, e.g. *a returned letter* (i.e. the letter has been returned) and *a returned soldier* (i.e. the soldier has returned). Often past participles with passive meaning appear in post-head position: *the relatives invited / the prisoners deported.* In such cases, the past participle retains more of its verbal character and can be interpreted as a reduced relative construction (cf. *the relatives who were invited / the prisoners who were deported*).

Special mention should be made of **denominal adjectives ending in the 'verbal suffix'** *-ed*: WINGED (*a winged animal*), WALLED (*a walled garden*), etc. Such adjectives have little verbal character. Instead they imply a prepositional *with*-group: 'an animal with wings', 'a garden with a wall', etc.

A number of adjectives and adverbs contain **the prefix** *a-*: AFLOAT, AFRAID, ALERT, ALONE, ASLEEP, ABROAD, AWAY, etc. One way of distinguishing between the *a*-adjectives and *a*-adverbs is to see whether they can follow the copula verb SEEM. If they can, they are adjectives (e.g. *the patient seemed afraid/asleep/*abroad/*away*). Conversely, if they can follow intransitive verbs of motion, they are adverbs (e.g. *She went *afraid /*asleep/abroad/ away*).

Adjectives may also derive from other adjectives: UNHAPPY, DISHONEST, INCOMPETENT, UNDER-SEXED, HYPERSENSITIVE, KINDLY, SMALLISH, etc. In some of these the prefix locally negates the basic adjective, as in the first three examples mentioned.

Compounding is an important factor too: MUCH-DEBATED, GOOD-LOOKING, HAND-MADE, etc. Note in this connection the frequent use of hyphens to signal adjectival status of nominal compounds and other complex constituents: *a remarkable last-ditch effort / the latest Clinton-for-President movement / a three-year-old girl / a small, what-else-can-you-expect nod.*

16.1.4. The external relations of adjectivals

Adjectivals typically have one of the following functions:

DEP	The *clever* girls told their *anxious* mother nothing.
Cs	Jane is *exceptionally intelligent.*

> Co   They drove him *mad*.

Naturally, adjectivals also function as conjoints in compound units, e.g.:

> CJT   She sent him a *long* and *rather boring* letter.

Adjectivals are often used as complements in verbless adverbial clauses:

> Cs   If *necessary*, I can help her.
>
> *However disagreeable* their presence, you have to let them in.

Adjectives serving as dependents in (pro)noun groups are called **attributive adjectives** while adjectives with subject or object complement function are called **predicative adjectives**.

In addition to attributive and predicative uses, adjectivals may assume **adverbial function**:

> A   *Unhappy with the result*, he decided to resign.
>
> Dicky hurried in *breathless*, wearing his new trenchcoat.
>
> *Expressionless* he drew his head back in again.

Adjectivals in this last category are sometimes referred to as 'independent' or 'free' complements rather than adverbials. They are borderline cases: on the one hand they assign a property to the subject or object, like genuine subject or object complements; on the other hand they are independent optional units providing supplementary background information, typically about the **state** of the entity involved, like many rather more typical adverbials.

Predicative adjectives (which normally take on subject complement function after copula verbs) are sometimes used in connection with verbs that are normally classified as **intransitive** rather than as **copula**:

(1)   The moon shone *bright*.

(2)   Hope springs *eternal* in the young man's breast.

In these examples, the italicized adjectives alternate with the adverbs *brightly* and *eternally*. The effect of using a complement adjective instead of an adverbial adverb is to change the status of the verb from intransitive to copula with a corresponding bleaching of the content. Alternation between complement adjective (describing the subject) and adverbial adverb (describing the situation) is especially common in connection with the verbs HANG, LIE, SIT and STAND:

(3)   The clouds hung *heavy* /*heavily*.

(4)   The guests stood *silent/silently*.

Like other constituent types, adjectivals may independently assume communicative functions such as exclamation (e.g. *Beautiful! / How sad!*).

Adjectives are sometimes **dislocated**:

(5)   *Tricky*, that's what writers are!

Note also that adjectives occasionally appear **after *as* and *than***:

(6)   They regarded him *as very competent*.

(7)   She was more hard-working *than clever*.

When used attributively, adjectivals typically serve as pre-head dependents: *a friendly doctor / a competent teacher / a very promising career*. Occasionally, however, they appear in post-head position: *things Italian / rivers navigable at this time of year*. We should therefore draw a distinction between **attributive pre-head** and **attributive post-head** adjectivals.

A further distinction should be drawn between those attributive post-head adjectivals which are **restrictive** and those which are **non-restrictive** (often referred to as **appositional**). While restrictive attributive post-head adjectivals (e.g. *the stars visible*) are directly attached to the head they modify, appositional adjectivals are separated from the head by e.g. a comma:

(8)   Problems, *political, environmental and moral*, were dealt with very casually by the new government.

16.1.5. Parataxis and hypotaxis

As already noted, adjectivals may realize conjoints in compound units:

(1)   In the distance he heard a laugh, *musical but malicious*.

(2)   The letter was *long and rather boring*.

Coordinated adjectives are **paratactically** related, i.e. they are at the same level of analysis. Whenever there are two or more adjectives in attributive post-head or predicative position, they are always paratactically related.

Parataxis is found also in attributive pre-head position:

(3)   He rather enjoyed her *dry and light* stage kisses.

(4)   What she saw was a *big, brutal, sweaty* boxer.

(5)   She was visited by a *tall dark handsome* stranger.

In (5), there are no overt markers of parataxis (coordinators, commas) but these could be supplied without changing the meaning of the construction (*She was visited by a tall, dark, handsome stranger*). In other cases there is **hypotaxis**, i.e. a relation between elements at different levels of analysis:

(6)   The *envious Republican* senators complained.

(7)   We had some *excellent Danish* cheese.

In these examples, the adjectives do not independently describe the head noun at the same level. Rather, the first adjective (*envious*; *excellent*) describes the combination of the following adjective and the head noun (*Republican senators*; *Danish cheese*).

Note finally that **distributive** sequences of adjectives, i.e. adjectives expressing properties in relation to different referents of the same head noun are always paratactically related and overtly linked: e.g. *French and Italian supporters / professional or non-professional advice*.

16.1.6. Descriptive, classifying and specifying adjectives

Adjectives are subclassified into **central** and **peripheral**. Central adjectives share the following characteristics:

(i) They are **gradable** and therefore allow of comparison and intensification by means of adverbs like VERY and EXTREMELY: *these (very) funny plays / (extremely) angry teachers / the cold(er) weather / the (most) beautiful song.*

(ii) They occur freely in both attributive pre-head position (as in the examples above) and in predicative position: *these plays are funny / the weather was cold / some of the teachers were angry.*

(iii) They often serve as conjoints in coordination, expressing different properties of the same referent: *his ugly and fat opponent / a high, tinny echo / those Indians are tough and mean-looking.*

(iv) They **describe** rather than classify or define the referent to which they assign a property.

Because of (iv), central adjectives are called **descriptive adjectives**. Peripheral adjectives do not conform to (some or all of) the criteria mentioned above: e.g. **very solar energy / *the onlier solution / *That nomination was presidential / *The student is former / *interesting and primary elections.*

There are two main types of peripheral adjectives: **classifying** adjectives and **specifying** adjectives. Classifying adjectives subcategorize the head they modify. For example, a *medical dictionary* is a special kind of dictionary and *solar energy* is a special kind of energy. Classifying adjectives thus help establish precisely what sort of thing is involved in the expression. By contrast specifying adjectives help single out or quantify the referent of the construction in relation to some context. For example, in *his main reason* and *my former colleague*, the specifying adjectives *main* and *former* have determiner-like properties.

It is important to note that the division of adjectives into descriptive, classifying and specifying adjectives is **function-based**. This means that it is often difficult to determine the precise subclass membership of adjectives examined out of context. In each case we have to consider the functional relationship between the adjective and the head it modifies. For example, in *an English university*, *English* is a categorizing adjective whereas in *a very English response* it is a descriptive adjective. Compare also *civil behaviour* vs. *a civil court* and *popular culture* vs. *a popular actress*.

16.1.7. Positional restrictions

Many descriptive adjectives freely allow of both **attributive pre-head** and **predicative** position, but not attributive post-head position in noun groups:

(1)   the new car / the car is new / *the car new
(2)   the happy children / the children are happy / *the children happy

Classifying and specifying adjectives normally appear only in attributive pre-head position:

(3)   the medical dictionary / *the dictionary is medical / *the dictionary medical
(4)   his main reason / *his reason is main / *his reason main

However, there is a lot of variation with respect to adjectival positions.

Occasionally attributive adjectives may appear in **post-head position** and thereby receive **end-focus**:

(5)   He had no patience with *problems hypothetical*.
(6)   Her weakness for *things Italian* is quite ludicrous.

This constituent order is found in indefinite noun groups if the meaning of the noun is highly general and the adjective subclassifies it. In indefinite pronoun groups, the head is so light and general that an attributive adjective is obligatorily placed in post-head position:

(7)   I am looking for *something different*.
(8)   Is there *anything interesting* on the front page?

Post-head position motivated by the principle of end-focus is also found in noun groups (definite or indefinite) containing **deverbal** adjectives:

(9)   Some agent *unnamed* had reached Schlema and gained access to the reports.

Post-head position of participial adjectives emphasizes their **verbal character**. The same is true of deverbal adjectives ending in *-able* or *-ible*, such as e.g. *the navigable rivers* vs. *the rivers navigable*. An additional implication in connection with attributive post-head adjectives is that the property they express may have **temporary** application. This can be illustrated by comparing *problems soluble* and *stars visible* with *soluble problems* and *visible stars*. In the former cases, the adjective describes a temporary property (e.g. 'right now', 'tonight'), in the latter a more permanent, generally valid property of the head. Adjectives ending in *-able* or *-ible* are particularly frequent in post-head position in noun groups premodified by a superlative or with a semantically related word such as ONLY:

(10)   They had the *greatest difficulty imaginable* getting there in time.

(11)   The *only room suitable* is the one on the third floor.

Sometimes more distinct meanings come to be associated with the position of the adjective relative to the head noun, compare:

(12)   She wrote a letter to the *parents concerned / concerned parents*.

(13)   He thanked all the *members present / present members*.

I leave it to the reader to sort out the different meanings of these examples.

   Adjectives with the prefix *a-* (such as AFLOAT, AFRAID, ALIKE, ALIVE, ALONE, ASLEEP, AWAKE, AWARE) tend to occur in predicative or attributive post-head position only:

(14)   The children were asleep. (*the asleep children)

(15)   Girls *aware* of such problems should seek medical advice. (*aware girls)

Occasionally we find the other *a*-adjectives in attributive pre-head position if they are premodified and/or used in a descriptive sense: *the barely afloat oil tanker / a most alive mind*.

   We often find **coordinated classifying or descriptive adjectives** in post-head position for the distributive expression of different entities by the head:

(16)   All sorts of problems, *political, environmental and moral*, would have to be solved if this bill is passed.

(17)   If I'm not allowed to make a profit on popular books, *good or bad*, I can't afford to publish less popular books for the discerning minority.

This constituent order, whereby the adjectives are added as an **apposition**, serves the purpose of highlighting the adjectives.

   Post-head position of coordinated non-distributive descriptive adjectives is common in literary style narration:

(18)   He was a big man, *square-shouldered and virile*.

(19)   The leaves, *so soft and yellow*, gave way to the gentle breeze.

On the whole there is a tendency to **avoid heavy pre-head modifiers** in English noun groups. Thus adjective groups containing dependent complementation or postmodifiers are placed in post-head position or in predicative position, or in discontinuous pre- and post-head position:

(20)   Professors *keen to take early retirement* should contact me immediately.

(21)   He was *afraid of his sisters*.

(22)   It falls into a *different* category *from the rest*.

16.2. Adjectival modification and positional ordering

We turn now to a closer examination of pre-head dependent adjectives. The general term used to describe the communicative function of dependent adjectivals is **modification** – one of the subfunctions described in connection with nominals, cf. section 14.1.3. Let us look again at the relevant part of the chart offered there for the functional description of nominals:

determination	modification	categorization	(multi-functional)

As this chart shows, the subfunctions of determination, modification and categorization are arranged in certain specific syntactic zones. In the following, we shall examine the way in which pre-head attributive adjectives occupy the modificational zone **between** determination and categorization.

16.2.1. Modificational zones

In section 16.1.6 we recognized three different kinds of adjective: specifying, descriptive and classifying. As pointed out, these three kinds of adjective are not (sub)classes in an ordinary sense: an adjective cannot be identified unambiguously as one or the other in isolation. In each case the relationship between the adjective and the head noun in a particular noun group must be carefully examined and interpreted. Rather than speaking of three subclasses of adjectives, it is more appropriate to operate with three **subfunctions of modification** which adjectives may assume in relation to a noun: **specification, description** or **classification**. This is supported by such data as:

CIVIL:	*civil reply*	(description)
	civil rights	(classification)
BLACK:	*black cloud*	(description)
	black coffee	(classification)
PRIMARY:	*my primary concern*	(specification)
	this primary election	(classification)
WOODEN:	*wooden bed*	(classification)
	wooden methods	(description)

In these constructions, one and the same adjective functions in two of the three different ways depending on how it relates to the head noun.

The three subfunctions of modification (specification, description and classification) are arranged in different syntactic zones between determination and categorization in noun groups. In other words, they impose a certain positional order on attributive pre-head adjectives: specifying adjectives precede descriptive adjectives, which in turn precede classifying adjectives, as shown in the table below. To emphasize the positional characteristics of the three subfunctions, we refer to specification as **Mod. I** (= 'modificational zone I'), description as **Mod. II** and classification as **Mod. III**. Each of these zones may accommodate zero, one, or more than one adjective.

Determination	Modification			Categorization
	Specification (Mod. I)	Description (Mod. II)	Classification (Mod. III)	
the	usual	sound	English	stock
her	own	handsome	naval	officer
the	same	beautiful	French	actress
the	next	interesting	congressional	procedure
	certain	serious	organic	diseases
the	last	mighty	German	attack
the	earliest	important	Aboriginal	carvings
	many	eager	medical	students
this	particular	informal	linguistic	rule
	other	horrid	psychological	tricks

In strings of premodifying adjectives belonging to different Mod. zones, it appears that those adjectives which are closest in function to determination, viz. specifying adjectives, are placed closest to the determiner and those adjectives which are closest in function to categorization, viz. classifying adjectives, are placed closest to the head of the noun group. This means that there is no strict separation between determination, modification and categorization but rather a continuum of values from determination to categorization: from the left determination fades into modification via specification and from the right categorization fades into modification via classification. In the middle we have modification at its purest: description. The term 'central adjective' (which was replaced by 'descriptive adjective') thus acquires new functional and syntactic significance: a central adjective appears in central position in the modificational zone and is functionally pure (i.e. left untainted by determination and categorization).

Adjective order is thus first and foremost a question of the functional characteristics of adjectives in relation to the head noun. It follows that the same adjective may appear in different positions depending on its sub-function. That this is indeed the case is shown in the following data:

(1a)	Scottish *popular* ballads	(III + III)
(1b)	*popular* Scottish ballads	(II + III)
(2a)	the *first* brilliant chapter	(I + II)
(2b)	the brilliant *first* chapter	(II + III)
(3a)	this *good* international turn	(II + III)
(3b)	this international *good* turn	(III + III)

In each of these constructions, the italicized adjective changes its modificational subfunction in relation to the noun (e.g. *popular*, which subclassifies *ballads* with respect to genre in (1a) and describes it in (1b).

16.2.2. Structure in and across Mod. zones

There are often more than one adjective in the same Mod. zone:

(1)	the first few primaries	(I + I)
(2)	the only other solution	(I + I)
(3)	a new, strange way	(II + II)
(4)	a healthy and virtuous girl	(II + II)
(5)	one Republican congressional leader	(III + III)
(6)	tactical nuclear weapons	(III + III)

To ascertain that the analysis of strings of non-central adjectives is correct, it is always possible to try to insert a central adjective (i.e. an adjective which typically serves as a Mod. II adjective, such as e.g. INTERESTING or INFLUENTIAL): if the original adjectives are to the left of the central adjective in its most appropriate position (as in *the first few interesting primaries*) then they are Mod. I adjectives; if the original adjectives are to the right of the central adjective, then they are Mod. III adjectives (as in *one influential Republican congressional leader*); and if the central adjective squeezes in between the original adjectives we have a Mod. I and a Mod. III adjective (as in e.g. *the only interesting Greek drama*).

Adjectives in Mod. I, in Mod. III and in combinations of Mod. I, Mod. II and Mod. III are **hypotactically** related, while adjectives in Mod. II are paratactically related. In Mod. II, many adjectives are separated by comma and/or conjunction. If they are not, it is always possible to separate them by such means without changing the meaning of the construction:

(7)	the sweet warm stale air
	= the sweet, warm, stale air
	= the sweet, warm and stale air

Adjectives from different Mod. zones are not normally separated:

| (8) | an interesting economic strategy | (II + III) |

(9)	the same beautiful girl	(I + II)
(10)	the first medical dictionary	(I + III)

When separation does occur, it is usually semantically significant, as in the following examples:

(11a)	a second context-sensitive rule	(I + III)
(11b)	a second, context-sensitive rule	

Here (11b) with the broken sequence differs in meaning from (11a) with the unbroken sequence. (11a), unlike (11b), implies the existence of a 'first context-sensitive rule'.

16.2.3. Zone-internal order

It is difficult to provide any hard and fast rules for the internal order in each Mod. zone. But there are certain tendencies:

A) Mod. I: In this zone we can distinguish four major groups of adjectivals which prove reasonably order sensitive:

(i) Precise and fuzzy ordinal numbers, like FIRST, SECOND, SEVENTH, NEXT, FINAL, etc.

(ii) Precise and fuzzy cardinal numbers, like TWO, FOUR, FEW, MANY, COUNTLESS, NUMEROUS, etc.

(iii) Compared forms like *older, smaller, better-known, finest, most beautiful*, etc.

(iv) Others, like ONLY, OWN, SAME, OTHER, SUBSEQUENT, FORMER, MAJOR, SIMILAR, DIFFERENT, MAIN, CHIEF, GENERAL, PRIMARY, SPECIFIC, CERTAIN, etc.

A string of two or more Mod. I adjectives provides **increasing specification**. There is a **tendency** for the adjectives in the four groups to appear in the order in which they have just been presented, i.e. '**ordinals** before **cardinals** before **compared forms** before **others**':

(1)	the first five primaries
(2)	the two major categories
(3)	six smaller children
(4)	the greatest subsequent importance

It is important to note, however, that some Mod. I adjectives may contract more closely with the definite article for the expression of definite specific reference, in which case they precede other Mod. I adjectives, irrespective of their membership of the four groups presented above: e.g. *the same particular phenomena / the other six more positive roles*.

B) Mod. II: Often the order in this zone seems random and can be reversed with little or no change of meaning (e.g. *a harsh thin light* vs. *a thin harsh light*). There are, however, certain **order preferences**:

(i) Short adjectives tend to precede long adjectives (therefore underived adjectives typically precede derived adjectives):

(5)   a deep quiet sleep
(6)   a slight disdainful smile

(ii) Deverbal adjectives tend to precede denominal adjectives:

(7)   predictable wishful distortions
(8)   quivering dusky maidens

(iii) Adjectives denoting size, height and length tend to precede others:

(9)   that big, tough guy
(10)   a tall, thin creature
(11)   long blank periods

(iv) Adjectives denoting size, length and height tend to appear in that order:

(12)   big, long things
(13)   big, high cheek bones
(14)   long, low sheds

(v) Emotionally loaded adjectives like BEAUTIFUL, WONDERFUL, LOVELY, HORRIBLE, DREADFUL, NASTY, etc. tend to precede others:

(15)   lovely soft hands
(16)   a nasty cold wind

Note in this connection that emotionally loaded adjectives occasionally enter a close relation to the following adjective and assume an adverb-like status:

(17)   a great big dog (= 'a very big dog')
(18)   an awful long trip (= 'a very long trip')

C) Mod. III: In this zone hypotaxis prevails, each adjective (sub)classifying the following adjective(s) and the head noun. Like the order in Mod. I, the order in Mod. III is relatively fixed. When variation does occur, it affects the way in which the head noun is (sub)classified, cf. e.g.:

(19)   classical Greek drama / Greek classical drama
(20)   paramilitary Protestant organizations / Protestant paramilitary organizations
(21)   therapeutic non-hypnotic techniques / non-hypnotic therapeutic techniques

But usually the order is fixed and can be described in terms of certain well-defined groups of adjectives:

(i) deverbal adjectives, like LEADING, SLEEPING, INTERNALIZED, RECOGNIZED, SUSCEPTIBLE, HYPNOTIZABLE, etc.

(ii) adjectives denoting colour, like GREEN, RED, YELLOW, BLACK, etc.

(iii) adjectives denoting nationality, like ENGLISH, FRENCH, CHINESE, etc.

(iv) (other) denominal adjectives, like INDUSTRIAL, PRESIDENTIAL, NUCLEAR, WOOLLEN, MEDICAL, CULTURAL, POLITICAL, FISCAL, etc.

(v) nominals serving as premodifiers, like METAL, SILK, FOREIGN POLICY, TOURIST, AIRLINE, etc.

The linear order is often **'deverbal** before **colour** before **nationality** before **denominal** before **nominal'**:

(22)	handwritten green pages
(23)	internalized linguistic representation
(24)	white American men and women
(25)	a yellow silk handkerchief
(26)	the increasing Russian military strength
(27)	an electronic metal detector

When typical Mod. I and Mod. II adjectives serve as Mod. III adjectives, they always immediately precede the nominal head, forming a compound-like relationship with it:

(28)	South-African *wild* birds
(29)	this international *good* turn
(30)	key *primary* states
(31)	the five-times-wed *former* actress

The same place is occupied by one of the inherent determiners when serving as a modifier: the classifying genitive (cf. section 14.3.8 [A]), as in:

(32)	a standard *tourist's* guide
(33)	artificial silk *women's* underwear

LITTLE, OLD and YOUNG often serve as Mod. III adjectives, in which case they seem to enter a compound-like relation with the head (e.g. *little girl, old man, young people*). When serving as Mod. II adjectives, they usually follow other Mod. II adjectives and precede Mod. III adjectives:

(34)	a very attractive little American girl
(35)	a handsome young Italian doctor

16.3. Comparison of adjectives

16.3.1. The basic system of comparison

The basic system of comparison in English looks like this:

(i) There are three members of the category:

positive	tall / beautiful
comparative	taller / more beautiful
superlative	tallest / most beautiful

(ii) There are two types of formal expression:

morphological comparison with the suffixes *-er* and *-est*

tall / taller / tallest

syntactic comparison with *more* and *most*

beautiful / more beautiful / most beautiful

(iii) A maximal comparative construction consists of three things:

comparative element	-er / -est // more / most
adjective (or adverb)	tall / beautiful
comparative basis	than I am / than me / of them all

Here are some examples:

(1)   The *younger* man was about twenty, with wavy hair and long sideburns.
(2)   I liked public phones, they were *more private than private ones*.
(3)   This was our *oldest* suitcase.

Using the terminology suggested above we can describe the instances of comparison in examples (1) to (3) in this way:

– in (1) we have morphological comparison; the comparative form *younger* consists of the adjective YOUNG and the comparative element *-er*; there is no explicit comparative basis.

– in (2) we have syntactic comparison; the comparative form *more private than private ones* consists of the adjective PRIVATE, the comparative element the adverb *more* and the comparative basis the preposition group *than private ones*.

– in (3) we have morphological comparison; the superlative form *oldest* consists of the adjective OLD and the comparative element *-est*; there is no explicit comparative basis.

Comparison involves the **ranking of entities** on the basis of the **degree** to which they possess some property. The kind of comparison dealt with so far assigns **a higher rank** or **the highest rank**. But there are also ways of expressing comparison assigning the same rank and a lower rank to an entity.

Assignment of the **same rank** is expressed by *as ... as* (or *so ... as*).

(4)   Let's see if you are *as good as you claim*.

(5)   She wouldn't be *so mean as him*.

In such constructions the first *as* (or *so*) is a degree adverb, the second *as* a conjunction (as in example (4)) or a preposition (as in example (5)).

Assignment of a **lower rank** is expressed by means of the irregularly compared forms of LITTLE, *less* and *least*), plus a positive form:

(6)   This was a *less agreeable* place than the railway station.

(7)   She is the *least pretentious* professor I know.

16.3.2. Irregular comparison

There are a few irregularly compared forms:

bad/ill	worse	worst
good/well	better	best
much/many	more	most

In some cases there are competing comparatives and/or superlatives:

far	farther	farthest
	further	furthest
late	later	latest
	latter	last
little	less	least
	lesser	
near	nearer	nearest
		next
old	older	oldest
	elder	eldest

As adjectives and adverbs both *farther/farthest* and *further/furthest* are used about 'distance' (e.g. *The village is further/farther than the border*), though the *-a-* forms are not frequent in BrE. Only the *-u-* forms are used in the 'additional' sense (e.g. *further evidence / without further delay*).

The regular forms of LATE (*later* and *latest*) are used about 'time' (e.g. *a later bus / his latest novel*) whereas the irregular ones (*latter* and *last*) are more specialized: in formal language *latter* is used in contrast to *former* about the second of two entities already mentioned (e.g. *Joan and Ruth were both dedicated to the cause: the former offered to take night shifts at the local hospital, the latter joined our first aid unit*). But it is also used to denote a 'period towards the end' (e.g. *In the latter part of the century / her latter years*). While *latest* means 'most recent', *last* is used to describe the final entity in a sequence (cf. *her latest/last novel*). But *last* is also used deictically in contrast to *next* (cf. *last/next week*) and with the meaning 'the one earlier than the one we are talking about' in contrast to demonstrative *this* (cf. *This meeting is more boring than the last one*).

The distinction between *nearest* and *next* is similar to the distinction between *latest* and *last*: the regular form *nearest* is used in the locational sense whereas *next* is used with sequential meaning.

The two comparatives of LITTLE typically differ in that *less* is used quantitatively, *lesser* qualitatively and in certain idiomatic expressions:

(1)   They gave me *less* money than I needed.

(2)   This is one of his *lesser* works.

(3)   To invite him along would certainly be *the lesser of two evils*.

As we saw in section 16.3.1, *less* and *least* are furthermore used in connection with comparison assigning a lower rank.

The compared *o*- forms of OLD (*older, oldest*) are used generally in comparative expressions involving the age of entities (e.g. *My car is much older than yours / Roger is my oldest colleague*). In predicative position only the *o*- forms are used. And only the *o*- forms can be modified, as in *much older* and *the very oldest*. The *e*- forms (*elder, eldest*) are used in attributive pre-head position (as well as 'substantivally', cf. section 16.4 below) as an alternative to the *o*- forms in expressions involving family or otherwise close relations (e.g. *My elder brother is now Ann's eldest relative*). Note finally the occasional use of *elder* in connection with proper names, e.g. *the Elder Matlock* and *Pliny the Elder*, and in the expression *an elder statesman*.

16.3.3. The choice between morphological and syntactic comparison

Most adjectives require or permit syntactic comparison with *more* and *most*. But some adjectives require morphological comparison and a not insignificant number permit morphological comparison. Here are the rules:

(i) Monosyllabic adjectives (e.g. BIG, CLEAN, FAST, GREAT, HARD, HIGH, QUICK, THICK, YOUNG) normally require morphological comparison:

kind	kinder	kindest
fine	finer	finest

Exceptions: JUST, LIKE, REAL, RIGHT, WORTH, WRONG and adjectives denoting nationality like FRENCH, DUTCH, SWISS, etc.

(ii) Disyllabic adjectives with the stress on the final syllable often but not invariably take morphological comparison:

polite	politer	politest
	(more polite)	(most polite)
profound	profounder	profoundest
	(more profound)	(most profound)

However, the following disyllabic adjectives almost always take syntactic comparison: ANTIQUE, BIZARRE, CONTENT, DEVOUT, ORNATE, those ending in *-esque* (e.g. BURLESQUE, GROTESQUE) and those with the prefix *a-* (AFRAID, ASLEEP, ALOOF, etc.).

(iii) Disyllabic adjectives ending in an unstressed vowel or syllabic [ɫ] (written *-er, -ow, -y, -le*) often take morphological comparison:

clever	cleverer	cleverest
	(more clever)	(most clever)
mellow	mellower	mellowest
	(more mellow)	(most mellow)
happy	happier	happiest
	(more happy)	(most happy)
simple	simpler	simplest
	(more simple)	(most simple)

So do COMMON, CRUEL, HANDSOME, PLEASANT, QUIET and STUPID:

common	commoner	commonest
	(more common)	(most common)

Other disyllabic adjectives normally require syntactic comparison:

urgent	more urgent	most urgent
careful	more careful	most careful
anxious	more anxious	most anxious

(iv) Adjectives in three or more syllables require syntactic comparison:

creative	more creative	most creative
melancholy	more melancholy	most melancholy
impressionistic	more impressionistic	most impressionistic

(v) Participles serving as adjectives such as MARKED, DETACHED, FELT, PLEASED, PRONOUNCED, SHAKEN, MESMERIZED, BORING, DYING, SOOTHING, WORRYING, etc. are always syntactically compared:

pleased	more pleased	most pleased
boring	more boring	most boring

(vi) Derived adjectives consisting of an adjectival stem which is normally compared morphologically and a negative prefix take morphological comparison but also permit syntactic comparison:

unkind	unkinder	unkindest
	(more unkind)	(most unkind)
untidy	untidier	untidiest
	(more untidy)	(most untidy)

(vii) The syntactic comparative of adjectives which permit both morphological and syntactic comparison is especially frequent in predicative position and when followed by a *than*-construction:

(1)   She was *more happy* than I thought.

The syntactic comparative is normally required in constructions comparing two properties in relation to the same entity:

(2)   She was *more happy /*happier* than *worried*.

Exceptions to this are HIGH, LONG, THICK and WIDE (and their antonyms), which are followed by a full *than*-clause:

(3)   The wall was *thicker than it was high*.

Morphological comparison is occasionally used for emotional effect in connection with adjectives normally requiring syntactic comparison:

(4)   She would give herself violently; then yawn at the *wrongest* moment.
(5)   He was shy and *awkwarder* than ever.

Note finally that when compared adjectives are coordinated, morphologically compared adjectives usually precede syntactically compared adjectives:

(6)   He bought the *largest* and *most successful* publishing house in England.
(7)   The second option was a *longer* and *more tedious* route.

For a string of adjectives some of which require, others permit syntactic comparison, syntactic comparison is sometimes extended to the whole string:

(8)   The solution was at once *more simple, economical and realistic*.

16.3.4. The use of compared forms

The positive form of adjectives is used in an **absolute sense** (i.e. simply to express a property in relation to an entity with no inherent association of comparison). By contrast, the comparative form is used in a comparison to assign to some entity a **higher rank** on the property scale defined by the adjective, and the superlative form is used in a comparison to assign the **highest rank** to some entity. The term 'property scale' is here used to emphasize the fact that comparison applies only to gradable adjectives, i.e. adjectives with scalar meaning. With both comparative and superlative forms it is important to notice that what is expressed is ranking on the property scale defined by the adjective rather than the presence of the property denoted by the positive form of the adjective. For example, in an expression like *Jack is bigger and older than Joan*, the speaker ranks Jack higher than Joan on the property scales of 'bigness' and 'oldness'. But this does not necessarily mean that the speaker ascribes the properties of 'big' and 'old' to Jack. Jack can be small and young even if he is bigger and older than Joan.

The comparative is found in expressions of **comparison between two**. More specifically it is used:

(i) to assign a higher rank on the property scale defined by an adjective to one entity (or set of entities) than to another:

(1)   He suspected that Henry was *cleverer* than David.

(2)   The incident amused some of the *older* members.

(ii) to indicate that an entity ranks higher on a property scale on one occasion than on another:

(3)   She did not look a day *older* than when they had first met.

(4)   Once darkness had fallen the house became *more mysterious and sinister.*

(iii) to assign a higher rank to an entity on one property scale than on another:

(5)   His eccentricities were *more repugnant than amusing.*

(6)   The letter was *more mischievous than threatening.*

The comparative form in English is not infrequently used in an **absolute sense** with an association of '(fairly) high degree' rather than 'higher rank'. In some examples inviting this analysis, the comparison signalled by the comparative form is left unspecified in the context and therefore implies a very general comparative basis: e.g. *This company produces larger tents* (i.e. 'larger than most') and *Our dog seems to like older people* ('older than average'). In such examples the distinction between 'fairly high degree' and 'higher rank' is difficult to draw precisely.

A gradually increasing degree of a property is expressed by repeating the comparative form (or marker) in a compound unit:

(7)   She sounded *angrier and angrier.*

(8)   He became *more and more irritating.*

The superlative is used in expressions of **comparison between more than two**. More specifically it is used:

(i) to assign a higher rank on the property scale defined by the adjective to one entity (or set of entities) than to **any** other (sets of) entities in a comparison, thus in effect ranking the entity as 'number one':

(9)   This is the *oldest* publishing firm in the country.

(10)   She was the *youngest* actress of them all.

(ii) to indicate that an entity (or set of entities) ranks higher on the property scale on one occasion than on **any** other occasion:

(11)   Children are *happiest* when they know from the start who is boss.

(12)   Do you have any political enemies, using that word in the *widest* sense?

The morphological superlative is occasionally used in an absolute sense, i.e. with an association of 'exceptionally high degree' rather than the usual association of 'highest rank':

(13)   Her face expressed the *liveliest* gratification.

The syntactic collocation of *most* and an adjective (or adverb) is often used for such purposes, especially in connection with the indefinite article:

(14)   It was a *most indecent* proposal.

(15)   I had a *most interesting* conversation with her the other night.

Note in this connection also standard expressions like: *With best wishes, at last, at least, my dearest Sarah*, etc.

    The superlative is often informally used instead of the comparative in expressions of 'comparison between two' when there is an explicit or implied *of*-construction as the comparative basis:

(16)   Joan is the *more/most considerate* of the (two) sisters.

(17)   He accepted the *smaller/smallest* sum.

16.4. The substantival use of adjectives

16.4.1. What is meant by 'substantival use'?

Traditionally, adjectives are said to be used substantivally when they serve as heads in entity-expressing constructions like the following:

(1)   The images ranged from *the grotesque* to *the obscene* to *the simply horrible*.

(2)   It was Astrid rather than Stu who was *the more influential* of the pair.

(3)   James hadn't told us *the worst* yet.

The term 'substantival use' is retained here because it aptly reflects the fact that when adjectives are used in this fashion, 'substance' is in some (concrete or abstract) sense added to the normal adjectival expression of a property: a property becomes an entity. In example (1), the three italicized constructions express general abstract properties **as if they were entities** (e.g. *the grotesque* = 'something grotesque' or 'that which is grotesque'). In example (2), *the more influential* refers to a particular person. Finally in example (3), *the worst* expresses a specific entity (e.g. 'the worst information'). In each of these instances, the adjective expresses a property (like other adjectives) but the property is not related to an entity expressed by a separate constituent but is itself used to establish an entity-like referent.

Substantivally used adjectives are a mixture of adjectives and nouns. Like nouns they are used to express entities, and they normally take the definite article, as we have seen. Like adjectives they can be modified by adverbs (cf. *the simply horrible*) and permit comparison (*the more influential / the worst*).

Substantivally used adjectives should be delimited from:

(i) Lexical items that serve as both adjectives and nouns, such as CRIMINAL, GERMAN, IMBECILE, PRIMARY and SAVAGE. Unlike these, substantivally used adjectives do not normally accept the indefinite article, nor do they accept the plural *-s* form or the genitive, e.g. *a criminal / criminals / this criminal's* vs. **a more influential / *more influentials / *this influential's*.

(ii) Elliptical constructions with adjectives missing their head nouns:

(4)   This is not a good solution but can you think of *a better* (one)?

(5)   Old furniture is sometimes more expensive than *new*.

In these examples we have anaphoric ellipsis (cf. section 5.2). Unlike substantivally used adjectives, *better* and *new* are here used as parallels to premodifying adjectives (*good/old*).

(iii) Pronoun groups with a demonstrative pronoun as head, cf. *the injured* (substantival use) vs. *those injured* (pronoun group with *those* as head). The former expresses a category of people, the latter has specific reference.

16.4.2. Generic and specific reference

Substantivally used adjectives may have either generic or specific reference. **Generic reference** is typically found in connection with:

(i) Descriptive (typical Mod. II) adjectives expressing an **abstract entity**:

(1)   He clearly felt he could no longer defend *the indefensible*.

(2)   'Even I can't manage *the impossible* at such short notice!'

(ii) Descriptive (typical Mod. II) adjectives expressing a **category of people**:

(3)   He accepts opponents without distinction – *the stupid, the wily, the vain, the cautious, the desperate, the hopeless*.

(4)   If the police waste time suspecting *the innocent* they'll have less chance of catching *the guilty*.

There is normally a clear association of plurality involved in such expressions, and as subjects they enter plural concord with the predicator (e.g. *The rich tend to prefer this area*).

Certain nationality terms and participles typically appearing in Mod. III may also be used substantivally to refer to a category of people: *the English / the French / the Irish / the Welsh / the Dutch / the Swiss / the Chinese / the Indonese / the Japanese / the Portuguese / the living / the dying / the injured*.

Specific singular or plural reference is typically found in connection with:

(i) Comparatives and superlatives (i.e. forms usually appearing in Mod. I):

(5)   *The older* of the two men turned out to be the poetry editor.
(6)   These clubs were by far *the most convenient* in London.

The use is particularly frequent in connection with an explicit or implied *of*-construction as the comparative basis.

(ii) Certain other adjectives typically appearing as Mod. I adjectives:

(7)   She promised to give me a call, but I knew that it would never be *the same*.
(8)   I went up to him and asked for *the usual*.

(iii) Certain fixed expressions: *the Almighty / the accused / the deceased / the condemned / the departed*:

(9)   The *accused* was/were greeted by many supporters.

As we have seen, substantivally used adjectives normally require the definite article. There are, however, exceptions to this, especially in the area of fixed expressions, e.g.: *to do one's best / at last / at least / my beloved / my intended / our poor / a bird feeding its young / a new class of rich*.

16.5. Adverbals

16.5.1. Preliminaries

The main function of adverbs is to express properties in relation to situations (as expressed by a verbal or a whole clause) or in relation to other properties (as expressed by adjectivals or other adverbals), e.g.:

(1)   She admires him *excessively*.
(2)   *Surprisingly*, no one turned up.
(3)   The debate was *highly* relevant.
(4)   She spoke *very* quickly.

In adverb groups, the head adverb may accept a pre-head dependent, a post-head dependent, a discontinuous dependent, or both a pre-head and a post-head dependent, as in the following examples respectively:

(5)   The boys are playing *very nicely.*

(6)   You just didn't look *carefully enough.*

(7)   That wiped out their armed forces *more efficiently than any nuclear bomb.*

(8)   *Very fortunately for me,* Jack had forgotten all about it.

Pre-head dependents in adverbals are typically **degree** adverbs (or adverb groups), as in (5). Frequent degree adverbs found in pre-head position are the ones which also premodify adjectives (see section 16.1.1): VERY, MUCH, QUITE, HIGHLY, EXTREMELY, RATHER, REALLY, SO, AS, TOO, MORE, MOST, LESS, LEAST. Pre-head adverbals may also occasionally express **viewpoint**, i.e. the respect in which something is done (e.g. *She reacted politically correctly*).

Post-head dependents are realized by *than*-clauses (in cases of morphological comparison), by the adverb ENOUGH (as in (6)), or by preposition groups.

Discontinuous dependents are found in cases of syntactic comparison:

(9)   Pundits were hedging *even more* blatantly *than usual.*

(10)   Mary danced *the most* elegantly *of them all.*

They may also be realized by constructions with *as ... as ...,* *so ... as ...,* *so ... that*-clause, *less ... than* and *too ... to*-infinitive clause, e.g.:

(11)   Mary dances *as* elegantly *as Joan.*

(12)   Kemp and Gore got along *so* famously *that it looked like a fraternity picnic.*

(13)   He is speaking *too* eloquently *to be entirely trusted.*

Adverbals express a variety of **meanings** (see also section 2.7 on the semantics of adverbials more generally). Some of these are illustrated here:

(14)   She was so surprised she stopped *right there.* (place)

(15)   She came to see me *yesterday.* (time)

(16)   You just didn't look *carefully enough.* (manner)

(17)   I love you *very much.* (degree)

(18)   These items are rare and *therefore* very expensive. (reason)

(19)   *Politically,* he is quite mad. (viewpoint)

Adverbals may also express **modal** meanings, cf. e.g. *Evidently they have slept here* (epistemic) and *Hopefully this is enough* (deontic).

16.5.2. The external relations of adverbals

Adverbals typically function as **adverbials** or as **dependents**. As adverbials they may realize adjuncts, disjuncts or conjuncts (cf. section 2.7):

(1)   Chi's arrival went *smoothly*. (adjunct)
(2)   *Quite frankly*, relations are no longer entirely satisfactory. (disjunct)
(3)   Your book has its flaws. *Nevertheless*, we're going to publish it. (conjunct)

A dependent adverbal most often modifies an adjective:

(4)   Moscow is having *unseasonably* warm weather.
(5)   He just isn't careful *enough*.

However, an adverbal may also modify an adverb or a (pro)nominal:

(6)   The rain smelled *ever so* faintly of home.
(7)   Vice President Al Gore intends to visit China *early* next year.
(8)   He will do *virtually* anything to kill the rest of us.

Some adverbals function as dependents in preposition groups:

(9)   She's just returned from *abroad*.

Note finally examples like *She went straight to bed* and *We finished well within time* where *straight* and *well* may be regarded as premodifiers in relation to a preposition.

In compound units realizing an adverbial or a dependent, adverbals may function as conjoints:

(10)   The weather is *unexpectedly* and *unseasonably* warm.

In non-clausal utterances adverbals may directly realize different speech act functions, such as statement (e.g. *Very badly* said in reply to *Has she been hurt?*), question (e.g. *Very badly?* said in reaction to *She's been hurt*) and directive (e.g. *Down* said to a dog).

Finally it should be mentioned that adverbals may function as subjects or objects in sentences where locative or temporal conditions are referred to:

(11)   *Indoors* is recommendable at this time of day.
(12)   I prefer *tomorrow*.

16.5.3. Morphology

Adverbs are morphologically **simple** (YET, ENOUGH, etc.), **complex** (BACKWARDS, BLATANTLY, etc.) or **compound** (NEARBY, THERE-ABOUTS, etc.). Complex adverbs constitute by far the largest of these subclasses, and most of them are formed by adding *-ly* to an adjective. This adverb-forming suffix is highly productive and much more so than the adjective-forming suffix -*ly* (FRIENDLY, COWARDLY, etc.). Adverbs in -*ly* frequently express manner. For example, the meaning of BLATANTLY is 'in a blatant way', and words like QUIETLY, RAPIDLY, FAINTLY, VIOLENTLY, SILENTLY, EASILY and NICELY can also be glossed 'in an [adjective] way'. In many other cases, however, and as demonstrated by the following examples, the meaning of an adverb in -*ly* is different:

(1)   He's *occasionally* late. (time-frequency)

(2)   There's a lot of crime *locally*. (place)

(3)   *Theoretically*, this is a good solution. (viewpoint)

Complex adverbs may also be formed by adding -*ly* to a present or past participle form, as in JOKINGLY and HEATEDLY, or to a noun, as in MONTHLY and YEARLY (which are matched by identical adjectives). But they cannot normally be formed by adding -*ly* to an adjective ending in -*ly*, i.e. from the adjective FRIENDLY one cannot freely derive *FRIENDLILY.

A large number of complex adverbs in -*ly* are matched by adverbs without this suffix, for example LOUDLY by LOUD:

(4)   A dog was barking *loudly*.

(5)   Read the letter out *loud*.

Other examples of such adverb pairs are CLOSE/CLOSELY, DEEP/DEEPLY, DIRECT/DIRECTLY, FLAT/FLATLY, HARD/HARDLY and HIGH/HIGHLY. While the variants in -*ly* in many of these pairs are usually unmarked and the more common, the short forms are largely restricted to idiomatic usage. Examples illustrating such usage are *hold me close*, *deep down*, *due east*, *take it easy*, *your memory is playing you false*, *aim high*, *pretty stupid*, *come as quick as you can*, *it serves you right*, *live rough*, *sleep tight* and *open your mouth wide*. In order to be sure of selecting the right form, the reader is advised to consult a good modern dictionary.

Some adverbs in -*ly* expressing time are matched by formally identical adjectives, for example EARLY, HOURLY, DAILY, WEEKLY, MONTHLY and YEARLY. While the -*ly* form is an adverb in a sentence like *I got up early today*, in a sentence like *She's in her early thirties* it is an adjective.

Complex adverbs may also consist of a noun followed by the suffix -*wise*. In examples like CRABWISE and CLOCKWISE, which express manner and direction respectively, this type of derivation is unproductive. However, adverbs may be freely formed – particularly in AmE – by adding -*wise* to a noun for the expression of **viewpoint**, i.e. in the sense of 'so far as [noun] is concerned'. Examples illustrating this type of formation are FOODWISE, DRINKWISE, MONEYWISE and WEATHERWISE. Some complex adverbs end in the suffix *-ward(s)* (the forms without *-s* being typical of AmE). As illustrated by WESTWARD(S), HOMEWARD(S) and BACKWARD(S), such adverbs express direction. Finally, a small group of complex adverbs begin with the prefix *a-*: ABROAD, APART, ASHORE, ASIDE, ASUNDER. This type of adverb formation is unproductive.

Simple adverbs (VERY, SOON, TOO, YET, etc.) constitute a fairly small class. Some simple adverbs, for example FAR, FAST, LITTLE, LONG, LOW, ONLY, STRAIGHT and WELL, are matched by formally identical adjectives:

(6)   Let's buy *low* and sell *high*. (adverbs)

(7)   Though in a *low* state of health, she's in *high* spirits. (adjectives)

Another group of simple adverbs, e.g. AFTER, BY, IN, NEAR, ON, OVER, THROUGH, UNDER and UP, are matched by formally identical **prepositions**:

(8)   Our relationship is *over*. (adverb)

(9)   She put her hand *over* my mouth. (preposition)

As illustrated by e.g. ABOARD, BENEATH, INSIDE, OUTSIDE and UNDERNEATH, such 'prepositional adverbs' may also be complex.

Compound adverbs constitute a relatively small class. A number of these have HERE or THERE as their first element and a preposition as their last, for example AFTER, BY, IN, OF, TO or UPON. Compounds ending in these prepositions may also begin with WHERE (e.g. *whereto*). Apart from HEREABOUTS, THEREABOUTS and THEREFORE, adverbs beginning with HERE or THERE are formal. Other examples illustrating this morphological subclass of adverbs are HALFWAY, NEARBY, OUTRIGHT, STRAIGHT-FORWARD and words composed of a preposition followed by a noun such as DOWNHILL, DOWNSTAIRS, INDOORS, OFFHAND and OUTDOORS.

16.5.4.   VERY versus MUCH

Among the simple adverbs VERY and MUCH are particularly common, and as these two words usually present difficulty to foreign learners of English, their distribution will briefly be dealt with. MUCH is used if the adverb functions as an adverbial, i.e. if it is closely connected with the verb. This use of MUCH is almost always restricted to non-assertive sentences:

(1)   We didn't enjoy the play *much*.

(2)   It doesn't *much* matter what you say.

VERY is used before positive adjectives and adverbs:

(3)   This is *very* useful.

(4)   You'll hear from me *very* soon.

MUCH, however, is used in constructions with *too* followed by a positive form and is sometimes preferred before positive forms with the prefix *a-*:

(5)   I was *much* too fond of her.

(6)   Her little brother was *much* afraid.

VERY is used as a pre-head dependent before an adjective or adverb in the superlative form while MUCH is used before the combination of the definite article and the superlative form:

(7)   This is our *very* lowest price.

(8)   This is *much* the noisiest place.

If the head of an adjective or adverb group is in the comparative form, however, it is MUCH which is required:

(9)   This is *much* better.

(10)   You'll notice *much* sooner than you expect.

Latinate 'comparatives' like SENIOR, JUNIOR, SUPERIOR, INFERIOR, etc. take MUCH if comparative meaning is expressed but otherwise VERY, cf.:

(11)   This paper is *much* superior to the last one you submitted.

(12)   This is *very* inferior stuff.

In accordance with the above rules a past participle form combines with MUCH if it is passive and with VERY if it is an adjectival non-passive:

(13)   Your attitude is *much* disliked by your colleagues. (S P- A -P A)

(14)   The case is *very* complicated. (S P C)

Before preposition groups we only find MUCH:

(15)   He was *much* in love.

(16)   She decided to meet with him again, *much* to my annoyance.

Finally it should be mentioned that MUCH is often premodified by VERY and in some idiomatic cases obligatorily so:

(17)   I like it *very much*.

16.5.5. Comparison

Adverbs with scalar meaning, such as EARLY, NEAR, QUIETLY and SOON (but not e.g. YET, NOW, CLOCKWISE), are capable of being compared. The type of comparison they select is usually **syntactic**, but a number of monosyllabic adverbs – all of which are matched by identical adjectives – take **morphological** comparison:

(1)   She couldn't bring herself to go any *closer*.

(2)   Jane stayed the *longest* of them all.

(3)   Let's see who can think of an answer *quickest*.

(4)   You'll see me *sooner* than you expect.

Among the derived adverbs in *-ly*, EARLY is compared morphologically while a couple of others, also matched by formally identical adjectives, vacillate between morphological and syntactic comparison:

(5)   Cole was injured *earlier* this season.

(6)   He speaks *kindlier / more kindly* to his children than he used to.

(7)   She is playing it *poorlier / more poorly* than she did yesterday.

Vacillation between morphological and syntactic comparison is also found in the case of a simple adverb like OFTEN:

(8)   I hope you'll come and see us *oftener/more often* next year.

In the large majority of cases, adverbs are compared **syntactically**, including virtually all the numerous adverbs formed by adding *-ly* to an adjective:

(9)   That's what prominent Republicans said, on the airwaves and *more vehemently* in private.

(10)   Mary danced the *most elegantly* of them all.

The compared forms *quicker/quickest* and *louder/loudest* are often found whether or not the positive forms of the adverbs would have lacked *-ly*:

(11)   You'll probably get a cab *quicker* by walking to Waterloo Road.

When compared forms are coordinated, morphologically compared adverbs usually precede syntactically compared adverbs:

(12)   Gore spoke *longer* and *more eloquently* than Kemp.

A small group of adverbs have **irregular comparison**:

badly	worse	worst
far	farther	farthest
	further	furthest
little	less	least
much	more	most
well	better	best

Examples:

(13)   All this happened when we *least* expected it.

(14)   I know their secrets *better* than anyone else.

For the use of compared forms see section 16.3.4.

Appendix: tips on pronunciation and spelling

A.1. Verbs

For many learners the -s suffix and the -ed suffix present difficulties with respect to pronunciation and spelling. The **-s suffix** is pronounced in three different ways:

(i) /ɪz/ (in some varieties /əz/) in verbs ending in a sibilant, i.e. in one of the consonants /s z ʃ ʒ tʃ dʒ/. Examples: *kisses, buzzes, wishes, rouges, watches, judges*.

(ii) /s/ in verbs ending in a voiceless non-sibilant, i.e. one of the consonants /p t k f θ/ (/h/ does not occur finally). Examples: *hops, bets, kicks, laughs, baths*.

(iii) /z/ otherwise, i.e. in verbs ending in a vowel or a voiced non-sibilant consonant. Examples: *sees, dies, goes / begs, sings, sells*.

The **-ed suffix** is also pronounced in three different ways:

(i) /ɪd/ (in some varieties /əd/) in verbs ending in an alveolar stop consonant, i.e. in /t/ or /d/. Examples: *heated, handed*.

(ii) /t/ in verbs ending in a voiceless consonant other than /t/. Examples: *stopped, watched, kicked, laughed, bathed* (in BrE in the sense of 'gave a bath to'), *kissed, wished*.

(iii) /d/ otherwise, i.e. in verbs ending in a vowel or a voiced consonant other than /d/. Examples: *kneed, died, glowed / begged, hanged, felled*.

Orthographically, the -s suffix has a variant -es, which occurs if the base form of the verb ends in a sibilant or in a single written *o*, cf. examples like *wish/wishes* and *go/goes*. Conversely, the -ed suffix has a variant without *e* which occurs if the base form ends in the letter *e*, as illustrated by *knee/kneed, referee/refereed* and *please/pleased*.

Apart from this orthographic variation in the suffix, it should be noted that the addition of a suffix may bring about a change of spelling in the base form. If -ing is added to a verb ending in 'mute' *e*, this letter is usually dropped, cf. examples like *live/living* and *fake/faking*. As shown by e.g. *age/ageing* and *dye/dyeing*, however, there are exceptions to this orthographic rule. If -ing is added to a base form ending in *ie*, secondly, this letter sequence is replaced by *y*, as in *die/dying, lie/lying* and *tie/tying*. The spelling of a verb may also be affected by -s and -ed. If either of these suffixes is added to a base form ending in a *y* preceded by a consonant, this *y* is changed to *i(e)*, for example in *try/tries/tried* (but not in e.g. *play/plays/played,* where *y* comes after a vowel letter).

A final consonant may also be **doubled** before *-ing* and *-ed.* This happens if the base form is monosyllabic and its final consonant is preceded by a vowel spelt with one letter, for example in *pat/ patting/patted* (but not in e.g. *sweat/sweating/sweated*), and it also happens if the base form is polysyllabic and has stress on the last syllable, for example in *propel/propelling/propelled.* In BrE, but not usually in AmE, consonant doubling is further found in some polysyllabic verbs whose last syllable is unstressed and ends in *l* or *m.* Examples illustrating this are *travel/travelling/travelled* and *program/programming/ programmed.* In polysyllabic words whose last syllable is unstressed and ends in *p* there is sometimes doubling but usually not (compare *worship/worshipping/worshipped* with *develop/developing/developed*). In a few verbs there is vacillating orthography, for example in *focus/focus(s)ing/ focus(s)ed.* Finally it should be mentioned that if a base form ends in *c,* there is 'doubling' in the shape of *ck* (as in *panic/panicking/panicked*).

A.2. Nouns

A.2.1. The regular singular/plural distinction

Number is a morphological category with the singular as the unmarked base form and the plural as the morphologically marked form. In speech, the plural is formed by adding:

(i) /ɪz/ to nouns ending in sibilants: e.g. *noses, niches, fringes*

(ii) /s/ to nouns ending in voiceless non-sibilants: e.g. *cats, kicks, taps*

(iii) /z/ to other nouns: e.g. *dogs, clans, shows*

In writing, the plural is usually formed by adding 's' to the base form (as in the examples above). Note however the following modifications to this simple spelling rule:

(i) *-s* **or** *-es.* Nouns ending in a sibilant take *-es* instead of simply *-s* unless they are written with a silent *-e: latch/latches, mass/masses,* etc. (but e.g. *bridge/bridges*).

(ii) Consonant doubling. There is doubling of the final consonant in *fezzes* and *quizzes.* Occasionally *bus* is pluralized as *busses* instead of the more regular *buses.* Note also that a number of abbreviations are pluralized by means of consonant doubling alone: e.g. *pp. 1-5* (= 'pages 1-5'), *exx.* (= 'examples'), *MSS* (= 'manuscripts').

(iii) *-y → -ies* or *-ys*. The plural form of nouns ending in written *-y* is *-ies* (as in *fly/flies, cry/cries, ally/allies,* etc.) except if *-y* is immediately preceded by another written vowel (as in *toys, delays, ways,* etc.). Exceptions to this rule are: most proper nouns (*Marys, Germanys, Julys*; but *the two Sicilies*) and members of other word classes (*stand-bys, the whys and wherefores*). Note also *soliloquies,* where *-qu-* is regarded as a consonant group.

(iv) *-o → -oes* or *-os*. Some nouns ending in *-o* take plural *-es*: *echoes, heroes, potatoes, tomatoes, vetoes*. Others (especially proper names, abbreviations and cases where *-o* is immediately preceded by another written vowel) take plural *-s* only: *Eskimos, Neros; kilos, photos, pianos; embryos, studios;* etc. There is vacillation in: *banjo(e)s, buffalo(e)s, cargo(e)s, commando(e)s, halo(e)s, motto(e)s, volcano(e)s,* and others. Note the difference between *bravos* (= applause) and *bravoes* (= bandits).

(v) *-s* or *-'s*. The plural form of letters is *-'s* rather than simply *-s*: e.g. *p's and q's*. With abbreviations and numerals written in figures there is vacillation with *-s* as the commoner form: *MP's* or *MPs, 1980's* or *1980s*. Quoted words usually take *-'s*: *There were too many but's in the passage*. Words which do not merely function as quotes but assume an integrated meaning in the sentence take *-s*: *Some of his whys are hard to answer*.

Pluralization sometimes results in a sound change:

(i) /-θ/ → /-ðz/. This change is very common in nouns like *baths, mouths, paths, youths*. There is vacillation (/-θs/ or /-ðz/) in *oaths, sheaths, truths, wreaths*. If *-th* is preceded by a consonant, or a short vowel, or a written *-r-* we only get /-θs/: *healths, lengths; deaths; moths; births, hearths*.

(ii) /-s/ → /-zɪz/. This change affects only one word: *houses*.

(iii) /-f/ → /-vz/. This change affects both the pronunciation and the spelling of nouns like *calf/calves, half/halves, knife/knives, leaf/leaves, life/lives, loaf/loaves, self/selves, shelf/shelves, thief/thieves, wife/wives, wolf/wolves*. However, most nouns ending in /-f/ take plural /-fs/: *beliefs, chiefs, cliffs, coughs, cuffs, flagstaffs, laughs, paragraphs, roofs, sniffs*. There is vacillation in: *dwarfs/dwarves, hoofs/hooves, scarfs/scarves, wharf/wharves*. Note the difference between *staffs* (= groups of people working together) and *staves* (= sticks, rods). Note also *still lifes*.

A. 2.2. Irregular plurals

There are a number of important exceptions to the rules of pluralization described above:

(i) Vowel change. This form of pluralization is found in the following nouns: *man/men, woman/women, foot/feet, goose/geese, louse/lice, mouse/mice, tooth/teeth*. Correspondingly, we find a vowel change in compounds containing these nouns (e.g. *dormouse/dormice, gentleman/gentlemen, chairwoman/chairwomen*). Note that there is normally no difference in pronunciation in compounds containing *-man*: both the singular and the plural is pronounced [mən]. Words containing *-man* which are not compounds take the regular plural: *Normans, Germans*.

(ii) *-en/-ren* plural. Only three nouns take the *-en/-ren* plural ending, two of them with additional vowel change: *child/children, ox/oxen* and *brother/ brethren* (used only about the members of a religious community; *brothers* is the normal plural of *brother*).

(iii) /-s/ (-ce) after voiced sound. This plural ending is found in two words: *dice* (the corresponding singular *die* is used only in standard phrases like *The die is cast*) and *pence* (used about amounts and 'small change', in contrast to *pennies*, which is used about the individual coins).

(iv) Foreign plurals. Many nouns of foreign, especially Latin or Greek, origin take foreign plural forms rather than the regular English plural form, though in many cases there is vacillation with the regular form as the less formal. Here are some of the most common examples:

- *-us* → *-i* (/aɪ/) or *-a* (/ə/):

alumnus/alumni, stimulus/stimuli; cactus/cacti or *cactuses, octopus/octopi* or *octopuses*. Note regular examples like: *campus/campuses, genius/ geniuses, virus/viruses. Corpus* and *genus* take the irregular plural form *corpora* and *genera* in formal, technical language.

- *-a* → *-ae* (/-iː/):

alumna/alumnae, larva/larvae, vertebra/vertebrae. Note regular examples like: *area/areas, villa/villas*. There is vacillation in *antenna/antennae* (of insects) or *antennas* (= aerials), *formula/formulae* (mathematical formulae) or *formulas* (more generally).

- *-um* → *-a* (/ə/):

addendum/addenda, bacterium/bacteria and others. Note regular *album/ albums, museum/museums, asylum/asylums*. Vacillation: *aquarium/aquariums* or *aquaria, symposium/symposiums* or *symposia*. Note that the plural form of *datum* is, strictly speaking, *data*, but *data* is increasingly used as a singular mass noun instead of *datum*, especially in scientific language, and especially about 'a collection of facts or examples'.

- *-ex* or *-ix* → *-ices*:

codex/codices, index/indices (in science) or *indexes* (more generally), *appendix/appendices* (in books) or *appendixes* (in anatomy), *matrix/ matrices* or *matrixes*.

- *-is → es* (/-i:z/):

analysis/analyses, axis/axes, basis/bases (the plural spelling thus coinciding with the spelling of *base/bases*), *crisis/crises, diagnosis/diagnoses, hypothesis/hypotheses*, etc. The regular English plural is rare: *metropolis/ metropolises*.

- *-on → -a* (/ə/):

criterion/criteria, phenomenon/phenomena but *demon/demons, electron/ electrons*, etc.

- Others:

portmanteau/portmanteaus or *portmanteaux, bureau/bureaus* or *bureaux, corps* (/kɔ:/)/*corps* (/kɔ:z/).

A.3. Adjectives: comparison

Certain orthographical changes occur in connection with morphological comparison:

(i) adjectives ending in written *e* require only additional *-r* and *-st* in the comparative and superlative, respectively:

fine	finer	finest
free	freer	freest

(ii) single final written consonants (except *w*) are doubled before *-er* and *-est* when the preceding vowel is stressed and spelled with a single letter, compare:

big	bigger	biggest
narrow	narrower	narrowest
neat	neater	neatest

Especially in BrE we get doubling of the final consonant also in:

cruel	crueller	cruellest

(iii) final written *-y* is normally changed to *-i-* when following a consonant but remains unchanged after a vowel, compare:

dry	drier	driest
grey	greyer	greyest

Especially in BrE, SHY, SLY, SPRY and WRY keep the *y*:

shy	shyer	shyest

Turning now to the spoken language, we begin by noting that the pronunciation of the suffixes *-er* and *-est* are [ə(r)] and [ɪst]. A number of phonetic changes occur when these suffixes are added to adjectival stems:

(i) final written *-r* is always pronounced when the suffixes are added:

    dear: [dɪə]   [dɪərə]   [dɪərɪst]

(ii) [ŋ] in *long, strong* and *young* becomes [ŋg] when the suffixes are added:

    long: [lɒŋ]   [lɒŋgə]   [lɒŋgɪst]

(iii) final syllabic dark *l* [ɫ] becomes non-syllabic clear l [l] when the suffixes are added:

    ample: [æmpɫ]   [æmplə]   [æmplɪst]

In such words morphological comparison thus does not increase the number of syllables.

A.4. Adverbs

The final *-y* of an adjective in more than one syllable is changed to *-i-* in a derived *-ly* adverb, as in PRETTILY (PRETTY). Furthermore, the final *-e* of the adjectives DUE and TRUE is dropped in the derived adverbs DULY, TRULY (but note that it is retained in e.g. PALELY and SOLELY). The letter *-e* is also omitted in adverbs derived from adjectives ending in *-le*, though here an *l* is dropped as well (except in WHOLLY): SUBTLY (SUBTLE), NOBLY (NOBLE), etc. Adverbs derived from adjectives in *-ic* end in *-ically*, as in PROBLEM-ATICALLY (PROBLEMATIC), except for PUBLICLY and POLITICLY. Note finally an adverb like OFFHANDEDLY, derived from the adjective OFFHAND. In this case, it should be added, the form without a suffix may also be an adverb, as in *I can't say offhand whether it's route 66 or 69*.

Select bibliography

Bache, Carl
   1978   *The order of premodifying adjectives in present-day English.* Odense: Odense University Press.

Bache, Carl
   1985   *Verbal aspect: a general theory and its application to present-day English.* Odense: Odense University Press.

Bache, Carl
   1986   "Tense and aspect in fiction", *Journal of Literary Semantics* 15: 66-70.

Bache, Carl – Mike Davenport – John Dienhart – Fritz Larsen
   1999   *An introduction to English sentence analysis* (3rd edition). Copenhagen: Gyldendal.

Davidsen-Nielsen, Niels
   1985   "Has English a future?", *Acta Linguistica Hafniensia* 21, 1: 5-20.

Davidsen-Nielsen, Niels
   1990   *Tense and mood in English: a comparison with Danish.* Berlin and New York: Mouton de Gruyter.

Dirven, René (ed.)
   1989   *A user's grammar of English: word, sentence, text, interaction.* Frankfurt am Main: Peter Lang.

Downing, Angela – Philip Locke
   1992   *A university course in English grammar.* New York and London: Prentice Hall.

Ferris, Connor
   1993   *The meaning of syntax: a study in the adjectives of English.* London: Longman.

Greenbaum, Sidney – Randolph Quirk
   1990   *A student's grammar of the English language.* London: Longman.

Harder, Peter
   1996   *Functional semantics: a theory of meaning, structure and tense in English.* Berlin and New York: Mouton de Gruyter.

Hartvigson, Hans – Leif Kvistgaard Jakobsen
   1974   *Inversion in present-day English.* Odense: Odense University Press.

Huddleston, Rodney
   1984   *Introduction to the grammar of English.* Cambridge: Cambridge University Press.

Huddleston, Rodney
   1988   *English grammar: an outline.* Cambridge: Cambridge University Press.

Jakobsen, Leif Kvistgaard
  1994   "Variation in the use of the definite article and the demonstratives as cohesive devices", RASK 1 (Odense University Press): 63-82.
Jespersen, Otto
  1909-49 *A modern English grammar on historical principles.* Copenhagen: Munksgaard, and London: Allen & Unwin.
Jespersen, Otto
  1929   *The philosophy of grammar.* London: Allen & Unwin.
Jespersen, Otto
  1933   *Essentials of English grammar.* London: Allen & Unwin.
Johansson, Stig – Per Lysvåg
  1986   *Understanding English Grammar* 1. Oslo: Universitetsforlaget.
Johansson, Stig – Per Lysvåg
  1987   *Understanding English Grammar* 2. Oslo: Universitetsforlaget.
Juul, Arne
  1975   *On concord of number in modern English.* Copenhagen: Nova.
Juul, Arne – Knud Sørensen
  1978   *Numerus i moderne engelsk.* Copenhagen: Schønberg.
Leech, Geoffrey
  1981   *Semantics* (2nd edition). Harmondsworth: Penguin.
Palmer, Frank
  1987   *The English verb* (2nd edition). London: Longman.
Preisler, Bent
  1992   *A handbook of English grammar.* Aarhus: Aarhus University Press.
Quirk, Randolph – Sidney Greenbaum – Geoffrey Leech – Jan Svartvik
  1985   *A comprehensive grammar of the English language.* London: Longman.
Schibsbye, Knud
  1970   *A modern English grammar* (2nd edition). Oxford: Oxford University Press.
Sinclair, John (ed.)
  1990   *Collins Cobuild English grammar.* London and Glasgow: Collins.
Steller, Poul – Knud Sørensen
  1974   *Engelsk grammatik* (2nd edition). Copenhagen: Munksgaard.
Swan, Michael
  1995   *Practical English usage.* (2nd edition). Oxford: Oxford University Press.
van Ek, Jan A. – Nico J. Robat
  1984   *The student's grammar of English.* Oxford: Basil Blackwell.
Vestergaard, Torben
  1985   *Engelsk grammatik.* Copenhagen: Schønberg.

Glossary

A: see **Adverbial**.

Absolute clause: a nonfinite or verbless adverbial clause with a subject and without a subordinator, e.g. *Ronald moved forward, Jenny staying behind* and *Ronald knelt down, his hands behind his back*.

Absolute comparative: a comparative which expresses '(fairly) high degree' rather than 'higher rank', e.g. *Our dog likes older people* (*older* = 'elderly').

Absolute superlative: a superlative which expresses 'exceptionally high degree' rather than 'highest rank', as in *Her face expressed the liveliest gratification* and *a most remarkable evening*.

Accusative with infinitive/participle: a traditional term for object infinitive or partiple clauses containing a subject, e.g. *I wanted her to leave*. When a personal pronoun is subject in the object clause it is in the objective ('accusative') form.

Action(ality): the category of action deals with the different (dynamic and stative) types of situation. The actionality of a construction is its situational nature (e.g. punctual, telic or habitual).

Active (voice): see **Voice**.

adj: see **Adjective**.

Adjectival: a form term covering both 'adjective group' and 'single adjective'.

Adjective (adj): adjectives typically express qualities in relation to nouns and pronouns (e.g. *a long letter / he is afraid*) and often allow comparison (e.g. *longer, longest / more afraid, most afraid*).

Adjective group: a group with an adjective as head, e.g. *My wife is very beautiful*.

Adjunct: an adverbial which is closely integrated in the sentence structure. Adjuncts typically express negation, time, place, manner, instrument, reason, purpose, condition, degree, etc. (e.g. *I left my wife in London*).

adv: see **Adverb**.

Adverb (adv): adverbs typically express qualities in relation to verbs (e.g. *Jack moved slowly*), adjectives (e.g. *very big*), other adverbs (e.g. *so gently*), or the rest of the sentence (e.g. *Fortunately, everybody was saved*). Adverbs are often derived from adjectives by means of the *-ly* suffix: e.g. *slow* →

slowly, gentle → *gently*. Like many adjectives, many adverbs allow comparison (e.g. *more slowly, most slowly*).

Adverb group: a group with an adverb as head, e.g. *She danced <u>very beautifully</u>*.

Adverbal: a form term covering both 'adverb group' and 'single adverb'.

Adverbial (A): a default clause/sentence function in that it is not a subject, predicator, object or complement. Adverbials fall into three major subclasses: adjuncts (e.g. *Jack left Rome <u>yesterday</u>*), disjuncts (e.g. *James is <u>undoubtedly</u> a talented piano player*) and conjuncts (e.g. *<u>However</u>, there are many other considerations*).

AFFECTED: a specific participant role; something/someone involved in, or affected by, a dynamic situation (e.g. *Jack fixed <u>the old motorbike</u>*).

AGENT: a specific participant role; a volitional (typically human) instigator of a dynamic situation (e.g. *<u>Jack</u> fixed the old motorbike*).

AmE: American English.

Anaphoric: a term for something that relates 'backwards' to an earlier constituent. In e.g. *Jack wanted to see her as soon as he got back*, the subject *he* in the subclause refers anaphorically to the subject *Jack* in the matrix clause.

Antecedent: a constituent referred to anaphorically. In an example like *I bought the book shortly after it was published*, the object *the book* in the matrix clause is the antecedent of the subject *it* in the subclause.

Appended coordination: coordination which provides additional information by means of a separate conjoint, as in *Barbara sings beautifully, <u>and Joan too</u>*.

Apposition: a post-head parenthetical dependent (e.g. *Jack Parker, <u>my neighbour,</u>* and *John, <u>who moved to Hove last year.</u>*).

art: see **Article**.

Article (art): articles typically combine with nouns to express definiteness (e.g. *<u>the</u> car, <u>the</u> idea*) or indefiniteness (e.g. *<u>a</u> car, <u>an</u> idea*).

Aspect: a category which enables the speaker/writer to present a situation as being in progress, i.e. with an internal focus (as in *It was raining in Dublin*) or as a fact, a complete unit, i.e. with an external focus (as in *It rained in Dublin*). Aspect is closely related to the category of tense. The combined tense-aspect system comprises the following four choices of verb form: present/past, future/nonfuture, perfect/nonperfect and progressive/nonprogressive.

Assertive pronoun: see **Partitive pronoun**.

Attitude: a psychological state (opinion, belief, love, hatred, liking, need, knowledge, supposition, etc.), cf. *George believes in God.*

Attraction concord: concord between a verb and a form closer to the verb than the head noun of the subject, as in *The situation in Bosnian mountain areas and forests now <u>seem</u> critical.* Such concord is erroneous, but is sometimes found when the verb is some distance from the subject head noun.

Attraction inversion: inversion triggered by a special initial constituent, e.g. a negative or restrictive constituent other than the subject, as in *Rarely <u>have</u> I set eyes on such a stunning beauty.*

ATTRIBUTE: a specific participant role representing three stative subroles: characterization (e.g. *Victoria is <u>beautiful</u>*), identification (e.g. *Bill is <u>the fellow standing over there</u>*) and classification (e.g. *Mick is <u>a dentist</u>*).

Attributive adjective: adjective serving as a dependent in a noun or pronoun group, e.g. *a <u>beautiful</u> woman* and *something <u>strange</u>*.

Autonomous genitive: a specifying genitive which does not relate to an overt head but rather by itself assumes an external function, as in *I met Jane at my <u>uncle's</u>*.

Autonomous pronoun: autonomous pronouns are either heads of pronoun groups (e.g. *<u>Someone</u> I like will be disappointed*) or syntactically independent (e.g. *<u>She</u> gave me <u>some</u>*).

Auxiliary verb: a verb that relates to and modifies full verbs (auxiliary verbs are sometimes called 'helping verbs'). The auxiliaries comprise BE, HAVE and DO as well as the modal verbs (*will /would, shall/should, can/could*, etc.).

Backshifting: the expression of indirect speech on the basis of direct speech, a process which involves changes of person, of tense-aspect (typically 'back' to some past form) and of other deictic elements, e.g. *Peter said that <u>his</u> commanding officer <u>would</u> regard <u>that</u> as cowardice* (cf. the original statement *<u>My</u> commanding officer <u>will</u> regard <u>this</u> as cowardice*).

Base form: the form of a word from which manifestation forms are derived (e.g. *love, loves, loved* and *loving* are manifestation forms derived from the base form LOVE). The base form of a word is its entry form in dictionaries.

Basic sentence structure: a typical constellation of obligatory sentence functions, e.g. S P O as in *Richard kissed Jessica.*

BE-passive: the 'normal' passive with BE as the auxiliary, e.g. *He was killed.*

BENEFICIARY: a specific participant role; someone/something for whose sake the dynamic situation is brought about (e.g. *He gave <u>me</u> the book*).

Binary: consisting of two parts.

BrE: British English.

Case: a category which applies to nouns and pronouns (personal, interrogative and relative). Three cases are recognized: the subjective, the objective and the genitive. Nouns are unmarked with respect to the distinction between subjective and objective but often take the genitive case to express possession or some other relationship with the head noun (e.g. *the boy's* book and *my sister's* idea). Some pronouns have specific subjective and objective forms (e.g. *he/him, they/them, who/whom*). Possessive pronouns can be regarded as the genitive form of personal pronouns: e.g. *his* and *their*.

Cataphoric: a term for something that relates to elements in the following text. For example, in *Deny it though he might, he dumped his wife in Paris*, the object *it* in the subclause refers cataphorically to the matrix clause.

Categorization: the expression of a category of things, persons, etc.; the central function of the head of a nominal is to categorize the referent.

Category: systematic formal variation affecting a large set of words. For example, the distinction between singular and plural, which applies to most nouns (*car/cars* and *girl/girls*), is referred to as the number category.

Catenative: a term sometimes used about (full) verbs which are chained together with (other) full verbs but which have a subordinate status, e.g. KEEP and GET in *She kept laughing* and *He got run over yesterday*.

CAUSE: a specific participant role; a non-volitional (typically non-human) entity bringing about a dynamic situation, cf. *The landslide* killed the old man.

Central adjective: adjective which is gradable and occurs freely in both attributive pre-head position and in predicative position. Central adjectives are often coordinated and they typically describe rather than classify or define the referent to which they assign a property. Examples: NICE, FUNNY, GOOD, ANGRY, COLD, etc. Central adjectives are also called descriptive adjectives.

Central determiner: the main, or only, determiner in a construction, as in *the fool* and *what a fool*.

Central pronoun: personal, possessive and reflexive pronouns are grouped together as central pronouns.

Central-M: adverbial medial position immediately following the operator, as in *Keith had never wanted her soul*. If there is no operator, Central-M position is simply between subject and predicator, as in *Keith never wanted her soul*.

CJT: see **Conjoint**.

cl: see **Clause**.

Class-member referent: see **Referent**.

Classification: a general term for the arrangement of things in categories or groups. It is sometimes used in a specialized sense to refer to a subfunction of modification, realized by classifying adjectives.

Classifying adjective: adjective which subcategorizes the head it modifies. For example, a *medical dictionary* is a special kind of dictionary. Classifying adjectives (unlike central adjectives) are not gradable.

Classifying genitive: a genitive which serves as a classifying modifier immediately preceding the head noun, as in *a women's magazine*.

Clausal complement(ation): the type(s) of clause (*that*-clause, infinitive clause, etc.) which a verb requires as object, adverbial or complement clause.

Clausal negation: see **Syntactic field of negation**.

Clause (cl): a complex form consisting of at least two clause functions (subject, predicator, object, etc.), one of which is almost always the predicator (e.g. *Jack left / Leave her now! / Would you care for a cup of tea? / If in doubt, ...*).

Cleft sentence: a sentence like *It was John who left early*, in which a constituent (*John*) is singled out for emphatic identification. This constituent is placed as a subject complement between provisional subject *it* + BE and a relative subclause as the real, extraposed subject.

Closed word class: closed word classes have relatively few members and rarely allow any new members. Pronouns, prepositions, conjunctions and articles are closed word classes.

CO: see **Coordinator**.

Co: see **Object complement**.

Co-reference: a relation between two or more expressions which have the same referent. In e.g. *She hated herself*, the subject and the object are co-referential.

Cognate object: an object whose head noun is derived from the verb preceding it, as in *to live a good life* and *to sing a song*.

Cohesion: a textual link between sentences, created by e.g. pro-forms or adverbials (especially conjuncts).

Collective noun: a number-inflecting noun (like *audience/audiences*) whose singular form can be interpreted in two different ways: a) as referring to a single unit (*The audience was impressed*), or b) as a collection of individuals (BrE *The audience were impressed*).

Comment: that which is stated about the topic, usually expressed by the predicate of a clause, as in *The parish vibrated with gossip the next day*.

Comment clause: a clause which adds a parenthetic comment to the content of the matrix, as in *It's private, you see*.

Common gender: the conflation of masculine and feminine gender, e.g. *writer*, *driver*, *teacher*, etc., which may equally well refer to males and females.

Common noun: a noun which refers to something regarded as a member of a class of things (e.g. KNIFE, BOY, PARENT, SCHOOL, BOOK, PEN, CUP, etc.).

Communicative function: the communicative function of a unit is its use in communication. For example, clauses are used to offer statements, ask questions, give orders, etc. Such functions are also referred to as illocutionary values.

Comparative: see **Comparison**.

Comparative basis: the standard against which a comparison is made. In e.g. *Joan is taller than Jack*, the comparative basis is expressed by *than Jack*.

Comparative element: the formal expression of comparison, i.e. either the suffixes *-er* and *-est* (as in *stronger/strongest*) or the adverbs *more* and *most* (as in *more beautiful / most beautiful*).

Comparison: a category which enables the speaker/writer to express the ranking of entities on the basis of the degree to which they possess some property, e.g. 'higher rank' or 'the highest rank'. For example, in *Jane is faster than Bob*, the subject *Jane* is ranked higher than *Bob* with respect to the property 'fastness'. Within the category of comparison three members are recognized: the positive (e.g. *fast*), the comparative (e.g. *faster*) and the superlative (e.g. *fastest*).

Complementation: a kind of subordination; a relationship between two constituents (e.g. a dependent and a head) where the subordinate constituent fills out the meaning of the superordinate element, as in *immune to criticism*, in which *to criticism* complements *immune*. If a complement is left out, it can be assumed to be understood in the context.

Complete semantic scope of negation: see **Semantic scope of negation**.

Complex coordination: coordination of conjoints which consist of more than one function, as in *She sold and I bought the house* (where each conjoint consists of both a subject and a predicator).

Complex form: complex forms require further syntactic analysis, i.e. analysis of their internal constituency. Complex forms include groups, compound units and clauses but not individual words (which are simple forms).

Complex-transitive predicator: a transitive predicator which takes an object plus either an object complement (as in *We painted the wall yellow*) or an obligatory adverbial (as in *I put the book on the shelf*). The basic sentence structures associated with complex predicators are S P O Co and S P O A.

Compound: a unit (typically nominal) made up by two or more independent parts, e.g. *classroom*.

Compound unit (cu): a complex form consisting of two or more conjoints (CJTs) typically linked by means of a coordinator (CO), e.g. <u>*Wendy and Kim*</u> *sat round the table* and *They saw* <u>*your daughter and my son*</u> *at the party*.

Concessive clause: a clause which expresses concession. Clauses are often marked as concessive by conjunctions like *(al)though, even if, whereas*, etc.

Concord: agreement in form between different constituents, e.g. the subject and the predicator, as in <u>*the boy*</u> <u>*is*</u> *clever* / <u>*the boys*</u> <u>*are*</u> *clever*.

conj: see **Conjunction**.

Conjoint (CJT): a constituent linked with another constituent by means of coordination in a compound unit. In e.g. *They saw your daughter and my son at the party*, the object *your daughter and my son* is a compound unit with two conjoints: *your daughter* and *my son*.

Conjunct: an adverbial which is peripheral to sentence structure. Conjuncts typically serve to relate the sentence to a previous sentence (e.g. <u>*However,*</u> *they both disappeared*) or they are used as discourse initiators (e.g. <u>*So*</u> *how are you today, Sally?*).

Conjunction (conj): conjunctions express relations between constituents. Coordinating conjunctions do so by combining constituents at the same level (e.g. *cars* <u>*and*</u> *books, clever* <u>*but*</u> *arrogant*). Subordinating conjunctions place one clause (e.g. *He didn't support her*) at a lower level in relation to another clause (e.g. *I said* <u>*that*</u> *he didn't support her*, where [he didn't support her] is at a lower level than, or embedded in [I said x]).

Constituent: a unit of analysis (e.g. a word, a group of words, or a clause) which is part of a larger construction. For example, *my* and *friend* are constituents of the group *my friend*, and *my friend* and *laughed* are constituents of the clause *my friend laughed*.

Contraction: the attachment of a reduced form to another form, e.g. operator-contraction as in: *it's* (= *it* + *is*) and *not* contraction, as in *hasn't* (= *has* + *not*).

CONTROLLER: a specific participant role; a volitional (typically human) participant for whom a state obtains for so long as he or she keeps it that way, e.g. *Roger is in London*.

Coordinating conjunction: see **Conjunction**.

Coordination: the linking together of constituents which have the same syntactic status and are at the same level of analysis, e.g. *Rolf and Werner were devious devils* and *She called Tim or Ruth the other day*. The coordinating conjunction (typically *and, or* or *but*) and the constituents it links form a compound unit. In a compound unit the constituents linked are analysed functionally as conjoints and the conjunction as a coordinator.

Coordinator (CO): a constituent which links conjoints to form compound units, e.g. *cars and books* and *clever but arrogant*. A coordinator is typically realized by one of the conjunctions *and, or* or *but*.

Copula predicator: a predicator which takes a complement, as in *Marion is such a nice person*. The basic sentence structure associated with copula predicators is S P C.

Count noun: a noun whose referent is conceived of as something individualized which we can count (e.g. BOOK, WINDOW, CAR, HOUSE, etc.).

Cs: see **Subject complement**.

cu: see **Compound unit**.

Dangling participle: see **Unattached participle**.

Declarative clause: a form type of clause typically used to express a positive or negative statement, e.g. *Bob inspected the book* and *He is not here*. Clauses are divided into declarative, interrogative, imperative and exclamatory.

Deixis (adj: deictic): a term used for meanings and categories that can only be interpreted in relation to the communicative event itself. For example, to interpret the personal pronoun *I*, we need to know who is speaking. Tense meaning is also deictic: we interpret present, past and future meaning in relation to the moment of communication. Another example involves demonstrative pronouns, which are used to refer to distant or near entities relative to the position of the speaker (e.g. *this book* versus *that book*).

Demonstrative pronoun: the central demonstrative pronouns are *this, these, that* and *those*. Demonstratives are mainly used to point to things. Two categories apply to them: number (singular *this* and *that* versus plural *these* and *those*) and deixis (near *this* and *these* versus distant *that* and *those*).

Denominal adjective: an adjective deriving from a noun, e.g. FRIENDLY.

Deontic: see **Modality**.

DEP: see **Dependent**.

Dependent (DEP): a subordinate group constituent which enters some relationship with the head of the group, e.g. *expensive* wine, *may* dance and *very* beautifully.

Description: a general term for saying in words what something is like.. It is sometimes used in a specialized sense to refer to a subfunction of modification, realized by descriptive adjectives.

Descriptive adjective: see **Central adjective**.

Determination: a kind of subordination; a relationship between a dependent and a nominal head where the dependent signals what kind of reference the noun group has, for example definite as in *the girl* and indefinite as in *a girl*. Such dependents are more specifically called determiners.

Determinative pronoun: determinative pronouns serve as DEP (as in *some people* and *her car*).

Determiner: see **Determination**.

Deverbal adjective: adjective deriving from a verb, e.g. RESISTIBLE.

Direct object: see **Object**.

Direct reference: involves strictly co-referential expressions, as in *John looked for the book, but couldn't find it*, where *it* refers directly to *the book*. Direct reference contrasts with indirect reference.

Direct speech: the quoting of what an original speaker said, as in *Sally said: "Simon has given up"*. Direct speech contrasts with indirect speech, as in *Sally said that Simon had given up*.

Directed(ness): directed situations progress towards a natural terminal point but do not include this point, cf. *Sally was building a garden shed*.

Directive: the communicative function of instructing the hearer to perform some action or to behave in a certain way, as in *Be quiet!*

Discontinuity: lack of linear continuity. A constituent whose parts are not all positioned together in the linear expression is said to be discontinuous. The predicator *was kissing* is continuous in *Jack was kissing the beautiful girl* but discontinuous in *Was Jack kissing the beautiful girl?*, where the subject *Jack* intervenes between the dependent and the head of the verb group.

Disjunct: an adverbial which is peripheral to sentence structure. Disjuncts typically convey the speaker's comment on the information expressed by the rest of the sentence or on the style or form of the expression itself (e.g. *To be frank, I do not want you to leave Hawaii yet*).

Dislocation: involves using a pro-form in the place of a constituent placed outside the sentence structure, either to the left, as in *Sally, she's an excellent pianist* (left-dislocation), or to the right, as in *I can't stand him, that friend of yours* (right-dislocation).

Distributive: a term used about an expression which refers to separate things, cf. e.g. the distributive plural *the sixteenth and seventeenth centuries*.

Ditransitive predicator: a transitive predicator which takes two objects, a direct and an indirect one, as in *Fred bought Sally a bunch of roses*. Ditransitive predicators contrast with monotransitive predicators, which take one object only. The basic sentence structure associated with ditransitive predicators is S P Oi Od.

DO-support: the use of auxiliary DO to form subject-operator inversion, as in *yes-no* questions (e.g. *Do you like me*), to form a negative clause (e.g. *She does not like me*), or to create emphasis (e.g. *She did like me after all!*).

DOER: a general participant role; someone/something bringing a dynamic situation about, e.g. *Jack fixed the old motorbike*.

Domain of negation: concerns the overall polarity of clauses; a distinction is drawn between global negation (negated unit = the clause as a whole) and local negation (negated unit = less than a full clause), cf. *He didn't apologize* (global) and *Jim pleaded not guilty* (local).

DONE-TO: general participant role; someone/something passively affected by a dynamic situation, e.g. *Jack fixed the old motorbike*.

Dual pronoun: a pronoun which implies a class of two members only, e.g. *both* and *either*.

Dynamic: a dynamic situation requires a continual input of energy and typically involves change, e.g. the situation of 'Jack fixing the old motorbike'.

Elaborative: a term used about dependents which enter an identity relation to the head but at the same time elaborate on the content of the head, as in *Jack Parker, my neighbour,* and *the idea that I should marry her*.

Ellipsis: a device for abbreviating expressions by leaving out constituents.

Embedding: the occurrence of complex forms within complex forms, e.g. clauses within clauses, as in *To see her is to love her*.

Emphatic DO-support: DO-support used to create emphasis, as in *She did like me after all*.

End-focus: the tendency to place new and important information at the end of a clause/sentence is called the principle of end-focus.

End-weight: the tendency, wherever possible, to place heavy (i.e. long) constituents last in a clause/sentence is called the principle of end-weight.

Endophoric reference: see **Textual reference**.

Epistemic: see **Modality**.

Exclamation: the communicative function of indicating emotional reaction (surprise, disapproval, pleasure, etc.), e.g. *How quiet John was!* and *Wow!*

Exclamatory clause: a form type of clause typically used to express exclamations, as in *What a big crowd turned up!* and *How delightful it is*.

Existential sentence: existential sentences state that something or someone exists somewhere, or comes into existence. Typically *there* is used as provisional subject and the predicator is realized by BE or a near synonym, as in *There was/remained a bottle of wine on the table*.

Exophoric reference: see **Non-textual reference**.

Extensive relation: a physical state, condition, location, position or possession obtaining for an entity, cf. e.g. *The village lies in a dark valley*.

EXTRA: default general participant role; anything that is not DOER, DONE-TO, SPECIFIER or SPECIFIED, e.g. *Jack was in London last week*.

Extraposed (real) (direct) object: see **Real object** and **Extraposition**.

Extraposed (real) subject: see **Real subject** and **Extraposition**.

Extraposition: involves the movement of a constituent (e.g. the subject or object) from its normal position to a position at the end of the clause, outside the basic clause structure. Real subjects and objects are often extraposed, as in *It was good to see you* and *I found it hard to work with her*.

Extrasentential: a term used about relations or phenomena outside a sentence.

Field of negation: see **Syntactic field of negation**.

Finite: a verb is finite when it formally expresses present tense (as in *they sing / she runs*) or formally expresses past tense (as in *they sang / she ran*). Other form types of verbs (such as infinitives, present participles and past participles) are nonfinite. There is only one finite verb in a finite predicator, and it always precedes any nonfinite verb (e.g. *She was being followed by us*).

Focalization: the postponement of a constituent for reasons of information structure (i.e. in order to give it end-focus).

Form: the make-up, or composition, of a constituent. Words, groups, compound units and clauses are form types. The manifestion form of a word is the morphological shape of its exact realization (e.g. *love, loves, loved* and *loving* are different manifestation forms of the verb LOVE).

Free (or implicit) indirect speech: indirect speech with the reporting clause left out, or parenthesized, as in *Would she be able to recognize this interpretation of herself, he wondered.*

Full (subject-predicator) inversion: see **Inversion**.

Full verb: the verb that carries the lexical content of a predicator (a full verb is often called a lexical verb), e.g. RUN / JUMP / LAUGH / WRITE / CONSOLE. Full verbs contrast with auxiliary verbs.

Function: the way a constituent is used in relation to other constituents. For example, subject, predicator and direct object are clause functions, and head and dependent are group functions.

g: see **Group**.

g-replacive *one*: group-replacive *one*; *one* used as a pro-form for a group rather than just a noun: e.g. *When she asked for a new key, I gave her one.*

Gender: a category which marks constituents as feminine, masculine, neuter or common. In English the category involves certain nominal and pronominal distinctions (e.g. *lion/ lioness* and *he/she/it*).

Generic referent: see **Referent**.

Genitive (case): see **Case**.

GET-passive: passive with GET used as the auxiliary verb, e.g. *He got killed.*

Global negation: see **Domain of negation**.

Gradable adjective: gradable adjectives denote scalar properties and thus take degree adverbs like VERY and EXTREMELY (e.g. NICE and RICH).

Grammar: the study of morphology and syntax, i.e. the study of how morphemes and words are combined to form higher-level constituents in meaningful ways.

Group (g): a complex form consisting of a head and one or more dependents. The head determines the nature of the group. Thus if the head is realized by a noun, the group is a noun group (e.g. *a nice party*); if the head is realized by a verb, the group is a verb group (e.g. *may have been dancing*), and so forth.

Group-replacive: see **g-replacive *one***.

H: see **Head**.

Habit: the product of a (dynamic or stative) situation occurring so regularly that it is conceived of as characteristic of someone or something, cf. *John teaches linguistics* and *Sally smokes*.

Head (H): a superordinate group constituent with one or more dependents. A head and its dependents form a group: e.g. *sad songs, may have been dancing* and *extremely miserable*. The head is an obligatory element which characterizes the group as a particular kind of group. Thus, for example, a group with a noun as head is a noun group.

HOLDER: specific participant role; a non-volitional (typically but not inevitably non-human) participant for whom/which a state obtains, e.g. *The village lies in a dark valley*.

Hypotaxis: a relation between elements at different levels of analysis. In e.g. *envious Republican senators*, there is a hypotactic relation between the two adjectives, *envious* modifying *Republican senators* rather than just *senators*.

Illocutionary: see **Communication function**.

Imperative: a mood realized by the base form of the verb. The imperative expresses something which needs to be made real, such as a directive or command (e.g. *Please come with me*).

Imperative clause: a form type of clause typically used to express a directive or a command, as in *Shut the door* and *You listen to me!*

Incomplete semantic scope of negation: see **Semantic scope of negation**.

Indefinite pronouns: a fairly complex subclass of pronouns comprising *every, some, any, no* and their combinations with *-one, -body, -thing* (e.g. *everyone, somebody, anything*, etc.). But there are other indefinite pronouns, the most important of which are *each, all, both, either, neither* and *one(s)*.

Independent relative clause: a relative clause with non-textual reference, i.e. without an antecedent. Independent relative pronouns can be interpreted as a fusion of a normal relative and an antecedent, as in *I gave her what was left*, where *what* means *that which*.

Indicative: a mood which has *-s* in the 3rd person singular of the present form of the verb and *-ed* in the past. The indicative basically expresses something real or factual (e.g. *Somebody opens/opened the door*).

Indirect object (Oi) a clause/sentence function which usually follows the predicator but precedes a direct object, as in *Fred bought Sally a bunch of roses*. It typically expresses a BENEFICIARY.

Indirect reference: reference to a non-identical, but related, antecedent, as in *I looked at the book but couldn't see the title*, where *the title* refers anaphorically but indirectly to *the book*.

Indirect speech: the reporting of what an original speaker said without offering a verbatim quote, as in *Sally said that Simon had given up*. Indirect speech contrasts with direct speech, as in *Sally said: "Simon has given up"*.

Infinitive: a verb form identical with the base form (also used as the entry form for verbs in dictionaries). Infinitives occur with or without the infinitive marker: e.g. *(to) write, (to) think, (to) work*.

Infinitive marker (infm): the word *to* when used in connection with an infinitive, as in *To see her is to love her*.

Inflection: morphological process whereby a word is marked by means of a morpheme to signal a grammatical relationship, e.g. *car - cars* (number), *walk - walked* (tense), *friend - friend's* (genitive), etc. Many manifestation forms are created by means of inflection. Thus, for example, the manifestation forms *loves*, *loved* and *loving* are inflectional variants of the base form LOVE.

Inflectional morphology: morphology involving inflection.

infm: see **Infinitive marker**.

Information structure: the way information is presented (e.g. the order in which constituents are placed).

Inherent adjective: inherent adjectives directly ascribe a property to the referent of the head they modify, e.g. *a beautiful girl* and *an angry man*.

INSTRUMENT: a specific participant role; entity or means used to bring about a dynamic situation, e.g. *Roger peeled potatoes with his pocket-knife*.

Intensive plural: a plural that intensifies the concept of the corresponding singular expression rather than simply quantifying the referent, e.g. *apologies, fears, skies, waters*, etc.

Intensive relation: either a description of an entity in terms of another or an assignment of a property to an entity, cf. *Ottawa is the capital of Canada* and *Victoria is beautiful*.

Interjection (intj): interjections are words which express emotional reaction (surprise, pleasure, annoyance, hesitation, etc.) like *huh, ouch, well, oh*, etc.

Interrogative clause: a form type of clause typically used to ask questions. There are two types of interrogative clause: *wh*-interrogatives (e.g. *Who killed the mocking bird?*) and *yes-no* interrogatives (e.g. *Did you like her a lot?*).

Interrogative pronoun: interrogative pronouns are used to form interrogative sentences, such as *Who wants to go?* and *What is this?*. The central interrogative pronouns are *who/whom/whose, which* and *what*.

Interrogative scope: concerns the set of possible answers to a question. The set is either limited or unlimited (quantitative selectivity), or it is of a special kind (qualitative selectivity). For example, the two expressions *Who is Roger Wilkinson* and *Which (of them) is Roger Wilkinson* are distinguished in terms of quantitative selectivity, the latter (but not the former) assuming a limited set of possible answers.

intj: see **Interjection**.

Intransitive predicator: a predicator which takes no object or complement, such as *Richard was sleeping*. Some intransitive predicators take an obligatory adverbial (e.g. *Jessica was in London*) and/or a number of optional adverbials (as in *Richard was sleeping heavily in the next room*). The basic sentence structures associated with intransitive predicators are S P and S P A.

Intrasentential: a term used about relations or phenomena inside a sentence.

Inversion: the reversal of the order of constituents. Typically the term is used in connection with a reversal of order in basic sentence structures. A distinction is drawn between (partial) subject-operator inversion (as in *Did you like her?*) and (full) subject-predicator inversion (as in *Here comes the bus*).

Irreversible coordination: coordination where the order of conjoints cannot be changed for formal reasons, or without also changing the meaning: e.g. *She went inside again and Philip drove off / Philip drove off and she went inside again.*

Iterative/iteration: iterative situations consist of a number of identical, or similar, consecutively realized subsituations, cf. *Someone was tapping me on the shoulder.*

Left-dislocation: see **dislocation**.

Left-hyphenation: the use of hyphenation before a label (e.g. -P:g) to indicate a discontinuous relationship between the unit it represents and a unit in the preceding linguistic context.

Lexical item: a word; the expression 'lexical item' is often used to refer to a word in its dictionary form, i.e. in its base form.

Lexicalization: the expression of meanings through words.

Limited negation: see **Syntactic field of negation**.

Linked coordination: coordination where the conjoints are explicitly connected by a coordinator, as in *John and Mary*.

Local genitive: an autonomous genitive referring to a home, building, institution, business or another place, as in *I met her at my uncle's*.

Local negation: see **Domain of negation**.

Main clause: corresponds to the whole sentence (or what could be a whole sentence), e.g. *Jenny would help me if she got the chance*. This main clause consists of the matrix *Jenny would help me* and the subclause *if she got the chance*. The subclause (*if she got the chance*) is said to be embedded in the main clause.

Mandative subjunctive: the deontic expression of compulsion in *that*-clauses after verbs, adjectives or nouns expressing demand, resolution, recommendation or the like, e.g. *I suggest that Smith leave at once*.

Manifestation form: the inflected or uninflected form of a word in actual speech or writing. The forms *love*, *loves*, *loved* and *loving* are manifestation forms of the base form LOVE.

Marked: atypical, unusual.

Mass noun: a noun whose referent is conceived of as something unindividualized which we cannot (or simply do not) count (e.g. WATER, SAND, BUTTER, FURNITURE, ADVICE, etc.).

Matrix clause: a main clause minus its subclauses. In e.g. *They discovered that Jack was a double agent*, the matrix is *They discovered*. The rest is a subclause.

Middle verb: a verb which appears not only in normal active and passive sentences but also in intransitive active, but notionally passive sentences with the AFFECTED participant as topicalized subject, e.g. *The door opened*.

Missing constituent: a constituent which has been left out to obtain economy of expression, as in *Ann became president and Jack __ vicepresident*. Cases of missing constituents are referred to as ellipsis.

Mod. I adjective: specifying adjective in modificational zone I.

Mod. II adjective: descriptive adjective in modificational zone II.

Mod. III adjective: classifying adjective in modificational zone III.

Modal verbs: auxiliaries which express modal meaning and which have no base form: *will/would, shall/should, can/could, may/might* and *must*.

Modality: modal meaning primarily involves two kinds of non-factual meaning: epistemic and deontic. Epistemic meaning concerns probability (logical possibility and necessity, hypothetical meaning, beliefs and predicta-bility), while deontic meaning concerns desirability (permission, obligation and volition). For example, MAY is epistemic in *The economy may get worse* (possibility) but deontic in *May I come in?* (permission).

Modification: a kind of subordination; a relationship between two constituents (typically a dependent and a head) where the subordinate constituent attributes a property to the superordinate constituent. A distinction is drawn between premodification (as in *beautiful* roses) and postmodification (as in *something beautiful*) depending on the position of the subordinate constituent relative to the superordinate constituent.

Mod(ificational) zone I: the zone containing specifying adjectives, e.g. *the same old English stock* and *the first few interesting talks*.

Mod(ificational) zone II: the zone containing descriptive adjectives, e.g. *the same old English stock* and *a tall dark stranger*.

Mod(ificational zone) III: the zone containing classifying adjectives, e.g. *the same old English stock* and *a new American medical dictionary*.

Monotransitive predicator: a transitive predicator which takes only one object (typically a direct object), as in *Jeremy kissed Sandra*. Monotransitive predicators contrast with ditransitive predicators, which take two objects (a direct and an indirect one). The basic sentence structure associated with monotransitive predicators is S P O.

Mood: a verbal category which can be used to define sentence/clause types according to how their meaning relates to reality. There are three moods: the indicative (e.g. *Somebody opens the door all the time*), the imperative (e.g. *Somebody open the door, will you*) and the subjunctive (e.g. *I suggest that somebody open the door*).

Morpheme: the smallest meaningful unit in language. Morphemes may be words (such as e.g. *my, the, old* and *shed*) or parts of words (as e.g. *un-* and *kind* in *unkind*, and *paint* and *-ed* in *painted*).

Morphological comparison: comparison by means of the *-er* and *-est* suffixes (e.g. *strong/stronger/strongest*).

Morphology: the study of how morphemes combine to form words, e.g. *un + kind = unkind* and *car + s = cars*.

n: see **Noun**.

n-replacive *one*: noun-replacive *one*; *one* used anaphorically as a pro-form for a noun rather than a whole group, as in *There were three visitors. The tall one left early.*

Nominal: a form term covering both 'noun group' and 'single noun'.

Nominal clause: a cover term for subject, object and complement clauses.

Nominalization: the expression of a situation as 'a thing' by forming a nominal constituent from a verbal or clausal one, as in *the killing of pigs*.

Non-assertive: see **Partitive pronoun**.

Non-gradable adjective: non-gradable adjectives denote categorial or determinative properties and are not normally compatible with intensification or comparison (e.g. ATOMIC, LINGUISTIC, MEDICAL, OWN, OTHER, etc.).

Non-inherent adjective: non-inherent adjectives relate by way of association to the meaning of the head they modify rather than ascribing a property to the referent as such, e.g. *a heavy sleeper* and *an animate noun*.

Non-recursive coordination: coordination where the number of conjoints is formally restricted to two. *But* is a non-recursive coordinator: e.g. *I like claret but not port* but not *I like claret but not port but Madeira*.

Non-restrictive relative clause: a relative clause which offers additional information about the referent of the antecedent, e.g. *Jim, who was brave, ran forward*.

Non-repetitive reference: anaphoric or cataphoric reference which does not involve the repetition of a form, as in *Jack said that he liked the idea*, where *he* refers anaphorically but non-repetitively to *Jack*. Contrasts with repetitive reference.

Non-textual reference: reference to something outside the text itself. Also called exophoric reference. Example: *He went to Paris*.

Nonfinite: a verb is nonfinite when it is not marked as present or past, i.e. when it has one of the following forms: infinitive (e.g. *(to) think*), present participle (e.g. *thinking*) or past participle (e.g. *(have) thought*).

***Not* contraction**: see **Contraction**.

Notional concord: concord determined by the notional number of the subject rather than its grammatical number, as in *My family love Australia*.

Notional passive: see **Middle verb**.

Noun (n): nouns typically express things or persons. In doing so they are often combined with articles and inflected for the expression of number (e.g. *the car* vs. *the cars*) and the genitive case (e.g. *Jack* vs. *Jack's*).

Noun group: a group with a noun as head, e.g. *My wife studies aboriginal art*.

Noun-replacive: see **n-replacive** *one*.

num: see **Numeral**.

Number: a category which enables the speaker/writer to express the distinction between singular and plural. The category applies to nouns (e.g. *car/cars*, *girl/girls*, etc.) and to certain pronouns (e.g. *this/these, I/we, he-she-it/they*).

Number-invariable noun: a noun that is invariably singular or plural, e.g. *furniture* (invariably singular) and *jeans* (invariably plural).

Number-transparent: a term used about a syntactic head which lets a dependent determine the number of the construction as a whole, as in *A lot of milk was needed* versus *A lot of eggs were needed*.

Numeral (num): numerals are words which express a number, such as *five*, *hundreds, 1993, tenth, twenty-first*, etc.

O: see **Object**.

Object (O), direct object (Od): a clause/sentence function which usually follows immediately after the predicator. It typically expresses the participant affected by the situation expressed by the predicator. Objects are identified by asking 'Who(m) or what' followed by the relevant partially inverted S P construction. Thus, to find the object in *Harris moved the bike*, we ask 'Who or what did Harris move?'. The answer is *the bike* (= the object).

Object complement (Co): a clause/sentence function which expresses further information about the referent of the object, as in *We painted the wall yellow*, where the object complement *yellow* describes the object *the wall* ('the wall became yellow'). The object complement is normally realized by an adjectival or nominal constituent.

Objective (case): see **Case**.

Objective genitive: a genitive relating to a verbal noun the way the object is related to the predicator in a corresponding clause, e.g. *Old Jack's release* (i.e. 'someone released Old Jack')

Obligatory constituent: a constituent which is syntactically indispensable. In e.g. *The small car stopped*, all the constituents except *small* are obligatory.

Od: see **Object, direct object**.

Op: see **Provisional object**.

Open word class: open word classes have indefinitely many members and admit new members whenever there is a need for them, e.g. nouns like LASER, SOFTWARE, etc. Nouns, verbs, adjectives and adverbs are open classes.

Operator: the finite auxiliary in a complex finite predicator: e.g. *may have lost*, *is working*, *have been running*, etc.

Operator-contraction: see **Contraction**.

Optative: the communicative function of expressing a wish or a benediction/ malediction, e.g. *If only I were you*.

Optional constituent: a constituent which is syntactically – though typically not semantically – dispensable. In e.g. *Richard slept heavily in the next room*, the two adverbials *heavily* and *in the next room* are optional.

Or: see **Real object**.

P: see **Predicator**.

Parataxis: a relation between elements at the same level of analysis. Parataxis typically involves unlinked or linked coordination. In e.g. *a tall dark handsome stranger* and *a tall, dark and handsome stranger*, the adjectives are paratactically related.

Partial inversion: see **Inversion**.

Participant: participants are referents (of especially nominal and pronominal constituents) involved in the situation expressed by the clause, e.g. DOER, SPECIFIER, CAUSE, BENEFICIARY, etc.

Participle: there are two kinds of participle in English: present participles (in the *-ing* form: *singing*, *beating*, etc.) and past participles (in the *-en* form: *broken*, *beaten*, etc.; the *-en* suffix is often realized as *-(e)d* (as in *loved* and *booked*) or irregularly with a change of vowel (as in *bought* and *told*), or not at all (as in *cut, put*)).

Partitive pronoun: a subtype of indefinite pronoun. There are two kinds of partitive pronoun: assertive (*some, somebody, someone, something*) or non-assertive (*any, anybody, anyone, anything*).

Passive (voice): see **Voice**.

Past: a tense-aspect form, e.g. *happened*.

Past future: a tense-aspect form, e.g. *would happen*.

Past future perfect: a tense-aspect form, e.g. *would have happened*.

Past future perfect progressive: a tense-aspect form, e.g. *would have been happening*.

Past future progressive: a tense-aspect form, e.g. *would be happening*.

Past participle: the *-en* form of a verb: e.g. *broken, beaten*, etc. The *-en* suffix is often realized as *-(e)d* (as in *loved* and *booked*) or irregularly with a change of vowel (as in *bought* and *told*), or not at all (as in *cut, put*).

Past perfect: a tense-aspect form, e.g. *had happened*.

Past perfect progressive: a tense-aspect form, e.g. *had been happening*.

Past progressive: a tense-aspect form, e.g. *was happening*.

Perception: a sense relation (visual, auditory, etc.), cf. *I saw her clearly*.

Perfect: a verb form consisting of HAVE and a past participle, e.g. *They have left* and *I have always loved her*.

Performative: the communicative function of 'doing by saying', e.g. *I (hereby) pronounce you man and wife*.

Peripheral adjective: an adjective which is not a central adjective. Peripheral adjectives are either classifying adjectives (e.g. SOLAR, MEDICAL, LINGUISTIC) or specifying adjectives (e.g. ONLY, SAME, FIRST).

Person: a category which enables the speaker/writer to express the distinction between speaker/writer (first person), listener/reader (second person), and others (third person), respectively). The category applies to personal pronouns, both singular (*I, you, he/she/it*) and plural (*we, you, they*), as well as derived forms, both possessive (*mine, your, his*) and reflexive (*myself, yourself, herself*).

Personal pronoun: personal pronouns refer to the interlocutors of a speech situation (*I, me; you*) and/or things and persons in relation to the interlocutors (*he, him; she, her; it; we, us; they, them*). Four categories apply to personal pronouns: case (e.g. subjective *she* versus objective *her*), number (e.g. singular *I* versus plural *we*), person (e.g. second-person *you* versus third-person *they*), and gender (masculine *he* versus feminine *she* versus neuter *it*).

Phoneme: distinctive individual language sound, e.g. $/k/ + /æ/ + /t/ = cat$.

Phrasal verb: a verb fused with a following adverb, as in *Julia gave in eventually*.

Phrasal-prepositional verb: a verb fused with a following adverb and preposition, as in (one reading of) *Cassandra looked down on the nurses*.

Positive: see **Comparison**.

Possessive pronoun: personal pronoun 'in the genitive'. There are two sets of possessive pronouns: determinative (*my, your, his, her, its, our, your, their*) and autonomous (*mine, yours, his, hers, ours, yours, theirs*), cf. *This is her Porsche* and *I parked my Porsche behind hers*.

Post-genitive: an autonomous genitive which appears in a postmodifying *of*-construction with a quantifying, partitive meaning ('of several'), e.g. *a friend of my sister's*.

Post-M position: adverbial position after the second or third auxiliary and before the head verb, as in *She may be secretly supporting their cause*.

Postcedent: a constituent referred to cataphorically. For example, in *When he had passed his degree, James left Paris*, the subject *James* in the matrix is the postcedent of the subject *he* in the subclause.

Postdeterminer: a determiner following another (central) determiner. *Every*, *such* and possessive pronouns are postdeterminers when they follow other determiners (e.g. *Jack's every wish* and *any such luck*).

Postmodification/Postmodifier: see **Modification**

Pragmatic function: general communicative function.

Pre-M position: adverbial position immediately before the operator, as in *I miss you, darling, I really do*.

Predeterminer: a determiner preceding another (central) determiner, e.g. *what a jerk*.

Predicate: a constituent comprising everything in a clause except the subject. In *Jack was fixing the old motorbike again*, the predicate consists of the predicator, the object and the adverbial: *was fixing the old motorbike again*. (Do not confuse 'predicate' with 'predicator' or 'predication'.)

Predication: a constituent comprising everything in a predicate except the operator. In *Jack was fixing the old motorbike again*, the predication consists of the nonfinite part of the predicator, the object and the adverbial: *fixing the old motorbike again*.

Predicative adjective: adjective with complement function, e.g. *I was rich*.

Predicator (P): a clause/sentence function always realized by one or more verbs expressing a situation, as in *Jack treated Sophia very badly* and *He can run a mile in six minutes*.

Premodification/Premodifier: see **Modification**.

prep: see **Preposition**.

Preposition (prep): prepositions express relations (often spatial relations) between constituents. They do so by relating a noun or group (e.g. *the table*) to another noun or group (e.g. *the book*) as in *the book on the table*, or to some action or state (*The book was placed on the table / The book is on the table*).

Preposition group: a group with a preposition as head, e.g. *to my suprise*.

Prepositional complement: the traditional name for a dependent in a preposition group, e.g. *to <u>my uncle</u>* and *without <u>their consent</u>*.

Prepositional verb: a verb fused with a following preposition, as in *Alfred's wife always <u>stood by</u> Jack*.

Present: a tense-aspect form, e.g. *happens*.

Present future: a tense-aspect form, e.g. *will happen*.

Present future perfect: a tense-aspect form, e.g. *will have happened*.

Present future perfect progressive: a tense-aspect form, e.g. *will have been happening*.

Present future progressive: a tense-aspect form, e.g. *will be happening*.

Present participle: the *-ing* form of a verb (*breaking, thinking*, etc.).

Present perfect: a tense-aspect form, e.g. *has happened*.

Present perfect progressive: a tense-aspect form, e.g. *has been happening*.

Present progressive: a tense-aspect form, e.g. *is happening*.

Primary verb: BE, HAVE and D O are called primary verbs because they function sometimes as auxiliaries (as in *She <u>was</u> laughing*), sometimes as full verbs, being alone in the predicator (as in *She <u>was</u> brave*).

pro: see **Pronoun**.

Proform: a form representing another constituent. Pronouns are common proforms, e.g. *My little sister saw <u>herself</u> in the mirror*.

Progressive: a verb form consisting of BE and a present participle, e.g. *She <u>was running</u>* and *They <u>are thinking</u> about it*.

Pronominal: a form term covering both 'pronoun group' and 'single pronoun'.

Pronoun (pro): pronouns are a rather heterogeneous word class, comprising personal pronouns (*I, me; you; he, him; she, her; it*, etc.), possessive pronouns (*my, mine; your, yours*, etc.), reflexive pronouns (*myself, yourself*, etc.), demonstrative pronouns (*that, those, this, these*), interrogative and relative pronouns (e.g. *who, which, what*) and indefinite pronouns (*some, something, any, anybody, no, nothing, every, everyone, all, (n)either, both*, etc.).

Pronoun group: a group with a pronoun as head, e.g. *There is <u>something rotten</u> in the state of Denmark*.

Proper noun: a noun written with a capital letter which is used as a name of e.g. a person (*Jack* and *Jenny*) or a place (*London* and *Spain*).

Provisional direct object: see **Provisional object**.

Provisional object (Op): a clause/sentence function always realized by *it* representing an extraposed real object (Or), as in *They found it difficult to work*, where *it* represents, or stands in the place of, the real object *to work*.

Provisional subject (Sp): a clause/sentence function realized by *it* or *there* in subject position representing a postponed real subject (Sr), as in *It was obvious that he disliked her* and *There were five books on the table*, where *It* and *There* are provisional subjects, representing the real subjects *that he disliked her* and *five books*, respectively.

Pseudo-cleft sentence: consists of a subject realized by an independent relative *what*-clause followed by BE and a subject complement, e.g. *What worries me is the poor quality of your work*.

Pseudo-coordination: coordination of conjoints which, formally, are completely identical, as in *There are teachers and teachers*.

Punctual(ity): punctual situations have little or no extension in time and hence not conceived of as having internal structure (e.g. *She hit me on the nose*).

Qualitative selectivity: concerns the interrogative scope of expressions like *What years are leap years?* and *Which years are leap years?*, which differ with respect to the kind of answers assumed. The former expression (unlike the latter) tries to elicit a characterization rather than just a list of years.

Quantification: the expression of meanings relating to number or quantity, as in *numerous cars, three books, some money* and *lots of beer*.

Quantifier: a word that expresses number or quantity, e.g. *some, three, many, lots*, etc.

Quantitative selectivity: see **Interrogative scope**.

Quantity partition: the quantification of the referent of a (mass or count) noun by means of a partitive *of*-construction preceded by a count noun, e.g. *a pint of beer*.

Question: the communicative function of seeking information, e.g. *Was John quiet?* (*wh*-question) and *Are you hungry* (*yes-no* question).

Raised subject: see **Raising**.

Raising: a term used when a function in a subclause (such as e.g. the subject or the object) appears in ('is raised into') the normal subject position in the matrix clause, e.g. *Alfred appears to be hungry* (cf. *It appears that Alfred is hungry*) and *His explanation was hard to believe* (cf. *It was hard to believe his explanation*).

Real object (Or): a clause/sentence function which presupposes the use of a provisional object (*it*). A real object is extraposed from the object position, as in *They found it difficult to work*.

Real subject (Sr): a clause/sentence function which presupposes the use of a provisional subject (*it* or *there*). A real subject is postponed or extraposed from the subject position, as in *There were five books on the table* and *It was obvious that he disliked her*, respectively.

Reciprocal: a term used about constituents expressing reciprocity, such as *each other* and *one another*.

Recursive: a term used to describe the repeated application of a rule to form indefinitely large complex constructions.

Recursive coordination: coordination with no formal restriction on the number of conjoints. *And* and *or* are recursive coordinators: e.g. *Would you like beer, white wine, port ... or Madeira?*

Reference: the communicative function of establishing something/someone as a referent.

Referent: something/someone referred to. Referents are divided into unique, generic and class-member. If a referent is conceived of as the only one of its kind (such as *Peter Schmeichel has decided to leave Manchester United*) it is unique. If it is seen as one of many similar things (e.g. *I parked my car near the library*) it is a class-member referent. If it is a kind or type of thing rather than an individual class-member, it is generic (as in *The funnel-web spider is very common in New South Wales*).

Reflexive pronoun: reflexive pronouns are *self*-forms (*myself, yourself, himself, herself, itself, ourselves, yourselves, themselves*). Reflexive pronouns are mainly used to express 'the same referent' as some other constituent, typically the subject (as in *Jack prided himself on his victory*).

Reflexive verb: a verb which requires a reflexive object, e.g. INGRATIATE (as in *He always ingratiated himself with his superiors*).

Relative (sub)clause: a (subclause) with a relative pronoun in it.

Relative pronoun: relative pronouns signal clausal subordination (like subordinating conjunctions) and at the same time they take on a clause function other than SUB in the relative subclause (e.g. subject or object) and have anaphoric reference: e.g. *They arrested Jeremy, who was on his honeymoon*. The central relative pronouns are *who/whom /whose, which, what* and *that*.

Repetitive reference: involves the repetition of a form, as in *A man and a woman entered the room. The man was laughing*.

Reporting clause: clause which introduces direct or indirect speech, as in <u>*He said*</u> *that Jane had left early* and <u>*He shouted*</u>*: "Jane left early"*.

Representation: the communicative function of 'standing for something'. In e.g. *I love you*, the personal pronouns represent the speaker and the hearer.

Restrictive relative clause: a relative clause which helps establish the referent of the antecedent, as in *The soldiers who were brave ran forward*.

RESULT: specific participant role; an entity created by the situation, e.g. *He dug <u>a hole</u>* and *She became <u>a raving lunatic</u>*.

Retrievability: the unique identification of a missing constituent.

Reversible coordination: coordination where the order of conjoints can be changed with no difference of meaning, e.g. *Jane and Albert arrived before noon / Albert and Jane arrived before noon*.

Right-dislocation: see **Dislocation**.

Right-hyphenation: the use of hyphenation after a label (e.g. P:g-) to indicate a discontinuous relationship between the unit it represents and a unit in the subsequent linguistic context.

S: see **Subject**.

Scope: the scope of a constituent is the extent of its semantic relations to other constituents (or of its influence over other constituents).

Self-contained/self-containment: self-contained situations are durative situations not having, or being directed towards, any natural point of completion, cf. *James and George were sailing along the coast*.

Semantic scope of negation: the extent of the semantic effect of negation; a distinction is drawn between complete (everything in the clause is included) and incomplete (not everything in the clause is included) scope, cf. *Jane didn't kill Bob deliberately* (complete) versus *Jane deliberately didn't kill Bob* (incomplete, *deliberately* being outside the semantic scope of negation).

Semantics: the study of meaning in language.

Semi-auxiliary: semi-auxiliaries are verbs which are difficult to classify unambiguously as either auxiliaries or full verbs because they share properties with both subclasses. Verbs like OUGHT (*to*), USED (*to*), DARE, NEED, HAVE (*to*), KEEP, GET, BE (*to*), BE (*about to*), BE (*going to*) are semi-auxiliaries.

Sentence: a string of words/constituents expressing a statement (e.g. *I love grammar*), a question (*What is grammar?*), a command (e.g. *Read this grammar carefully*) or an exclamation (*What a wonderful grammar teacher she is!*).

Sentence function: sentence functions form sentences. The main sentence functions are subject, predicator, direct object, indirect object and adverbial.

Sentential relative clause: a relative clause which refers back to a superordinate clause, e.g. *The twins don't look alike, which puzzles me.*

Simple coordination: coordination of constituents which by themselves would serve only one clause or group function: *Jane and Albert left* (= *Jane left* and *Albert left*). Simple coordination contrasts with complex coordination.

Simple form: a form which does not require further syntactic analysis, i.e. an individual word.

Situation: a cover term for the many different dynamic and stative meanings that sentences express (e.g. punctuality, iteration and habituality).

Sp: see **Provisional subject**.

Specification: the communicative function of singling out, or determining the extent of, a referent. In e.g. *his decision*, the possessive pronoun *his* has a specifying value. Specification is also a subfunction of modification, realized by specifying adjectives.

SPECIFIED: general participant role; someone/something for whom/which a state exists or is true, e.g. *Jack is in London.*

SPECIFIER: general participant role; determines the nature of a state (relation) in conjunction with the predicator, e.g. *Jack is in London.*

Specifying adjective: adjective which singles out or quantifies the referent in relation to some context, e.g. *his main reason* and *my former colleague.*

Specifying genitive: a genitive that serves as a central definite determiner, as in *my sister's degree.*

Split infinitive: an infinitive construction where an adverbial intervenes between infinitive marker and infinitive verb, as in *to suddenly resign.*

Sr: see **Real Subject**.

Standard negation: negation expressed by NOT in central-M position, as in *Jack has not apologized* and *She didn't love him any more.*

Statement: the communicative function of giving information, e.g. *John left.*

Stative: a stative situation 'exists' or is 'true' of someone/something rather than 'takes place' or 'happens', cf. e.g. *Ottawa is the capital of Canada.*

Stranded preposition: a preposition whose complement in an active clause (e.g. *Alice slept in the bed*) serves as the subject of a passive clause, so that the preposition no longer has a complement (*The bed was slept in*).

Subclause/subordinate clause: a clause which functions within a main clause, either by realizing a clause function (such as the subject in *Being with you is far more important*) or by realizing some lower-level function (such as the DEP in *The house which my parents bought last year*).

Subject (S): a clause/sentence function which typically expresses the person or thing which the predicator says something about. In statements the subject precedes the predicator. We can identify the subject by asking 'Who or what' immediately followed by the predicator. Thus if we want to find the subject in *The parish vibrated with gossip the next day*, we ask 'Who or what vibrated?'. The answer is *The parish* (= the subject).

Subject complement (Cs): a clause/sentence function which expresses further information about the referent of the subject, as in *My brother looks very intelligent*. Subject complements can always be realized by an adjectival constituent, but often have nominal realization (e.g. *Jack became very friendly / Jack became my best friend*).

Subject-operator (partial) inversion: see **Inversion**.

Subject-predicator (full) inversion: see **Inversion**.

Subjective (case): see **Case**.

Subjective genitive: a genitive relating to a verbal noun the way the subject relates to the predicator in a corresponding clause, e.g. *Dr. Daruwalla's estimation* (i.e. 'Dr. Daruwalla estimated').

Subjunctive: a mood which is realized by the base form of the verb (or by *were*), and which typically expresses something non-factual or hypothetical (e.g. *It is essential that Pitt leave at once* and *If only I were rich and famous*).

Subordinate clause: see **Subclause**.

Subordinating conjunction: subordinating conjunctions place one clause (e.g. *He didn't support her*) at a lower level in relation to another clause (e.g. *I said that he didn't support her*), or in relation to the head of a group (e.g. *The claim that he didn't support her was obviously false*).

Subordination: relationship between constituents which have a different syntactic status. In groups there is subordination between head and dependent(s), the latter being the subordinate constituent(s) (e.g. *nice colours*, where *nice* is subordinate to *colours*). At clause level, subordination is often marked explicitly by means of a subordinating conjunction (e.g. *I said that he didn't support her*, where [he didn't support her] is subordinate to [I said]). There are three main kinds of subordination: determination, complementation and modification.

Substantival use of adjectives: adjectives expressing properties as if they were 'things' or 'persons', as in *The poor hadn't heard the worst yet*.

Superlative: see **Comparison**.

Suffix: a morphological ending added to the base form of a word, e.g. *-s*, *-ed* and *-ing* (LOOK: *looks/looked/looking*).

Syllable: a unit of pronunciation typically larger than the phoneme but smaller than the word. Syllables often consist of a vowel and a number of consonants, e.g. *po* and *lite* in *polite*.

Syntactic comparison: comparison by means of the adverbs *more* and *most* (e.g. *beautiful / more beautiful / most beautiful*).

Syntactic field of negation: concerns the syntactic material acutally negated; a distinction is drawn between clausal negation (stadard negation with NOT, as in *He didn't give us the tickets*) and limited negation, where a negative clause function other than the predicator makes the clause as a whole negative, as in *No one gave us the tickes* and *He gave us no tickets*.

Syntactic zone: see **Zone**.

Syntax: the study of how words combine to form sentences, e.g. *Everybody + likes + chocolate = Everybody likes chocolate*.

Tag (question): an interrogative construction like *is it* and *can't we* added to a statement: e.g. *It is not urgent, is it?* and *We can leave now, can't we?*

Telic(ity): telic situations are durative (i.e. non-punctual) leading up to and including a natural terminal point (cf. *Jack fixed the old motorbike*).

Tense: a category which enables the speaker/writer to express assignment to situations of 'location in time', e.g. present time location *Linda lives in Stockholm* versus past time location *Linda lived in Stockholm*. Tense is closely related to the category of aspect. The combined tense-aspect system comprises the following four choices of verb form: present/past, future/nonfuture, perfect/nonperfect and progressive/nonprogressive.

Textual reference: reference to something in the text itself, or to something already established as a referent elsewhere in the text. Also called endophoric reference. Example: *Jack killed himself*.

Topic: the person or thing a predicator says something about, usually expressed by the subject, as in *The parish vibrated with gossip the next day*.

Topicalization: the fronting of a constituent to highlight it as topic, e.g. *This book I can't stand*).

Transferred negation: negation which is moved from a subclause where it belongs semantically to a superordinate clause, e.g. *I don't think it is raining.*

Transitive predicator: a predicator which takes an object, as in *Richard kissed Jessica*. The basic sentence structure associated with transitive predicators is S P O.

Unattached participle: a participle in a subjectless participle clause where the implied subject is not the subject of the matrix clause, e.g. *Known primarily as the author of 'Changing Places', many consider Lodge a humourist.* Also called 'dangling participle'. Generally viewed as unacceptable English.

Unique referent: see **Referent**.

Universal pronoun: a subtype of indefinite pronoun. There are two kinds of universal pronoun: positive (*every, everybody, everyone, everything; all*) and negative (*no, nobody, no one, nothing, none*).

Unlinked coordination: coordination with no overt coordinator, as in *Who blew the landing party, the coordinates, the beach, the time?*

Unmarked: most typical, usual.

v: see **Verb**.

Valency: the number and kinds of participants associated with verbs.

Verb (v): verbs express dynamic or stative situations and inflect for tense and aspect (e.g. *write* vs. *wrote*), person and number (e.g. *write* vs. *writes*).

Verb group: a group with a verb as head, e.g. *may have been dancing* and *having been examined*.

Verbal: a form term covering both 'verb group' and 'single verb'.

Verbless clause: a clause without a predicator, e.g. *When in Rome, ...*

Vocative: an expression used to address the hearer, as in <u>Bob</u>, *please go now.*

Voice: a category allowing the speaker to present information in two different ways, in the active voice or in the passive voice: e.g. *Her parents might have saved her* (active) / *She might have been saved by her parents* (passive).

w: see **Word**.

Word (w): a conventional unit of expression consisting of one or more morphemes, e.g. *kind* and *unkind*.

Word class: a collection of words which share morphological, semantic and/or syntactic characteristics, e.g. nouns, which are a collection of words which typically express things or persons (semantics), which are often combined with articles (syntax), and which are usually inflected for the expression of number (morphology). There are eight main word classes: nouns, verbs, adjectives, adverbs, pronouns, prepositions, conjunctions and articles.

Yes-no question: a question which tries to elicit a *yes* or a *no* for an answer, e.g. *Do you like me?*.

Zero (form): a missing constituent represented by the symbol Ø (e.g. *He said Ø he was hungry*).

Zone: an area with a particular function which may be realized by one or more items, e.g. pre-head adjectival modification in nominals.

Subject index

Word index

fly 62
foodwise 255
fool 164
for 179
forceps 192
foreign policy 243
forever 136
former 241
four 241
French 243, 246, 252
friend 164, 167
friendly 231, 255
fry 86
funds 192
furniture 167
further 245, 258
furthest 245, 258

gallows 191
gander 165
gasworks 191
general 241
German 251
get 24, 85-6
girl 164
glasses 192
go 24, 62
god 165
goddess 165
golden 230
good 222, 230, 230, 245
good-looking 232
goods 192
goose 165
government 100
great 246
green 230, 243
gross 190
grotesque 247
grouse 190
grow 24

had 60, 147
half 172-73
halfway 256
hand-made 232
handsome 247
hang 62, 117, 233

happen 17
hard 109, 246
hard 255
hardly 69, 255
have 12-15, 59, 89, 91, 118, 131-32
have got 59
have to 119, 154-55
he 99, 199, 200, 202, 203
head 190
headquarters 191
hear 128
heatedly 255
heir apparent 163
helper 164
hen-pheasant 165
her 170
herd 100
here 62, 256
hereabouts 256
hero 164
heroine 164
high 246, 248, 255
highly 229, 253, 255
his 170
historic 231
historical 231
hit 134
hold 134-35
homeward(s) 256
hope 115
horrible 242
horse 164
horsepower 190
hourly 255
house 167
how 215, 217-18, 220
humorous 231
hundredweight 190
hypersensitive 232
hypnotizable 243

I 99, 201, 202
idea 167
if 43, 64, 65, 111
ill 245
imagine 114
imbecile 251
imply 102

www.ingramcontent.com/pod-product-compliance
Lightning Source LLC
Chambersburg PA
CBHW080917100426

42812CB00007B/2302